# SALES MANAGEMENT

C.L. TYAGI
ARUN KUMAR

ATLANTIC
PUBLISHERS & DISTRIBUTORS

Published by

**ATLANTIC**
PUBLISHERS & DISTRIBUTORS
B-2, Vishal Enclave, Opp. Rajouri Garden,
New Delhi-110027
Phones : 25413460, 25429987, 25466842

Sales Office
7/22, Ansari Road, Darya Ganj,
New Delhi–110002
Phones : 23273880, 23275880, 23280451
Fax : 91-11-23285873
web : www.atlanticbooks.com
e-mail : info@atlanticbooks.com



ISBN 81-269-0311-2



Printed in India
at Nice Printing Press, Delhi

# Preface

Sales management in any enterprise is an art. It deals with the problems like recruiting, training and motivating today's top sales talent and develop them into a top performing cohesive sales unit. But this art cannot be acquired without a good book on the subject. "I don't think myself, books think for me" is a famous saying. This is the reason for writing this book in spite of the fact that a number of books are available in the market at present. The book does not claim originality. But the subject matter has been drawn from a number of eminent authors. The book is a comprehensive treatise on the subject and covers syllabus prescribed for marketing students. It contains chapters on sales talks, sales records, sales field, sales force management and remuneration and sales recruitment, usually missed in many text books. Besides, it contains theory and practice of sales promotion, channels of distribution, marketing strategy, motivation and psychology of sales. The book will prove an all time guide for undergraduate and graduate business students seeking to work in the enthusing field of sales management.

Suggestions, if any, for the improvement of this book in the next edition shall be highly appreciated.

In the end, we are thankful to Dr. K.R. Gupta, Chairman of Atlantic Publishers and Distributors, New Delhi, with whose effort the book has seen the light of the day.

**C.L. TYAGI**
**ARUN KUMAR**

# CONTENTS

# 1

# Introduction

Originally sales management was referred to as the direction of sales force personnel. Later, in addition to the management of personal selling, "sales management" came to mean management of all marketing activities, including advertising, sales promotion, marketing research, physical distribution, pricing, and product merchandising. In due course, business, adopting academic practice, started using the term "marketing management" in place of "sales management" to describe the broader concept. However, the Definitions Committee of the American Marketing Association agreed that sales management meant "the planning, direction, and control of personal selling, including recruiting, selecting, equipping, assigning, routing, supervising, paying, and motivating as these tasks apply to the personal sales force."[1]

This definition made sales management synonymous with management of the sales force, though the modern sales managers have considerably broader responsibilities. Today sales managers are in charge of personal-selling activity. Their primary assignment is management of the personal sales force. However, as personal-related tasks do not comprise their total responsibility, their personal-related responsibilities are called "sales force management."

## RESPONSIBILITIES OF SALES MANAGERS

Sales managers are responsible for organizing the sales effort, both within and outside their companies.

**1. Within the Company.** The sales manager builds formal and informal organizational structures that ensure effective communication not only inside the sales department but in its relations with other organizational units.

1. American Marketing Association. Committee on Definitions. *Marketing Definitions* (Chicago: American Marketing Association), p. 60.

**2. Outside the Company.** The sales manager serves as a key contact with customers and other external public and is responsible for building and maintaining an effective distribution network.

**3. Other Responsibilities.** Sales managers are responsible for participating in the preparation of information critical to the making of key marketing decisions, such as those on budgeting, quotas and territories. They participate in decisions on products, marketing channels and distribution policies, advertising and other promotion, and pricing. They are both administrators in charge of personal-selling activity and members of the executing group that makes marketing decisions of all types.

## PROBLEMS OF SALES MANAGEMENT

In many types of enterprises sales management is a key function. Manufacturing and wholesaling enterprises encounter a wide range of problems in sales management. Small and large retail institutions have sales management problems, even though when compared to the problems of manufactures and wholesalers the differences are so great that at least in the academic world retailing problems are ordinarily considered separately. Some retailers have sales management problems akin to those of manufacturers and wholesalers than to those of other retailers, for example — the automobile dealer, the real-estate broker, and the direct-to-consumer marketer. Firms selling intangibles, such as the insurance company, the stockbroker, the mutual fund, and the airline, have problems in sales management. Even in companies not employing sales personnel sales management problems exist. For example, in the company that uses manufacturers' agents rather than its own sales personnel to reach its markets, the problems of managing a sales force of "independent outsiders" are often more complex than when sales personnel are on the company payroll.

The four factors, according to James B. Weitzul, that are critical in the development of sales organisation are (a) Motives (Sales Person); (b) Management (Sales Management); (c) Money (Compensation to Salesforce) and (d) Market place (Market research and feed back). A Sales manager, like other jobs, require SKAP profile to be successful S—Skill, K—Knowledge, A—Ability and P—Personal Characteristics.

## OBJECTIVES OF SALES MANAGEMENT

**1. To boost Sales and Profits.** From the company viewpoint, there are three general objectives of sales management: sales volume, contribution to profits, and continuing growth. Sales executives do not carry the full burden of these objectives, though they make major contributions. Being accountable for the success or failure of the entire enterprise top management has the final responsibility. Top management is accountable for supplying an ever-increasing volume of "socially responsible" products that final buyers want at satisfactory prices.

It delegates powers and functions to marketing management, which then delegates these to sales management with sufficient authority to achieve the three general objectives. Objectives are translated into more specific goals. In the process they are broken down and restated as definite goals that the company has a reasonable chance of reaching. During the planning that precedes goal setting, sales executives provide estimates on market and sales potential, the capabilities of the sales force and the middlemen, and the like. Once these goals are finalized, it is up to sales executives to guide and lead the sales personnel and middlemen who play critical roles in implementing the selling plans.

**2. To encourage Growth and Development.** Sales management is influential in charting the course of future operations. It provides higher management with informed estimates. It provides facts for making marketing decisions and for setting sales and profit goals. It is on sales management's appraisal of market opportunities that targets are set for sales volume, gross margin, and net profit in units of product and in dollars, with benchmarks of growth projected for sales and profits at specific future dates. Achievement of these targets are reached depending upon the performance of sales and other marketing personnel.

**3. To show Good Financial Results.** An objective of sales management is to show good financial results. Financial results are stated from two basic accounting formulas:

sales – cost of sales = gross margin

gross margin – expenses = net profit

Sales management influences the "numbers cranked into these formulas."

(i) *Sales, Gross Margin and Expenses* : Affected by the caliber and performance of sales management, these are the major determinants of net profit. The cost-of-sales factor cannot be affected directly by sales management. It can be affected indirectly since sales volume must be large enough to permit maintenance of targeted unit costs of production and distribution. These formulas become the company operating statement used by the board of directors, and by stockholders, in appraising top management's performance. In judging the effectiveness of sales management top management uses these formulas.

(ii) *Sales Volume* : In instances when sales executives stress sales volume while neglecting gross margin and expenses, even though sales volume increases, gross margin declines, expenses increase proportionately, and net profits are reduced. Profits disappear and losses appear if these conditions prevail for long. The best treatment for this situation is to shrink sales volume and expenses. Skilled sales management can reduce expenses and raise gross margin, sufficiently to convert a loss into a profit even with a lower sales volume.

Because of a preoccupation with percentage relationships it is possible to overemphasize high gross margins and low expenses. Percentages of gross margin and expenses are important, but sales management should be more concerned with dollar relationships. The important net profit is dollar net profit, not the percentage of net profit. If total sales volume and net profits are inadequate it is small consolation to have satisfactory gross margin and expense percentages. Sales management should worry more about sales and profit dollars than about percentage relationships.

**4. To provide Optimum Relationship among Four Factors.** The company maximizes its net profits if it obtains an optimum relationship among the four factors. Both in its planning and operating roles, sales management aims for an optimum relationship among the *three* factors it can directly affect: sales, gross margin, and expenses. Sales management works with in charge of production and advertising to assure that sales volume is sufficient to attain targeted *cost of sales*, the fourth factor.

## FUNCTIONS OF SALES MANAGEMENT

**1. Formulation of Objectives.** The sales management formulates the objectives for the sales department, subordinate to the top management and responsible for the fulfilment of the objectives set by the top management. The corporate objectives are broken down into specific goals, targets and measures. Power is delegated to the subordinate departments to discharge their respective responsibilities. The sales manager exercises the power and authority delegated to the sales department and discharges all the duties and responsibilities of the sales department. As he alone cannot perform all the functions, he is authorised to recruit, train, motivate and control the sales force.

The sales objectives are formulated on the basis of the information and data collected by the sales force and, market researcher. Market opportunities market conditions, competition, etc., are analysed to formulate the market objectives. The individual target for each sales force is decided according to the market potentials, sales force capability, cost and other component functions. The individual targets, the group goals of sales management and top management objectives are framed, to exploit the market opportunities. The sales management increases the net margin, arrived at by deducting the cost of production and sales expenses from the total value of sales. The sales manager tries to maximize sales and minimize expenses. The functions of the production manager are production maximisation and cost minimisation. Both co-operate to achieve the objective of the maximisation of the net profit. Co-ordination among the different departments is necessary so that the net profit may be maximised. Basically responsible for the volume sales, expenses and the cost of maintaining the sales force, the sales management formulates policies bearing on sales planning and control, recruitment and selection, training, organisation and motivation of sales force.

**2. Sales Planning.** A plan is a blueprint for future action. The success of an action depends on suitable planning. The sales management should formulate concrete, useful and effective plans, including objectives. Forecasting, budgeting, strategy, programming and controlling. The plan should be specific and properly classified in relation to time, objectives and budget.

(i) *Setting Objectives* : The first and foremost function of sales planning is to determine the sales objectives. The internal as well as external factors of environment are evaluated to find out how far they would assist in the achievement of objectives.

The objectives should be specific and framed within the limits of the corporate objectives. Sales objectives are subordinate to corporate objectives. They are broken down in periodical targets, territorial goals and departmental objectives so that each unit may specifically know its respective targets and goals. Specific and well-defined objectives can be easily achieved. Under sales objectives and planning are decided the channels of distribution, the duties and responsibilities of the sales force, the need for a sales force, recruitment, training and motivation and many other functions of the sales management. Territorial planning and sales force planning are important elements in sales planning. The, sales manager should formulate meaningful objectives for each territory and salesman.

(ii) *Forecasting* : Sales forecasting about the volume of sales, the quality, design of the product decides the sales objective and sales process. These are forecast for the total market and for each market, on the basis of records of past years, sales records by territory, local conditions in each market, information on one's strengths and weaknesses. As data are compiled at the' head office, specific forecasting is made about the sales volume expected to determine their influence on the sales volume in each territory. The probable effects of all the factors are assessed.

In sales forecasting, salesmen collect all' the information bearing on the customers, competition, potential' markets, products, and so on. They forecast on realistic assumptions and factual information. The sales manager makes the necessary modifications in their forecasts. On the basis of the information and data he prepares a useful and final sales forecast.

(iii) *Budgeting* : "Budgeting" refers to the inflows and outflows of resources estimated by planners. It includes money, materials and manpower. The "sales budget" refers to the volume of sales to be achieved during a particular period, *viz.*, a month, a year. Actual sales are compared with the budgeted sales to discover deviations. Sales expenses are budgeted to rationalise the funds allocation. They are divided into manpower expenses, travel expenses, administrative expenses, and so on. The sales budget is prepared for each territory, salesman and branch. Periodical estimates are made about the sales performance of the budget.

(iv) *Strategy* : As a comprehensive and concrete strategy assists in the achievement of sales objectives, the sales manager decides it in the light of the suggestions made by sales representatives and recommendations of the top management. It may determine how to approach the buyer and organise a sales group. It guides the sales persons in contacting various persons in the buying and selling organisations. Before, during and after the sale, technical salesmen may approach customer. Before a programme of organisational development is launched the number and quality of men in the sales force are decided.

(v) *Programming* : "Programming" refers to the specific activities to be performed by workers in future. It determines the sequence in which specific activities are to be performed by sales persons. It decides the resources to be allocated between the sales force and branch offices. Procedures are means and methods of performing activities. Sales programming is an action plan. Each salesman decides how to achieve the pre-determined objectives. The programming includes customer classification, product line emphasis, sales approach and new designs of sales functions.

(vi) *Sales Control* : Planning controls the sales functions. It indicates the necessary action to be initiated to correct imbalances. A control device includes control of money, materials, methods and management functions. Decided by the sales people the sales force controls mechanism including control of the sales volume, travel expenses, territorial coverage and activities of sales persons.

**3. Recruitment.** While planning indicates the number of persons to be recruited by the sales manager, the sales force structure, the sales force size and work allocation are decided under recruitment and selection.

(i) *The Sales Force Structure* : It includes territorial-structured sales force, territory size, product structured sales force, customer-structured sales force and complex sales force structures. In territorial-structured sales force, each sales person is assigned an exclusive territory, defining the salesman's responsibility and increasing his incentive to develop local rapport for the expansion and utilisation of the market potential. Administrative expenses are minimised. The sales representatives are supervised by the local or regional sales manager who is controlled by the sales manager at the head office.

(ii) *Territory Size* : It is decided on the basis of equal sales potential or equal workload. The equal sales potential provides equal income to sales representatives. Their ability to influence customers is judged on the basis of the differences in the sales volume achieved by each of them. They are encouraged to work at their maximum capacity. The product-structured sales force is useful to the company as it influences product lines. Product specialisation is required for the expansion of sales and profit. To meet the requirements of consumers and realise the maximum utilisation of the market potential, the size of the customer-structured sales force is determined.

(iii) *The Size of the Sales Force* : It influences the volume of sales. If the number of salesmen increases the sales are expected to rise provided they have been well trained. The size is decided on the basis of the existing workload of salesmen, the potential development of sales and the existing capability and size of the sales force. The average number of sales per salesman determines the appointment of the number of salesmen by the top executive and the sales manager.

(iv) *Process of Recruitment* : Recruitment is the process of looking out for prospective employees and stimulating them to apply for a job. It involves identifying the sources of recruits and choosing suitable methods of recruiting sales persons.

(a) ***The Number of Persons to be Recruited*** : The average productivity of a person is a guiding factor in the decision bearing on the number of recruits to be taken up. The turnover of each recruit is compared with the costs of the sales to determine the marginal productivity and number of recruits.

(b) ***Characteristics and Quality of the Representatives to be Recruited*** : They must be energetic, self-confident, enthusiastic and high-spirited. Mayer and Greenberg are of the opinion that the sales persons should have empathy and ego drive. The management determines the number and kind of sales persons required, the sources of recruitment and the selection of competent persons for field work.

(v) *Methodology* : The sales manager may invite names from current sales representatives, employment agencies, competitors, advertisement agencies and recommendations from colleges and universities.

**4. Selection.** Selection is the process of choosing the right persons from among those who have applied for jobs. Its purpose is to ascertain the qualities and abilities of applicants. That is why the number and kind of sales force required, planning and selection procedures are considered under selection.

(i) *Number and type* : The management should employ competent and able men to perform the sales function as the kind of sales personnel employed has a direct bearing on the volume of sales. The top management fixes the number and quality of sales force. Salesmen have to sell products as well as identify the customer's needs and, convince them for purchasing particular products. They collect market information and transmit it to the top management so that the latter might arrive at correct marketing decisions. The kind of job a salesman has to perform determines the kind of person to be appointed. He has to perform sales jobs, counter-sales jobs, travelling sales jobs, promotional sales jobs, technical sales jobs and other jobs to augment the turnover of the company and assist in winning customer and goodwill for it. He is a full-time employee. As he represents the company, his performance may make or mar the reputation of the company. He is a motivator, who persuades a shopkeeper to sell the maximum number of his products and to educate customers about the utilities of those products. He should have a persuasive skill to induce the customers who are generally unaware of their needs and may feel that they do not require a particular product. He creates a demand among the customers. By adopting an offensive strategy he should adopt the counter practice of repeating the purchases by customers. As he is required to travel extensively he should be physically strong and healthy so that he might stand up against the strain. He should have technical knowledge to explain the virtues and qualities of the product. Technical knowledge may help in creative selling. Properly selected sales persons understand the problems of customers and can develop satisfactory customer relations. Right selection ensures a strong position for the sales organisation. The management recognises the importance of well-qualified and well-trained sales persons.

(ii) *Selection Planning* : The top management prepares the selection Plan together with the sales manager. An efficient plan incorporates the job analysis, job description, job specification and job evaluation.

(a) ***Job Analysis*** : Job analysis is a detailed study of a job, breaking it down into small components and understanding the qualifications or qualities required for the effective performance of the job. It requires a systematic collection and study of information. It determines the objectives of the job, relations with customers and relations of the sales department with other departments of the company. It provides a complete picture of the roles of salesmen to be successfully played in the sales world. It provides an idea about the work and the salary, training, working methods of personnel, and the direction and control of sales functions. A valuable guide to employees, it fixes the responsibility of each employee. It makes possible the appointment of the right persons to the right jobs.

(b) ***Job Description*** : Job description is a compact statement of duties, simple and concise written statements, explaining the content and essential components of a job. It includes job identification and title, job summary, duties to be performed, supervision, relation to other jobs, the methods, machines and working conditions required for the performance of a job. It produces a precise picture of task content and occupational requirements. On the basis of job description a description in detail of the job is given to salesman.

(c) ***Job Specification*** : Every job has two aspects, *i.e.* job description and job specification. A job description merely describes the job content but a job specification is the standards required of the man to be placed in the job. "Job specification" specifies the required qualifications for the performance of the salesman's job efficiently and effectively. It describes the qualifications required for the job, the physical standards, educational qualifications, experience, aptitude and other job requirements. A job specification is a description of the essential qualities of the persons required for the job. Job specifications are used to indicate the minimum acceptable qualities required for getting employment. Job specifications stipulate the minimum educational qualifications, the qualities of the product and technical knowledge of the job. A specification of the job ensures the success and smooth performance of duties and responsibilities by salesman.

(d) ***Job Evaluation*** : "Job evaluation" refers to the classification of a job. It is the rating of the various jobs on the basis of duties and responsibilities. Categories of cadres are established under it. Salary and compensation are fixed on its basis. Jobs may be classified as very highly skilled jobs, highly skilled jobs, skilled jobs, semi-skilled jobs and unskilled jobs. The grade or remuneration is fixed for each category. Job evaluation indicates the skill required, the responsibility involved, the effort required, the qualifications and experience needed and the working conditions.

(iii) *Selection Procedure* : Though the selection procedure may vary from company to company, there is a standard selection procedure adopted by most companies to select salesmen; such as inviting applications, conducting written tests and interview, and asking for references.

(a) ***Applications*** : Application calls for information of age, sex, qualifications, status, experience and other relevant material from the applicants. The posts are advertised and applications are invited from prospective candidates. Application forms include all the pertinent information required for a job. The applicant may be required to attach to his application certificates from previous employees, salary drawn, special qualifications, and other relevant information.

(b) ***Written Tests*** : Written tests are conducted to evaluate the mental alertness of the applicants and their ability to discharge the duties and responsibilities of the job efficiently and effectively. The tests may be in language, mathematics and general understanding. Written tests may evaluate the applicant's attributes such as IQ, aptitude, and general knowledge. The applicants below a minimum standard may be rejected and above that level accepted on the basis of merit rating. The tests for the selection of salesmen are different from those for the selection of managers and clerks. Aptitude tests and psychological tests are conducted to select salesmen.

(c) ***Interview*** : The interview is a widely used method of selection under which aptitude and psychological tests can be scientifically administered to evaluate the attributes of salesmanship in the applicant. The interview is conducted by a committee of experts in the areas of salesmanship, psychology and management. Many companies have a selection committee which is able to judge a candidate's ability in oral communication, personal appearance, manners, aptitudes and his flair for salesmanship, as well as his educational qualifications and career and family background. The interview committee may be composed of the managing director, the sales manager and other executives in the areas of sales.

(d) ***References*** : References may be used to evaluate the past experience, conduct, reputation, honesty and interpersonal relationships of the candidate. Sometimes the referees provide confidential reports used to assess the integrity and honesty of the candidate. Application forms, written tests and interviews do not reveal the information obtained through references.

The candidate is asked to mention two or three names in the application form to whom a reference may be made about him. The employer sends a prescribed form to the referees, asking about the ability, integrity, personal behaviour and character traits of the candidate. As the referees may give biased information for or against a candidate, the reports should he thoroughly evaluated before their acceptance.

**5. Training.** A formal sales training contributes significantly to sales. It may be imparted to the newly-recruited salesmen and to the older sales people, for it increases their productivity and efficiency. A supervisor has to devote much less time and effort on trained men. The trainees are motivated and morally pushed up to achieve the targets of the organisation. Though costly, the training programme is essential for the success of the sales force. An effective training programme should have a clear definition of objectives, decisions on programme content, selection of training methods and execution of the actual training programme. Professional sales trainers call these steps the A-C-M-E procedure-aim, content, method and execution.

(i) *Objectives of Training* : The main objective of a training programme is to increase the efficiency and productivity of the sales people. By product knowledge and knowledge of salesmanship, it provides a base for the measurement of the productivity of each salesman. As the salesman achieving high productivity is given a higher salary and allowance, his morale increases. He acquires a detailed knowledge of the rules, regulations and procedures. The minimum level of productivity and a knowledge of specific rules and regulations exercise a proper control over his activities. He has to promote goodwill for the company, through good relations with customers. Training keeps him abreast of new developments in the sales field. Sales promotion can be handled by a specially trained group of salesmen.

(ii) *Contents* of *Training Programme* : Though the contents of the training programme vary from company to company, some useful items are included in all training programmes such as product knowledge, an awareness of the importance of the industry, sales techniques, knowledge of the company and of markets.

(a) ***Product Knowledge*** : *The* salesman should know the attributes and want-satisfying characteristics of the product. He should have a detailed knowledge of the qualities and attributes of the product he sells so that may convince about the worthwhileness of the product. Technical as well as non-technical products have some inherent qualities which should be known to salesmen so that they might demonstrate them to customers. Salesmen may spend a few weeks at the factory to acquaint themselves thoroughly with the production process.

(b) ***Importance of Industry*** : *The* trainees should know the product as well as the importance of the industry very thoroughly. Every industry has some unique features which distinguish it from other industries.

(c) ***Sales Techniques*** : Salesmen acquire a knowledge of the processes of the sales techniques. They receive training in the principles of salesmanship. They acquire a knowledge of salesmanship by demonstration, learning, reading and practice. The methods of operating a machine are demonstrated by the salesman. The selling points are emphasised intelligently to motivate buyers.

(d) ***Knowledge about the Company*** : The trainees are told about the objectives, policies and philosophy of the company. Salesmen can build goodwill for, and the reputation of the company. They know the marketing strategies of the company, its pricing policies, product techniques, promotion policies and distribution systems. A knowledge of working conditions and career opportunities encourage them to improve their job performance.

(e) ***Knowledge about Market*** : Salesmen are given adequate knowledge of the market, of the demand for the product, of the competition and of potential areas, so that they should know the customers, their locations, buying habits and financial position.

(f) ***Knowledge of Competition*** : Salesmen should be made aware of the competitors' policies and techniques. The methods of beating competition, their uses and applications as well as methods of winning the confidence of customers under competitive situations are made known to them.

(iii) *Methods of Training* : There may be on-the-job training, vestibule school, apprenticeship training, special courses, conferences and seminars, case discussions and other methods of training.

(a) ***On-the-Job Training*** : In it salesmen are placed under the supervision of an experienced senior salesman who guides them at every stage of their training. The main purpose of this method is demonstration of the work, observation of the job performed by salesmen and how improvements may be effected in performance. The underlying principles of this method are co-operation, sympathy, instruction and mutual assistance.

(b) ***Vestibule School*** : Management institutes, marketing institutes, universities and professional institutes provide training in salesmanship to new as well as old salesmen, in all the areas of management, *viz.*, marketing, production, personnel and finance.

(c) ***Apprenticeship*** : Apprentices are given theoretical and practical insights into the discipline of salesmanship. They are trained to accept the job on agreement. They may be absorbed in the organisation after their training.

(d) ***Special Courses*** : To acquire an in-depth knowledge of salesmanship the salesman can be offered special courses. Correspondence courses are provided by several educational and private institutions, because salesmen who cannot attend regular courses may find correspondence courses very useful.

(e) ***Conferences and Seminars*** : The existing salesmen may be given training by permitting them to attend conferences and seminars, where sales problems and solving techniques are discussed. Conferences and seminars discuss the latest techniques of solving problems.

(f) ***Case Discussion Method*** : The case discussion method discusses individual cases and problems. Before discussing the actual cases, some hypothetical cases are framed and discussed at a higher level. The discussion is designed to involve all the salesmen with a view to finding suitable solutions.

(g) ***The Role Playing, Brain Storming and Round Table Method*** : The role playing method involves salesmen to act in contrived problem situations. The brain storming method involves discussion of a problem without contradicting the arguments of other participants. The round table method involves the discussion among all the trainees who try to improve their performance.

**6. Organising.** Salesmen can be organised on the basis of geographical area, product types and customer classification. There may be one sales manager for each area to organise his market. In the geographical organisation the chief sales manager looks after the sales functions of each region. If the business is very heavy, one area sales manager may be appointed for each region. Similarly, a product organisation is organised on the basis of product types. The customer organisation is achieved on the basis of wholesaling, retailing and institutional marketing. In territorial organisation the salesmen are organised on a territorial basis to perform their respective jobs. The cost of maintaining a geographical organisation may be higher than that of other types of organisation, though it has been productive of substantial rewards for the sales management.

**7. Supervision.** "Supervision" refers to an activity which directs and motivates the sales force to do a better job. Working on commission basis the salesmen may need some sort of supervision to guide them to achieve higher targets of sales. The area sales manager has to see that no salesman is overburdened or travels unnecessarily. The purpose of supervision is to achieve maximum sales at minimum cost without affecting the efficiency of the sales personnel. The sales manager has to direct, motivate and supervise the sales force to improve their competitive qualities. He has to evaluate their performance and tell them where and how improvements can be effected by them. As excessive supervision can retard the growth of business, supervision should be exercised within some limits to motivate salesmen at developing customer targets, prospect targets and time efficiency.

The sales manager classifies customers into several categories according to their purchasing behaviour. Prospect targets are decided to invite new persons to purchase the product. The prospecting methods are determined by the supervisor. Annual call schedules, market development, sales generating activities, market protection activities are considered to evaluate time efficiency. Time is allocated for travel, waiting, selling, administration, food and breaks.

**8. Compensating.** Compensation is essential for the purpose of retaining and motivating the sales force. Monetary incentives may be in the form of salary, commission, bonus, etc. A minimum amount of salary is guaranteed to salesmen to ensure the safety of, and satisfaction with the job. Commission and salary are combined to compensate salesmen and stimulate them to achieve the targets. The salaries are commensurate with the responsibility and nature of job. Travel and out-station allowances are adjusted properly to motivate them. Compensation may be in the form of a straight salary plan, a straight commission plan, a salary-plus-commission plan, a salary-plus-bonus plan, and a salary-plus-bonus-commission plan.

(i) *Straight Salary Plan* : It offers the maximum security to salesmen. The management guarantees payment of at least a minimum salary and expects minimum productivity. This method is based on the time-wage system. Salesmen are paid travelling expenses and other expenses incurred by them in the discharge of their duties. They are assured of a minimum amount every month. It gives them a sense of security and promotes their loyalty to the organisation. They are motivated to explore new areas of sales because they work seriously to develop an untapped area into full-fledged market. They are not required to adopt aggressive salesmanship procedures. They may devote more time to satisfy customers and understand their requirements. Supervision and other managerial jobs can be assigned to them.

The straight salary method does not offer any incentive to salesmen. There is no direct relationship between the volume of sales and the cost of sales. Salesmen do not take up any difficult task because that does not yield any extra remuneration to them.

(ii) *Straight Commission Plan* : It incorporates payment of compensation on the basis of sales performance. The commission may be paid on the net sales or on the total number of units sold. The compensation based on commission varies from salesman to salesman, depending upon their sales performance. It provides a maximum direct financial incentive. This is the most suitable method of expanding sales. It attracts those people who are energetic, industrious and enthusiastic. The selling cost is controlled in relation to the sales volume. This plan suffers from certain defects. The aggressive selling method is used without caring for the reputation of the company. Salesmen may concentrate on easy sales, and may not devote time to the exploration of new markets. They may lack creative salesmanship.

(iii) *Salary Plus Commission Plan* : It combines two methods a fixed salary paid to all salesmen and a commission at a fixed rate on the total sales effected by them. Salesmen are satisfied with the fixed regular salary because it assures safety and security, while industrious, energetic, efficient and enterprising salesmen earn a larger amount on the basis of their sales performance.

(iv) *Salary Plus Bonus Plan* : In this plan, bonus is paid when a particular sales quota is achieved, or when promotional activities are undertaken, or when the objectives are attained and all the assigned jobs have been performed. The salary plan offers safety and satisfaction, while bonus is an additional incentive for the attainment of targets. Bonus is a satisfactory incentive. However, the procedure for bonus payment should be determined clearly and fairly.

(v) *Commission Plus Bonus Plan* : Salesmen are motivated to earn a higher amount by way of bonus on higher sales.

(iv) *Salary Plus Commission and Bonus Plan* : Salesmen may be given salary as well as commission on their regular sales. If their performance exceeds the prescribed level, they are rewarded with a bonus. The bonus stimulates; the commission gives incentives, and the salary ensures security. Thus, the three elements are combined to ensure the highest performance.

**9. Co-ordinating.** Co-ordinating is an orderly arrangement of group effort, done by grouping similar activities under one head. Committees are formed to integrate the activities of sales people. Personal relationships and voluntary co-ordination are established for co-ordinating the sales activities of different salesmen in different regions. Staff meetings, conferences, programmes, etc. are organised to co-ordinate the activities of salesmen.

**10. Control.** The sales manager has to adopt suitable methods for controlling sales performance. The control mechanism includes budgetary control, planning control, cost control and operational control. The sales performance, profitability and other evaluation techniques are used to examine the performance of sales representative. The comparison of the performance of a salesman with that of other salesmen or with the standard performance is made to determine the efficiency of a salesman. Qualitative achievements are examined to evaluate the performance of the sales people.

The control mechanism enables the management to improve the efficiency and performance of sales representatives.

## SALES EXECUTIVE AS CO-ORDINATOR

In terms of sales volume, net profits, and long-term growth optimum marketing performance requires co-ordination. Sales executives play significant roles in co-ordinating. They have responsibilities for co-ordination involving (1) the organisation, (2) the planning, and (3) other elements in the marketing strategy. Higher-ranking sales executives are most concerned with obtaining effective co-ordination, while sales executives at all organisational levels have some responsibility for co-ordinating.

**1. Co-ordination in Organization.** Co-ordination in personal selling, advertising, and so forth is achieved through a single responsible, top-ranking executive. Generally, marketing vice-president, director of marketing, or marketing manager is responsible for minimizing the possibility that the different order-getting departments work at cross-purposes or work toward sales goals independently.

From the department head on down, all sales executives are responsible for co-ordinating the organizational units under their control inside the sales department. Generally democratic administration is the rule in sales departments that functions smoothly. Subordinates affected by a decision are consulted in advance and are allowed to participate in making it. This reduces the tendency to resist directives issued by superiors. There are minimum opportunities for misunderstandings to occur. Subordinates as well as superiors both visualize the circumstances giving rise to decisions.

**2. Co-ordination in Planning.** Having specialized knowledge of the market and of the capabilities of the sales force the sales executive is involved in achieving co-ordination in marketing objectives and draft plans that achieve desired results at optimum cost. He determines the personal selling, advertising, and so forth that make up the marketing program, apportioning the relative amounts of each to equate its marginal effectiveness with that of other elements. Co-ordination among the marketing planners is essential to lay out specific programs for achieving pre-determined sales, profit and growth objectives. As a member of the planning group the sales executive seeks to secure a marketing program which is appropriate for market conditions and reflects the probable contribution of the sales force.

**3. Co-ordination of other Elements in the Marketing Program.** The sales executive is related to co-ordinating personal selling with other order-getting methods.

(i) *Personal Selling*: If the total marketing effort is to achieve the desired results, personal-selling efforts must be co-ordinated with advertising, display, and other promotional efforts. As they must build co-ordination into the marketing plan, so they must achieve co-ordination during the plan's implementation.

(ii) *Adverising* : Synchronizing personal selling with advertising is particularly important, because unless the sales force capitalizes upon the interest aroused advertising may prove uneconomic. In explaining details that might be explained by advertising, personal-selling effort is wasted. But promotional impact is magnified when sales personnel and the advertising use the same appeals. Both the timing and sequence with which different phases of the personal-selling and advertising efforts are executed affect the firm's chances for marketing success like personal-selling effort, an advertising effort should be implemented within the context of the larger marketing effort.

(iii) *Other Promotional Efforts* : Sales executives are involved in co-ordinating other promotional efforts with the personal-selling effort. Point-of-purchase displays, are set up in retail stores where customers see them at the precise time that tie-in advertisements appear in national and local media. The sales force achieves this timing and co-ordination. The sales personnel alerts dealers to special couponing or sampling efforts so that they can benefit from heightened customer interest.

**4. Distributive Network Co-ordination.** Sales executives co-ordinate personal selling with the marketing efforts of the middlemen, whose most important aspects are; product distribution, dealer identification, reconciliation of business goals and sharing of promotional risks.

(i) *Product Distribution* : Sales executives are responsible for obtaining distribution, when a new product is introduced, unless the product is sold directly to final users. Sometimes, middlemen refuse to stock a new product unless the manufacturer's sales staff presents convincing arguments of its salability. Some manufacturers succeed in "pulling" their products through the distribution channel by means of heavy advertising to final buyers, though such instances of "forced distribution" are rare. The manufacturer of a new product, faces distributor lethargy and dealer indifference for which he must use missionary selling. It frequently happens in marketing a new consumer product that even missionary selling is handicapped because corporate chains and other integrated retailers do not permit decentralized calls on their individual outlets. Therefore the manufacturer of a new product has to build to demand for it in as many outlets as are initially willing to handle it. He must prove the existence of a established market demand to the remaining "desired outlets" before adequate distribution is secured. The sales executive must ensure that the manufacturer's initial promotional efforts are tied in with those of the middlemen who first stock the product. He must see to it that progressively larger shares of the promotional burden are shifted to the middlemen. The product is made available in more outlets, co-ordinating the promotional efforts of the manufacturer and its middle men grows increasingly important. The sales executives must adjust their co-ordinating efforts accordingly.

(ii) *Dealer Identification* : To further the chances of success of the personal-selling effort the sales executive must ensure that final buyers know as to which local outlets stock the product. No sales will give any result if final buyers cannot find the source that stock it even if advertising succeeds in pre-selling the product. Inadequate dealer identification leads to clogged distribution channels from the dealer's stockroom to the factory, while dealers take the initiative in publicizing the availability of the product. In most cases, sales personnel promote dealer identification through providing store sign, furnishing preprints and reprints of advertisement, supplying advertising mats for local insertions, and assisting in building merchandise displays. In other cases, sales executives arrange for the placing of local advertising over the dealers' names.

In marketing many consumer products, particularly those distributed through self-service retailers the sales force plays a related role. Once in the right retail stores consumers can locate the product with minimum difficulty. Display at the point of purchase bridges the gap between advertising impact and the retail sale. Sales executives must teach sales people how to obtain the retailer's permission to use them, whenever merchandising aids, such as interior display pieces or shelf markers, are used. Timing is important in securing permission, for example, at the start of a special promotional campaign—retailers are more willing to allow the creation of display than they are during slow selling seasons.

(iii) *Reconciliation of Business Goals* : Skillful co-ordination by sales executives and the sales force minimizes the natural friction that develops because of imaginary or real conflicts between the business goals of the manufacturer and middlemen.

The less the manufacturer and the middlemen work at cross-purposes, the greater is the return to both parties.

(a) ***The Manufacturer Shares Business Information with the Middle Men*** : Certain information is imparted through trade advertising, but sales people personalize much data for middlemen. For example, when the results of marketing research studies have special reports prepared for personal presentation and explanation by the sales force.

(b) ***The Manufacturer Needs Information on the Operating Situation and Problems of the Middle Men*** : Through regular and special reports sales personnel serve as the vehicles of communication. Sales executives recognize that it is possible to provide them with effective promotional and other assistance, if timely information is available on the needs and attitudes of middlemen. In the light of information provided by sales people in the field the sales executive makes periodic appraisals of existing marketing policies. This ensures that current as well as newly formulated policies are appropriate for the total marketing situation.

(c) ***Sales Executive Ensure that Sales Personal are Fair and Impartial in their Dealings with Middlemen*** : No outlet should be favoured at the expense of another; all should receive equitable treatment. Sales people need continual training to keep them abreast of correct operating policies, practices and procedures. They require effective supervision to apply them fairly as well as properly. It is the responsibility of sales executives to provide this training and supervision.

(iv) *Sharing of Promotional Risks* : The marketing program often calls the manufacturer and the middle men to share promotional risks such as in case of co-operative advertising. The sales executives ensure that the sales personnel make effective presentations designed to convince dealers to participate. Manufacturers utilizing selective or exclusive agency distribution gain the most from sharing promotional risk with middlemen. The sales executives and the sales force play roles in the initial selection of middlemen as well as in obtaining their consent to share promotional risks. Manufacturers using mass distribution do not find it feasible to delegate much promotional authority to their middlemen. However, regardless of the company's distribution policy, the sales executive takes steps to make the job of the middlemen more interesting, profitable and challenging. This facilitates the task of co-ordination.

**5. Overall Marketing Strategy Co-ordination.** Problems in co-ordination occur in timing and securing the best sequence of execution of the various phases when the overall marketing strategy is being put into effect. When a new product is to be introduced at a trade show or exhibition, the sale executive co-ordinates with advertising executives to ensure that the proper interval elapses before advertisements appear or sales people make calls on dealers in the product's behalf. Similar coordinating action ensures proper spacing of the advertising in relation to the call schedules of sales people. The sales executives ensure that field sales personnel integrate every phase and segment of the promotional programs of distributors and dealers.

Introduction of a new brand successfully in the market is a test of the mettle and the level of competence possessed by members of the marketing management team, including sales executives. It requires policies, strategies, and detailed plans, appropriate to the company's marketing situation. Launching a brand at the wrong time, or faulty timing at any state, kills or reduces the changes for success. Proper timing of the stages in the introduction plan is important. All the promotional efforts for the new brand require co-ordination of advertising with personal selling and the manufacturer's total promotion with middlemen activities.

While executives should know the techniques and problems of new-brand introduction, they must also be capable of putting the plans into action and implement them effectively. They must skillfully execute the program of market introduction.

## PHASES OF CONTROL

Sales executives control the personal-selling effort of the organizational units under them to ensure that sales department objective are reached, like planning, organizing, and co-ordinating. The following phases of control are presented in the normal sequence though some of these may occur simultaneously or overlap in time.

**1. Sizing up the Situation.** Starting by reviewing the personal-selling objectives of the firm, sales executives analyze these objectives with respect to the present, the past, and the future to answer the following four questions.

(i) Where are we now?

(ii) How did we get here?

(iii) Where are we going?

(iv) How do we get there?

After satisfying themselves that the company's long range and short range personal-selling objectives are reconcilable sales executives appraise them about the plans, policies, and procedures that have been used, or are intended to be used to reach personal-selling objectives. In the course of sizing up the situation, sales executives find and correct weaknesses or imperfections in the sales plans and the policies and procedures used in theft implementation.

**2. Setting Quantitative Performance Standards.** The sales executives set quantitative standards against which to measure performance. This requires continual experimentation. Most standards are far from precise. The ultimate test of a particular standard's appropriateness is whether it contributes more to personal-selling efficiency than it costs.

Intelligent standard setting requires identification of the individuals responsible for the activity or group of activities being put under control. Even though they may operate in identical circumstances no two salespersons or executives perform exactly alike. Thus, standards are often expressed as ranges to acceptable performance. Though it is convenient to think of a standard as a fixed value, there should be an upper and lower limit within which human variation may take place. When the performance of an organizational unit passes these control limits, the danger flag is up, signalling that the situation is out of control.

**3. Gathering and Processing Data on Actual Performance.** Though the type and amount of information needed for controlling sales depend upon the standards selected, it should not be in excess of sales management's real needs, nor should its cost of collection and processing be more than its worth. At regular intervals sales management determines whether the reported information is sufficiently important and enough to justify its costs. Sales executives remember that changes in executives, basic policies, or other matters may change the usefulness of information. They look for cases where the same or similar information is being obtained from more than one source, representing opportunities for savings through eliminating duplications in reporting. Savings are realized through reducing or lengthening the intervals at which information is gathered and processed.

Sales executives must have information on actual performances soon enough to permit timely corrective action. An efficient system of sales control furnishes information necessary to managerial evaluation of performance. It also promptly relays it, together with suggestion for actions, to the appropriate organizational unit. However information on actual sales performance is often slow in arriving on the sales executive's desk. This considerably delays performance evaluations. For example, many companies, require sales personnel to make weekly sales reports. In such cases, a week or more may pass before the sales executive acts on the report. However, progress is being made in improving the timeliness of sales control information. Utilization electronic of data-processing systems for handling sales control data has sped up information evaluation and feedback.

**4. Evaluating Performance.** Evaluation of performance includes comparing actual result with standards. Though it is difficult to compare individual performances due to differences in territorial and other conditions it is possible to explain each individual salesperson's variations from standard. These are classified into uncontrollable and controllable variations.

(i) *Uncontrollable Variations* : These include those caused by rapid and unexpected changes in economic conditions; changes in government activities, and wars, strikes, floods, and other natural disasters.

(ii) *Controllable Variations* : These include obtaining proper sales coverage, following up leads, selling a balanced line, securing adequate credit information, and the like. As subordinates should not be held responsible for uncontrollable conditions it is important to exclude them in appraising performance.

**5. Action to Correct Controllable Variation.** Management corrects the controllable variations and takes steps to move the individual's performance in the direction of the standards. Though the specific actions taken differ with the nature of the variation, management's actions assume one or more of three forms: (*i*) Direction, or Pointing out more effective ways to perform certain tasks; (*ii*) Guidance, or providing additional instructions training; and (*iii*) Restraint, or the installation of procedures and practices aimed at keeping results within desired bounds.

**6. Adjustment for Uncontrollable Variation.** The amount of uncontrollable variation in the comparison indicates the need for adjusting sales plans and policies. If it suggests that the present sales objectives are unrealistic or not in line with current expectations, basic revisions in the objectives are made. Thus adjustment of standards to attainable levels is in order, if a comparison of results with standards reveals substantial controllable variation.

## INFORMAL SALES CONTROL

Under some circumstances awareness of the changing situation, and the ability to analyze it, are adequate devices. In such a situation effective sales executives have their "fingers on the pulse of the business". They have uncanny ability to detect situations requiring attention. However, in a large company with a higher administrative hierarchy it is hard to use "fingertip" control. Formal control is required as the business grows and the structure of the sales organization becomes more complex. A growing business needs dependable machinery to provide the facts making workable decisions and for formulating appropriate policies.

## FORMAL SALES CONTROL

The appearance of sales policies in writing is an evidence of the introduction of formal sales controls. No enterprise can survive for long without policies, though smaller firms often operate satisfactorily, even though they do not put their policies in writing. As the sales organization grows, the limits are one spelled out in detail within which action is to take place in given situations. A large organization has more complex problems than a small organization. There is less chance that everyone will know what to do in every circumstance. Therefore a large organization needs written sales and marketing policies to ensure substantial uniformity of action, essential for both different persons handling similar problems and the same persons handling similar problems at different times. Written policies conserve executive's time. More time can be used for planning and making decisions on problems not covered by existing policies. Sales executives reserve time for handling "policy exceptions". A new policy is formulated and is put into writing if they encounter enough exceptions of similar nature.

## TYPES OF FORMAL SALES CONTROL

**1. Policy Formulation and Review.** The process of policy formulation and review illustrates the formal control. A good policy evolves from thorough study and evaluation to tangible information, though many sales policies deal with subjects on which quantitative data are lacking, especially when management is experimenting with new ideas. When objectives are not set clearly because of lack of information results vary from the standard because of "uncontrollable variations" being evaluated. Thus, sales management reviews the original plans along with the scaling down of objectives. Policies initially based on inadequate data often become appropriate and "good" through successive revisions.

**2. Formal Control Over Sales Volume.** Introduced early in the history of a firm one formal control is that over sales volume. Both for planning and control estimating how much of a product can be sold in a specified future period is pre-requisite. Sales volume performance is best appraised by comparing it with potential sales volume. Thus, "sales or market forecast," serves as a standard for evaluating sales performance, though the periodic forecast of sales is not enough for effective control over sales volume. Sales management monitors industry sales trends, activities of competitors, and share-of-the-market percentages during the intervals between forecasts. Significant changes in these factors require changes in sales objectives, plans, policies and procedures.

**3. Budgetary Control.** Formal control requires sales budgetary controls and setting up of sales territories. Budgetary control represents an extension of control over sales volume to control margins and expenses and, hence, over profits. Through it sales management can project individual profit-and-loss statements for such units as sales territories, products, marketing channels, and classes of customers. Sales management sets standards for controlling individual expense items and the grant margin through such estimating devices as standard costs of distribution. Sales management appraises sales performance against pre-determined standards through marketing costs analysis. Thus the areas of below par sales performance are brought to management's attention reducing the time between drops in performance and corrective action.

**4. Decentralization.** In the decentralized sales organization, greater control is exercised by executives lower in the hierarchy than is true in the centralized organization. The higher up executives in the organization they deal with "policy" or "control" exceptions than with the control mechanism itself. Situations falling outside the control limits are handed up to that executive who has authority to deal with them. The power to make decisions is delegated as far down in the organizational structure as is consistent with the caliber and experience of executives.

## TYPES OF SELLING

Selling is the outcome of a marketing process. The sales process should be seen in the context of customer problem-solving rather than as merely selling a product. The relationship based selling creates difficulties in assessing the role of the sales persons. A better appreciation of variations in sales approaches can be obtained by viewing them as part of a continuum as shown below :

*Alternative Approaches in Selling*

Conditioned — insight

Sales oriented — customer oriented

Order taker — order maker

Direct — indirect/continuing

Transaction based — relationship based

Derch Newton classifies sales as four types : Trade, missionary, technical and new business selling. Sales person's performance can be judged according to this classification. McMurry and Arnold's classification is of nine types, namely : (1) Inside order sales; (2) Delivery sales; (3) Outside order sales; (4) Missionary sales; (5) Technical sales; (6) Creative sales (tangibles); (7) Creative sales (intangibles); (8) Political sales and 9. Multiple sales. A modern classification of sales is in two types : (a) Direct and (b) Indirect. Direct and indirect both may further be subdivided into (i) Consumer sales; (ii) Industrial sales; (iii) Government sales; (iv) National sales and (v) International sales.

## SALE AND MARKETING

Some of the misconceptions about selling are now gone *e.g.* that selling is not a worthwhile career or good products will sell themselves and that earning through sales is immoral activity. Sales efforts influence and are influenced by decisions taken on the ingredients of company's marketing mix, which in turn effect its overall marketing efforts. Sales are a part of the activity of marketing function. Selling is only a part of the total marketing programme of the company.

## QUESTIONS FOR EXERCISE

1. Define sales management and discuss its objectives.
2. Describe the functions of Sales Management.
3. Explain the functioning of sales executive as co-ordinator.
4. Define the phases of control of the personal selling effort of the organisation units by the sales executive.
5. Distinguish between informal and formal sales control.

# 2

# SALESMANSHIP AND THEMES OF SELLING

Salesmanship is one aspect of personal selling. Personal selling is a broader concept than salesmanship. Personal selling, along with other marketing elements such as pricing, advertising, product development and research, marketing channels, and physical distribution, is a means for implementing marketing programs. Salesmanship is one of the skills used in personal selling.

## DEFINITION OF SALESMANSHIP

1. Irving J. Shapiro. "It is the art of successfully persuading prospects or customers buy products or services from which they can derive suitable benefits, thereby increasing their total satisfaction."

At one time, the emphasis in salesmanship was almost wholly on persuasion; today while recognizing the significance of persuasion, the emphasis is on the benefits attractive to prospects and customers. One variation of benefit-oriented salesmanship is "consultative selling"—creating long-term, mutually beneficial sales relationships with customers by helping them to improve their profits through products and services.

2. Ripley. "Salesmanship is the power to persuade plenty of people pleasurably and permanently to purchase your product at a profit."

3. H.W. Horignton. "Salemanship is a personal service rendered to the community in connection with the marketing of goods. It is a service which is essential to the producer and distributor of goods as well as to the consumer."

4. T.S. Knox. "Salesmanship is the ability to change need into human wants."

5. Harold White-head. "The art of presenting and offering that the prospect appreciates the need for it and that a mutually satisfactory sales follows".

6. W.M. Scott. "It is a part of salesman' business to create demand by demonstrating that the need does exist although before his visit there was no consciousness of that need."

7. Harry L. Hansen. "Salesmanship is that act of persuading people to accept an idea."

8. D.D. Cough. "Salesmanship is the science of creating in the mind of your prospect desire that only possession of your product will satisfy."

9. American Marketing Association. "Salesmanship is the process of including and assisting a prospective buyer to buy a commodity or service or to act favourably upon an idea that has commercial significance to the seller." It has been defined as the ability to persuade people to buy goods or services at a profit to the seller and with benefit to the buyer.

10. Pederson and Wright. "Salesmanship is "the process whereby the seller ascertains and activates the needs or wants of the buyer and satisfies these needs or wants to the mutual continuous advantage of both the buyer and the seller." As a positive effort at persuading people to buy, salesman benefits both the seller and the buyer.

## ESSENTIALS OF SALESMANSHIP

**1. No Exploitation.** Good salesmanship does not exploit an innocent customer. It aims at charging reasonable prices irrespective of sex, rank, status or age of the customer.

**2. No Haggling.** Haggling indicates suspicion on the part of the buyer that the prices are higher. The salesman should state clearly and frankly that the prices are uniform for all.

**3. Tolerant Persuasion.** Good salesmanship considers that customer is always right. Having his interest in mind the customer studies the merits of the proposition from his point of view. He notices various defects which the salesman ordinarily does not care to know. An honest salesman must be prepared to listen to all criticism and try to understand defects of the goods with an open mind.

**4. Serving the Customer.** Good salesmanship aims at serving the customer. The salesman advises the customer how to use, preserve and maintain the things and also to set right the things if they are out of order.

**5. No Pressure Tactics.** A good salesmen does not use pressure tactics. Shy customers often accept goods reluctantly because of a feeling of guilt that they have taken the time of the salesman and that it is not proper to leave the shop without buying. Such customers may not visit the shop again.

**6. Standard.** A good salesman sets standards for sellers. However, he never comes down from his high standards. He sets an example to others.

**7. Mutual Benefit.** After the purchase the customer should feel that he has not suffered a loss or wasted his money. He should be induced to desire goods and buy them at a price profitable to both the parties.

## UTILITY OF SALESMANSHIP

(i) *To Manufacturers* : An efficient sales force ensures high profits to industrialists and agriculturists. Good salesmanship is an incentive to higher production.

(ii) *To Society* : Salesmanship increases production, enhances profits to the middlemen, gets higher dividends for the shareholder and higher emoluments to employers also get-more profits. Thus the whole society reaps advantage by salesmanship.

(iii) *To the State* : When industries make high profits, the government also benefits in the form of high quantum of taxation. It gets income by way of excise duty on production, sales tax on sales, freights on account of transport.

(iv) *To Consumers* : Higher production brings in competition which in its turn lowers prices. Consumers are able to purchase better quality of goods in the market and enjoy a number of services from salesmen and companies.

(v) *To Salesmen* : The salesmen themselves are profited directly and indirectly, increasing their commission.

## PROSPECTING

### Meaning

The planning of work, essential in eliminating calls on non-buyers, is called "prospecting." Efficient organization of time and thorough planning of work are earmarks of above-average sales persons. They look for a way to "stretch" productive selling time. They arrange travel and call schedules to economize the time spent *en route* and distance travelled. They make appointments to avoid prolonged waiting for call backs. They do not waste time trying to sell to people who cannot buy or are not likely to do so.

Improvement in prospecting increases productive selling time. Sales personnel who devote too little time to prospecting spend too much time to calling on non-prospects. Salespersons proficient in prospecting apply their selling efforts productively. They do not call on non-prospects but devote their full attention to those likely to buy.

Some companies use specialized personnel for prospecting and most regard it as one of the salespersons' responsibilities. Even though salespersons may not do "all" the prospecting, they often have access to information on likely prospects.

### Steps in Prospecting

The steps in prospecting are (1) formulating prospect definition, (2) searching out potential accounts, (3) qualifying prospects and determining probable requirements and (4) relating company products to each prospect's requirements.

**1. Formulating Prospect Definition.** Prospective customers must have the willingness, the financial capacity, and the authority to buy. They must be available to the salesperson. Salespersons only waste time in attempting to sell to individuals who have neither need for the product nor money to pay for it. They waste time if they try to sell to the wrong persons. It is important to ascertain which persons in each firm have the authority to buy. Although individuals may qualify as prospects in other respects they may be inaccessible to the salesperson. For example, the president of a large corporation may need insurance and be willing and able to pay for it, but a particular salesperson may have no way to make the contact.

Besides meeting the stated requirements, there are requirements unique to each company's customers. Starting with data on the profitability of present accounts, the characteristics typical of profitable accounts but not shared by unprofitable accounts should be detected. These should be recognizable from information appearing in directories or lists. For example, prospects in many businesses and professions are readily identified from classified listings in telephone and city directories. The prospect definitions are the key characteristics that identify profitable accounts and are assembled into descriptions of the various classes of customers.

**2. Searching out Potential Accounts.** With the help of the prospect definitions, the salesperson reaches different sources for the names of probable prospects, or "suspects," as they are called. Important sources of prospect information are directories of all kinds, news and notes in trade papers and business magazines, credit reports, membership lists of chambers of commerce and trade and manufacturers' associations, lists purchased from list brokers, and records of service requests; responses to company advertising, sales personal of non-competing firms calling on the same general classes of trade, conventions and meetings, bankers and other "centers of influence," and the salesperson's own observations. For example, salespeople selling services and insurance find' out prospects among their acquaintances; members of their professional, religious, and social organizations; and the referrals of friends. Another source of prospects is the "endless chain" of satisfied customers.

**3. Qualifying Prospects and Determining Probable Requirements.** While information is assembled on each tentative prospect it is easier to estimate the probable requirements of each for the types of products sold by the company. Prospects with too small requirements to represent profitable business are rejected from further consideration. Additional information required to qualify certain prospects may be gathered by personal visits of salespersons. These visits save time, as prospects are separated from non-prospects.

**4. Relating Company Products to Each Prospect's Requirements.** The final step in prospecting is to plan the strategy for approaching each prospect. It is usually possible to determine each prospect's probable needs from the information assembled. The salesperson selects those that seem most appropriate for a particular prospect from what he or she knows about the company's products, their uses and applications.

Now, the salesperson's presentation is tailored to fit the prospect. He should have clear ideas' about specific objections the prospect may raise and other obstacles to the sale. He should be ready to contact the prospect, by making an appointment, deciding how to open the presentation and determining how to persuade the prospect to become a customer.

## SALES RESISTANCE

By pointing out real or imagined obstacles, and by voicing, sincere or insincere prospects show sales resistance for analyzing which, the salesperson needs skill in the accurate and rapid appraisal of people and their motivations. A prospect's expressed sales resistance may be either an obstacle or an objection. While the obstacle may be real or unreal; the objection may be sincere or insincere.

**1. Obstacles to Sales.** Obstacles are real or apparent reasons due to which the prospect is not buying a commodity. A real obstacle precludes the consummation of the sale. But there are ways to circumvent apparent obstacles. When prospect says that a temporary shortage of cash is preventing buying — it is an obstacle, not an objection. The salesperson may help the prospect in circumventing by pointing out a method for financing the purchase. When an obstacle arises, the salesperson determines whether or not there is a way to get around it. If he recognizes the specific obstacle and knows a way to circumvent it, he should present the solution to the prospect.

**2. Sales Objections.** Though no good reasons for failing to complete the sale, objections always divert the salesperson's presentation from its main course. It requires a satisfactory answer; otherwise, it blocks the sale. Effective salespeople show adroitness in handling objections.

(i) *Sincere Objections* : Sincere objections point out incompleteness, inaccuracy, or vagueness in the sales presentation. Prospects may not recognize the nature of their needs. They may have doubts about the appropriateness of the product to fulfil those needs. They may be confused in some respect. They may react unfavourably to the salesperson's personality. These sincere objections are overcome by patient and thorough explanations.

(ii) *Insincere Objections* : The objectives of insincere objections are to discourage salespersons, to get rid of them, to test their competence, and false excuses for not buying. In the face of an insincere objection sales persons seek to regain the offensive as soon as possible. They do not permit it to provoke an argument which is the surest way to lose a sale.

Some sales executives maintain that every objection, no matter how insincere, should be treated with the utmost courtesy. Others believe that insincere objections should be ignored. As the best defensive strategy is a strong counter attack, the salesperson should seek to regain the initiative as soon as he or she can gracefully do so.

## CLOSING SALES

Low-pressure sales are closed more easily than are high-pressure ones. In low-pressure sales, prospects feel that they are reaching the buying decisions themselves, primarily through rational processes of thought. Therefore, there is no need for extra push just before the sales are consummated. In high-pressure sales, the main thrust is to the prospects emotions. Therefore, salespersons attempt to propel' prospects into buying decisions. As the sale nears its climax, often the prospect regains normal perspective. In this case, the salesperson needs unusually effective persuasion to close the sale.

While closing sales either the sales person sells the prospect an order or the prospect sells the salesperson a "no sale." Closing time is an opportunity to show tangible proof of selling skill. Even the best salesperson must rely upon closing skill to make the sale.

Well done prospecting puts the salesperson in the frame of mind for the close. He feels that a real service is being performed for the prospect, not that " a bill of goods is being sold." He thinks that the product is the best solution to the prospect's problems.

No difficulty is met in closing the sale when the sales presentation is complete and clear. All obstacles and objections to the sale have been removed to the prospect's entire satisfaction. Basic agreement has been reached. The prospect is ready to accept the proposal.

But in spite of thorough prospecting and some excellent presentation prospects refrain from positive commitments. Many people let inertia guide their reactions — others are happy to leave things as they are. Unless they jolt these prospects into buying salespersons leave empty-handed. The skilled closer gives the extra push that triggers a buying response. Poor prospecting, inept presentations and ineffective closing all lead to failures to get an order result.

If an attempted close fails, the salesperson should try another as the refusal does not necessarily imply an unwillingness to buy. It may indicate the prospect's need for additional information or for clarification of some point. Sales personnel should attempt as many as five closes before giving up. Early closing attempts should be expressed in such a way that a refusal will not out off the presentation.

## FACTORS GOVERNING BUYER-SELLER INTER-RELATION

**1. Advertisement and Personal Selling.** Salesmanship involves buyer-seller interactions. Interacting with each other, the salesperson and the prospect constitute "buyer-seller dyad." Both in advertising and personal selling, the seller seeks to motivate the prospective buyer to behave favourably toward him. It depends upon the nature of the interaction whether or not the buyer reacts as the seller desires. The opportunity for interaction is less in advertising than in personal selling though, advertising and personal selling often supplement or support each other, and the buyer reacts to their combined impact.

**2. Similarity of Characteristics and Factors.** Similarity of physical characteristics like age and height, objective factors like income, religion and education and variables that relate to personality factors such as politics, affect sales interaction. Whenever possible, sales personnel should be assigned to prospects whose characteristics are similar to their own. This will improve the chance of successful dyadic relationships. Pairing salespersons with customers of similar backgrounds can be easily accomplished in industrial selling, where there are fewer prospects about whom information is needed, than in consumer-goods selling, where the number of prospects and customers per salesperson is much larger.

**3. Ideal Performance.** In Henry Tosi's studies of dyads of wholesale drug salespeople and retail pharmacists who made buying decisions, when the buyer perceived the salesperson's performance to be similar to his or her concept of "ideal" performance, the number of sources from which purchases were made was low. Customer satisfaction with the salesperson's behaviour did allow the salesperson to get into the store. Tosi concluded that, in addition to the physical characteristics and personality and objective factors cited by Evans, the customer's perception of what that behaviour should be is a necessary condition for the continuation of dyadic interaction.

**4. Initial Conditioning.** The buyer's initial conditioning with respect to selling is another factor influencing buyer-seller dyadic interactions. Salespeople have been maligned, and the butt of nasty stories for generations. People are taught from childhood to beware of the tricky salesperson. Salespeople leave much to be desired in the impact they make on customers. Studies of the attitudes of buyers and purchasing agents reveal that many are critical of the salesperson's lack of product knowledge, failure to follow up, general unreliability, slavish adherence to "canned" presentations, blatant use of flattery, bad manners, commercial dishonesty, and so forth.

The sales process is influenced by both sales person and buyer, each a focal person influenced by personal characteristics and role requirements. Personal characteristics include personality, values, attitudes, past experiences, and the like. Role set requirements (for example, formal authority and organisational autonomy) interact with personal characteristics to shape needs and expectations. Based on individual needs and expectations, each focal person develops a strategy to negotiate favourable exchange which may include persuasion, ingratiation, communication of facts or offers, friendship and other elements. If the strategies are compatible, an exchange takes place. Otherwise, the salesperson and the buyer may stop interacting. Or both may adapt by altering strategy, attempting to adjust needs and expectations, or modifying role requirements. As role requirements, as well as needs and expectations are determined by forces beyond the focal person's control, so one or both may find it impossible to adapt. For instance, a salesperson may need to set prices to meet a buyer's expectations, yet this may be against company policy and beyond the salesperson's control.

## DIVERSITY OF PERSONAL-SELLING SITUATIONS

As much diversity exists among personal-selling situations, it is helpful to distinguish between service and developmental selling. Service selling aims to obtain sales from existing customers whose habits and patterns of thought are already conducive to such sales. Developmental selling aims to convert prospects into customers. It seeks to create customers out of people who do not currently view the salesperson's company favourably, and who are resistant to changing present sources of Supply.

### Sales Position

Different sales positions require different amounts and kinds of service and developmental selling. McMurry and Arnold classified positions on a spectrum ranging from the very simple to the highly complex and categorized sales positions into three mutually exclusive groups each containing subgroups, a total of nine subgroups in all.

**Group A (Service Selling)**

**1. Inside Order Taker.** "Waits on" customers; for example, the sales clerk behind the neckwear counter in a men's store.

**2. Delivery Salesperson.** Mainly engages in delivering the product; for example, persons delivering milk, bread, or fuel oil.

**3. Route or Merchandising Sales person.** Operates as an order taker but works in the field—the soap or spice salesperson calling on retailers is typical.

**4. Missionary.** Aims only to build goodwill or to educate the actual or potential user, and is not expected to take an order; for example, the distiller's "missionary" and the pharmaceutical company's "detail" person.

**5. Technical Salesperson.** Emphasizes technical knowledge; for example, the engineering salesperson, who is primarily a consultant to "client" companies.

**Group B (Developmental Selling)**

**6. Creative Salesperson of Tangibles.** For example, salespersons selling vacuum cleaners, automobiles, siding and encyclopaedias.

**7. Creative Salesperson of Intangibles.** For example, salesperson selling insurance, advertising services, and educational programs.

**Group C (Basically Developmental Selling, But Requiring Unusual Creativity)**

**8. Political", "Indirect", or "Back-Door" Sales person.** Sells big-ticket items, particularly commodities or items with no truly competitive features. Sales are consummated through rendering highly personalized services (which have little or no connection with the product) to key decision makers in customer's organisations; for example, the salesperson who lands large orders for flour from baking companies by catering to key buyers' interests in fishing, golfing, blondes, or the like.

**9. Sales Person Engaged in Multiple Sales.** Involves sales of big-ticket items where the salesperson must make presentations to several individuals in the customer's organization, usually a committee, only one of which can say "yes", but all of whom can say "no"; for example, the account executive of, an advertising agency who makes presentations to the "agency selection committees" of advertisers — even after the account is obtained, the salesperson has to work to retain it.

The amount and kind of developmental selling depends upon the natures of prospects and customers, and the nature of product. The easiest sales are self-service sales. Customers know their needs, know the products capable of satisfying these needs, sell themselves, and go through the check-out line. The most difficult sales require development selling *and* creativity — where sometimes the sales must be made on something other than the product's merit, or "multiple" sales are necessary to get the order, and where continual effort is required to keep the account.

## SELLING AS AN ART AND SCIENCE

Is selling a science or an art learned through experience? In a survey by J.H Goldstucker, and others it was found that of 173 marketing executives 46 percent perceived selling as an Art, 8 percent as a Science, and 46 percent as an Art evolving into a Science. Selling considered an art by some and a science by others has produced two contrasting approaches to the theory of selling.

**1. Selling is an Art.** This approach distilled the experiences of successful salespeople and, advertising professional. Many such persons, succeeded because of their grasp of practical, or learned-through-experience psychology and their ability to apply it in sales situations. These selling theories emphasize the "what to do" and "how to do" rather than the "why." Based on experiential knowledge accumulated from years of "living in the market" rather than on a systematic, fundamental body of knowledge, these theories are subject to Howard's dictum, "Experiential knowledge can be unreliable."

**2. Selling is a Science.** This approach borrowed findings from the behavioural sciences. The late E.K. Strong, Jr., professor of psychology at the Stanford Graduate School of Business, was a pioneer in this effort. John A. Howard of the Columbia Graduate School of Business was in the forefront of those who adapted the findings of behavioural science to analyse buying behaviour.

Both these approaches led to four theories. The first two, the "AIDAS" theory and the "right set of circumstances" theory, are seller oriented. The third, the "buying-formula" theory of selling, is buyer oriented. The fourth, the behavioural equation, emphasizes the buyer's decision process but also takes the salesperson's influence process into account.

## THEORIES OF BUYING AND SELLING

The buying process has five stages—need identification, search for product or service, evaluation of alternatives, actual purchase and finally use. Various models have been developed to explain the buyer's behaviour, mostly in case of new products. The main components of buyer's behaviour are four : (a) Personal; (b) Psychological; (c) Cultural; and (d) Social and group influences. Personal factors are age, occupation, income and economic status, geographic and area location and life style. The psychological factors are personality, motivation, perception, attitudes and learning. Culture, social class like middle, poor, rich etc.

In case of organizational buyers, the buying decisions are influenced by many people. They may be actual users in production department or higher authorities.

In case of sales, stimulus-response theory works in direct selling. AIDAS formula, explained below, may be used. Rackham gives 'SPIN' formula for larger sales—situation questions, problem questions, implication questions and need pay off questions. The seller uses situation questions to establish a context so that buyer reveals implied needs which are developed in implication questions. This makes the buyer feel the problem questions are clear by and acutely so that buyer states explicit needs (need pay off questions) allowing seller to state the benefits. The sales person should follow these steps : (a) Identity prospects; (b) Pre-call planning; (c) Approach; (d) Presentation; (e) Overcome objections; (f) Closing the sale and (g) Follow up.

## SELLER ORIENTED THEORIES OF SELLING

### 1. AIDAS Theory of Selling

The term AIDAS includes the initials of the five words used to express it: attention, interest, desire, action, and satisfaction. These provide the basis for many sales and advertising texts. It is the skeleton around which many sales training programs are organized. The psychological writings of William James support this theory. Its construct is based upon experiential knowledge. It was in existence as early as 1898. According to this theory, during the successful selling interview the prospect's mind consciously passes through five successive mental states :

attention, interest, desire, action, and satisfaction. The sales presentation must lead the prospect through steps in the right sequence if a sale is to result.

(i) *Securing Attention* : In order to put the prospect into a receptive state of mind, the first few minutes of the interview are crucial. The salesperson has to have a reason, or an excuse, for conducting the interview.

If he has previously made an appointment, this phase presents no problem, though experienced sales personnel say that even with an appointment, a salesperson must possess considerable mental alertness, and be a skilled conversationalist, to survive the start of the interview. As the prospect realizes that the caller is bent on selling something, the salesperson must establish good rapport at once. He needs an ample supply of "conversation openers." Among other things, favourable first impressions are assured by proper attire, neatness, friendliness, and a genuine smile just before the interview. Skilled sales personnel often decide upon conversation openers so that those chosen are as timely as possible. It is advantageous if the opening remarks are about the prospect or if they are favourable comments about the prospect's business. A good conversation opener causes the prospect to relax and sets the stage for the total presentation.

(ii) *Gaining Interest* : Many techniques are used to intensify the prospect's attention so that it evolves into strong interest. Some sales people develop a contagious enthusiasm for the product or a sample. Sales portfolios, flipcharts, or other visual aids serve the same purpose when the product is bulky or technical.

One should search out the selling appeal that is most likely to be effective. Sometimes, the prospect drops hints, which the salesperson then uses in selecting the best approach. Some salespeople devise stratagems to elicit revealing questions to encourage hints by the prospect. Others ask the prospect questions designed to clarify attitudes and feelings toward the product. But before identifying the strongest appeal even experienced sales personnel do considerable probing, usually of the question-and-answer variety. The prospects' interests are affected by basic motivations, closeness of the interview subjects to current problems, its timeliness, and their receptive, skeptical or hostile mood. In selecting the appeal to emphasize the salesperson must take all these into account.

(iii) *Kindling Desire* : The salesperson must keep the conversation running along the main line toward the sale to kindle the prospect's desire to ready-to-buy point. The development of sales obstacles, the prospect's objections, external interruptions, and digressive remarks may sidetrack the presentation during this phase. Obstacles must be faced and ways found to get around them. Objections need answering to the prospect's satisfaction. Time is saved, and the chance of making a sale improved if objections are anticipated and answered before the prospect raises them. Good salespeople summarize what has been said earlier before continuing. Digressive remarks should be disposed of tactfully, with finesse, but sometimes distracting digression is best handled bluntly for example, "Well; that's all very interesting, but to get back to the subject...."

(iv) *Inducing Action* : If the presentation has been perfect, the prospect is ready to buy. However, buying must be induced. Experienced sales personnel do not close until the prospect is fully convinced of the merits of the proposition. The trial close, the close on a minor point, and the trick close are used to test the prospect's reactions. For fear of getting a "no," from which they think there is no retreat some sales personnel never ask for a definite "yes" or "no." But it is better to ask for the order straight forwardly.

(v) *Building Satisfaction* : The salesperson should reassure the customer that his buying decision is correct and that the sales person merely helped in deciding. The order is the climax of the selling situation. Building satisfaction means thanking the customer for the order, and attending to such matters as making certain that the order is filled as written, and following up on promises made.

### 2. "Right set of Circumstances" Theory of Selling Importance of Circumstances

This theory is summed up as "Everything was right for the sale". It sometimes called the "situation-response" theory. It having its psychological origin in experiments with animals. This theory holds that the particular circumstances prevailing in a given selling situation cause the prospect to respond in a predictable way. The more skilled the salesperson is in handling the set of circumstances, the more predictable is the response. If he succeeds in securing the attention and gaining the interest of the prospect, and if he presents the proper stimuli or appeals, the desired response that is, the sale will result.

The set of circumstances includes factors external and internal to the prospect. At least four factors internal to the prospect affect the response. These are the presence or absence of desires. For example: (1) to have a cup of coffee; (2) to have it how, (3) to go out and (4) to go out with the sales person.

Proponents of this theory stress external factors at the expense of internal factors. They emphasise selling appeals that evoke desired responses. In many selling situations sales personnel experience difficulties traceable to internal factors which are not readily manipulated. A seller-oriented theory, this theory stresses the importance of the sales person controlling the situation. If he does not handle the problem of influencing factors internal to the prospect, and fails to assign appropriate weight to the response side of the situation-response interaction, he fails.

### 3. "Buying formula" Buyer Oriented Theory of Selling

Recognizable versions of this theory appear in a number of early books on advertising and selling by authors who had experiential knowledge of salesmanship. Several psychologists have advance explanations similar to the buying formula. The name "buying formula" was given to this theory by the late E.K. Srong. Jr. This theory emphasizes the buyer's side of the buyer-seller dyad; the buyer's needs or problems. The salesperson's role is to help the buyer find solutions.

**Elements of buying formula**

It is schematic representation of a group of responses, arranged in psychological sequence. It emphasizes the prospect's responses which are strongly influenced by internal factors. It de-emphasizes the external factors. It is based on the assumption that being naturally conscious of the external factors the salesperson will not overlook them. As the salesperson's normal inclination is to neglect the internal factors, the buying formula is a convenient way to help him remember.

The mental processes involved in a purchase are :

Need (or problem) → Solution → Purchase

The outcome of a purchase affects the chance that a continuing relationship will develop between the buyer and the seller. Nearly all sales organizations are interested in continuing relationship. Therefore it is necessary to add a fourth element. The four elements then, are

**1. Need.** The individual is conscious of a deficiency of satisfaction whenever a need is felt, or a problem recognized. 'The solution will always be a product or service or both, and they will belong to a potential seller.

**2. Solution.** The "solution" involves two parts : (1) product (and/or service) and (2) trade name (name of manufacturer, company, or sales person).

**3. Purchase.** The purchase proceeds mentally from need or problem to product or service, to trade name, to purchase.

**4. Satisfaction.** Upon using the product or service, he or she experiences satisfaction or dissatisfaction. When a buying habit is being established, the buyer must know why the product or service is an adequate solution to the need or problem, and why the trade name is the best one to buy. The buyers also must have a pleasant feeling toward the product or service and the trade name. After definite buying habit has been established the buying formula is:

Need or Problem → Product/Service and/or Trade name → Purchase → Satisfaction/dissatisfaction

The product or service and the trade name must be considered to ensure purchase. The buyer must experience a pleasant feeling of anticipated satisfaction when thinking of the product and/or service and the trade name. An item viewed as adequate is also liked in many cases and *vice versa*, but this is not always so. Some products and services that are quite adequate are not liked, while some things are liked and bought that are admittedly not as good as competing items. Similar reasoning applies to trade names. Some sources of supply are both adequate and liked, others are adequate but not liked, still others are liked but patronized even though they are inadequate compared to competing sources.

Including adequacy and pleasant feelings the buying formula becomes:

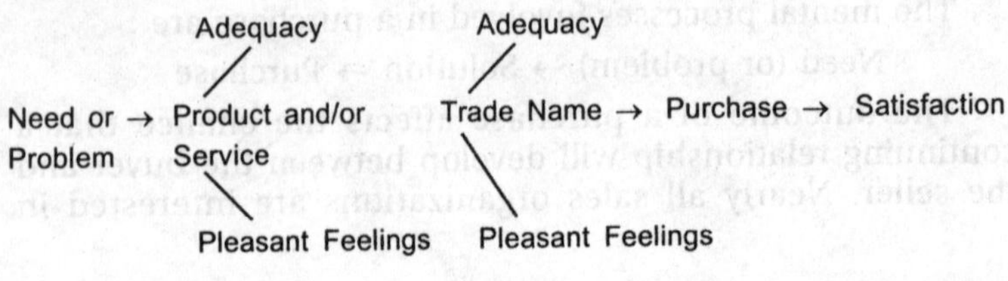

The buyer needs reasons to defend the purchase whenever the buyer's buying habit is challenged by a friend's remark, a competing salesperson's presentation, or a competitor's advertisement. In addition, he or she needs a pleasant feeling toward both the product or service and the trade name.

The primary elements in a well-established buying habit are those connected by solid lines, on the central line of the formula. Reasons and pleasant feelings constitute the elements of defence in the buying habit. Repeat buying occurs as long as present.

The buying formula implies answer to each selling problem. Differences among answers are differences in emphasis upon the elements in the formula.

**Circumstances of Emphasis**

The emphasis to be placed depends upon the following variety of circumstances :

**1. Need.** If the prospect does not feel a need or recognize a problem that can be satisfied by the product or service, the need or problem should be emphasized.

**2. Association.** If the prospect does not think of the product or service when he or she feels the need or recognizes the problem the association between need or problem and product or service should be emphasized.

**3. Trade Name.** If the prospect does not think of the trade name when he or she thinks of the product or service, the association between product or service and trade name should be emphasized.

**4. Purchase and Use.** If need or problem, product or service, and trade name are well associated, emphasis should be put upon facilitating purchase and use.

**5. Adequacy.** If competition is felt, emphasis should be put upon establishing in the prospects' minds the adequacy of the trade-named product or service, and pleasant feelings toward it.

**6. Every Element.** If sales to new prospects are desired, every element in the formula should be presented.

**7. Reminder.** If more sales to old customers are desired, the latter should be reminded.

## "BEHAVIOURAL EQUATION" THEORY

J.A. Howard explains buying behaviour in terms of the purchasing decision process, viewed as phases of the learning process. He uses a stimulus-response model (a sophisticated version of the "right set of circumstances" theory), and incorporates findings from behavioural research.

### Essential Elements of the Learning Process

Included in the stimulus — response model are four essential elements of the learning process — Drive, Cue, Response, and Reinforcement.

**1. Drives.** These are strong internal *stimuli* that impel the buyer's response. Drives are of two kinds :

(i) *Innate Drives* : These stem from the physiological needs, such as hunger, thirst, pain, cold and sex.

(ii) *Learned Drives* : Learned drives such as striving for status or social approval are acquired when paired with the satisfying of innate drives. They are elaborations of the innate drives, serving as a facade behind which the functioning of the innate drives is hidden. The learned drives are dominant in economically advanced societies.

**2. Cues.** These are weak *stimuli* that determine when the buyer will respond. Cues are of two types :

(i) *Triggering Cues* : These activate the decision process for any given purchase.

(ii) *Nontriggering Cues* : These influence the decision process but do not activate it. These may operate at any time even though the buyer is not contemplating a purchase. Non-triggering cues are of three kinds :

(a) ***Product Cues*** : These are external stimuli received from the product directly, for example, colour of the package, weight, or price.

(b) ***Informational Cues*** : These are external stimuli that provide information of a symbolic nature about the product. Such *stimuli* may come from advertising, conversations with other people (including sales personnel), and so on.

(c) ***Specific Product and Information Cues*** : These may also function as triggering cues when price triggers the buyer's decision.

**3. Response.** It is what the buyer does.

**4. Reinforcement.** It is any event that strengthens the buyer's tendency to make a particular response.

### Behavioural Equation

Howard incorporates these four elements into an equation :

$$B = P \times D \times K \times V$$

where $B$ = Response or the internal response tendency, that is, the act of purchasing a brand or patronizing a supplier.

$P$ = Pre-disposition or the inward response tendency, that is force of habit.

$D$ = Present drive level (amount of motivation).

$K$ = "Incentive potential," that is, the value of the product or its potential satisfaction to the buyer.

$V$ = Intensity of all cues: triggering, product or informational.

The relation among the variables is multiplicative. Thus, if any independent variable has a zero value, $B$ will also be zero and there is no response. There is no response no matter how much $P$ there may be, for example, if the individual is unmotivated ($D = 0$).

Whenever pre-disposition ($P$) increases in value there is a response — a purchase — in which satisfaction ($K$) is sufficient to yield a reward. Reinforcement occurs when the satisfaction yield a reward. Technically, what is reinforced is the tendency to make a response in the future to the cue that immediately preceded the rewarded response. After reinforcement, the buyer has learned that probability increases that the buyer will buy the product or patronize the supplier the next time the cue appears.

### Impact of Reinforcement

A salesperson and a buyer, each can display a rewarding of reinforcing behaviour to the other. When the salesperson provides the buyer with a product and the necessary information about it and its uses this satisfaction of the need is regarding to the buyer. He can reward the salesperson by buying the product. Each can also reward the other by providing social approval. The salesperson provides social approval to a buyer with friendly greetings, warm conversation, praise and the like displaying high regard.

**Social Aspect of Inter-relation**

It is helpful to separate economic aspects from social features while understanding the salesperson-client relation. While the salesperson wishes to sell a product, and the buyer wishes to buy it — both also place a value and cost upon the social features consisting of sentiments or expressions of different degrees of liking or social approval. By changing their own behaviour or getting buyers to change theirs salesperson may receive rewards or reinforcements.

**Impact of Salesperson**

The process by which the salesperson influences the buyer may be explained in terms of the equation $B = P \times D \times K \times V$. The salesperson directly influences $P$ (pre-disposition) through interacting with the buyer in ways rewarding to the buyer. However, the greatest effect on $P$, comes from using the product. The salesperson exerts strong influence through $D$ (amount of motivation), when the buyer seeks information in terms of informational cues. By helping to clarify the ends to be served or the buyer's goals, the salesperson exerts influence through D. When the buyer has stopped learning and his buying behaviour becomes spontaneous — the salesperson influences D by providing triggering cues. When the buyer narrows down the choices to a few sellers, the salesperson by communicating the merits of the company brand, lines to make it appear relatively better, and thus affect $K$ (its potential satisfaction for the buyer). Finally, by varying the intensity of his or her effort, the salesperson can make a difference in $V$ or the intensity of all cues.

**Reducing Buyer Dissonance**

According to Festinger's theory of cognitive dissonance anxiety or dissonance will almost always occur when individuals choose between two or more alternatives because the decision has unattractive as well as attractive features. After decisions, the people expose themselves to information that they perceive as likely to support their choices, and to avoid information likely to favour rejected alternatives.

Festinger meant his theory to apply only to post-decision anxiety, but it seems reasonable for pre-decision anxiety as well. Hauk writes that a buyer may panic on reaching the point of decision and rush into the purchase as an escape from the problem or put it off because of the difficulty of deciding. Thus, he can experience either pre-decision or post-decision dissonance, or both.

The salesperson reduces pre and post-decision anxiety or dissonance. Recognizing that the buyer's dissonance varies according to whether the product is an established or a new one, and whether the salesperson-client relationship is ongoing or new, following are four types of cases according to Howard involving the salesperson's role :

**1. An Established Product.** An ongoing salesperson-client relationship. Unless the market is unstable, the buyer tends toward automatic response behaviour, in which no learning is involved and thus experiences little, if any, dissonance; but insofar as it does occur, the salesperson is effective because the salesperson is trusted by the buyer.

**2. An Established Product.** A new salesperson-client relationship. The salesperson, being new, is less effective in reducing dissonance.

**3. A New Product.** An ongoing salesperson-client relationship. Unless the buyer generalizes from personal experience with an established similar product, the buyer experiences dissonance, especially if it is an important product. Because of the established relationship with the buyer, the salesperson can reduce dissonance.

**4. A New Product.** A new salesperson-client relationship. The buyer needs dissonance reduction, and the salesperson is less capable of providing it.

There are two ways a salesperson facilitates the buyer's dissonance reduction: (1) to emphasize the advantages of the product purchased, while stressing the disadvantages of the foregone alternatives and (2) to show that many characteristics of the chosen object are similar to products the buyer has foregone but which are approved by the reference groups.

As Industrial Revolution generated specialised activities in the area of business, the production no longer remained the twin action of marketing due to large-scale production and world-wide marketing. Production is no more guided by the existing market but by the untapped markets uncovered by the marketing people. New and fresh demands are created by them. The specialised activities of marketing lead to the establishment of several departments: advertising, sales promotion, marketing, research, distribution, pricing, merchandising, packaging, transporting, communicating, etc. Production and the marketing activities were divorced from each other. As middlemen came in between the producer and the consumers, wholesalers, import-export houses, retailers, and several other channels were developed for distribution of production. Advertising, research, merchandising, transporting etc. today require a proper management of the sale of products.

Sales management is concerned with the direction and control of the sales force. It refers to the management of sales personnel, though sometimes, it covers advertising, distribution, pricing and product designing, which are elements of marketing management.

Thus, sales management is a part and parcel of marketing management. It refers to the direction and control of salesmen, the planning, recruiting and selection, training, organising, supervision, compensating and co-ordinating of the sales force.

The term "marketing" refers to the business activities through which ownership of products is transferred from the producer to the consumers. Marketing includes sales management as well as other important functions. The marketing problems are carefully analysed, described and interpreted so that producers and consumers may be benefited to the maximum extent. While consumers want to pay the lowest possible price producers and middlemen or marketing men strive for me maximum possible profit.

Marketing management is a broader term which covers sales management and marketing functions. Marketing management includes several activities of marketing such as pricing, promotion, physical distribution, product and sales personnel management. However, sales management is mainly concerned with the sales personnel management. A subordinate of the marketing manager the sales manager advises the marketing manager in sales force management and other marketing functions in general. According to Louis, E. Boone and David L. Kurtz: "Sales management effort may be exerted in the direction of securing, maintaining, motivating, supervising, evaluating and controlling an effective field sales force". The modern concept of sales management revolves around the development of human resources.

## QUESTIONS FOR EXERCISE

1. Define salesmanship and describe its essentials and utility.
2. Explain prospecting and analyse steps in it.
3. Write short note on Sales Resistance and Closing Sales.
4. What factors govern buyer-seller inter-relation?
5. Is selling an Art or a Science? Explain seller oriented theories of selling.
6. Explain buyer oriented theory of selling.
7. Which buying theory emphasises both buyer and seller? Give details of such a theory.
8. Distinguish sales management marketing and marketing management.

# 3

# SALES PROMOTION

Simultaneously with other marketing mix decisions, promotion decisions involve finding target markets, determining objective and tasks, budgeting for promotion, selecting promotional media, evaluating promotional effectiveness and controlling the promotion elements. According to McCarthy E. Jerome, "Promotion, one of the four major variables with which the marketing manager works, is communication of information between seller and buyer to change attitudes and behaviour." The four major variables are product, price, physical distribution and promotion.

## THE PROMOTION MIX

The marketing manager is concerned with the effective utilisation of the promotion mix, together with other kinds of marketing mix. The promotion mix includes four ingredients, sales promotion, personal selling, publicity and advertising. The promotion mix is used to achieve the objectives of promotion, which are information, persuasion and reminding. Promotion is responsible for awakening and stimulating consumer demand for a product. Persuasive communication informs potential customers of the existence of products and persuades and convinces them that the products have want-satisfying capabilities. All marketing communications or forms of promotion aim at influencing consumer attitudes, beliefs, values and preferences, life styles and ways of living.

**1. Sales Promotion.** It induces purchasers to buy a product. It involves demonstrations, contests, prices-off, coupons, free samples, special packaging and money refund offers. Its activities are designed to encourage resellers and sales people to sell the product. Different from personal selling and advertising sales promotion is non-recurrent in nature and is for a short period. This type of promotion mix is complementary to the other kinds of promotion mix.

**2. Personal Selling.** It involves interpersonal communication aiming at informing and persuading customers to know and buy products. A face-to-face relationship between sellers and potential customers, it provides immediate feedback helping sales persons to adapt the sales techniques to the needs of the situation. A powerful promotional tool in informing, persuading and reminding the people it provides an effective opportunity to sales people to talk back, to answer questions and meet objections. These advantages are not available in other kinds of promotion mix.

**3. Publicity.** Publicity is non-personal communication about the product. It reaches people because it is newsworthy. The manager may plan a press release and external communication. Publicity generates more inquiries than advertising. It is treated as a form of advertising without payment. Whereas advertising is paid for and controlled publicity is unpaid and less controlled.

**4. Advertising.** It is mass communication transmitted through the mass media, such as radio, television, magazines and newspapers. Having identified sponsor advertising has objectives, issues and message development. It is characterised by media selection and evaluation of advertising effectiveness.

## MEANING OF SALES PROMOTION

Sales promotion is an action which increases the volume of sales. In a broad sense, the term 'sales promotion' refers to promotion having all the activities of personal selling, publicity, advertising and sales promotion leading to the enhancement of sales. However, the meaning of sales promotion has been technically defined to include display, demonstration, contests and trading stamps. To quote, Boone, E Louis and Kurtz, L. David, "It applies to assorted, non-recurrent and somewhat extraordinary non-personal selling efforts". Many authors have defined sales promotion as non-personal selling and it is also known as non-recurring promotional efforts. According to Philip Kotler, "Sales promotion consists of a wide variety of promotional tools designed to stimulate earlier and/or stronger market response. They include tools for consumer promotion (*e.g.*, samples, coupons, money-refund offers, prices-off, premiums, contests, trading stamps, demonstrations), trade promotion (*e.g.*, buying allowances, free goods, merchandise allowances, co-operative advertising, push money, dealer sales contests) and sales force promotion, (*e.g.*, bonuses, contests, sales rallies)." Directed at final consumers sales promotion efforts are designed to motivate, persuade and remind them of the goods and services that are offered. Sales persons adopt several techniques for sales enhancement. Creative sales promotion can be very effective.

## OBJECTIVES OF SALES PROMOTION

To specify promotion objectives and policies is the marketing manager's responsibility. Though sales promotion objectives are consistent with marketing objectives, they may vary with the type of target market and points of channel.

**1. Objectives for Retailers.** To carry new items, encourage off season buying, offset competitive promotions, build brand loyalty and so on.

**2. Objectives for the Sales Force.** To encourage a new product or model, stimulate off-season sales, persuade more prospective buyers, and so on.

**3. Objectives for Consumers.** To encourage more usage and purchases of a larger number of units and attract competitors' brand users.

## FUNDAMENTAL OBJECTIVES OF SALES PROMOTION

These objectives are attained through effective communication.

**1. To Inform.** Informing is to educate the consumers about the product. They must have some knowledge about the product offered by the producer. They should, therefore, be informed of the new product and told that the new product works better than all similar existing products. Free samples may be distributed to leading consumers who may be a source of advertisement for other prospective consumers.

**2. To Persuade.** Sales persons persuade consumers to buy products. They develop or reinforce a favourable set of attitudes and influence their buying behaviour. They supply comparative information on various products so that consumers may be willing to purchase the products promoted by them.

**3. To Remind.** Reminding leads the firms to reinforce the previously satisfactory behaviour of the customer. For this purpose, it provides suitable knowledge for recollection. Reminding the consumers of their past satisfaction will persuade them to stay with the product and prevent them from shifting to competitors.

## IMPORTANCE OF SALES PROMOTION

Sales promotion has been accepted as an effective sales tool. Internal and external factors assist in the adoption of sales promotion successfully. While other promotional media are costly and not very effective sales promotion is both economical and more effective. Sales promotion ideas as mass advertising carry the entire promotion load. Personal selling has a limited scope. It has not been properly utilised for the benefit of manufacturing organisations. More personal than mass advertising sales promotion provides more opportunities for the development of sales. Sales persons meet several queries and answer specific questions. They sell only those ideas which may be sold and not just what is told them to sell. Sales promotion offers greater chances of the acceptability of a product. It stimulates the primary demand for the company's product. Mass sales promotion persuades consumers to purchase goods and services.

Sales promotion permanently alters the market share. It persuades the buyers of the competitors' product to shift to the product of the company. It helps develop brand loyalty. It becomes more effective when used together with advertising. Sales promotion is an important tool in developing product symbolization, which is significant in increasing the value of the products that consumers use in self-expression. It may create awareness, interest and adoption of the product because it provides an opportunity for evaluation, trial and confirmation of brand loyalty.

## FORMS OF SALES PROMOTION

Sales promotion may take any or all of the three forms tools, or methods of sales promotion — consumer promotion, trade promotion or sales force promotion.

**1. Consumer Promotion.** It includes samples, coupons, money refund offers, prices-off, premiums, contests, demonstrations and trading stamps. These tools are well utilised by marketing management.

(i) *Samples* : These are free distribution of a product for the purpose of obtaining consumer acceptance. This may be done on a door-to-door basis, *via* demonstrations, or by mail. It is useful for promoting new products.

(ii) *Coupons* : These offer a discount on new purchases of a product. They are certificates entitling the bearer to a discount on the purchase of a specific product.

(iii) *Money-Refund Offers* : These are granted to cash purchasers.

(iv) *Prices Off*: Sometimes, customers are given the product at a price below the normal rate.

(v) *Premiums* : These are merchandise offered at relatively low prices.

(a) Free-in-the mail premium is an item mailed to the consumers.

(b) A self-liquidating premium is an item sold below normal price.

(vi) *Contests* : Firms may offer contests to attract customers by offering substantial cash or merchandise price cuts.

(vii) *Demonstrations* : These are made to inform the public or consumers in the target market about the attributes and utilities of the product.

(viii) *Trading stamps* : These are a special type of premium received by customers, which can be redeemed for merchandise through stamp redemption.

**2. Trade Promotion.** It encourages buyers to buy a larger quantity of the product. It is also known as buying allowance because it is an offer of some discount on each item of purchase above a minimum quantity. It may take the form of free goods, merchandise allowances, co-operative advertising, dealer sales contests and push money.

(i) *Free Goods* : These are offered to public and dealers after the purchase of certain items. They boost the sales of a commodity by offering some additional commodities free of cost. For example, a bar of soap is sold by offering a match box free of cost; the sale of a coffee jar of 500 gms. is accompanied by a free steel cup and so on.

(ii) *Merchandise Allowance* : It is offered to compensate dealers for disposing of the manufacturer's products.

(iii) *Advertising Allowance* : It compensates dealers for advertising the product.

(iv) *Dealer Sales Contests* : Sales competitions are arranged, prizes are announced or special offers are made on the sale of new products.

(v) *Push Money* : It is offered to the purchaser or agents to increase the sale of a product.

**3. Sales Force Promotion.** Salesmen are motivated to sell products by offering bonuses, contests and sales rallies.

(i) *Bonus* : They are offered a bonus if the sale increases above the minimum level.

(ii) *Sales Contests* : These are organised as an effective measure of ales promotion. The main purpose of sales contests is to increase the sales through retailers or sales persons. An off-season sale can be motivated by such contests. When the volume of sales is declining, it creates a sense of security and stability. It is also useful in getting repeat orders from present and past customers. Cash awards, merchandise prizes, travel and special honours make the contest prizes more effective than the cash awards because more contestants are attracted to participate in the contest. Young energetic sales personnel are tempted by travel awards, particularly when their spouses are offered this award to visit an exotic land.

(iii) *Sales Rallies* : These encourage open participation by retailers and salesmen. They are publicly honoured at the winning positions. Sales rallies should be designed in such a way as to ensure that every participant has a fair chance of winning the award.

## MAJOR DECISIONS IN SALES PROMOTION PROGRAMME

In using sales promotion, a company must establish the objectives, select the tools, develop the program, prctest the program, implement and control it and evaluate the result.

**1. Establishing the Sales Promotion Objectives.** Sales promotion objectives are derived from basic marketing communication objectives, which are derived from more basic marketing objectives developed for the product. The specific objectives set for sales promotion vary with the type of target market.

(i) *For Consumers* : These objectives include encouraging more usage and purchase of larger size units, building trial among non-users and attracting competitors' brand users.

(ii) *For Retailers* : The objectives include inducing retailers to carry new items and higher levels of inventory, encouraging off-season buying, encouraging stocking of related items, offsetting competitive promotions, building brand loyalty of retailers and gaining entry into new retail outlets.

(iii) *For the Sales Force* : The objectives include encouraging support of a new product or model, encouraging more prospecting and stimulating off-season sales.

**2. Selecting the Sales Promotion Tools.** Many sales promotion tools are available to accomplish these objectives. The promotion planner should take into account the type of market, sales promotion objectives, competitive conditions and cost effectiveness of each tool. The main tools are described below.

(i) *Samples, Coupons, Price Packs, Premiums and Trading Stamps* : These tools make up the bulk of consumer promotions.

(a) ***Samples*** : These are offers of a free amount or trial of a product to consumers. The sample might be delivered door to door, sent in the mail, picked up in a store, found attached to another product, or featured in an advertising offer. Sampling is the most effective and most expensive way to introduce a new product. For example, Lever Brothers had so much confidence in their new mouth wash called Signal that in 1978 they distributed free samples to two out of three American households, at a cost of $ 15 million.

(b) ***Coupons*** : These are certificates entitling the bearer to a stated saving on the purchase of a specific product. In U.S.A. over 81 billion coupons were distributed in 1979, about 1,200 per household. Only 4 per cent were redeemed. Coupons can be mailed, enclosed in other product, or inserted in ads. They can be effective in stimulating sales of a mature brand and inducing early trial of a new brand. Experts believe they should provide a 15 to 20 per cent saving to be effective. P&G's plan for breaking into the Pittsburgh market in 1977 with its Folger brand included a thirty-five-cent discount coupon on a one-pound can mailed to area homes and a coupon it can for ten cents off.

(c) ***Price Packs*** : Also called cents-off deals these are offers to consumers of savings off the regular price of a product, flagged on the label or package. They may take the form of a reduced-price pack, which in single packages sold at a reduced price (such as two for the price of one) or a banded pack, which is two related products banded together (such as a toothbrush and toothpaste). Price packs are very effective in stimulating short-term sales, even more than coupons.

(d) ***Premiums*** : These are merchandise offered at a relatively low cost or free as an incentive to purchase a particular product.

(a) ***With-Pack Premium*** : It accompanies the product inside (in-pack) or (on-pack) the package. The package itself, if a reusable container, may serve as a premium.

(b) ***Free-in-the-Mail Premium*** : It is an item mailed to consumers who send in a proof of purchase, such as a box top.

(c) ***Self-liquidating Premium*** : It is an item sold below its normal retail price to consumers who request it.

Manufacturers now offer consumers all kinds of premiums bearing the company's name.

(e) ***Trading Stamps*** : These are a special type of premium received by customers making purchases, which they can redeem for merchandise through stamp redemption centers. The first merchants who adopt trading stamps usually attract new business. The other merchants adopt them defensively and eventually they become a burden to everyone, with some merchants deciding to drop them and offer lower prices instead.

(ii) *Point-of-Purchase (POP) Displays and Demonstrations* : POP displays and demonstrations take place at the point of purchase or sale. Unfortunately many retailers do not like to handle the hundreds of displays, signs and posters they receive from manufacturers. Manufacturers are responding by creating better POP materials, typing them in with television or print messages and offering to set them up.

(iii) *Trade promotion* : Manufacturers use a number of techniques to secure the co-operation of wholesalers and retailers.

(a) ***Buying Allowance*** : It is an offer of cents-off on each case purchased during a stated period of time. The offer encourages dealers to buy a quantity or carry a new item that they might not ordinarily buy. The dealers can use the buying allowance for immediate profit, advertising or price redemptions.

(b) ***Merchandise Allowance*** : It is offered to compensate dealers for featuring the manufacturer's products.

(c) ***Advertising Allowance*** : It compensates dealers for advertising the manufacturer's products.

(d) ***Display Allowance*** : It compensates them for carrying special displays of the product.

(e) ***Free Goods*** : Manufacturers may offer free goods, which are extra cases of merchandise, to middlemen who buy a certain quantity.

(f) ***Push Money*** : They may offer push money, which is case of gifts to dealers of their sales force to push the manufacturer's goods.

(g) ***Speciality Advertising Items*** : These carry the company's name, such as pens, pencils, calendars, paperweights, matchbooks, memo pads, ashtrays and yardsticks.

As they are unhappy about the amount of consumer deals they have to handle, food retailers strongly prefer trade deals to consumer deals. According to Chevalier and Curhan : "Retailers view promotional efforts initiated by manufacturers as encouraging profitless brand switching rather than increasing sales or profits. Manufacturers, on the other hand, complain that retailer-initiated promotions sometimes damage brand franchises which have been carefully and expensively nurtured over many years. Worse yet, manufacturers complain that retailers frequently take advantage of them by 'absorbing' deals without passing their benefits along to consumers."

(iv) *Business Conventions and Trade Shows* : Industry associations organize annual conventions and typically sponsor a trade show at the same time. Firms selling to the particular industry display and demonstrate their products at the trade show. In USA fifty-six hundred trade shows take place every year, drawing approximately 80 million people. The participating vendors expect several benefits, including generating new sales leads, maintaining customer contacts, introducing new products, meeting new customers and selling more to present customers.

(v) *Contests, Sweepstakes and Games* : These devices present to consumers, dealers, or sales forces the chance to win something — such as cash, trips or goods — as a result of luck or extra effort.

(a) ***Contest*** : It calls for consumers to submit an entry — a jingle, estimate, suggestion — to be examined by a panel of judges who will select the best entries.

(b) ***Sweepstake*** : It calls for consumers to submit their names, in a drawing.

(c) ***Game*** : It presents consumers with something every time they buy — bingo numbers, missing letters — which may or may not help them win a prize.

(d) ***Sales Contest*** : It is a contest involving dealers or the sales force to induce to redouble their sales efforts over a stated period, with prizes going to the top performers.

**3. Developing the Sales Promotion Program.** The marketer must make following additional decisions to define the full promotion program :

(i) *Size of incentive* : The marketer has to determine how much to offer. A certain minimum incentive is necessary if the promotion is to succeed. A higher incentive level will produce more sales response but at a diminishing rate. Some of the large consumer-packaged-goods firms have a sales promotion manager who studies the effectiveness of past promotions and recommends appropriate incentives to brand managers.

(ii) *Conditions for Participation* : Incentives might be offered to everyone or to select groups. A premium might be offered only to those who turn in box tops. Sweepstakes might not be offered in certain states or to families of company personnel or to persons under a certain age.

(iii) *Distribution Vehicle for Promotion* : The marketer must decide how to promote and distribute the promotion program. A fifteen per-cents-off coupon could be distributed in the package, store, mail or advertising media. Each distribution method involves a different level of reach and cost.

(iv) *Duration of Promotion* : If the sales promotion period is too short, many prospects will not be able to take advantage, since they may not be repurchasing at the time. If the promotion runs too long, the deal will lose some of its "act now" force. According to Arthur Stern, the optimal frequency is about three weeks per quarter and optimal duration is the length of the average purchase cycle.

(v) *Timing of Promotion* : Brand managers need to develop calendar dates for the promotions. The dates will be used by production, sales and distribution. Some unplanned promotions will also be needed and will require co-operation on a short notice.

(vi) *Total sales Promotion Budget* : The sales promotion budget can be developed in two ways. It can be built from the ground up, where the marketer chooses the individual promotions and estimates their total cost. The cost of a particular promotion consists of the administrative cost (printing, mailing and promoting the deal) and the incentive cost (cost of premium or cents-off, including rate of redemption), multiplied by the expected number of units that will be sold on deal.

In the case of coupon deal, the cost would take into account the fact that only a fraction of the consumers will redeem the coupons. In the case of an in-pack premium, the deal cost must include the costs of procurement and packaging of the premium, offset by any price increase on the package.

The more common way to develop the sales promotion budget is to use a conventional percentage of the total promotion budget. For example, toothpaste may get a sales promotion budget of 30 per cent of the total promotion budget, whereas shampoo may get 50 per cent. These percentages vary for different brands in different markets and are influenced by the stages of the product life cycle and competitive expenditures on promotion.

Multiple-brand companies should co-ordinate their sales promotion activities, such a making single mailing of multiple coupons to consumers. In his study of company sales promotion practices, Strand found three major budgeting inadequacies :

1. Lack of consideration of cost effectiveness.

2. Use of simplistic decision rules, such as extensions of last year's spending, percentage of expected sales, maintenance of a fixed ratio to advertising and the "left-over approach" where promotion gets what is left after advertising is set.

3. Advertising and promotional budgets being prepared independently.

**4. Pretesting the Sales Promotion Program.** Although sales promotion programs are designed on the basis of experience, pretests should be conducted to determine if the tools are appropriate, the incentive size optimal and the presentation method efficient. A survey by the Premium Advertisers Association USA indicated that fewer than 42 per cent of premium offerers ever tested their effectiveness. Strange maintains that promotions can usually be tested quickly and inexpensively and that some large companies test alternative strategies in selected market areas with each of their national promotions. Sales promotions directed at consumer markets can be readily pretested. Consumers can be asked to rate or rate of rank different possible deals. Or trial tests can be run in limited geographical areas.

**5. Implementing and Controlling the Sales Promotion Program.** Implementation and control plans for individual promotion should be established. Implementation planning must cover lead time and sell-off time. Lead time is the time necessary to prepare the program prior to launching it. According to Kurt H. Schaffir and H. George Treten, "It covers initial planning, design and approval of package modifications or material to be mailed or distributed to the home, preparation of conjunctive advertising and point of sale materials, notification of field sales personnel, establishment of allocations for individual distributions, purchasing and printing of special premiums or packaging materials, productions of advance inventories and staging at distribution centers in preparation of release at a specific date and finally the distribution to the retailer."

Sell-off time begins with the launch and ends when approximately 95 per cent of the deal merchandise is in the hands of consumers, which many take one to several months, depending on the deal duration.

**6. Evaluating the Promotion Results.** According to Strang, "evaluation of promotion programs receives...little attention. Even where an attempt is made to evaluate a promotion, it is likely to be superficial.... Evaluation in terms of profitability is even less common. However, evaluation is a crucial requirement."

Manufacturers can use four methods to measure sales promotion effectiveness.

(i) *Comparison of Sales Before, During and after a Promotion* : Suppose a company has a 6 per cent market share in the pre-promotion period which jumps to 10 per cent during the promotion, falls to 5 per cent immediately after the promotion and rises to 7 per cent after some time. The promotion evidently attracted new triers and also stimulated more purchasing by existing customers. After the promotion sales fell as consumers worked down their inventories. The long-run rise to 7 per cent indicates that the company gained some new users. If the brand's share returned to the pre promotion level, then the promotion only altered the time pattern of demand rather than the total demand.

(ii) *Consumer Panel Data* : It would reveal the kinds of people who responded to the promotion and what they did after the promotion.

(iii) *Consumer Surveys* : These can be conducted to learn how many recall the promotion, what they thought of it, how many took advantage of it and how it affected their subsequent brand-choice behaviour.

(iv) *Experiments* : Sales promotions can also be evaluated through experiments that vary such attributes as incentive value duration and distribution media.

Sales promotion plays an important role in the total promotion mix its systematic use requires defining the sales promotion objectives, selecting the appropriate tools, constructing the sales promotion program, pretesting it, implementing it and evaluating the results.

## PUBLICITY FOR SALES PROMOTION

### Meaning of Publicity

A major promotion tool of publicity involves "securing editorial space as divorced from paid space, in all media read, viewed or heard by a company's customers or prospects, for the specific purpose of assisting in the meeting of sales goals."

### Use of Publicity

Publicity's results can sometimes be spectacular. It is used to promote brands, products, persons, places, ideas, activities, organization and even nations. Trade associations use publicity to rebuild interest in declining commodities such as eggs, milk and potatoes. Organizations employ publicity to attract more tourists, foreign investment and international support.

### Publicity and Public Relation

Publicity is part of a larger concept, that of public relations. Company public relations has several objectives, including obtaining favourable publicity for the company, building up a good "corporate citizen" image for the company and handling adverse rumours and stories that break out. Public relations departments use following tools to carry out these objectives.

**1. Press Relations.** Their aim is to place newsworthy information into the news media to attract attention to a person, product or service.

**2. Product Publicity.** It involves various efforts to publicize specific products.

**3. Corporate Communications.** It covers internal and external communications and promotes understanding of the institution.

**4. Lobbying.** It involves dealing with legislators and government officials to promote or defeat legislation and regulation.

**5. Counselling.** It involves advising management about public issues and company positions and image.

Those skilled in publicity are usually found not in the company' s public relations department and not in marketing department. The public relations department is typically located at corporate headquarters. Its staff is so busy dealing with various persons — stockholders, employees, legislators, city officials — that publicity to support product marketing objectives may be neglected. One solution is to add a publicity specialist to the marketing department.

Because of its limited and sporadic use publicity is often described as a marketing stepchild. Yet publicity can create a memorable impact on public awareness at a fraction of the cost of advertising. The company does not pay for the space or time in the media. It pays for a staff to develop and circulate the stories. If the company develops an interesting story, it could be picked up by all the media and be worth millions of dollars in equivalent advertising. It would have more credibility than advertising.

**Major Decisions in Publicity**

Management should establish the publicity objectives, choose the publicity messages and vehicles that will implement the publicity plan and evaluate the publicity results, in considering when and how to use product publicity.

**1. Establishing the Publicity Objectives.** Publicity can contribute in a number of ways to the overall promotion program. Its potential contribution can be especially strong in the following circumstances :

(i) *Newsworthiness* : Products with interesting stories are the best candidates for publicity.

(ii) *Stimulus for Sales Force and Dealers* : Publicity can help boost sales-force and dealer enthusiasm. Stories about a new product before it is launched will help the sales force sell it to consumers.

(iii) *Need for Credibility* : Publicity adds credibility by communicating the message in an editorial context.

(iv) *Small Budget* : Publicity costs less than mail and media advertising. The smaller the company's promotion budget, the stronger the case for using publicity to gain share of market.

Specific objectives should be set for every publicity campaign. For example, the Wine Growers of California hired the public relations firm of Daniel J. Edelman, Inc., to develop a publicity campaign to convince Americans that wine drinking is a pleasurable part of good living and to improve the image and market share of California wines. The following publicity objectives were established : (1) develop magazine stories about wine and get them placed in top magazines (Time, House, Beautiful) and in newspapers (food columns, feature sections); (2) develop stories about wine's many health values and direct them to the medical profession; and (3) develop specific publicity for the young adult market, college market, governmental bodies and various ethnic communities. These objectives were refined into specific goals so that final results could be evaluated.

**2. Choosing the Publicity Messages and Vehicles.** Now, the publicist identifies interesting stories to tell about the product. Suppose a relatively unknown college wants more public recognition. The publicist will search for possible stories. The stories chosen should reflect the image this college wants. If the number of stories is insufficient, the publicist should propose newsworthy events that the college could sponsor. Here the publicist gets into creating news rather than finding news. The ideas include hosting major academic conventions, inviting celebrity speakers and developing news conferences. Each event is an opportunity to develop a multitude of stories directed at different audiences.

Event creation is a particularly important skill in publicizing fund-raising drives for non-profit organizations. Fund raisers have developed a large repertoire of special events, including anniversary celebrations, art exhibits, auctions, benefit evenings, bingo games, book sales, cake sales, contests, dances, dinners, fairs, fashion shows, parties in unusual places, rummage sales, tours and walkathons.

**3. Implementing the Publicity Plan.** Implementing publicity requires care. Take the matter of placing stories in the media. A great story is easy to place. But most stories are less than great and may not get past busy editors. One of the chief assets of publicists is their personal relationship with media editors. Publicists are often ex-journalists who know many media editors and know what they want. Publicists look at media editors as a market to satisfy so that these editors will continue to use their stories.

Publicity requires extra care when it involves staging special events such as testimonial dinners, news conferences, and national contests. Publicists need a good head for detail and for coming up with quick solutions when things go wrong.

**4. Evaluating the Publicity Results.** Publicity's contribution is difficult to measure because it is used along with other promotion tools. If it is used before the other tools come into action, its contribution is easier to evaluate.

(i) *Exposures* : The easiest measure of publicity effectiveness is the number of *exposures* created in the media. Publicists supply the client with a clipping book showing all the media that carried news about the product and a summary statement.

Exposure measure is not very satisfying. There is no indication of how many people actually read or heard the message and what they thought afterward. There is no information on the net audience reached, since publications overlap in readership.

(ii) *Awareness/Comprehension/Attitude Change* : A better measure is the change in product awareness/comprehension/ attitude resulting from the publicity campaign after allowing for the impact of other promotional tools. This requires surveying the before-and-after levels of these variables. In USA the Potato Board learned, for example, that the number of people who agreed with the statement "Potatoes are rich in vitamins and minerals" went from 36 before the campaign to 67 per cent after the campaign, a significant improvement in product comprehension.

(iii) *Sales and Profit Contribution* : Sales and profit impact is the most satisfactory measure, if obtainable. For example, 9-Lives sales increased 43 per cent at the end of the "Morris the Cat" publicity campaign. In USA however, advertising and sales promotion had also been stepped up and their contribution has to be allowed for.

## SALES PROMOTION STRATEGIES

**1. Communication.** The purpose of communication is to persuade potential customers to purchase the product. Persuasibility is related to feelings of inadequacy and social inhibitions. Different audiences perceive the same message in different ways and interpret it differently.

**2. Elements of Communication Process.** The communication process has five elements : source, encoding, message channel, decoding and receiver.

(i) *The Source* : It delivers the message in different ways. What is communicated may not be received properly and correctly by the receiver unless the message and methods of communication are effective and properly determined by experts. Noise may disturb the communication at any stage. It is extraneous interference with communication and makes it less effective. A distracting remark or action by another may interfere with the message's reception. On the reverse, feedback provides effective communication. It may be a two-way communication to determine communication effectiveness. It tells us whether the message sent was the message received or whether the receiver interpreted the message differently. It may be in the form of nodding, expression of interest, a smile from the listener, etc. Marketing management needs it to identify and rectify the causes of noise.

(ii) *Encoding*: An error in encoding or decoding may distort the message. An expression or word may convey different meanings in different parts of the country.

(iii) *Message Channel* : The source of communication has much influence on the receiver who is extraordinarily alert when he knows that the message is coming through some indirect channel. If the message is coming through a reputed newspaper or on the radio, the receiver will give weightage to these sources. The announcement of discount and other sales promotion techniques in an ordinary or dubious newspaper may distort the message. The design of the message and presentation of communication technique differ for the hierarchy of the adoption process, which may be innovators, early adopters, early majority, late majority and laggards. The hierarchy of effects assumes that there is a logical progression from stimulus to response.

(iv) *Decoding and Receiver* : An Action Oriented Model is employed to create interest among the existing buyers and potential buyers because it arouses attention, holds interest, arouses desire and obtains action. The potential customer becomes aware of the company's product at the attention-strategy stage of the communication. Holding interest is necessary to build the prospect's interest in the product and promote a liking for it. Arousing desire favourably affects the evaluation process. Obtaining action includes building conviction with a view to ensuring a purchase. The communication process varies in accordance with each adoption-stage.

**2. Objectives and Tasks.** The marketer determines the message to be aimed at the target market to gain product acceptance. The overall marketing objectives define the role of communication in sales promotion. Identifying the target audiences is the main task of a sales promotion communication. The audience's feeling about the message source helps determine the message's effectiveness. The marketer should determine his sales promotion objectives and tasks mentioning what is to be accomplished and what kind of buyer responses are desired. Sales promotion tasks should be objective-oriented, informing, persuading and reminding the customers about the products. The marketer should inform consumers about his product. He should show how it works better than all similar existing products. He should persuade customers to buy it. If customers have positive attitudes, a reminding objective should be endorsed. It leads to reinforcing previously satisfactory behaviour and preventing the customer from shifting to competitors.

**3. Media.** Sales promotion may involve different methods of approaching people. While deciding a particular method of sales promotion strategic variables are taken into account. Consumer promotion has been considered a very effective mode of sales promotion. Potential consumers are offered samples, coupons, trading stamps, etc. to promote sales. The point-of-purchase display is a silent strategy to trigger off buying decisions. Retailers rely on in-store displays to familiarize customers with their products. A showroom display makes it easy for prospective buyers to familiarize themselves with the different features of the product. Trade promotion through buying allowances, free goods, merchandise allowances, push money, etc., help to enhance sales by retailers and traders. Packaging is another important form of promotion, particularly for consumer goods. It may carry selling messages and information about the product. A good package design uses a proper blend of colour design and type and attracts the shopper's attention away from other products. Sales force promotion motivates the sales persons to enhance their sales quota and get the benefits of bonus on additional sales. Special premiums have attractions for the people.

**4. Budgets.** Before resorting to sales promotion activities it is very essential to determine sales promotion budgets. The resources and sales potentials are estimated before the formulation of budgets. Sales promotion budgets should be adequate so that they might achieve promotion objectives. Some marketing managers use arbitrary budgeting methods based on trial and error.

Sales promotion is the cause and not the effect of sales. If the sales have increased because of external factors, the increase in sales promotion budget has no logical background for it. However, budgeting is commonly used in sales promotion activities. The expenditure on sales promotion is a long term investment which may enhance the name and fame of the company. Therefore, many companies favour maximum expenditure on sales promotion. A competitive atmosphere also dictates that there should be maximum expenditure. On the basis of the various expenditures on fixed assets, the marketing manager fixes the limit of the sales promotion budget.

The total expenditure on all sorts of promotion is fixed on the basis of the return on investment in the past five to ten years averaged to arrive at the standard rate of return. The maximum limit on the promotion budgets is discounted on this basis. The promotion budget is rationally divided into sales promotion, personal selling, publicity and advertising. The total expenditure on sales promotion is fixed on the basis of objectives and tasks. The marketing manager chooses the technique best capable of enabling him to *attain* the objectives. It foretells the amount required to *attain* the objectives. The sales promotion objectives and budgets are decided at the time the objectives and budgets of other methods of promotion are evaluated and fixed.

The expenditure on sales promotion and other methods is determined on the basis of expenditure on it in the industry. Competition determines the volume of expenditure on sales promotion. The responsiveness of the budget is evaluated on the basis of the return in industry on promotion expenditure. The market share of the company is taken as a guide for fixing the amount of expenditure. A crude evaluation of responsiveness may be done by the comparative analysis method of additional promotion expenditure and additional sale realisation. However, because of the different sales promotion activities, costs of production and sales, quality of the product, promotional plans and external environmental variables, it is difficult to evaluate the impact of promotion expenditure as a whole. The responsiveness also varies in accordance with the life cycle of the product. Industry sales are less responsive to promotion during maturity and more responsive to promotion during the introduction stage.

**5. Promotional Mix.** Promotional mix refers to the combination, types and amount of promotion used by the marketing manager. An individual form of promotion is seldom effective or efficient. If accompanied by publicity, advertising and personal selling or a combination thereof, the sale promotion programme may be more effective than an individualistic approach to promotion. The promotion mix depends on the notion that promotion elements are interchangeable and some promotion mixes are more suitable for the attainment of certain objectives. Therefore, attempts are made to select the optimum combination of the methods of promotion.

The trial-and-error method, past performances and corporate policies may influence the appropriate promotional mix. With the application of appropriate combinations of the promotion media many firms have increase their sales. Sales promotion and personal selling are supported with publicity. As promotion mix is a variable in the marketing strategy. It should be clearly decided how far a particular element should be used in combination with other promotional methods.

**6. Strategic Approach.** The kind of promotional mix employed determines the promotional strategy. A particular combination, type of amount of sales, promotion, personal selling, publicity and advertising is brought into the promotional mix, which becomes the promotional strategy in the course of implementation. Promotional objectives, policies and programmes as a whole and individual approach of each combination blend into the promotional strategy. The marketing strategy as such guides the determination of the promotional strategy. It may be divided into sales promotion strategy, personal selling strategy, publicity strategy and advertising strategy. The strategies may be push-and-pull promotional strategies, sustaining promotional strategy, developmental promotional strategy or promotional appropriation.

(i) *Push and Pull Strategies* : These may be used to enhance sales. The push strategy concentrates on middlemen or retailers who push the sale of the product to the final consumers. It covers co-operative advertising, attractive terms of sale, coupons, and discount facilities. The pull strategy is directed toward the final buyers. It persuades the buyers to go to the sellers to buy. Sales promotion, particularly customer promotion, is an important form of the pull strategy, which asks the sellers or retailers to attract the buyers. Trade promotion is the main form of the push strategy. Trade promotion refers to buying allowances, free goods, co-operative advertising, push money, sales contests, merchandise allowances and so on. The marketing manager has to adopt both these strategies to promote sales.

(ii) *Sustaining Promotional Strategy* : The market share should not decline after a higher level of sale has been attained. The sustaining promotional strategy stabilises the market share. Sales force promotion by way of bonus and other incentives may contain the market. Steps are taken to prevent the sales force from going across to the competitors. Brand loyalty of customers is fostered and reinforced. An appropriate promotional mix may contain the market.

(iii) *Developmental Promotional Strategy* : The introduction of new products may require expansion of the market. New products or brands are popularised by offering trade discounts, cash rebates, premiums, money refunds and so on. The new consumers are given several after-sales services. Consumer-franchise building is done with developmental promotional strategy. The promotional mix for a brand with insignificant marketing penetration may require emphasis on both personal selling and sales promotion.

(iv) *Promotional Appropriation* : Promotional objectives determine promotional appropriation, under this strategic approaches are determined — the forms of promotion, the costs of each component of promotion, the activities to be performed and appropriations on personal selling sales promotion, advertising and publicity. The marketing manager has to arrive at the optimum promotional mix of the evaluation. The effectiveness of the promotional mix and stimulation are considered only in the light of sales achievements.

Before the formulation of an appropriate sales promotion strategy, product attributes, brand differentiation, purchase frequency, the nature of the market, the size of market and its location, the nature of prospective buyers, purchase frequency distribution and price strategies are evaluated.

7. *Evaluation and Control of Sales Promotional Strategy* : Sales promotional strategies should be evaluated at the stages of implementation and final performance. Implementation controls suggest improvements during the application of the

promotional strategy. Performance control is a guide for the future. Implementation control covers initial planning, objectives, promotional packages and printing of special premiums and packaging materials, distribution to retailers, etc. 95 per cent of implementation control improved sales results, although very few firms adopt this strategy. Performance or sales results are evaluated in the light of planned objectives. Consumer panel data, consumer surveys and consumer experiments are used to evaluate the performance of particular form of sales promotion. These evaluation techniques show how far the sales promotion techniques have been effective in increasing sales through motivating consumers and sellers.

## SALES TARGETS

The purposes of setting sales targets are :

1. To evaluate sales performance.
2. As an incentive to salesmen.
3. As a means of remuneration.
4. To control selling activities.

The methods used to determine sales targets are :

(a) Based on economic or leading indicators (new car sales, population trends) in the market.

(b) Historical data based on last year sales plus a desired percentage.

(c) Managerial judgment.

(d) Salesmen set their own target.

(e) Target based on territory potential.

Sales targets may be of two types : (1) Quantitative sales targets and (2) Qualitative sales targets. Quantitative sales targets are based on : (a) Sales by volume or value; (b) Sales by products; (c) Expenses to sales ratio; (d) Gross margin on orders; (e) On basis of market share; (f) On basis of daily or weekly calls or call frequency ratio; (g) Average order size and (h) Return on investment.

Qualitative sales targets depend on the corporate, marketing and sale objectives *e.g.* technical advice, to train sales persons and to locate new customers. A good target should be clear, concise, measurable and attainable, cover objectives and both quantitative and qualitative.

## QUESTIONS FOR EXERCISE

1. Explain marketing variables and the promotion mix.
2. Discuss the meaning, objective and importance of sales promotion.
3. Explain various forms of sales promotion.
4. Explain major decisions in sales promotion programme.
5. Discuss and explain publicity as a major tool of sales promotion
6. Explain and discuss important sales promotion strategies.

# 4

# Marketing Management

According to Philip Kotler, "Marketing management is the analysis, planning, implementation and control of programs designed to create, build, and maintain beneficial exchanges and relationships with target markets for the purpose of achieving organizational objectives." Marketing management takes place when at least one party to a potential exchange gives thought to objective and means of achieving desired responses from other parties.

Marketing management occurs in an organization in connection with any of its markets. Consider an automobile manufacture. The vice-president of personnel deals in the labour-market. The vice-president of purchasing deals with the raw materials market. The vice-precedent of finance deals with money market. After these they have to set objectives and develop strategies for producing satisfactory results in these markets. Traditionally, these executives were not called marketers nor were they trained in marketing. Instead, marketing management was identified with tasks and personnel dealing with the customer market. Today, marketing applies to all markets.

In the customer market, marketing is carried out by sales managers, sales representatives, advertising and promotion managers, marketing researchers, customer-service managers, product managers, market managers and the marketing vice-precedent. Each job position carries well-defined tasks and responsibilities. Many of these jobs are concerned with particular marketing resources such as advertising, sales people, or marketing research. On the other hand, product managers, market managers and the marketing vice-precedent manage programs through analyzing, planning and implementing programs that produce a desired level and mix of transactions with specified target markets.

Generally, the marketing manager is considered as someone whose task is primarily to stimulate demand for the company's products. This is too limited a view of the range of marketing tasks carried out by marketing managers. Marketing management has the task of influencing the level, timing and composition of demand in a way that will help the organization achieve its objectives. Thus, marketing management is demand management.

## STATES OF DEMAND AND CORRESPONDING MARKETING TASKS

Following are eight different common states of demand and the corresponding tasks facing marketing managers :

**1. Negative Demand.** If a major part of the market dislikes the product and may even pay a price to avoid it, a market is in a state of negative demand. People have a negative demand for vaccinations, dental work, vasectomies and gall bladder operations. Employers feel a negative demand for ex-convicts and alcoholic employees. Here, the marketing task is to analyze why the market dislikes the product and whether a marketing program can change the market's beliefs and attitudes through product redesign, lower prices and more positive promotion.

**2. No Demand.** Target consumers may be uninterested in or indifferent to the product. For example, farmers may not be interested in a new farming method. College students may not be interested in taking foreign language courses. Here, the marketing task is to find ways to connect the benefits of the product with the person's natural needs and interests.

**3. Latent Demand.** A substantial number of consumers may share a strong desire for something that cannot be satisfied by an existing product or service. For example, there is a strong latent demand for unharmful cigarettes, safer neighbourhoods and more-fuel-efficient cars. Here, the marketing task is to measure the size of the potential market and develop effective goods and services that would satisfy the demand.

**4. Falling Demand.** Sooner or later every organization faces falling demand for one or more of its products. For example, churches see their membership decline. Private colleges see their applications fall. Here, the marketer must analyze the causes of market decline and determine whether demand can be restimulated through finding new target markets, changing the product's features or developing more effective communication. The marketing task is to reverse the declining demand through creative remarketing of the product.

**5. Irregular Demand**. Demand varies on a seasonal, daily or even hourly basis, causing problems of idle capacity or overworked capacity. In mass transit, much of the equipment is idle during the off-peak hours and insufficient during the peak travel hours. Museums are undervisited during weekdays and overcrowded during weekends. Hospital operating rooms are overbooked early in the week and under-booked toward the end of the week. Here the marketing task is to find ways to alter the time pattern of demand through flexible pricing, promotion and other incentives.

**6. Full Demand**. Organizations face full demand when they are pleased with their amount of business. Here, the marketing task is to maintain the current level of demand in the face of changing consumer preferences and increasing competition. An organization must keep up its quality and continually measure consumer satisfaction to make sure it is doing a good job.

**7. Overfull Demand.** There is a demand level that is higher than organizations can or want to handle. For example, the Golden Gate Bridge carries a higher amount of traffic than is safe. The Yellowstone National Park is terribly overcrowded in the summertime. The marketing task of finding ways to reduce the demand temporarily or permanently is called demarketing. Demarketing does not aim to destroy demand but only reduce its level. General demarketing seeks to discourage overall demand. It consists of such steps as raising prices and reducing promotion and service. Selective demarketing consists of trying to reduce the demand coming from those parts of the market that are less profitable or less in need of the service.

**8. Unwholesome Demand**. Unwholesome products attract organized efforts to discourage their consumption. For example, "No SALE" campaigns have been conducted against cigarettes, alcohol, hard drugs, handguns, X-rated movies and large families. Here, the marketing task is to get people who like something to give it up using such tools as fear communication, price hikes, and reduced availability.

The organisation forms an idea of a desired transactions with a target market. The actual demand level may be below, equal to, or above the desired demand level. There may be no demand, adequate demand and excessive demand. The marketing management has to cope with these different states.

## COMPANY CONCEPTS OF MARKETING

Marketing activities should be carried out under some well-thought out philosophy that spells out responsive and responsible marketing. Following are five concepts under which business and other organizations can conduct their marketing activities.

**1. The Production Concept.** According to Philip Kotler, one of the oldest concepts guiding sellers, "the production concept holds that consumers will favour those products that are widely available and low in cost. Management in production-oriented organizations concentrates on achieving high production efficiency and wide distribution coverage."

In at least two types of situations consumers are primarily interested in product availability and low price holds:

(i) Where the demand for a product exceeds supply and therefore customers are more interested in obtaining the product than in its fine points. The suppliers will concentrate on finding ways to increase production.

(ii) Where the product's cost is high and has to be brought down through increased productivity to expand the market.

In connection with developing the market for automobiles Texas Instruments, the Dallas-based electronics firm, is the leading American exponent of the "get-out-production, cut-the-price" philosophy that Henry Ford pioneered in the early 1900s. Ford put all of his talent into perfecting the mass production of automobiles to bring down their costs. Texas Instruments put all of its efforts in building production volume and improving technology in order to bring down costs. It uses its lower costs to cut prices and expand the market size. It usually achieves the dominant position in its markets. To Texas Instruments, marketing means bringing down the price to buyers. As this orientation is also found in many Japanese companies, Texas Instruments is well prepared to compete with them in world markets.

Among service organizations, medical and dental practices are organized on assembly-line Principles as are unemployment offices and license bureaus. This type of management is open to the charge of impersonality and consumer insensitivity though it results in handling many cases per hour.

**2. The Product Concept.** According to Philip Kotler, "The product concept holds that consumers will favour those products that offer the most quality, performance, and features. Management in these product-oriented organizations focus their energy on making good products and improving them over time."

Assuming that buyers admire well-made products, appraise product quality and performance and are willing to pay more for product "extras", many of these managers caught up in a love affair with their product fail to appreciate that the market may be less "turned on" and they may even be moving in a different direction. Saying "we make the men's finest tailored suits" or "we make the finest television sets" they wonder why the market doesn't appreciate this. An office-files manufacturer complained that his files should be selling better because they are the best in the world. "They can be dropped from a four-story building and not be damaged." "Yes," agreed his sales manager, "but our customers aren't planning to push them out of four-storey buildings."

One of the most common manifestations of the product concept occurs with new products that a company invents. Management gets enamored of the product and often loses perspective. Believing that building a better mousetrap will lead people to beat a path to its door, they fall into the "better mousetrap fallacy."

The product concept leads to an undue concentration on the product rather than the need. For example, Railroad management thought that users wanted trains rather than transportation and overlooked the growing challenge of the airlines, buses, trucks and automobiles. Slide-rule manufacturers thought that engineers wanted slide-rules rather than calculating capacity and overlooked the challenge of pocket calculators. Colleges assume that high school graduates want a liberal arts education and overlook the shift of preference to vocationally-oriented education. Churches, symphonies and the post office assume that they are offering the public the right product and wonder why their sales falter. According to Philip Kotler, "These organizations too often are looking into a mirror when they should be looking out of the window."

**3. The Selling Concept.** According to Philip Kotler, "The selling concept holds that consumers, if left alone, will ordinarily not buy enough of the organization's products. The organization must therefore undertake an aggressive selling and promotion effort." Selling concept assumes that consumers typically show buying inertia or resistance and have to be coaxed into buying more. It believes that the company has available a whole array of effective selling and promotion tools to stimulate more buying. It is undertaken most aggressively with "unsought goods," that buyers normally do not think of buying such as goods insurance, encyclopedias and funeral plots. Many industries have perfected various sales techniques to locate prospects and hard sell them on the benefits of their product. Hard selling also occurs with sought goods, such as automobiles.

The fund raisers, college admissions offices, and political parties use the selling concept practiced in the nonprofit area. A political party vigorously sells its candidate to the voters, a fantastic person for the job from early morning to late evening. The candidate stomps through voting precincts holding hands, kissing babies, meeting donors, making breezy speeches. Countless rupees are spent on radio and television advertising, posters, and mailings. Any flaws in the candidate are shielded from the public because the aim is to get the sale, not worry about post-purchase satisfaction. The new official continues to take a sales-oriented view toward the citizens even after the election. With little research into what the public wants, there is a lot of selling to get the public to accept policies that the politician or party wants.

Most firms practice the selling concept due to overcapacity. Their aim is at selling what they can make rather than making new things to sell. In most industrial economies, productive capacity is built up to a point where most markets are buyer markets and sellers have to scramble hard for customers. Prospects are bombarded with television commercials, newspaper ads, direct mail and sales calls. Someone is trying to sell something at every turn. The public identifies marketing with hard selling and advertising.

People are surprised to learn that selling is not the most important part of marketing. As Peter Drucker puts it, "There will always, one can assume, be need for some selling. But the aim of marketing is to make selling superfluous. The aim of marketing is to know and understand the customer so well that the product or service fits him and sells itself. Ideally, marketing should result in a customer who is ready to buy. All that should be needed then is to make the product or service available."

Thus, to be effective, selling must be preceded by needs assessment, marketing research, product development, pricing, and distribution. If the marketer does a good job of identifying these effectively his products will sell very easily. When Eastman Kodak designed its instamatic camera, when Atari designed its first video game and when Mazda introduced its RX-7 sports car, these manufacturers were swamped with orders because they had designed the "right" product based on the marketing homework they had done.

Marketing based on hard selling wrongly assumes that customers coaxed into buying the product will like it and if they don't they won't bad-mouth it to friends or complain to consumer organizations. And they will possibly forget their disappointment and buy it again. These are indefensible assumptions.

**4. The Marketing Concept.** As a business philosophy, the marketing concept arose to challenge all previous concepts.

According to Peter Drucker, marketing was invented in Japan around 1650 by the first member of the Mitsui family to settle in Tokyo as a merchant and to open what might be called the first department store. He anticipated by a full 250 years basic Sears, Roebuck policies, which are : to be the buyer for his customers; to design the right products for them and to develop sources for their production; the principle of your money back and no questions asked and the idea of offering a large assortment of products to his customers rather than focusing on a craft, a product category or a process. Marketing appeared in the West in the middle nineteenth century at the International Harvester Company. The first man in the West to see marketing clearly as the unique and central function of the business enterprise and the creation of a customer as the specific job of management, was Cyrus H. McCormick (1809-1884). The history books mention that he invented a mechanical harvester. But he also invented the basic tools of modern marketing such as market research and market analysis, the concept of market standing, pricing policies, the service salesman, parts and service supply to customer and installment credit.

Another fifty years passed before the marketing discipline emerged on the academic scene in America. In 1905 W.E. Kreusi taught a course entitled. "The marketing of Products" at the University of Pennsylvania. In 1910 Ralph Star Butler offered a course entitled "Marketing Methods" at the University of Wisconsin. He said, "In considering the whole field of selling I developed the idea that personal salesmanship and advertising had to do simply with the final expression of the selling idea. My experience with the Procter & Gamble company had convinced me that a manufacturer seeking to market a product had to consider and solve a large number of problems before he ever gave expression to the selling idea by sending a salesman on the road or inserting an advertisement in a publication."

Marketing departments within companies first appeared in the early twentieth century in the form of marketing research departments. In 1911 the Curtis Publishing Company installed the first marketing research department called commercial research at the time under the direction of Charles C. Parlin. Marketing research departments were subsequently established at U.S. Rubber (1916) and Swift and Company (1917). Viewed as adjuncts to the sales department they tried to develop information that would make it easier for sales departments to sell. Gradually, marketing research departments accepted additional responsibilities such as sales analysis and marketing administration. Later, companies began to combine marketing research, advertising, customer services, and other miscellaneous marketing functions into marketing departments.

## ESSENTIALS OF MARKETING

According to Philip Kotler, "The marketing concept holds that the key to achieving organizational goals consists in determining the needs and wants of target markets and delivering the desired satisfactions more effectively and efficiently than competitors." The marketing concept has been expressed in the following ways:

1. "Find wants and fill them."
2. "Make what you can sell instead of trying to sell what you can make."

3. "We have to stop marketing makeable products and learn to make marketable products."

4. "Love the customer and not the product."

5. "Have it your way" (Burger King).

6. "You're the boss" (United Airlines).

7. "To do all in our power to pack the customer's dollar full of value, quality and satisfaction" (J.C. Penney).

Drawing sharp contrast between the selling and the marketing concepts, Levitt has said, "Selling focuses on the needs of the seller, marketing on the needs of the buyer. Selling is preoccupied with the seller's need to convert his product into cash; marketing with the idea of satisfying the needs of the customer by means of the product and the whole cluster of things associated with creating, delivering and finally consuming it."

While selling concept deals with the company's existing products and calls for heavy selling and promoting to achieve profitable sales, the marketing concept starts with the company's target customers and their needs and wants. The company integrates and coordinates all the activities that will affect customer satisfaction. The company achieves its profits through creating and maintaining customer satisfaction. To conclude with Philip Kotler, "the marketing concept is a customers' needs and wants orientation backed by integrated marketing effort aimed at generating customer satisfaction as the key to satisfying organizational goals."

The marketing concept expresses the company's commitment to consumer sovereignty. What is to be produced should not be in the hands of the companies or in the hand of government but in the hands of consumers. The companies produce what the consumers want. They maximize consumer welfare and earn their profits. However, even in USA, only a small number of companies are master practitioners of the marketing concept. These include Procter and Gamble, IBM, Avon, McDonald's, General Mills, General Foods, Gillete, Kodak, General Electric, Caterpillar and John Deere. These companies are organized to respond effectively to changing customer needs. They have well-staffed marketing departments. Their manufacturing, finance, research and development, personnel, purchasing departments, all accept the concept that the customer is the king. They have marketing culture with deep roots in all of their departments and divisions.

Most of the U.S. companies have not arrived at full marketing maturity. They have a marketing vice-president, product managers, sales force, advertising budgets and so on. Yet they fail to adapt to changing consumer needs and changing competition. International Harvester is on the verge of bankruptcy; Chrysler almost collapsed and companies like Harley Davidson, Xerox and Zenith, one-time leaders in their respective fields, are all rapidly losing market shares to Japanese competitors.

## REASONS FOR MARKETING CONCEPT

Most companies embrace the marketing concept driven by following reasons :

**1. Sales Decline.** Companies become desperate and start looking for answers when they experience falling sales. For example, as more people turn to television news, newspapers show falling circulation. Publishers who are beginning to realize that they know very little about why people read newspapers and what they want out of newspapers are commissioning consumer research and attempting to redesign newspapers to be contemporary, relevant, and interesting to readers.

**2. Slow Growth.** Slow sales growth gives companies an impetus to cast about for new markets. They recognize a need for marketing know-how if they are to successfully identify, evaluate, and select new opportunities. In USA, Dow Chemical wanting new sources of profits, decided to enter consumer markets and invested heavily in acquiring marketing expertise to carry out the job.

**3. Changing Buying Patterns.** Companies living through increasingly turbulent markets marked by rapidly changing customer wants, seek more marketing know-how if they are to continue producing value for buyers.

**4. Increasing Competition.** Complacent companies are suddenly attacked by powerful marketing companies and forced to learn marketing to meet the challenge. For example, American Telephone and Telegraph (A.T & T) remained a regulated marketing naive company until the 1970s, plunged into the marketing waters and hired the best people it could find to go down the marketing learning curve as fast as possible when other companies were allowed to sell telecommunication equipment to A.T & T customers.

**5. Increasing Marketing Expenditure.** When companies find their expenditures for advertising, sales promotion, marketing research and customer getting out of hand, their managements decide to rationalize the marketing function.

## HURDLES IN MARKET ORIENTATION

A company will face organized resistance, slow learning, and fast-forgetting in the course of converting to a market-oriented company.

**1. Organized Resistance.** Some resistance to departments in the company, particularly manufacturing and R & D to marketing department is seen because it threatens their own power in the organization. Initially, the sales/marketing function is seen as one of several equally important business functions in a check-and-balance relationship. A dearth of demand leads marketers to argue that their function is somewhat more important than the others. A few marketing enthusiasts say that marketing is the major function of the enterprise, for without customers, there would be no company. They put marketing at the center with other business functions serving as support functions, while other managers do not think of themselves as working for marketing. Enlightened marketers clarify the issue by putting the customer rather than marketing at the center of the company. They argue for a customer orientation in which all functions work together to sense, serve and satisfy the customer. Finally, some marketers say that if customers needs are to be correctly interpreted and efficiently satisfied, marketing needs should command a central position in the firm. They argue as follows:

(i) The assets of the firm have little value without the existence of customers.

(ii) The key task of the firm is therefore to create and hold customers.

(iii) Customers are attracted through promises and held through satisfaction.

(iv) Marketing's task is to define an appropriate promise to the customer and to ensure the delivery of satisfaction.

(v) The actual satisfaction delivered to the customer is affected by the performance of the other departments.

(vi) Marketing needs influence of control over these other departments if customers are to be satisfied.

Marketing resistance is especially conspicuous in industries where marketing is being introduced or proposed for the first time, such as in the legal professions, libraries, hospitals or colleges. Colleges have to face the hostility of professors and hospitals have to face the hostility of doctors, because each group thinks that marketing their service would be degrading.

**2. Slow Learning**. Companies build up the marketing function in their organization in spite of resistance in many quarters. The company president gives enthusiastic support to the function. New job positions are created. Outside marketing talent is hired. Key members of management attend marketing seminars to gain a deeper understanding of marketing. The marketing budget is substantially increased. The marketing, planning and control systems are introduced. However, the learning as to what marketing really is comes slowly.

**3. Fast Forgetting.** Even after strong marketing is installed in an organization and matures through the various stages, management tends to forget marketing principles in the wake of marketplace success. In the 1950s and 1960s a number of major American companies entered European markets expecting to achieve outstanding success with their sophisticated products and marketing capabilities. A number of them failed because they forgot the marketing maxim "Know your market and know how to satisfy it". Instead of redesigning them on the basis of what the market needed American companies came into these markets with their current products and advertising programmes. American marketers failed to appreciate the major cultural variations between and even within European countries and the need to start where the consumers are not where their products are. To quote Sorenson, in the United States, the marketing concept appears to be well into the mature phase of its own life cycle. It is increasingly being questioned, criticized and in some instances—ignored or discarded. By contrast, the marketing concept in Europe is alive and vigorous and just entering the rapid growth stage of its life cycle.

According to Philip Kotler, "The societal marketing concept holds that the organization's task is to determine the needs, wants and interests of target markets and to deliver the desired satisfactions more effectively and efficiently than competitors in a way that preserves or enhances the consumer's and the society's well-being." The social marketing concept calls upon marketers to balance company profits, consumer want satisfaction, and society interests in setting their marketing policies. Originally, companies based their marketing decision largely on immediate company profit calculations. Gradually, they began to recognize the importance of satisfying consumer wants. This introduced the marketing concept involving society's interest in their decision making. The societal marketing concept calls for balancing all three considerations. Through adopting and practising the societal marketing concept, many companies have achieved notable sales and profit gains.

## AREAS OF MARKETING MANAGEMENT

**1. Business Sector**. Marketing entered the consciousness of different companies at different times. In the business sector, General Electric, General Motors, Procter and Gamble and Coca-Cola were among the leaders in USA. Marketing spread most rapidly in USA in consumer packaged goods companies, consumer durables companies and industrial equipment companies. Producers of commodities such as steel, chemicals and paper came later. Within the last decade consumer-service firms, especially airlines and banks, have moved toward modern marketing. Marketing is also beginning to excite the interest of insurance and stock brokerage companies. Professional service provides such as lawyers, accountants and architects are the most recent business groups to take an interest in marketing.

**2. Non-profit Sector**. Marketing is increasingly attracting the interest of nonprofit organizations such as colleges, hospitals, departments, museums, and symphonies.

As these organizations have marketplace problems, their administrators are struggling to keep them alive in the face of changing consumer attitudes and diminishing financial resources. Many institutions have turned to marketing as a possible answer to their problems. Indian government agencies are showing an increased interest in marketing.

**3. International Sector**. Multinationals have introduced and spruced modern marketing practices throughout the world. Smaller domestic- companies in various countries have started looking into ways to strengthen their marketing muscle to compete with the multinationals. In socialist countries various functions of marketing, such as marketing research, branding, advertising and sales promotion are now spreading rapidly.

## QUESTIONS FOR EXERCISE

1. Explain the meaning of personnel and functions of marketing management. Describe states of demand and the corresponding marketing tasks.
2. Discuss various company concepts toward the marketplace.

# 5

# PHYSICAL DISTRIBUTION

Physical distribution is the science of business logistics whereby the proper amount of the right kind of produce is made available at the place where demand for it exists. It is the key link between manufacturing and demand creation. It is generally used to describe a series of interrelated activities. It includes :

(i) *Various interrelated activities* : These are inventory controls, storage, transportation, material handling, order size control and order processing.

(ii) The total distribution system.

## DEFINITION OF PHYSICAL DISTRIBUTION

1. Philip Kotler. "Physical distribution comprises the tasks involved in planning and implementing the physical flows of materials and final goods from points of origin to points of use or consumption to meet the needs of customers at a profits."

2. William J. Stanton. "Physical distribution involves the management of the physical flow of products and the establishment and operation of flow system."

3. Cundiff and Still. "Physical distribution involves the actual movement and storage of goods after they are produced and before they are consumed."

## UTILITY OF PHYSICAL DISTRIBUTION SYSTEM

**1. Control on Distribution Cost.** A detailed analysis of transportation and storage costs is made in view of controlling or minimising the distribution cost under an efficient system of physical distribution. It aims at reducing the sale price to the consumers. Hence, stress is laid on improvement in packaging, control over channels of distribution, simplification of distribution system and technical improvements.

**2. Increase in Sales Volume.** Physical distribution seeks to increase sales volume by inventory control. It reduces the quantity of stock held by the consumer as he is assured of regular supply. On the other hand, a concern can produce more with the same amount of finance because of low inventory and reduction in distribution cost.

**3. Coordination of Demand and Supply.** Physical distribution facilitates the coordination between demand and supply. Two main factors are involved in the process, *i.e.*, time factor and place factor.

The industries producing articles having seasonal demands such as woollens or fans produce throughout the year only because modern storage facilities are available and are supplied in the sufficient quantity in the season. On the other hand, where production is seasonal as in case of sugar or wheat, storage facilities play a dominant role in order to maintain their supply throughout the year.

As quick and modern transportation system makes it possible to transport even the perishable goods to the consumer places in no time, all the commodities are available in all seasons throughout the year. Sea foods are made fresh available even at distant places due to efficient transport system.

Thus, an efficient physical distribution system establishes equilibrium between demand and supply at reasonable rates.

**4. Stabilisation of Prices.** Control over supply position helps in stabilizing the prices in the market. If demand exceeds at any time the supply available in the market, additional supplies can be released from the warehouses. On the other hand, if supply position improves, the production may be kept in storage in order to arrest the fall in prices. Transportation system also helps to maintain the price-level. The supply can be transported from the place of abundance to the place of shortage which equalizes the prices of two places.

**5. Help in Product Planning.** Activities of physical distribution affect the product planning. Transportation and storage facilities-their type, nature and place-are considered vigorously while taking a decision regarding size, weight, packing, price, etc.

**6. Help in deciding Channel of Distribution.** Physical distribution system affects the decision on channels of distribution. If the product requires storage, it should be sold out through wholesalers who own their own godowns or storing facilities. If a company decides to manage its warehouses, it should decide the points where to establish them and what type of transport facility should be arranged to carry the goods to the warehouses of its own or of middlemen. These factors are important while taking the decision on channel of distribution.

**7. Help in deciding Size of Inventory.** If transport facilities are good, the size of inventory may be kept at low level because goods can be purchased as and when it is required. Storage and transport facilities are short, heavy stock of raw materials shall be preserved to maintain continuous flow of production.

Thus, the development of physical distribution facilities has made the production possible throughout the year at lower cost of production and distribution.

## DECISION AREAS

Decisions in following areas are taken in order to achieve the various objectives and advantages of physical distribution :

**1. Size of Inventory.** Inventories are reservoirs of goods held in anticipation of sales, *i.e.*, of filling demands along the marketing channels. Incoming quantities of product or completed stock production increase the inventory and outgoing quantities of product or sale reduce it. Thus, the inventory fluctuates with every unit of production or purchase and of sale. The fluctuation in inventory is always on with every change in rates and quantities of input and output. Hence, in deciding on inventory size, the management must determine both maximum and minimum allowable extreme limits. This involves two main considerations: (i) Sales considerations and (ii) Cost considerations.

(i) *Sales Considerations* : The inventory management aims at meeting the market demand, *i.e.*, to make sales and to file the customers' orders. As inventories are kept in anticipation of demand, the upper and lower limits should be set on the basis of sales forecasts. The more accurate the sales forecasts, the greater the opportunity is for gain from economical inventory levels. In this regard the two following additional factors need attention:

(a) ***Management's Concept of Acceptable Level of Customers Service*** : The proportion of orders of the customers that the ready stock can satisfy without delay has a definite bearing on the upper inventory limit.

(b) ***Distribution System Responsiveness*** : Distributors should be able to communicate their needs to the producer and get needed inventory into the field. The amount of management responsiveness determines how quickly the firm can adjust inventory to demand changes. This responsiveness influences the lower limit of the inventory.

(ii) *Cost Considerations* : Following three main types of costs are related to the inventory :

(a) ***Holding Costs*** : These include warehousing and storage charges, cost of capital blocked in inventory, cost of adverse price movement, obsolescence, spoilage, pilferage and taxes and insurance on inventory.

(b) ***Costs of Shortages*** : These include special clerical, administrative and handling costs, losses of specific sales, of goodwill and even of some customers.

(c) ***Costs of Replenishing Inventory*** : These differ in composition depending upon whether a business does its own manufacturing. These include labour and machine set up costs, cost of materials used during set up testing, cost of production, time lost during set up, clerical and administrative costs, transportation and unloading, placement in warehouses and performing necessary related activities etc.

Inventory decisions should seek to balance all the above mentioned three types of costs. The holding costs bear a direct relation to the size of inventory. The costs of shortages and replenishment have negative correlation with the size of inventory. Thus all the three costs are related to inventory size.

**2. Storage and Inventory Locations.** The next area of decision regarding physical distribution is the decision on storage and inventory location. It closely relates to the decision on inventory size. Reduction in the size of inventory will require less storage space. Marketers use following three important storage decisions:

(i) Geographic deployment of inventory.

(ii) Comparison of inventory concentration and dispersion.

(iii) Ownership of warehouse facilities.

(iv) Number and location of warehouses.

(i) *Geographical Deployment of Inventory* : Following are the three decision alternatives on geographical deployment of inventory :

(a) Concentration at or near the plant or at some other control location.
(b) Dispersion at several distribution points located in or closer to the main markets, and
(c) Concentration of substantial inventory at a few distribution centres and redistribution to a large number of distribution points dispersed throughout the market.

Among these, while the first two alternatives are opposite extremes the third one is a compromise between them.

(ii) *Comparison of Inventory Concentration and Dispersion* : It reveals opposite sets of strengths and weaknesses. The firm which concentrates its inventories can minimise the number of customers' orders unfilled because of stock outs. On the other hand, it may increase the transportation costs and delay customer services. If it decides to disperse its inventories it may reduce its total inventory investment and use sub-inventories to be sold in a particular market. This reduces total transportation charges and speeds up customer services. As dispersion decision needs a larger enough reserve stock maintenance at each branch each marketer should combine these two alternatives.

(iii) *Inventory Dispersion and Warehouse Ownership* : If the manufacturer decides for the dispersion of inventories, he may choose between maintaining its warehouses or using public warehouses. The choice depends upon the various factors, such as the amount of sales originating in a particular market, fixed and variable warehousing costs, degree of flexibility, relative warehousing efficiency and the market channels. These factors are interrelated to each other. The manufacturer should prefer owned warehouses if the volume of goods moved is substantial with little seasonal fluctuations.

As the public warehouses charge on the basis of time taken and space occupied, these can be preferred only when less goods are handled or large volume of goods is handled through seasons.

(iv) *Number and Location of Warehouses* : The decision about the number and location of warehouses is influenced by several important variables such as customers' buying patterns and delivery expectations, freight rate structure, transport service available, warehousing costs, location of factories, production capacities, productmix, suitable renting of warehousing in different localities etc.

**3. Modes of Transportation.** Decision on modes of transportation largely depends upon the size of inventories and the location of the storage both of which are interrelated because economy in transportation charges may increase the storage cost or vice versa, the overall cost of physical distribution and not only the cost of one aspect should be borne in mind.

With the increase in transportation services the manufacturer should take a decision about the mode of transportation, such as road, rail, air or sea, taking into account their comparative freights and other related costs. Cost and time factors should be considered well before deciding the mode of transportation.

**4. Material Handling.** Among the areas of physical distribution Material handling decisions have experienced the greatest change and improvement in efficiency. Two major changes which took place in this area are (i) elimination of man handling, and (ii) Containerization.

(i) *Elimination of man handling* : The first improvement was the replacement of man handling by machine handling though it is still used in retail or final buyer stage. Improved conveyer systems and left equipments has changed to total mechanisation.

(ii) *Containerization* : Containerization is a method by which a large number of units of a product are combined into a single compact unit for storage and transportation. It reduces material handling cost and time spent. Use of improved handling equipments and containerization will increase the efficiency and reduce the wastage and costs. It will make possible best utilisation of space in storage.

**5. Order-size.** Orders of quantities less than a container will increase the cost of handling because the handling process will be done entirely by hand instead of machines. It will increase costs and consume more time. Less than container size orders increase the costs of storage and inventory control and add to their complexity. They also affect the cost of transportation because transportation charges are lower for bulk quantity. Hence, the management must make order size decisions concerning minimum order sizes, units in increment in order sizes, and preferred order sizes.

**6. Order Processing.** The methods of processing customers' orders affects a concern's service to them in two ways:

(i) Recorder time is affected and

(ii) Consistency of Delivery time is affected.

Variations in these two variables affect the profits of the buyers through changing their required investment in inventory, their ordering costs and the probability that they will be out of stock. Therefore, the buyers tend to shift their orders to other suppliers providing better processing services.

## APPLICATION OF OPERATIONS RESEARCH (OR)

Physical distribution decisions involve an attempt to optimise several variables. Business community today uses new approaches like mathematical stimulation; linear programming, heuristic programming and integer programming etc.

**1. Mathematical Stimulation.** By mathematical stimulation the whole physical distribution system can be managed through computers. Various schemes of management can be tested for improvement in distribution methods or lowering of distribution costs. The management after comparing such stimulation on the alternatives selects that which fulfils the need. These can be tested on warehouse for shipping arrangements. Though these stimulations can schedule the shipments, it may not prove to be in favour.

**2. Linear Programming.** Transportation is used in planning shipment from one destination to the other for minimizing the total shipping costs through linear programming. These destinations include factory, warehouse, distribution centre, store or customer. It is to decide which warehouse will supply to which customer for minimising costs. Cut and dry method was applied before transportation technique.

The simplest method to find solutions to multidimensional problems includes various time periods, different products and one or more intermediate storage points in the distribution system.

**3. Heuristic Programming.** It is used to reduce problem solving effort. A particular problem to be solved is a collection or combination of sets of instructions making possible computerised solutions to problems. Heuristic programming finds out a way to solve a complex problem in physical distribution with less computational effort.

**4. Integer Programming.** The optimal solution giving 'whole numbers' determines the optimum solutions from among considerable large number of alternatives than with linear programming and without excessive time and effort. Recently several companies have used this method.

## QUESTIONS FOR EXERCISE

1. What do you understand by Physical Distribution? Discuss its utility in the business world?
2. Explain the decision areas in the management of Physical Distribution.
3. Describe the various applications of operations research to Physical Distribution Problems.

# 6

# SALESMEN-RECRUITMENT

A salesman occupies a strategic place in the sales organisation. The competitive strength of the organisation depends on its salesmen. Therefore their proper selection contributes to the survival and growth of a sales organisation.

On the other hand, poor selection is quite expensive. It creates a high turn over of salesman. It has an unfavourable effect on prospects. It involves the organisation in wastage of expenditure incurred on selection and training.

It is difficult to measure the success or failure of the salesman. It normally takes more than a year to assess his effectiveness or otherwise. In recruiting and selecting salesman, the sales manager has to determine the best candidates from among the applicants.

**Value of Personality.** Nothing can be farther from truth that "good salesmen are born not trained". No doubt certain individual possess qualities by birth which make it easy for them to do a good job of selling. Personality which includes the emotional, social, mental and physical development of a person is a born trait of a person. Some people do have a natural distinct flair for selling with their pleasing personality pushing nature and affectionate, sympathetic convincing approach. They catch the imagination of their prospect more easily and effectively than others. Their personality traits render them much more likeable by those whom they approach. But their success as a good salesman cannot be a matter of personality alone. Personality creates for them the most favourable background. However, they can use their favourable background for effective selling only if they possess the knowledge of goods selling techniques. To possess technique they must acquire the knowledge of the products and of the customers. They may possess the natural qualities for the selling job but to obtain maximum sales volume they must get the proper training.

**Need of Training**

In these day of competitive marketing with ever increasing variety of new products coming in the market, personality alone cannot make a good salesman. As whitehead has said "personality only helps to open the door to good selling. It does not make sales". Between a person with extremely good, highly pleasing personality without requisite training and another with good training but inferior personality, the latter is bound and prove a better salesman. Training makes one a good salesman.

**Objectives of Recruitment**

According to Bolling salesmen are the 'active striking power' of the sales department. Recruitment of the right type of salesmen in sufficient number is necessary to carry on the selling functions of a firm. Salesman possessing necessary qualities have to be recruited to meet the following objectives :

1. To replace those salesmen who are removed from the job as unfit.
2. To fill up the vacancies caused by the resignations, deaths or disability of the salesmen on roll.
3. To add to the existing sales force to organise the sale of a new product.
4. To introduce a new line of products to open new market.
5. To educate dealer-middlemen.
6. To take up other sales promotion works.

The need of salesmen and the frequency with which they are to be recruited vary from firm according to the products to be sold, the rise of the firm, the choice of the channel of distribution, the firm's financial position and the nature of market to be covered. However salesmen must be hired to make sales contacts the qualifications of men who make such contacts must be determined before they are appointed. This makes recruitment of salesmen an important function which has to be performed caution. As success or failure of the firm depend upon the type of salesmen selected, therefore selection must be made very carefully.

## RECRUITMENT PROCESS

Recruitment of salesmen involves the following steps :

(1) Job analysis.

(2) Personal analysis.

(3) Tapping the various sources of recruitment.

(4) Selection of the candidates.

(5) Appointment agreement.

**1. Job Analysis.** This concerned with the determination of nature of duties and responsibilities to be performed. The sales manager must first know the job for which the salesman has to be recruited. Duties of wholesaler's salesmen will be different from those of the manufacturer's salesmen or retailer's salesmen. The responsibilities of counter salesmen will differ from those of the outdoor salesmen. Duties of salesmen selling shopping goods differ from the duties of salesmen of speciality goods. Job analysis is concerned with preparing a well thought out plan of recruitment of salesmen on the basis of thorough analysis of the duties to be assigned to the salesmen, to be appointed. It is helpful in scientific selection and training of a salesmen.

**2. Personal Analysis.** Qualities required of a good salesman are character traits, human and mental qualities, maturity appearance and impressiveness. Sales manager has to determine the order of preference of specific qualities needed for the performance of the job. This is known as personnel specifications or job specifications. For determining the qualities, the personal traits are divided in to three groups :

(i) *General Qualities* : These include good personality, sound health, intelligence, honesty and integrity of character, sociability and power of observation.

(ii) *Particular Qualities* : These include educational qualifications past experience, knowledge of the product, customers and markets.

(iii) *Technical Knowledge* : It includes the knowledge about the chemical or mechanical aspects of the products to be sold. Knowledge of legal implication involved in the sales activities and the languages should be know to the candidates.

**3. Sources of Recruitment.** Choice of sources of recruitment has to be made after the job analysis and personal specifications. Every possible source should be tapped for the purpose. Various sources are Own staff, competiting firm, other firms, customers and their employees, school and colleges, situations wanted columns, casual candidates etc.

(i) *From Company's Own Staff* : This is a common method followed in most organisations. The employees working in other departments should be considered if they are promising and innate talents. This method has following advantages :

(a) Greater loyalty and cooperation from staff is ensured.

(b) Very little training is required as the person is already familiar, with the company and its products.

(c) The candidate need not be paid a high remuneration.

**Disadvantages**

(a) New ideas and thoughts can not be implemented as the employees might already has developed certain biases.

(b) The employees not having any potentialities for a sales job demand the post as a personal right and privilege

(ii) *From Competing Firm* : The practice of enticing away a man from the competing company is bad on ethical grounds. But such a salesman would be of great assistance for a new firm producing an existing product, for he would be having sufficient back ground in the sales of the same product. No training is needed for him. but the cost involved could be greater as the enticing is done only by offering a higher remuneration. The greatest drawback in this type of selection is that such a salesman may again be lured away.

(iii) *Employment Agencies* : Employment exchanges sponsored by the government from a major source of recruitment. But applicants generally available through them are untrained and inexperienced. Proper training might be necessary for them.

(iv) *From Educational Institutions* : Fresh graduates from colleges and institutes could be called for the job and person with real aptitude than be selected.

(v) *Through Press Advertisements* : This is the most usual and commonly employed form of recruiting salesmen.

(vi) *From Casual Applicants* : Large firm usually keep on getting a number of applications for different jobs. Such applications can also be considered.

(vii) *Recommended Candidates* : Sometimes the wholesalers and retailers etc. may recommend eligible candidates. The firm may select suitable persons on the basis of necessity.

**4. Selecting a Proper Salesman.** Next step is screening of the applications. The applicants who satisfy the job description and men of specifications are considered. After preliminary screening the selected applicants are further closely using the following methods :

(i) *Application Form* : Most companies prefer to have a standardised application form known as 'Application Blank'. In this form are listed only qualities and information considered essential for a particular job. This enables a quick elimination of obvious misfits. Weighted application forms are also used by some firms.

(ii) *Personal Interview* : Personal interview is highly essential since a salesman must have certain physical qualities. The interview helps the firm to find out whether or not what the applicant has stated in his application form is true. The interview may take any one of the two forms — (i) Non patterned interview and patterned interview. In the former form the candidate is persuaded to talk and answer twisted questions, in the latter form of interview all the candidates are asked the same questions.

(iii) *Psychological Tests* : Latest psychological tests are conducted such as intelligence or general apitute tests.

(iv) *Inviting Reference* : The candidates are asked to provide the referees with whom references could be made. The referees may be previous employers or reputed persons in society.

**5. Finalising the Employment.** The selected candidate may be called once again for a final interview and a medical examination. The candidate is asked to submit the certificates in original and an appointment order is issued stating clearly job description, designation, salary and allowances, nature of duties and mode of appointment.

The sources of recruitment are : (1) Advertisement; (2) Personal contacts; (3) Employment agencies and exchanges; (4) Internal recruitment; (5) Educational institutions. The selection tools employed may be : (a) application forms; (b) references; (c) interviews; (d) physical/medical test; and (e) psychometric and other tests like intelligence tests.

**THE RECRUITMENT PROCESS**

Job analysis

Manpower planning

Future — Existing

Quantitative — Qualitative

Job description

Job specification

Recruitment

Screening

Selection

**Duties and Responsibilities of a Salesman**

A salesman's job is to get an order. But while getting an order a good salesman serve the buyers. He must benefit both the parties — the buyer and the seller. This is possible if the attitude of service dominates all his activities.

Duties and responsibilities of a salesman depend upon the type of selling job but a list of duties and responsibilities almost common to all salesmen has been given below.

**1. Selling.** It includes meeting the prospects, taking orders demonstrating products, increasing sales to the existing customers, sincerity in quoting prices and terms of sales of sales and consistently following the approved policies and methods of his firm.

**2. Travelling.** A salesman has to undertake journey to cover the territory assigned.

**3. Collecting.** A salesman may be required to make collections of the bills relating to products sold by him.

**4. Reporting.** He has to prepare and send daily, weekly and monthly reports to his firm. These reports contain the expenses incurred, calls and sales made, service rendered, customers lost to the firm, competition if any, business condition, mileage of the journey made and route schedules followed.

**5. Handling Complaints.** He is expected to attend to the complaints of the customers. He may settle the claims himself or recommend terms on which the head office should finalise settlement.

**6. Collection of Credit Information.** Some firms depend upon their salesmen for the information about the credit worthiness of their customers.

**7. Advising and Counselling.** Salesmen give advice to the customers on matters relating to the products and marketing problem.

**8. Organising.** Salesmen are expected to take active interest in preparing the route and time schedules for their sales journey to put in systematised sales efforts.

**9. Attending Sales Meetings.** Salesmen have to attend the meetings held at periodic intervals to keep the salesmen well informed about the new products, new sales policies etc.

**10. Promotion of Goodwill of the Firm.** It is the duty of the salesman to cultivate customers, keep them satisfied and thus maintain and further increase the goodwill of the firm by enhancing its prestige in the eyes of the customers.

## QUALITIES OF GOOD SALESMEN

To perform all his functions a salesman must possess certain basic qualities. As the duties of a salesman vary materially from industry to industry and with in the same industry, from firm to firm, qualities needed of a salesman also vary much. Nevertheless, the following list of qualities prepared by the Educational Committee of the Sales Managers Association Philadelphia is commonly accepted pattern of qualities which go to make a salesman an ideal one.

**1. Basic Character Qualities.** These include: (i) Dependability i.e. trustworthiness and honesty; (ii) Stability; (iii) Courage; (iv) Initiative; (v) Diligence; (vi) Thoroughness; (vii) Ambition; and (viii) Self control.

**2. Human Qualities.** These include : (i) Liking for people; (ii) Understanding of people; (iii) Tactfulness; (iv) Loyalty; (v) Straight-forwardness; (vi) Enthusiasm; (vii) Cheerfulness; (viii) Team spirit; and (ix) Constructive outlook.

**3. Mental Qualities.** These include : (i) Teachability; (ii) flexibility: (iii) Judgement : (iv) observation; (v) Analytical ability; (vi) Fore sight: (vii) Business sense; (viii) Imagination and (ix) Resourcefulness.

**4. Appearance and Impressiveness.** These would depend upon : (i) Health; (ii) Energy; (viii) Voice and speech; (iv) Poise and self-confidence; (v) Dress; and (vi) Neatness.

**5. Maturity connoting the following :**

(i) Ability to assume responsibility.

(ii) Capacity to tolerate criticism and to hear praise gracefully.

(iii) Capacity to appreciate and understand the rights of others and to realise ones own social and civic obligations.

(iv) Ability to rise above ones own narrow, personal, selfish ends.

According to Bill Donaldson attributes of sales persons can be divided into five types :

1. Personality Characteristics—dominance, endurance, ego strength, social recognition and empathy.
2. Personal and Physical Characteristics—Age, height, weight, formal education, hobbies/membership of organizations.
3. Enthusiasm, confidence, intelligence and self-worth.
4. Knowledge—of product, competitors, market, company.
5. Skills—of communicating, matching, persuasive.

## TYPES OF SALESMEN

There are mainly four types of salesmen :

1. Manufacturer's salesman;
2. Wholesaler's salesman;
3. Retailers' salesman;
4. Outdoor salesman;
5. Staple salesman;
6. Speciality salesman;
7. Exporter salesman.

**1. Manufacturer's Salesmen.** Manufacturer's salesmen sell either directly to consumers (or users) or to the middlemen. Those selling, directly to consumers are like speciality salesmen.

Manufacturer's salesmen selling to middlemen (dealers or distributors) may be grouped into three following classes :

(i) Pioneer salesmen;

(ii) Dealer servicing salesmen and

(iii) Merchandising salesmen.

(i) *Pioneer Salesmen* : Manufacturer's salesmen engaged in creating market for new products unknown to wholesalers, distributors and dealers is called pioneer salesman. He has to convince the whole salers and retailers about the usefulness and suitability of the new product. He has to persuade them to believe that the product possesses necessary quality and features to find favour of the ultimate consumer. The pioneer salesman has to do aggressive selling. He must be self reliant and self generating. His work is difficult and needs high skill and persuasive capacity.

(ii) *Dealer Servicing Salesmen* : He sells products to wholesalers, retailers or distributors. Products sold by dealer servicing salesman already an established market. His job is to retain and expand the market already created. He calls on the middle men traders at regular intervals and books orders. Thus his main job is to keep the established group of whole salers and dealers well served.

He is expected to explain important features of the product which the dealers can use as the selling points in their talks with their customers. He needs not do aggressive selling. Even in a competitive market, he is required to do defensive selling. A dealer servicing salesman must possess enough energy, consistency and capacity for persistent efforts. Enthusiasm and friendly personality are the qualities needed by such salesmen. He may sell shoes, hardware, tooth paste, packaged foods orderings or any other product which requires constant contact with the dealer.

(iii) *Merchandising Salesmen* : These salesmen carry on the activities of sales promotion of the firm rather than collecting or directly securing orders, their main job is to collect information and give advice on the various problems connected with selling. They visit the middlemen, make enquiries about their stock position, discuss their marketing problems advise them on matters relating to sales.

Merchandising salesmen are helpful in creating and enhancing the reputation of the product. They must possess high educational qualifications and be well informed. They have to deal with well educated men. Sometimes they may take orders from the customers and pass them on the concerned middle men for execution. Such merchandising salesman are also known as 'missionary salesmen's.

**2. Whole Salers Salesmen.** Many whole salers appoint their own salesmen to call on the retail dealers at regular intervals and book their orders. They are expected to visit the retail dealers occasionally, take down orders accurately and thus ensure constantly smooth flow of goods from the stocks of the whole saler to retailer's shop. They have to advice retailers regarding their sales. They must be friendly in their attitude and purctual in action. Effectiveness of this type of salesmen is measured in terms of repeat sales over a long period of time. The wholesaler salesman need not be aggressive. He should be friendly, dependable, and reliable, he should make regular calls.

**3. Retailer's Salesmen.** (i) Counter salesman (ii) Outdoor salesman.

(i) *The Counter Salesman* : He works in the retailer's shop and sells to the customers who came to the shop to buy products they need. He should have adequate knowledge of the stock, prices and products and selling points. He must be courteous, considerate and salient in persuading the visiting customers to buy particular products.

(ii) *Outdoor Salesman* : He goes to the prospective customers rather than the customers coming to him as is the case with the counter salesmen. They carry samples of goods with them and persuade customers to buy the goods of the firm represented by them. Only retail houses operating on very large scale can afford to employ outdoor salesmen.

**4. Speciality Salesmen.** Salesmen employed to sell speciality items are called speciality salesmen. Speciality goods have higher unit cost, are relatively durable and are not purchased regularly. Buyers of speciality goods prefer to make careful selection. This requires the speciality salesmen to have a considerable amount of initiative, drive, product knowledge etc. He should have an extensive training in the art of salesmanship. His job is most onerous. Usually he is helped by proper advertising and marketing research.

**5. Staple Salesman.** The speciality articles become staple articles when they are common in use. Staple salesman generally concentrates on selling necessaries like food, clothes, stationery etc. these articles are sold in bulk. Furthermore, these articles are already desired by the customers and there is no necessity for salesmen to create the demand. His job is further reduced because this kind of goods require intensive distribution and a long chain of middlemen. Unlike the speciality salesman, the area of operation of the staple salesman is restricted and limited. But his job is not easy since he may have to work in highly competitive market. The profitability of the staple salesman depends upon the turnover of large business.

**6. Exporter's Salesman.** The foreign trade involves a large number of problems on account of different nationalities, different currency units etc. the greatest among the problems is to find a market for the product where the manufacturer has roots. From early times special agencies know as 'Indent House' have been working in this field. They act as agents as well as middlemen for a manufacturer. For the import of goods also such indent houses render valuable services.

It is aptly said that 'nothing happens, until somebody sells something.' Selling is the major contributor behind all human progress. It has given the highest level of comforts in the world. A salesman is really an artist who paints mental pictures with a verbal brush.

## QUESTIONS FOR EXERCISE

1. "The fortune of the concern depends on sales which in turn depends on the Salesman." Discuss the statement explaining the importance of recruiting the right type of salesman.
2. How do the duties and responsibilities of a Salesman depend upon the type of selling job?
3. What are the main types of salesmen and their duties and responsibilities?

# 7

# PERSONAL SELLING

Personal selling is the oldest form of marketing when peddlers moved from door to door to sell their products. They themselves created demand and evaluated the purchasing power of potential consumers. They used to carry the products on their heads. When they joined together they formed caravans. Cartload merchants were respected by the prospective consumers. Gradually merchants started selling goods on credit which was collected when they came after a year or so in the same village or city. Travelling merchants were considered persons capable of meeting the requirements of the local population. Subsequently, the merchants started charging higher prices and exploited the debtors. The practice of money-lending and indigenous banking developed. The consumers were exploited therefore they resorted to purchasing from local businessmen. Now, traditional peddlers faced competition with the local people.

In USA, the cartload merchants, known as wagon peddlers, used to leave home in early spring and roam the countryside to sell their products and return to their homes in the beginning of winter. Gradually, they settled down in particular localities for their businesses. They became retailers and owned small stores. The small craftsmen functioned at their residence. A sort of local market developed. Some persons worked as links between the producers and the consumers. The Americans called them greeters or drummers. The greeters became representatives of wholesalers and manufacturers. The drummers or factors in marketing were suspect because they resorted to unethical practices to promote sales.

During the first quarter of the twentieth century personal selling declined because of heavy demand by the public. The producers were confronted by the great depression of the twenties. The end of the First World War gave a set-back to the demand of civilian as well as war materials. The factors and commission agents acquired greater importance. The Second World War produced a strain on the market. As rationing was introduced in all the countries involved in the war and the need for personal selling was extinguished. The end of the Second World War witnessed a crisis. In all the countries prices increased tremendously. The producers earned huge margins following the growing demand for their products. The governments resorted to a reconstruction of their economies. Many backward countries embarked on development of their economies. Increasing production called for the exercise of fresh function. In obedience to the requirements of changing conditions marketing strategies were moulded. After the mid twentieth century the role of personal selling increased tremendously. As the sales people became more professional they adopted customer oriented techniques of sales promotion.

Personal selling is an oral presentation of goods to one or more prospective customers to promote sales. It helps in the transfer of the title from the seller to the buyer. It involves a face-to-face relationship or inter personal interaction or communication between a sales person and the buyer. As the sales people become aware of the problems of the buyers they suggest suitable products or services to satisfy their wants.

## CHARACTERISTICS OF PERSONAL SELLING

The fundamental characteristics of personal selling are high pressure_tactics, persuasion, winning the buyer's confidence, service to the buyer, mutual benefit, educative process and creative process.

**1. High Pressure Tactics**. Buyers are pressurised and influenced by sales talk and sales motivation. They are prevailed upon to purchase products which are not really required by them. The multinationals adopt high pressure techniques to sell out automotive consumer goods and electric appliances though only a few people can afford to buy these goods. Sales techniques and advertisements lure those people to buy. Buyers are often led to favorable buying decisions by high pressure sales tactics when the buyer's psychology and attitudes are used to create "imaginative" demand for the products which are ultimately accepted by consumers.

**2. Persuasion**. Many techniques are persuasive and not pressure building.

**3. Winning the Buyer's Confidence.** The salesman can succeed in his mission only when he wins the confidence of the buyers. Misrepresentation, dishonesty, cheating, etc. should be avoided by sales persons. The ignorance or credulity of the buyer should not be exploited.

**4. Service to the Buyer.** Consumers should be educated, informed and reminded of the basic elements of the products to be sold. The salesman should solve the problems of the buyer. He should discover the problems of the buyer and provide effective solutions by suggesting suitable goods and services.

**5. Mutual Benefits.** Instead of making profits out of the ignorance of people true salesmanship believes in mutual benefit. The buyer is made aware of the problems by the seller who also gains by the sale of the products. The seller makes a reasonable profit.

**6. Educative Process.** The salesman educates the customers or potential customers about their needs and ways of satisfying them. The utility of each product is outlined to the potential customers so that they can purchase commodity appropriate to satisfy their wants.

**7. Creative Process.** The salesman is responsible for the creation of demand. He helps solve the buyer's problem by suggesting suitable products. The modern concept is to guide, help or persuade the buyers to purchase a particular product. It creates a need and promotes an awareness of the need to stimulate sales.

## IMPORTANCE OF PERSONAL SELLING

Today 40 per cent of the total sales are effected through personal selling and this percentage is rising because of its inherent advantages. Thus personal selling is an important ingredient in the promotion mix and a dynamic element in the marketing mix.

When other sales promotional activities cannot reach them the salesman pinpoints the prospective buyers with a minimum waste of effort and time. He arouses, holds and sustains the attention and interest of the prospect. He has flexibility. Sales talks can be fitted to the individual needs and motives of the buyers. In personal selling, the salesman understands the reactions in response and objections of the prospects. He adjusts the sales presentation in response to their reactions and objections. He closes the sales talk at the finalization of the sales task. Effecting sales is a two way communication. The top management can find out the weakness of the sales force and sales technique while acknowledging the wishes of potential buyers. Feedback which is absent in other means of sales communication is possible in personal selling. Salesmen offer personalised services to customers and retailers and enhanced sales.

Personal selling has become a vital element in the success of marketers in western countries. Sales persons gather adequate information and feedback for subsequent sales and marketing plans. This helps management control, planning and execution. Salesmen can easily find the target consumers. They approach them with a helping hand. They formulate suitable strategies and effective policies and programmes for increasing sales.

## LIMITATIONS OF PERSONAL SELLING

As personal selling involves substantial costs of travel, literature publication, samples, surveys, management and control, it has become less attractive for small companies. Many sales persons do not take much interest in sales promotion. They waste time and shift to other organisations on lucrative salaries. They disclose the sales strategies of their organization to competitors. The companies face the problems of sales defection. Therefore, they should manage their sales force effectively and systematically. Many companies have a sad experience of bad sales persons. Thus, personal selling can be effective only when sales persons are carefully selected on the basis of merit, proper training and adequate motivation.

## PERSONAL SELLING — QUALITIES

Personal selling requires special qualities and capabilities such as hard work, initiative, sales techniques and knowledge.

**1. Hard Work.** Only a hard working sales person can succeed. Hard working sales persons improve the image and goodwill of the company. They have ideas, philosophy and personality. They understand the needs, desires and attitudes of the buyers and can motivate them to purchase goods and services.

**2. Initiative**. The sales process is full of rebuffs and disappointments. The sales person should have initiative and the urge to persuade people to purchase the goods. If a sales person is unable to sustain, he cannot succeed. He should take the problems and obstacles as challenges and directions for a deep understanding of potential buyers. He should suggest suitable products to meet the requirements of the buyers. Though initiative is inborn or inherent in a person; but it can be developed by training and motivation. A sales person may be motivated to work hard and diligently.

**3. Sales Techniques.** A sales person should know the sales techniques and he should have the willingness to follow them. Prospecting, preparation, presentation and post-sales activities are included in the sales techniques. Protecting is a' 'seeking' function of marketing. It is "matching the supply with demand." Presentation is the "buying process of consumers". The salesman should maintain contacts with the buyers after the sale of the product.

**4. Knowledge.** The sales persons must have adequate knowledge of their company, its products, competition customers and processes. The company is the main factor in sales presentation as salesmen are regarded as representatives of the company. They should know everything about the company, its policies, procedures, service facilities, discount, and guarantees offered by the company. They should have the capability to deal with customer inquiries in a satisfactory way. Knowledge of the product will enable them to motivate the potential customers to buy their products. They should also have knowledge of competing products. If they have adequate knowledge of the customer's wants and desires, they may suggest appropriate products for purchase. They should have adequate knowledge of the buying motives, patronage, rational and emotional. Knowing several sales processes, they may use adequate and suitable products at a given time. They should have the capability for introspection. They can improve their effectiveness as sales persons if they critically evaluate their activities.

## EFFECTIVE PERSONAL SELLING

Most of the sales-training approaches try to convert a sales person from being a passive order taker to an active order getter. Order takers operate on some assumptions such as customers know there needs; they would resent any attempt at influence; and they prefer salespersons who are courteous and self-effacing. For example, a salesmen would be of an order taking mentality who knocks on dozens of doors each day, simply asking if the consumer needs any detergent.

**Basic Approaches to Training**

In training salespersons to be order getters, there are two basic approaches:

**1. Sales Oriented Approach.** It trains the salesperson in high-pressure techniques such as those used in selling encyclopedias or automobiles. The techniques include overstating the product's merits, criticizing competitive products, using a slick canned presentation, selling yourself and offering some concession to get the order on the spot. This form of selling assumes that the customers are not likely to buy except under pressure that they are influenced by a slick presentation and ingratiating manners and that they will not be sorry after signing the order or if they are, it doesn't matter.

**2. Customer Oriented Approach.** This approach trains sales personnel in customer problem solving. This approach assumes that customers have latent needs that constitute company opportunities, that they appreciate good suggestions and that they will be loyal to sales representatives who have their long-term interest at heart. This sales person learns how to identify customer-needs and propose effective solution. The problem solver than the hard seller or order taker is a more compatible image for the salesperson under the marketing concept.

**Steps in Effective selling**

No sales approach works best in all circumstances though most sales-training programmes agree on the major steps involved in any effective sales process. These steps have been discussed below :

**1. Prospecting and Qualifying.** The first step in the selling process is to identify prospects. Although the company supplies leads, sales representatives need skill in developing their own leads which can be developed in the following ways :

(i) Asking current customers for the names of prospects.

(ii) Cultivating other referral sources, such as suppliers, dealers, non competing sales representatives, bankers and trade association executives.

(iii) Joining organizations to which prospects belong.

(iv) Engaging in speaking and writing activities that will draw attention.

(v) Examining data sources (newspapers, directories) in search of names.

(vi) Using the telephone and mail to track down leads.

(vii) Dropping in unannounced on various offices (cold canvassing).

Sales representatives must know how to screen out poor leads. Prospects can be qualified by examining their financial ability, volume of business, special requirements, location and likelihood of continuous business. The salesperson should ring or write to prospects to see if they are worth pursuing.

Buying styles are just as varied as selling styles. Buyers vary in their concern for the purchase and concern for the sales person. Some buyers couldn't care less; some are defensive; some will only listen to salespersons from well-known companies. Blake and Mouton argue that no one type of sales style will be effective with all buyers. The view that effective selling depends on matching the seller's style to the buyer's style means that salespersons should not be trained in only one style of selling. Evans found selling as a dyadic process, where the outcome depends on the match of buyer and seller characteristics as well as on buying and selling styles. He found that people bought insurance from people very much like themselves in such factors as age, height income, political opinions, religious beliefs and smoking. The perceived similarity mattered more than the actual similarity. Evans proposed that insurance companies should hire all types of salespersons if they want to achieve broad market penetration. The only requirement is that they exhibit the intelligence and kinds of abilities effective in selling insurance.

**2. Preapproach**. About the prospect company : what it needs, who is involved in the purchase decision and its buyers, their personal characteristics and buying styles, the salespersons should learn as much as possible. He can consult standard sources such as Moody's Standard and Poor, Dun and Broadcaster, etc. acquaintances and other, to learn about the company. He should set call objectives which might be to qualify the prospect or gather information or make an immediate sale. He should decide on the best approach which might be a personal visit, a phone call or a letter. He should think about the best timing because many prospects are busy at certain times. Finally, he should give thought to an overall sales strategy for the account.

**3. Approach**. To get the relationship off to a good start, the salesperson should know how to meet and greet the buyers.

This involves the salesperson's appearance, the opening lines and the follow-up remarks. He should wear clothes similar to what buyers wear, show courtesy and attention to the buyer and avoid distracting mannerisms such as pacing the floor or staring at the customer. His opening line should be positive, such as "Mr. Mohan, I am Satish from the ABC company. My company and I appreciate your willingness to see me. I will do my best to make this visit profitable and worthwhile for you and your company." This might be followed by some key questions or the showing of a display or sample to attract the buyer's attention and curiosity.

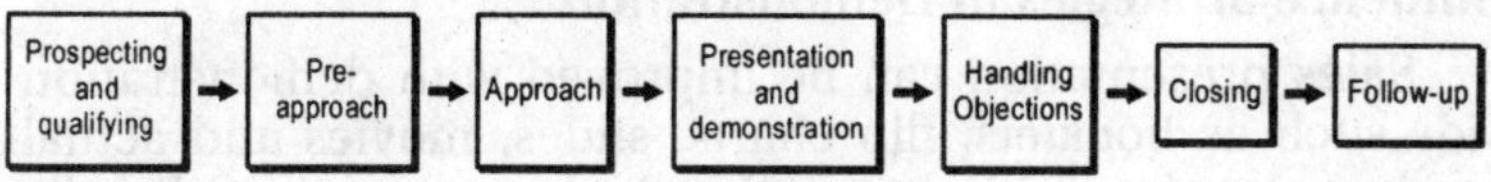


**4. Presentation and Demonstration.** Following the AIDA formula of getting attention, holding interest, arousing desire and obtaining action, the salesperson now tells the product "story" to the buyer. He emphasizes throughout customer benefits, bringing in product features as evidence of these benefits. A benefit is any advantage, such as lower cost or less work. A feature is a characteristic of a product, such as its weight and size. A common mistake in selling is to dwell on product features instead of customer benefits.

**Styles of Sales Presentation**

(i) *The Canned Approach* : It is the oldest approach which is a memorized sales talk covering the main. points. It is based on stimulus-response thinking, that is the buyer is passive and can be moved to purchase by the use of the right stimulus words, pictures, terms and actions. For example, an encyclopedia salesperson might describe the encyclopedia as "a once-in-a-lifetime buying opportunity" and hoping to trigger desire for the encyclopedia focus on some beautiful four-colour pages of sports pictures. Canned presentations are used primarily in door-to-door and telephone selling.

(ii) *The Formulated Approach* : It is also based on stimulus-response thinking. It identifies the buyer's needs and buying style and then uses a formulated approach. He initially draws the buyer into the discussion that indicates the buyer's needs and attitudes. Then he moves into a formulated presentation that shows how the product will satisfy the buyer's needs.

(iii) *The Need Satisfaction Approach* : It starts with a search for the customer's real needs by encouraging the customer to do most of the talking. It calls for good listening and problem solving skills. According to Mark Human it is well described by an IBM sales representative: "I get inside the business of my key accounts. I uncover their key problems. I prescribe solutions for them, using my company's systems and even at time components from other suppliers. I prove beforehand that my system will save money or make money for my accounts. Then I work with the account to install the system and make it prove out."

**Influence Strategies in Demonstration**

Sales presentation can be improved with demonstration aids such as booklets, flip charts, slides, movies and actual product samples. To the extent that the buyer can see or handle the product, he or she will better remember its features and benefits. According to Rosann L. Spiro and William D. Perreault, Jr., the salesperson can draw on five influence strategies during the demonstrations.

(i) *Legitimacy* : The salesman emphasizes the reputation and experience of his or her company.

(ii) *Expertise* : He shows deep knowledge of the buyer's situation and company's products, doing this without being overly "smart"

(iii) *Referent Power* : He builds on any shared characteristics, interests and acquaintances.

(iv) *Ingratiation* : He provides personal favors (a free lunch, promotional gratuities) to strengthen affiliation and reciprocity feelings.

(v) *Impression Management* : He conveys favourable impression of himself or herself.

**4. Handing Objections.** During the presentation or when asked to place an order, customers almost always pose objections. Their resistance can be psychological or logical.

(i) *Psychological Resistance* : It includes resistance to interference, preference for established habits, apathy, reluctance to giving up something, unpleasant associations about the other person, tendency to resist domination, predetermined ideas, dislike of making decision and neurotic attitude toward money.

(ii) *Logical Resistance* : It might consist of objections to the price delivery schedule or certain product or company characteristics. To handle these objections the salesperson maintains a positive approach, asks the buyer to clarify the objection, questions the buyer in a way that the buyer has to answer his or her own objection, denies the validity of the objection, or turns the objection into a reason for buying. The salesperson needs training in the broader skills of negotiation of which handling objections is a part.

**DEALING WITH OBJECTIONS**

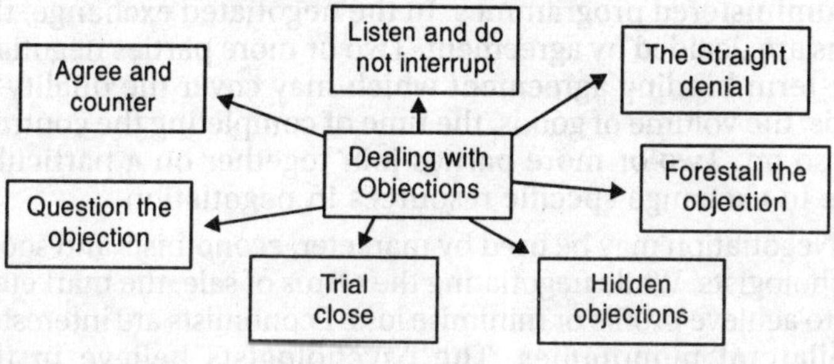


**5. Closing.** Now the salesperson attempts to close the sale. Some sales people lack confidence or feel guilty about asking for the order. They do not recognize the right psychological moment to close the sale. They need to know how to recognize closing signals from the buyer, including physical actions, statements or comments and questions. They can use one of several closing techniques. They can ask for the order, recapitulate the points of agreement, offer to help the secretary write up the order, ask whether the buyer wants A or B, get the buyer to make minor choices such as the colour, size or indicate what the buyer will lose if the order is not placed now. They may offer the buyer specific inducements to close, such as a special price and extra quantity at no charge or a gift.

**6. Follow Up.** If the salesperson wants to ensure customer satisfaction and repeat business, follow up is necessary. Immediately after closing, he should complete any necessary details on delivery time, purchase terms and other matters. He should schedule a follow-up call when the initial order is received, to make sure there is proper installation, instruction and servicing. This visit would detect any problems and assure the buyer of the salesperson's interest. It would reduce any cognitive dissonance that might have arisen.

## TYPES OF PERSONAL SELLING

The process of personal selling is adopted in the light of the objectives of personal selling and sales promotion. Personal selling may be by negotiation selling strategy, AIDAS approach and stimulus response approach.

**1. Negotiations.** To arrive at an agreement on the price and other terms and conditions of sale personal selling is effected through negotiation. Negotiation skills are applied to customers, suppliers and middlemen. A negotiated exchange is different from a routinized exchange where the terms are established by administered programmes. In the negotiated exchange, the terms are decided by agreement. Two or more parties negotiate long-term binding agreement which may cover the quality of goods, the volume of goods, the time of completing the contract and so on. Two or more parties join together on a particular issue to exchange specific resources in negotiation.

Negotiation may be used by marketer, economists and social psychologists. While negotiating the terms of sale, the marketers aim to achieve profits or minimise loss. Economists are interested in bilateral monopolies. The psychologists believe in the structural context of the agreement, the behavioral pre-dispositions of agreement, interference of agreement and use of social-influence strategies. The salesman should know when and how to negotiate the terms. He should build and manage strong relationships with key customers. This is relationship management because it affects the future sales of the company. Customers are guided by their cordial relationships with the salesman who is ready to visit them on significant social occasions. The salesman should be ready to understand the problems and difficulties of his customers. He should share even non-business problems with customers. He may offer lunch, picnic or dinner to develop personal relationships with customers.

Negotiation or bargaining should be guided by an effective hard or soft strategy, which is a commitment to achieve objectives. Some believe in principled strategy which is hard on merits and soft on people. A principled negotiation involves the separation of the people from the problem and a focus on interests, finding options for mutual gain and on instance on objectives. Bargaining tactics employed by the salesman to gain the customer's willingness to purchase his product are to act crazy or as a big shot or as a prestigious ally or as one having limited authority; to divide and conquer, stall for time and to be patient, etc,

**2. Selling Strategy**. Personal selling operations involve selling strategy which is more effective than negotiation, for it involves determining personal selling objectives, sales policies, formulation of sales strategies determining the personal selling appropriation and management of the sales force.

(i) *Selling Objectives* : Personal selling have short and long-term objectives. Short-term objectives are specific and related to promotional programme and marketing strategy Long-term objectives are broad and general, related to the overall objectives of the company. The selling strategy should be concerned with searching out new customers, maintaining customer's co-operation and providing technical advice and assistance to customers. The objectives of personal selling strategy should be clearly laid down so that they might be systematically attained within the prescribed time.

(ii) *Sales Policies* : Sales policies are framed to guide sales management in the formulation of sales strategies, definition of sales jobs and decision on the size of the sales force. These should be consistent with personal selling objectives. These describe the method of achieving these objectives. These are formulated for the attainment of objectives that is, for an adaptation of sales policies and personal selling decisions in a particular marketing situation. Although sales people in different companies perform similar duties and have similar responsibilities, they have to adopt different strategies and policies for their varied selling objectives. In determining the sales strategy, the complexity of the product line is an important factor. The order-giving or order taking procedure differs from company to company. As the types of customer, *viz.*, industrial users and consumer users, have different needs, the sales person has to adopt different sales strategies. On the basis of the present capability of the sales force the sales management may fix the number of persons required to meet the sales needs. Sales potential and work load are evaluated to estimate the number of persons required for sales purposes. While quantitative objectives are decided by the sales management these have to be achieved by the sales force.

**3. AIDAS Approach**. The AIDAS approach includes attention, interest, desire, action and satisfaction. It is a buyer-oriented formula emphasizing the customers needs and problems.

(i) "Attention" makes customers aware of the product as well as the image of the company.

(ii) "Interest" refers to the prospects or the customer's interest in the product.

(iii) "Arousing desire" refers to the preferences or liking of the customers.

(iv) "Action" means building conviction or obtaining a trial order. Promotion insures continuing action. Different promotion blends are required for different segments of the market. Many customers are motivated by a continuous AIDAS approach to purchase the product of the company.

(v) "Satisfaction" is mainly concerned with the problem-solving technique. The AIDAS approach solves the problems of the customers. The sale is made in the mind of the buyer. The need-problem, its solution, the purchase of the product and the satisfaction flowing from the purchase are the basic elements. The solution, i.e., the company's product, should satisfy the needs of the customer. It should create a pleasant feeling in the buyer's mind. The sales presentation should be made in such a way as to ensure that the customers willingly purchase. Consumers can develop pleasant feelings for the product which lead to consumer loyalty to it. Thus, repeat sales are ensured. The salesman has to convince his customer that his product offers a real solution to his need-problem.

**4. Stimulus-Response Model.** The stimulus-response model has four components — Drive, Cues, Response and Reinforcement.

(i) *Drive* : The term "drive" refers to the strong stimuli which impel the buyer to purchase the product. The salesman should know that there are certain needs which stimulate the buyer to purchase a particular product. The need may be dictated by hunger, thirst, safety or self-esteem. The drive may be primary or learnt. The primary drive is felt by all persons; and may be for food, clothing and shelter. The learnt drives are felt by economically advanced people. The self-esteem, ego recognition and status symbol are some of the learnt drives. A salesman should be aware of these various drives if he is to motivate successfully the different classes of people.

(ii) *Cues* : Cues indicate when the prospect or customer will respond to a stimulus. They are subsidiary to the main drive. The salesman should be able to recognize the cues and motivate the buyer accordingly to purchase the product. There may be different types of cues stimulating the buyers. They may be product cues, informational cues, activator-cues and non-activator cues. Non-activator cues are dormant cues which influence the buyer at a later stage. The triggering cues influence the purchase decision. Price, package and service may be the triggering cues.

(iii) *Response* : When the salesman has administered the drive and cues, the buyer may respond positively or negatively. Negative responses are evaluated and assessed to convert them into positive responses.

(iv) *Reinforcement* : The salesman has to reinforce the decision of the buyers to continue to buy his products. The drive should be effectively utilized to motivate the buyer.

## NEGOTIATION

Salespersons trying to stimulate customer interest in their product must apply their negotiation skills. The two parties should reach agreement on the price and the other terms of sale. Salespersons should win the order without making concession that will hurt profitability.

Negotiation skills apply to dealing not only with customers but also with suppliers, middlemen and agencies, store buying committees, other departments in the company and various publics.

Marketing is concerned with exchange activities and the terms of exchange. One can distinguish two general types of exchange :

(i) *Routinized Exchange* : In it the-terms are established by administered programmes of pricing and distribution.

(ii) *Negotiated Exchange* : In it price or other terms of exchange are set via bargaining behaviour. According to Johan Arndt, a growing number of markets are coming under negotiated exchange, in which two or more parties negotiate long-term binding agreements such as joint venturers, franchises, subcontracts, vertical integration, etc. These markets are moving from being highly competitive to being highly "domesticated," that is, being less available to competitors.

Price is most frequently the object of negotiation activities. Other objects of negotiation include time of contract completion; quality of goods or service offered; volume of goods sold; responsibility for financing, risk taking, promotion and title; and safety of product with government agencies. The number of negotiation-related topics and parties is virtually unlimited.

**Features of Bargaining**

Phillip Kotler, Ian Merely and Geoffrey Stephenson use the terms bargaining and negotiation interchangeably.

1. At least two parties are involved.

2. The parties have a conflict of interest with respect to one or more issues.

3. The parties are at least temporarily joined together in a special kind of voluntary relationship.

4. Activity in the relationship concerns the division or exchange of one or more specific resources and/or the resolution of one or more intangible issues among the parties or among those whom they represent.

5. The activity usually involves the presentation of demands or proposals by one party and evaluation of these by the other, followed by concessions and counterproposals. The activity is thus segmental rather than simultaneous.

For successful implementation of marketing strategies the marketing managers must have negotiation skills.

**Impact of Various Disciplines**

Game theory, economics, social psychology and experimental perspective have contributed to bargaining which has received attention in a variety of disciplines including economics, applied mathematics, international relations, industrial relations and social psychology.

**1. Game Theorists**. In their work theory of games and economic behaviour, John von Neuman and Oscar Morgentern in the work *Theories of Games and Economic Behaviour* have examined the results of rational actor's strategies in situations involving interdependent decision making and have given a well-written general survey of game theory. In their book, *Games and decisions*, R. Duncan Lace and Howard Raiffa, assumes that each actor has an objective such as loss minimisation, and the payoffs depend on the decision of his or her opponent. The major purpose of game theory is to describe the set of decision rules by which rational actors choose the best strategy. The following books have applied game theoretic models to analyzing actual bargaining situations : John Denni McDonald, *The Game of Business* (New York Doubleday Co. 1975) and Thomas C. Schelling, *The Strategy of Conflict* (Cambridge Mass. Harvard University Press, 1960).

**2. Economists.** Economists study the bargaining process through the concept of "bilateral monopoly." They see the process as a sequence of offers and counteroffers by the participants. They pay less attention to manipulative tactics, power and bargaining skills of the participants.

**3. Social Psychologists.** These have studied the effect of several independent variables on bargaining effectiveness. In their exhaustive review of social psychological studies on bargaining behaviour, Rubin and Brown summarized the impact of four major variables—the structural context of bargaining, the behavioral predispositions of bargainers, the interdependence of bargainers and the use of social influence strategies—on bargaining effectiveness. Bargaining effectiveness is usually measured by the number of cooperative or competitive choices made throughout the total number of trials and/or the magnitude of the outcomes obtained by the bargainers. The behavioral approach focuses on the concepts of power, tactical action, and bargaining settlements.

The experiential approach to the discussion of bargaining has the advantages of being based on first hand experience in negotiation settings. Literature lists the traits that effective negotiators should possess. The most important traits are preparation and planning skill, knowledge of subject matter being negotiated, ability to think clearly and rapidly under pressure and uncertainty, ability to express thoughts verbally, listening skill judgement and general intelligence, integrity, ability to persuade others and patience.

### When to Negotiate?

Lee and Dobler have listed the following instances when negotiation is an appropriate procedure for concluding a sale.

1. When many variable factors bear not only on price, but also on quality and service.

2. When business risks involved cannot be accurately predetermined.

3. When a long period of time is required to produce the items purchased.

4. When production is interrupted frequently because of numerous change order.

Young has developed a "bargainers calculus," which mathematically demonstrates the point at which bargaining is an appropriate method of accomplishing objectives.

According to Philip Kotler, bargaining is appropriate whenever the five definitional conditions are met and a zone of agreement exists which can be considered as the range of acceptable outcomes that exist simultaneously for all bargaining parties. If two parties say a manufacturer and one of its dealers are negotiating a price, each privately establishes the threshold value that he or she needs. The seller has a reservation price, which is the minimum he or she will accept. Any final contract value, x, represents a price that is worse than not reaching an agreement at all. For any $x > s$, the seller receives a surplus. Obviously the seller desires as large a surplus as possible while maintaining good relations with the buyer. Likewise the buyer has a reservation price, b, that is the maximum he or she will pay; any x that is above b represents a price that is worse than no agreement. For any $x < b$ the buyer receives a surplus. If the seller's reservation price is below the buyer's, that is, $s < b$ then a zone of agreement exists and bargaining will determine where x will fall within the zone.

In knowing or problematically assessing the other party's reservation price and in making one's own reservation price seem higher (for a seller) or lower (for a buyer) than it really is there is an obvious advantage. However, the openness with which buyers and sellers reveal and use their reservation prices or otherwise practice strategic misrepresentation is often dictated by the personalities of the bargainers, the circumstances of the negotiation and the expectation of future relations.

## THE PRINCIPLED NEGOTIATION APPROACH

In the Harvard Negotiation Project, Roger Fisher and William Ury arrived at four points for conducting "principled negotiations" that have a high chance of concluding successfully for both parties. They are described below :

**1. Separate the People from the Problem.** Because people are conducting the face-to-face bargaining, it is easy for emotions to become entangled with the objective merits of the issue being negotiated. Framing negotiation issues in terms of the personalities involved rather than the interests of the parties can lead to ineffective bargaining. Negotiation deteriorates when it becomes a test of wills instead of a joint problem solving activity. Separating the people from the problem first involves making accurate perceptions. Each party must understand empathetically the power of the opponent's viewpoint and try to feel the level of emotion with which they hold it. Second, emotions brought into or evolving out of negotiations should be made explicit and acknowledged as legitimate. Openly discussing emotions of both parties while not reacting to an emotional outburst helps keep negotiations from degenerating into unproductive name-calling sessions. Third, clear communications must exist between parties. Listening actively and acknowledging what is being said, communicating about problems rather than the opponent's shortcomings and directly addressing interests rather than speaking first just to be heard are methods of improving the chances of jointly beneficial solutions by better communication techniques. In general, separating the people from the problem means looking at the issues side by side rather than face to face.

**2. Focus on Interests not Position.** The difference between positions and interests is that one's position is something one decided upon, while one's interests are what caused one to adopt the position. Thus a bargaining position may be that a contract must include a stiff penalty for late shipment; but the party's interest is to maintain an unbroken flow of raw materials. Reconciling interests works better because for every interest there usually exist several possible positions that could satisfy that interest. Also, opposing positions may hide shared and compatible interests (e.g., we want the predictability of a steady flow of order, you want the security of an unbroken flow of raw materials). Making certain that interests are understood by all parties and then being flexible as to the means of achieving these interests, while negotiating firmly for the interests themselves is an effective strategy. As fisher and Ury state it: "Fighting hard on the substantive issues increases the pressure for an effective solution; giving support to the human beings on the other side tends to improve your relationship and to increase the likelihood of reaching agreement. It is the combination of support and attack which works; either alone is likely to be insufficient."

**3. Invent Options for Mutual Gain.** Inventing options for mutual gain involves searching for a larger pie rather than arguing over the size of each slice. Developing options require innovative thinking such as brainstorming sessions where judgement of options is undertaken only after many options have been invented. Looking for options which offer mutual gain facilitates the desirable condition of side-by-side bargaining and helps identify shared interests.

**4. Insist on Objective Criteria.** When an opposing negotiator is intransigent and argues his position rather than his interests, a good strategy is to insist that the agreement must reflect some fair objective criteria independent of the position of either side. This will help reach solutions on principle, not pressure. By discussing objective criteria instead of stubbornly held positions, neither party is yielding to the other; both are yielding to a fair solution. Such objective criteria may be market value, depreciated book value, competitive prices, replacement costs, wholesale price index, etc. This approach works best when each issue is seen as requiring a joint search for objective criteria and each party is open to reason as to the standards best reflecting objectivity. Deviation from a fair, objective standard should be made only when a better one is offered, not because the opposing party is applying pressure, threats or other means of imposing his will.

## BARGAINING TACTICS

### Classic Bargaining Tactics

From a list of over 200 tactics prepared by professor Donald W. Hendon of the University of Hawaii in his seminar, 'How to Negotiate and Win' following are some standard bargaining tactics :

**1. Acting Crazy.** Put on a good show by visibly demonstrating your emotional commitment to your position. This increases your credibility and may give the opponent a justification to settle on your terms.

**2. Big Plot.** Leave yourself a lot of room to negotiate. Make high demand at the beginning. After making concessions, you'll still end up with a large payoff than if you started too low.

**3. Get a Prestigious Ally.** The ally can be a person or a project that is prestigious. You try to get the opponent to accept less because the person/object he or she will be involved with is considered "prestigious."

**4. The Well Is Dry**. Take a stand and tell the opponent you have no more concessions to make.

**5. Limited Authority**. You negotiate in good faith with the opponent and when you're ready to sign the deal you say, "I have to check with my boss."

**6. Whipsaw/Auction.** You let several competitors know you're negotiating with them at the same time. Schedule competitors' appointments with you for the same time and keep them all waiting to see you.

**7. Divide and Conquer**. If you're negotiating with the opponent's team, sell one member of the team on your proposals. That person will help you sell the other members of the team.

**8. Get Lost/Stall for Time**. Leave the negotiation completely for a while. Come back when things are getting better and try to renegotiate then. Time period can be long (say you're out of town) or short (go to the bathroom to think).

**9. Wet Noodle**. Give no emotional or verbal response to the opponent. Don't respond to his or her force or pressure. Sit there like a wet noodle and keep a "poker face."

**10. Be Patient**. If you can afford to outwit the opponent, you'll probably win big.

**11. Let's Split the Difference**. The person who first suggests this has the least to lose.

**12. Play the Devil's Advocate**. Argue against the opponent's proposal by stating, "Before I say yes or no, let's look at all the bad things that could possibly happen if we did what you want." This lets you show the opponent your better way of achieving his or her objectives without directly opposing the opponent's viewpoint.

**13. Trial Balloon**. You release your decision through a so-called reliable source before the decision is actually made. This enables you to test reaction to your decision.

**14. Surprises**. Keep the opponent off balance by a drastic, dramatic, sudden shift in your tactics in general. Never be predictable—keep the opponent from anticipating your moves.

**Modern Bargaining Tactics**

According to Philip Kotler, Bargaining tactics can be defined as manoeuver to be made at specific points in the bargaining process.

1. In both scholarly and "how-to" books, threats, bluffs, last chance offers, hard initial offers and other tactics are discussed. Many sources offer checklists of tactical dos and dont's such as "Don't tip your hand too early" and "Do negotiate on home ground whenever possible." Usually a shotgun blast of widely varied actions and these lists of possible tactics are rarely consistent with specific overriding bargaining strategy.

2. On the other hand, Fisher and Ury have offered some tactical advice that is consistent with their strategy of principled negotiation. Their first piece of tactical advice concerns what should be done if the other party is more powerful. The best tactic is to know one's BATNA (Best Alternative To a Negotiated Agreement). If a settlement is not reached by identifying one's alternatives it sets a standard against which any offer can be measured. It protects one from being pressured into accepting Unfavourable terms by more powerful opponent.

3. Another tactic comes into play when the opposing party insists on arguing his or her position instead of his or her interests and attacks one's proposals or person. While the tendency is to push back hard when pushed against, the better tactic is to deflect to attack from the person and direct it against the problem.

4. Another series of bargaining tactics concerns responses to opposition tactics that are intended to deceive, distort or otherwise influence the bargaining to their own advantage. When the other side uses a threat or a take-it-or-leave-it tactic or puts the other party on the side of the table with the sun in her eyes, a negotiator should recognize the tactic, raise the issue explicitly and question the tactic's legitimacy and desirability, negotiating over it. Negotiating the use of the tactic follows the principled negotiation procedure. Question the tactic, ask for the reasons why the tactic was used, suggest alternative courses of action to mutually pursue, suggest the principle behind the tactic as a negotiation rule. Finally if all else fails one should resort to one's BATNA and terminate the negotiation until the other side ceases to employ these tricky tactics. Meeting these tactics by defining principle is more productive than counterattacking with tricky tactics.

## RELATIONSHIP MANAGEMENT

The principles of personal selling and negotiation are transaction oriented. Their aim is to help marketers effect an immediate sale to customer. Relationship management is a larger concept that may guide the seller's dealings with its customers. The seller who knows how to build and manage strong relationships with key customers has plenty of future sates from them.

A key skill needed by marketers, relationship management is not appropriate with those customers and publics who can most affect the organization's future. The top five or ten customers account for a disproportionate share of the company's sales in many companies. Relationship manager, sales people working with key customers must do more than call when they think customers might be ready to place orders. They should call or visit at other times, taking customers to dinner, making useful suggestion about their business, and so on. They should follow the fortunes of these key accounts, know their problems and opportunities and be ready to serve them in a number of ways. This type of salesperson is often called a relationship manager, a national account manager or a customer manager. In the evolution of the sales person he represents the latest step. Originally salespersons were order takers who involved into order getters, aggressively seeking business from purchasing agents. Later they evolved to account representatives dealing with a number of people in the buying organization who could influence purchases. Today they are evolving into relationship managers who plan and service the entire relationship with the customers.

Because of increased buyer concentration relationship management will play a larger role in the future. As the buyers in an industry become fewer and larger, it is highly desirable that a relationship manager be assigned to each important customer. He would plan and coordinate the company's services to serve the customer well.

## STEPS IN A RELATIONSHIP MANAGEMENT PROGRAM

**1. Identifying the Customers Meriting Relationship Management.** The company can choose the five or ten largest customers and designate them for relationship management. Additional customers can be added who show/exceptional growth or who pioneer new developments in the industry and so on.

**2. Assigning a Skilled Relationship Manager to Each Key Customer.** The salesperson who is currently servicing the customer should receive training in relationship management or be replaced by someone who is more skilled in relationship management. The relationship manager should have characteristics that match or appeal to the customer.

**3. Developing a Clear Job Description for Relationship Managers.** It should describe their reporting relationships, objectives, responsibilities and evaluation criteria. The relationship manager is responsible for the client, is the focal point for all information about the client, and is the mobilizer of company services for the client. Each relationship manager will have only one or a few relationships to manage.

**4. Appointing an Overall Manager to Supervise the Relationship Managers.** This person will develop job description, evaluation criteria and resource support to increase the effectiveness of this function.

**5. Each Relationship Manager Developing Long-range and Annual Customer-relationship Plans.** The annual relationship plan will state objectives, strategies, specific action and required resources.

In managing their relationship with the managers of other organizations, the company's managers need skill. An organization must focus as much on managing its customers as its products.

## QUESTIONS FOR EXERCISE

1. Trace the history of personal selling. Describe the meaning and characteristics of salesmanship.
2. Examine the importance and limitation of personal selling and explain the qualities of sales force.
3. Explain steps in an effective the process.
4. Discuss various types of personal selling.
5. Discuss negotiation approach to bargaining.
6. Explain the principled negotiation approach to bargaining. Describe important classical and modern bargaining tactics.
7. Write short note on Relationship Management.

# 8

# WHOLESALING

Wholesaling is not necessarily the work of wholesale middlemen alone. The manufacturers who sell directly to retailers or to other manufacturers are also involved in wholesaling. If in a transaction the buyer is buying for purposes of resale, or to further his business operations, the seller in that same transactions is engaged in wholesaling.

## DEFINITION OF WHOLESALING

1. Cundiff and Still. "Wholesalers buy and resale merchandise to retailers 'and other merchants and to industrial, institutional and commercial users, but do not sell insignificant amounts to ultimate consumers."

2. Morris E. Hurley. "Wholesalers are marketing middlemen who occupy a position midway between retailer and the producer or manufacturer."

3. William J. Stanton. "Wholesaling or wholesale trade includes the sale and all activities directly incidental to the sale of products or services to those who are buying for the purpose of resale or business use."

On the basis of above definitions one may conclude that the wholesaler is a person who invariable buys in large quantities and sells them to the retailers for resale or to industrial and commercial consumers with a view to earn profits. However, the wholesaler may be identified on the basis of the purpose of sale or the nature of purchaser and not on the basis of quantities sold.

## CHARACTERISTICS OF WHOLESALING

1. **Direct Large Buying.** Wholesalers generally buy merchandise direct from the producers in large quantities mainly in cash.

**2. Sale Through Agents.** Wholesalers are trading concerns having an army of agents and stock the large quantities of goods, supply or sell goods to the retailers directly or through their agents in small quantities.

**3. Good Financial Position.** Generally, wholesalers possess good financial health. They purchase goods in cash from the manufacturers and sell to the retailers on credit.

**4. Small profit margin.** Wholesalers' profit margin is very small so that they maximise their sale-volume to earn maximum profit.

**5. Limited Product Line.** Wholesalers deal in limited, generally in one or two products or product-line. More often they deal in products of one manufacturer.

**6. Warehouses.** Wholesalers maintain warehouses and godown at different places in the country to facilitate the trade at minimum transportation charges.

**7. Grading.** Wholesalers sometimes make grading of the goods under their own name or brand.

## CLASSIFICATION OF WHOLESALERS

1. **Functional**, on the basis of Functions.
2. **Geographical**, on the basis of Area served.
3. **Service**, on the basis of Services rendered.

### 1. Functional Classification

(i) *Manufacturer Wholesalers* : Such wholesalers also engage in manufacturing activities. They not only sell their own products to retailers but may also make large scale purchasing from other manufacturers to meet the demands of the retailer. The wholesalers carry a comprehensive stock of goods to increase their turnover considerably. By their dual role they reduce their overhead expenses and increase their profits.

(ii) *Retailer Wholesalers* : Retailer wholesalers purchase goods in bulk direct from the producers or manufacturers and retail them to the consumers through their own shops. Thus, they combine the twin functions of wholesaling and retailing.

(iii) *Wholesalers Proper or Pure Wholesalers* : They are also called distributors. Such persons are the merchants who carry the business of purchasing and selling in large quantities and do not engage in manufacturing or retailing activities. They maintain their godowns or warehouses in the well located part of the city. The goods are collected and stocked from different manufacturers and supplied to the retailers.

From the point of view of their specialisation of dealing, the pure wholesalers can be further classified into three categories :

(a) ***Mill Supply Wholesalers*** : Such wholesalers sell a wide variety of goods to the mills or manufacturers for their production of consumer goods. They purchase and stock the materials and equipments from a large number of producers and keep them in store for supply to the industrial consumers. They advertise their stock and sell their goods through their agents throughout the state or country.

(b) ***Single line Wholesalers*** : These wholesalers deal in the different varieties of a particular line of goods such as cloth wholesalers or paper or hardware wholesalers. They purchase and stock goods from different producers of the line and sell them to retailers for different purposes.

(c) ***Complete-line Wholesalers*** : Such wholesalers deal in a complete line of goods required by a particular industry or trade. For example, hospital supply companies may supply all requirements of hospitals.

**2. Geographical Classification**

(i) *Local Wholesalers*: The trade of local wholesalers is limited to the boundaries of a particular town or city. They supply their purchases to the local retailers and specialise in the distribution of nationally advertised goods and unbranded staple.

(ii) *Provincial Wholesalers* : Sometimes called district or state distributors, they sell goods to retailers or a particular district or a state.

(iii) *National Wholesalers* : National wholesalers distribute goods all over the country. They supply goods to local or provincial distributors.

**3. Classification on the Basis of Services Rendered**

(i) *Jobbers Wholesalers* : Jobbers wholesalers purchase goods from the producers or producer, stock them in their own godown and then sell to the retailers. We may call them pure wholesalers.

(ii) *Processors* : Processors purchase the goods from manufacturers or producers for grading and processing. They sell the goods in small packets. Sometimes, they develop their own brand.

(iii) *Exporters* : Exporters purchase the goods from country-manufacturers and export them in the foreign markets either in the same form or after processing. They often create demands for Indian goods in foreign countries.

(iv) *Importers* : Importers import the goods from foreign producers and sell them to country wholesalers, manufacturers or retailers.

(v) *Industrial Distributors* : Industrial distributors act as wholesale distributors of particular mill or producer.

## FUNCTIONS OF WHOLESALERS

**1. Assembling.** The wholesaler collects varieties of a product from different manufacturers and keeps them in stock for sale to the retailers. Some wholesalers collect product only from a single producer.

**2. Dispersion.** The products assembled and kept in stock to be distributed to the retailers or manufacturers or producers are kept in stock in warehouses pending their sale to the retailers.

**3. Warehousing.** The goods assembled from manufacturers or producers are kept in stock in warehouses pending their sale to the retailers.

**4. Transportation.** The wholesalers have to move the goods from the place of production to their godowns or warehouses and from there to the place of retailers. They arrange and maintain their own vans for the movement of goods.

**5. Financing.** Wholesalers sometimes finance the manufactures and retailers. They purchase goods from the manufacturers in cash or deposit security to assure the purchase of goods. They also supply goods, to the retailers on credit.

**6. Grading and Packaging.** The wholesaler performs the task of sorting out different grades of products purchased either from one producer or from different producers according to quality and other considerations and packing the goods into smaller lots for retailers.

**7. Pricing.** The retailer determines the price to be charged from customers on the basis of the price fixed by the wholesaler. Wholesalers can say more particularly about the produce and also suggest the price to be fixed by the producer.

**8. Risk-Assuming.** Wholesaler undertakes the risk of manufacturers and retailers. Having purchased the goods from the manufacturers in large quantities, he assumes the risks arising out of changes in demand and spoilage or destruction of goods in his warehouse. He takes the credit-risk by selling the goods to the retailers on credit.

## WHOLESALER'S SERVICES

### 1. Services to Manufacturers

(i) *Help in Concentration on Production* : By taking over the marketing function from the manufacturer, the wholesaler enables him to concentrate on the problems of production.

(ii) *Help in large Scale Production* : The manufacturer gets the benefit of large orders for goods of more or less standard type through the wholesalers. The wholesalers either purchase goods in bulk from the manufacturers for resale or collect orders from the retailers and pass them on to the manufacturers. Thus wholesalers enable the manufacturers to produce goods on large scale.

(iii) *Distribution Facilities* : Wholesaler is a vital link between manufacturers and consumers. The manufacturer does not have to take the trouble of collecting small orders and supplying them to a large number of retailers scattered widely.

(iv) *Demand Analysis and Forecasting* : The manufacturers can regulate their production and estimate their sale or demand according to the changes in the direction and pattern of demand, indicated well in time by the orders placed by the wholesalers. Wholesalers remain in touch with the consumers through retailers and keep themselves informed about the changes in task, fashion and demand.

(v) *Financing* : Wholesalers provide financial assistance to the manufacturers by purchasing the goods in bulk in cash and by depositing security with the manufacturers.

(vi) *Warehousing* : The manufacturer is saved from the problem of warehousing large stocks of finished goods as the wholesalers purchase the goods in bulk as soon as they are ready and stock them till they are sold to the retailers in smaller lots.

(vii) *Help in Production* : The wholesalers help the manufacturers in maintaining an even pace of production by placing advance orders for periods which are generally characterised by slack demand.

(viii) *Help in Sales Organisation* : The wholesaler also helps the manufacturer by having his own sales organisation as the wholesaler generally has a ready sale organisation of his own.

(ix) *Help in Price Determination* : Wholesalers who are in constant touch with buyers through retailers know the needs and reactions of the customers and also what the customer can pay. Hence, they can suggest the manufacturer the best price he can fetch in the market for his goods.

(x) *Advertisement* : Generally dealing in one or two items, the wholesalers advertise for the goods they deal in. The manufacturers are also benefitted by this activity of wholesaler because their product draws more attention of buyers.

(xi) *Grading and Standardisation of Goods* : Where the manufacturer produces unstandardised goods, the wholesalers purchase them in lots and grade them according to their quality. They sometimes pack them in smaller, lots and after standardisation and processing give a brand name to them.

(xii) *Widening of Market* : Wholesalers widen the markets for the goods of the producers. They sell their goods in new markets through their own sales organisation. They create demand of the product in foreign markets and thus increase the goodwill of the producers.

**2. Services of Wholesalers to Retailers**

(i) *Purchasing Facilities* : Wholesalers stock the goods from different manufacturers and provide the facility to the retailers to buy their requirements at convenient intervals without much difficulty. A retailer has a large number of customers to deal with. He has, therefore to keep a wide variety of products in store to cater the individual needs. It is not feasible for him to purchase such a variety of products from a number of producers directly.

(ii) *Low Inventory* : The retailers generally suffer from the dearth of capital and of storage facilities. It is not possible for them to purchase goods in bulk and store them to maintain the steady supply in the market. The wholesaler himself warehouses the goods and releases them in smaller lots to the retailers who require low inventory.

(iii) *Risk Taking* : Wholesalers assume most of the risk of marketing the goods. As the wholesaler warehouses the goods and takes the risks of market fluctuations in prices or spoilage of goods in warehouses due to pesticides and natural calamity, he saves the retailers from such risks.

(iv) *Financial Assistance* : Wholesalers finance the bulk of retail trade by supplying goods on credit. Due to small capital, most of the retailers buy goods on credit from wholesalers and pay them only after they collect the money by selling the goods to the ultimate customers. Thus, the wholesalers enable the retailers to trade without much working capital.

(v) *Information about New Product* : Through his travellers and salesmen employed for this purpose the wholesaler brings to the notice of the retailers the new types of goods which are being manufactured. Trade circulars, advertisement in papers and showroom also help in this function.

(vi) *Benefits of Specialisation* : The wholesalers generally specialise in a few lines of goods and buy from the manufacturers who produce the best and the cheapest goods. The advantage of such specialisation is automatically passed on to retailers who purchase their goods from them.

(vii) *Advantage of Advertisement* : The wholesalers advertise their goods very extensively and create the demand in the market which is virtually met by the retailers. Thus retailers need not advertise. They are directly benefitted from the advertisement by wholesalers.

(viii) *Consultancy Services* : Wholesalers provide consultation or advice to the retailers on various marketing activities such as displaying of goods on the shop etc. They also supply the advertisement materials to retailers which explain the qualities of the products.

(ix) *Transport Facilities* : Wholesalers generally have their own transport to supply the goods to the retailers according to their requirements. As they more often deliver the goods on the shop of the retailers on the basis of traders collected from them the retailers save the transport charges.

(x) *Stability in Prices* : Wholesalers hold the price line by maintaining the demand and supply equilibrium. They release the goods when they are in short supply and stock them when they are not in demand. This saves the retailers from the risk caused by fluctuations in prices.

Thus, the wholesaler is a valuable link between the producer and the consumer in the channels of distribution.

## SHOULD WHOLESALER BE REMOVED?

Some critics believe that the institution of wholesaler is a wasteful and avoidable link between the producer and the retailers and it should be eliminated immediately. This opinion is based mainly on the following grounds :

**1. Responsible for increasing the Cost of Distribution.** If there are more than one wholesalers in the chain of distribution, their commission or their profit margin is included in the price of the commodity before it finally reaches the hands of final consumers. It is additional burden for the consumers. Wholesalers are, therefore, called parasites thriving at the expense of the consumers.

**2. Create a Long Chain Between the Actual Producer and Consumers.** Thus, they prevent the two classes of people who are mutually interdependent to came into direct touch. Hence, the producer is not in a position to know the actual demand for the grievances of the consumers. The consumers cannot approach the producer to enlighten him about the actual trend of the market.

**3. The Producers are Kept in Dark About the Actual Demand Potentials.** Wholesalers generally suppress the market trend in favour of their interest. Due to the main relations of these wholesalers, the producers are not able to conform production to demand and it often results in over production or under-production.

**4. Encourage Black Marketing by Cornering All the Available Supply of Goods.** Wholesalers corner the available supply of commodities and then dictate any price which the consumers have to pay or go without it. This is against all business ethics. The situation becomes more aggravated if the commodity is food, drink and clothing or any other essential commodity.

**5. Against the Modern Trend towards Direct Marketing of Merchandise from Producers to Consumers.** The growth of multiple shops, departmental stores, super bazars, etc. is one step in the direction of elimination of wholesalers. In India, several producers such as DCM, Bata, Liberty etc. have started their multiple retail stores which have proved successful. This practice may be extended to other commodities replacing wholesalers.

**6. Develop Their Own Brand and earn Goodwill for Themselves on the Cost of Producers.** Most of the producers have in recent years begun to develop their own trademark and advertise that. It is therefore not necessary to depend on the wholesalers for selling the produce.

**7. Do not serve Much to the New Entrants in the Field of Manufacturers.** As the wholesalers generally prefer dealing in popular products the selling of which is not a problem they do not make much efforts for selling new products which generally, die in their infancy.

**8. Generally Interested in Higher Profits.** Wholesalers sell the commodities of producers who offer them lucrative commission irrespective of the quality of goods. This tendency is neither beneficial to producers nor to consumers.

From the above arguments, it seems that the wholesalers are useless in the channels of distribution and they should be eliminated as soon as possible. With the development of large scale retailing and cooperative movement their necessity has been minimised. On the other hand, they render some disservices and create many problems to the producers and the consumers. However, their invaluable services to manufacturers and retailers cannot be ignored. Their elimination from the chain of distribution will create hardships. This agency should be properly controlled through proper legislations. The dependence of producers on them for marketing functions should be reduced. Thc existence of wholesalers does not depend on the manufacturers or customers. They exist due to their services rendered to various parties.

## QUESTIONS FOR EXERCISE

1. Define wholesaler. How would you classify wholesaling middlemen? Explain the functions of wholesaler.
2. Outline the services of wholesalers to manufacturers and retailers. Should the wholesalers be abolished?
3. It is said that the wholesaler is a parasite and, therefore, an unuseful link in the chain of middlemen from the producer to the consumers. Explain with reference to the services rendered by the wholesaler to the manufacturer and to the retailer.

# 9

# RETAILING

Dictionary define retailing as "the sale of goods in small quantities to ultimate consumers." The word retailer is of French origin meaning "to cut again". Thus literally retail trade is one that cuts off smaller portion from large lump of goods. From the bulk of products procured by the wholesaler, small lots are cut and distributed through retailers. In the chain of distribution between the manufacturers and the ultimate consumer the retailer is the last link. Retailers make the goods of industry conveniently available to millions of consumers. There could be no mass production without them. Even the Industrial Revolution would not have taken place in the absence of retailers. The retail shops are the oldest and most widely used business establishments in any country of the world.

## DEFINITION OF RETAILING

1. R.S. Davar. "Retail outlets are shops from whom the consumer ultimately buys."

2. Report of the Definition Committee U.S.A. "Retailing includes all activities incidental to selling to the ultimate consumer."

3. William J. Stanton. "A retailer or a retail store is a business enterprise which sells primarily to the ultimate consumers for non-business use."

4. Cundiff and Still. "Retailing consists of activities involved in selling directly to ultimate consumers."

5. McCarthy. "Retailing is selling final consumer products to householders."

## DIFFERENCE BETWEEN RETAILER AND RETAILING

A retailer or a retail store, also known as a dealer, is a business enterprise which sells to ultimate consumers. Retailing, on the other hand, includes all activities directly related to the sale of goods or services to the ultimate consumer, irrespective of who sells. The distinction of retailing is made on the basis of to whom the products are sold. For example, if a manufacturer sells; direct to the consumer that also is retailing. Even a wholesaler is said to be engaged in retailing when he sells directly to an ultimate consumer. Therefore it is remarked, "If the buyer in the transaction is an ultimate consumer, the seller in the same transaction is engaged in retailing." Thus, regardless of what he calls himself any one selling to the ultimate consumers is performing the functions of a retailer.

Retailers are the buying agents for their customers. They are the marketing or merchandising arm of many manufacturers. Retailing is subjected to constant changes which increase both the risk and opportunities of the participants. It is influenced by many forces such as population growth and the mobility of consumers (social forces), increased personal income, changes in the distribution of income, consumer credit and competitive changes etc. (economic forces). Technological innovation also affects retailing. It is also influenced by Government policies which prevail over social, economic and scientific influences.

## RETAILING FUNCTIONS

**1. Assembling.** Assembling of goods from various wholesalers.

**2. Transport.** The physical movement and storage of goods for the supply to the final consumers to meet their needs and requirements.

**3. Information.** The providing of information concerning the nature and use of goods to the wholesalers and producers. It also informs about the market trend.

**4. Standardisation, Grading and Processing.** The standardisation, grading and final processing of goods which have been left ungraded or unstandardised by wholesalers.

**5. Provision.** The provision of ready availability of goods of various qualities and of various manufacturers.

**6. Risk Bearing.** The assumption of risk concerning the price, nature and extent of demand of goods as long as they remain unsold.

**7. Financing.** The financing or inventory and the extension of credit to consumers for a short period.

## SERVICES RENDERED BY THE RETAILERS

**1. Stocking.** The retailer keeps stock of different varieties of goods. An average consumer cannot afford to stock goods that he requires for every day use. By holding stocks of these goods the retailers relieve the consumer of performing this function for himself.

**2. Variety of Choice.** The retailer keeps a good assortment of various varieties of a products manufactured by different firms. In this way, he provides a variety of choice to his customers.

**3. Creation of Demand.** Most of the demand creation methods are undertaken by retailers for the manufacturers and wholesalers. They arrange for the display of goods, supply necessary information to the customers and provide various similar services.

**4. Distribution.** The retailer is an expert in the distribution of consumer goods. Out of his experience, training and intimate knowledge of the goods he is in a position to help the customers in the proper selection of goods. His success in his business ultimately rests on the effective rendering of these services.

**5. Credit Facilities.** The retailer often extends credit facilities to the consumers. These alone account for larger sales volume.

**6. Personal Services.** The retailer provides many personal services to the customer such as home delivery, after-sales-service, liberal exchange of goods, etc.

**7. Information.** For the manufacturers, a retailer collects information about trends in marketing, change in fashions, tastes, etc. It is through the retailer that a customer meets the manufacturer.

**8. Other Services.** Besides the above services rendered by the retailers, they make available goods according to season, give advice to their customers, provide facility or return of goods, increase in the knowledge of customers and periodical services.

## ESSENTIALS FOR A SUCCESSFUL RETAILING

**1. Selection of Proper Goods.** A retailer should be able to select proper goods which can meet the requirements of his customers. He should exercise his foresight, use his past experience and keep in view the changing fashions for proper selection.

**2. Perfect Knowledge About Goods.** A retailer should have though knowledge about the goods he deals in order to be able to satisfy his customers and answer their questions.

**3. Proper Sales Policy**. A retailer should adopt the policy of buying in bulk and increase his sales by satisfying himself with a lower margin of profit. By this policy he can also face any local competition from other retailers in the market.

**4. Adequate Capital**. A retailer should command adequate capital at his disposal because he has to allow some credit facilities also to his customers.

**5. Suitable Business Location**. It is very necessary that a suitable business location easily accessible to the customers should be selected. A suitable location will depend on the nature of goods one deals in. For example posh colonies should be selected for sophisticated goods.

**6. Business Education**. The retailer should be well versed with the art of salesmanship. He should underline the habits and temperaments of his customers.

**7. Attractive Display and Advertisement**. In order to attract more customers the retailer should arrange things in an attractive style. Goods should be prominently displayed and advertised.

**8. Credit Facility**. In modern tunes providing credit facilities has also become necessary, for which the retailer should know the financial position of his customers and their habits also.

**9. Provisions of Other Facilitics**. The retailer should also provide free advice, facility of return of goods if possible, home delivery facility and periodical services or repairs etc. of durable items.

## FORMS OR RETAILING

Retailing has changed very drastically during the last two decades. Some institutions have disappeared whereas newer ones have been added. This process of deletion and addition still continues in newer forms. Large-scale retailing shops are working simultaneously with very small units. There range from hawkers and dealers who have no permanent place to well organised settled shop like chain-stores, departmental stores, super bazaar, etc.

Following is the classification of the important kinds of retailing business units on the basis of their place of business :

1. Itinerant retailers and
2. Fixed shop retailers.

## 1. Itinerant Retailers

Itinerant Retailers have no fixed business places and move about from place to place as the season changes. They sell low-priced items in very small lots. They invest a very small capital and do not stick to a particular line of business. Some of them are as follows :

(i) *Hawkers and Pedlars* : Sale by hawkers and pedlars is of a very old origin. They carry the goods from place to place with the help of a beast of burden or a hand cart and sell them at the very doors of the customers. The same function is done even by pedlars with the difference that they carry their goods on their persons. Both of these retailers do not have any fixed place of business. They keep on moving from locality to locality on the basis of prospects of the business. They generally handle cheap goods with low unit value like pens, handkerchiefs, knives, combs, cheap cosmetics, toys, etc. There is no guarantee about the quality of goods which are of inferior variety. Hence, while buying goods from hawkers and pedlars one must be careful about their quality. These retailers sell goods at very tempting prices considerably lower than the market rate. Hawkers and pedlars are found in streets of busy cities, towns and villages and at places where exhibitions, fairs are held. They are seen outside the temple or bathing ghats where people throng in large numbers.

(ii) *Market Traders* : These are retailers who open their shops at different places on fixed days known as market days like Som Bazaar, Mangal haats etc. Such days are fixed on weekly, fortnightly and monthly basis. Such traders carry on their business in one locality or at different places on different days when the market is open. They open their shops on important festivals and have roaring business on those days.

(iii) *Cheap Jacks* : A cheap jack has independent shop in a business locality. His shop is not of permanent nature and he may shift it if he finds that another locality is more profitable.

(iv) *Street Traders* : Street traders carry on their business in the busy streets or foot paths of busy town roads. They are often seen near railway stations, bus stops, and similar places where there is huge floating population. They handle only light goods that are largely in demand. They mainly deal in one kind of goods at a time.

## 2. Fixed Shop Retailers

Fixed shop retailers generally retain permanent places of business. These may be classified on the basis of their size of operations, *i.e.*, small scale and large scale.

### A. Small Scale Retailing

(i) *The Street Holders* : These have their stalls in a street where they may find heavy traffic. They exercise much care in selecting the location as the site once selected is more or less permanent. These retailers get their supplies from the wholesalers as well as from local suppliers. They handle goods on a very small scale. They deal in different types of articles like pen, towels, underwear, socks, etc.

(ii) *Second Hand Goods Dealers* : These dealers deal in second hand goods or articles like books, furnitures, clothes, etc. They purchase and sell goods particularly to those customers who cannot afford to buy new goods at higher prices. They mainly get their supplies from public auction. They do not take any responsibility either for durability or quality of the goods.

(iii) *Speciality Shops* : These shops sell goods of particular variety. The dealers specialise and deal only in one line of goods. Some examples are shops exclusively meant for books, leather goods, toys, medicines, readymade garments etc.

(iv) *General Shops* : These shops sell the whole list of products required for every day use. Their size is generally decided on the basis of population they have to serve. They claim permanent local customers.

(v) *Independent Store* : These are small non-integrated retail establishments having a lesser degree of specialisation in their management. The owner himself manages the business. He maintains intimate personal contact with customers. He gets supplies from the wholesalers. Independent stores may be classified into : (a) general stores, (b) single line stores and (c) speciality stores.

(vi) *Automatic Vending Machines* : Vending machines sell a variety of products through coin operated machines, automatically, without the aid of any sales assistant. The use and importance of such type of retailing is yet to prove its viability in India.

(vii) *Discount Houses* : During post-war period the discount houses grew out of the practice of manufacturers giving large discount to retailers on certain types of goods. A discount house is a retailing business unit which features consumer durable items like jewellery, household appliances and wares and similar merchandise. These houses operate on a relatively low make-up and a minimum customer service.

(viii) *Syndicate Stores* : It is an extension of the chain and mail order house but relatively on a small scale. One of its chief characteristic is that while it offers a variety of merchandise to customers, it seldom sells well-known brands. Most of the merchandise it sells would be of unknown. They buy unbranded merchandise which are sold under their own brands later on.

**B. Large Scale Retailing**

These days, several types of large scale retail organisations have sprung up in a bid to eliminate the wholesaler middlemen and to get the economies of large scale operations. Some of the large scale retail organisations are : (1) Departmental Stores, (2) Chain stores or multiple shops, (3) Mail order business, (4) Hire purchase and installments, (5) Consumers' cooperative stores, (6) Super bazaars, and (7) Malls.

## DEPARTMENTAL STORES

**Meaning**

The departmental stores are considered to be of French origin. It is stated that in Boa March'e and the other places departmental stores came into existence and flourished during the period of the Second French Empire (1852-1871).

The departmental store is a large-scale retailing business unit which handles a wide variety of shopping and speciality goods and is organised into separate departments for the purpose of promotion, service and control. It has decentralised selling. Technically it is a horizontally integrated retail institution. It has many departments with each department specialising in one kind of merchandise such as cloth department, drugs department, stationary department, readymade garments, toys department, etc. In it each unit resembles a speciality shop. All these departments are centrally controlled and work under one roof. The main idea behind the departmental stores is to supply all requirements from a single place. It is said that a departmental store is a place where one could get articles ranging from 'pin to plane'.

**Characteristics of Departmental Stores**

**1. From Pin to Plane.** It is a place where a consumer can get all his daily needs from pin to plane except probably some easily perishable items.

**2. Departmental.** The working of the store is organised on the departmental basis, *i.e.,* departments are established to deal in different items. Each department works under the supervision of a manager.

**3. Centralised Management and Control.** In spite of the fact that each department is independent in its day to day working all the departments are owned, managed and controlled centrally.

**4. Large.** The departmental store is large in size, centrally located and capable of attractions to a large number of customers.

**5. Convenient Services.** Services towards customers such as recreational facilities, free home delivery, post and telegraph, etc., are provided conveniently.

**6. Central Location.** This is the most important element that decides the successful existence of a departmental store. Being a large-scale institution its profit depends upon the large turnover. There would be a flow of customers only if the location is freely accessible. Further, the building must be capable of providing car parking, recreational and other facilities.

**Organisation**

Departmental stores usually adopt Joint Stock Company form organisation. The management of the departmental store as a whole is vested in the hands of a Managing Director or a General Manager. Each section or department is controlled by a manager under the direct control of the General Manager. The activities of a department store are divided into the following five major sections or divisions to facilitate smooth working of the store :

**1. Merchandise Section.** It looks after buying and selling goods.

**2. Store Section.** It undertakes advertisement and publicity, window display and other demand creational methods.

**3. Service Section.** It is concerned with the maintenance of the properties of the stores.

**4. Establishments Section.** It supervises selection and appointment etc. of the employees.

**5. Accounting and Finance Section.** It takes charge of all financial matters.

**Advantages**

**1. All Facilities under One Roof.** The departmental store provides all facilities under one roof to enable the customer to buy all his requirements.

**2. Central Location.** Its central location attracts a good number of customers which increases the sales turnover.

**3. Variety of Goods.** A large variety of goods in one line are stored. This has a special attraction to the customers (particularly house-wives).

**4. Financially Strong.** The financial strength of a departmental store enables it to have expert in all sections. It, therefore, can achieve a high level of efficiency.

**5. Lower Cost.** Centralised buying helps it to get merchandise at lower cost together with advantages in transporting, storing, etc.

**6. Standardised Goods.** The departmental store plays mainly on the these services by providing more or less standardised articles and other services, not offered by its other counterparts.

**7. Advertising.** Being a large scale organisation departmental store can afford to have effective advertising through press and other media of publicity.

**Disadvantages**

**1. High Operating Cost.** It is estimated that the operating cost of these stores works out to be 35% of sales. Therefore, they often run at a loss.

**2. Problem in Location.** There are problems in finding out proper location particularly because of the need to have large premises which bear high rents.

**3. Stiff Competition.** Stiff competition from other forms of retailing organisations stands in the way of its progress.

**4. Losses.** Certain departments have to be retained in spite of their recurring losses.

**5. Impersonality.** There is a lack of personal element in departmental stores. A customer may not be attended twice in succession by the same salesman.

**6. Hired Employees.** Departmental stores are generally run by hired employees far from the sense of ownership. It causes losses and leaks.

**7. High Overhead Charges.** The exotic and elaborate services provided, high operating cost, leakage, waste, etc., tend to increase the overhead charges which compel them to mark-up high prices on the articles.

### Departmental Stores in India

There are a few departmental stores in India like Spencers Ltd, and Army and Navy Stores Ltd. of Madras, Lainlaw Ltd. of Bombay, Kamlalaya Stores Ltd. Calcutta, and K.G. Thakurdas and Co. Kanpur. These departmental stores are in no way comparable to the giant stores of U.K. and U.S.A. Because of the following reasons the departmental stores are not much popular in India :

**1. Dearth of Capital.** Dearth of capital in India hinders the growth of departmental stores.

**2. High Prices.** Prices in such stores are high due to increased operating cost.

**3. Building Problcm.** Acquiring big building in the midst of the city is also difficult.

**4. Limited Needs.** There are limited needs of people in India.

**5. Ignorance.** Indians are quite ignorant of the importance of the departmental stores.

## MULTIPLE SHOPS OR CHAIN STORES

**S.E. Thomas** has defined the multiple shops as "a system under which there is a large number of retail shops owned by the same proprietor which are scattered over the various places of a particular city of a country and are engaged in the same line of activity." The name 'multiple shops' itself indicates that under this organisation similar shops are established in multiples by the same management. A chain stores system consists of four or more stores which carry the same kind of merchandise. These are centrally owned and managed. Usually goods are supplied to all of them from one or more central warehouses. A chain store is one of the retail units in chain store system. This chain store or multiple shops is a group of retail stores of the same type, centrally owned and with some degree of centralised control. In Europe, this system is called as multiple shops. The Americans call it 'chain stores'.

The main idea under the multiple or chain shop arrangement is to approach the customers and not to draw the customer to it as is practised in the case of the departmental store. In order to draw a large number of customers, attempts are made to open a large number of shops in the same city at different places.

In India examples of chain stores system are offered by Bata shop, Usha sewing machines, etc. Such multiple shops have "centralised buying with decentralised selling." They specialise in one product or products of one producer but with all its varieties or models. Their success depends upon how the selection of goods is made. The following considerations are important in selecting goods for retail through such stores :

(i) The articles are of every day use with popular appeal;

(ii) The articles are branded and

(iii) The articles are portable and have a rapid turnover.

This type of retailing is gaining momentum because it is a system through which the manufacturers can easily eliminate the wholesalers and establish a direct contact with consumers. Of late, manufacturers themselves have started opening their own retail shops of this kind. In such cases they are called "manufacturer retailers". They are known as middlemen multiple shops. When controlled by wholesalers, the chain store system can also be categorised as vertically integrated institution as it takes over and performs for itself functions which would otherwise be performed by separate wholesale institutions.

**Important Characteristics**

**1. Similar Product.** Each such shop deals in the same type of products.

**2. Articles of Daily Use.** The products dealt in are generally that of day to day use.

**3. Central Purchase.** All purchases are effected through the central organisation and uniform sale policy is followed by all stores.

**4. Uniform Policies.** All shops are managed and controlled from the head office, *i.e.*, all policies are decided by the head office and carried out by the shops. Thus, there are uniform policies.

**5. Same Style.** Each shop is decorated in the same setting and style. A high degree of standardisation and uniformity is attained in the interior lay out of stores, window dressing and outward appearance.

**Advantages of Chain Stores**

1. **Lower Selling Prices.** This is made possible due to economy in buying operation, etc.

2. **Economy in Advertising.** Common advertisements covering all the units are feasible which reduces publicity expenditure. Advertisement for one becomes an advertisement for all other shops.

3. **Ability to Spread Nest.** Unlike the departmental stores the principle here is not "to lay all the eggs in one basket." By trial and error a unit sustaining losses may be shifted from one place to another or be even dropped.

4. **Economical Buying.** As supplies are made to all the shops through the central office, it is in a position to gain the economies of large scale buying It can purchase goods direct from the manufacturers.

5. **Speedy Turnover.** As chain stores are mainly located in different localities therefore they are in direct touch with the actual customers and know current trends in demand. They can have such stock as sell fast. Multiple shops can achieve a rapid turnover target.

6. **Economical Operation.** Multiple stores generally work with lower operating costs than many of their competitors duc to the following factors (i) rapid turnover, (ii) elimination of bad debts, (iii) no need for maintaining accounts for credit sale, and (iv) common advertisement.

7. **No Bad Debts.** As it works on cash basis bad debts and detailed accounting processes are avoided in chain stores.

**Disadvantages**

1. **Inflexible in Practice.** Multiple shops deal only in standardised products. This creates inflexibility in offering wide varieties. Each unit is controlled by the central office which prevents the unit from adjusting to local conditions.

2. **Personnel Problems.** Being a large scale organisation it is susceptible to problems associated with large-scale business. Transfer and promotion etc. bring inefficiency to the organisation.

3. **Pool Public Image.** Various consumer services such as credit facility, door delivery, etc. are absent in a chain store. In

addition to desiring low price the present day consumers prefer to have more services than quality.

**4. Attempt to eliminate Retailers.** Multiple shops represent an attempt on the part of the wholesalers and manufacturers to eliminate retailers.

**5. Rise in Operation Costs.** As the number of shops in the chain increases, the control and supervision becomes lose and the disadvantages of large scale operations begin to appear. The increase in the size of chain leads to disproportionate size of operations costs, cost of supervision and cost of delivery.

**6. No Set off.** According to W.J. Stanton "Price compensation is not possible as such stores are handling only limited items."

## DEPARTMENTAL STORE *VS.* MULTIPLE SHOPS

**1. Location.** Whereas central location is essential in the case of a departmental stores multiple shops could be located in any place where the consumers are adequate. The former institution attracts customers to its place of business whereas latter moves nearer to consumers.

**2. Clientale.** Basically departmental stores are meant for rich people whereas multiple shops do not maintain such distinctions.

**3. Prices.** Departmental stores charge high prices on account of various services rendered for customers. As multiple shops do not provide such facilities their prices are comparatively low.

**4. Variety.** Departmental stores provide a good variety of goods to their customers who are enabled thereby to make all their purchases under one roof. The multiple shops, on the other hand, specialise in a limited range of merchandise only.

**5. Source.** Departmental stores sell products manufactured by various manufacturers. The multiple shops, on the contrary, sell only one merchandise of one or a very few manufactures.

**6. Risks.** While the departmental stores run greater risks of business in as much as they sell goods only at one place, on the multiple shops reduce their risks by selling goods through different branches at different places.

**7. Advertisement.** While the departmental stores advertise only in restricted local areas because they are interested only in local customers, the multiple shops organise their advertisement campaign on nation wide or at least regional basis.

## MAIL ORDER BUSINESS

According to F.F. Clark "A mail order house is that type of retail institution which solicits patronage by means of catalogues of merchandise offered for sale."

Mail order trading also referred to as "Non-store impersonal retailing or shopping by post," is done through the post office and personal selling is avoided. The orders are collected and goods are delivered at the very doors of the customers through the medium of post. No help of middlemen is sought. The seller takes all the necessary steps to introduce the product by sending catalogues, circulars or other printed matter to the prospective customers. Publicity through other media is also undertaken. No personal contact is possible between the buyer and the seller.

### Types of Mail Order Houses

**1. The Manufacturing types.** In it products are sold direct to the public by the manufacturer and there is no middlemen.

**2. The Departmental types.** In addition to selling goods through different departments the departmental store starts selling goods by mail.

**3. The Middlemen types.** Run by wholesalers this is the proper and true mail order business. As and when orders are received by post the goods are brought from the manufacturer or other wholesalers and dispatched to the respective parties.

Selling through mail depends on how effectively the customers are persuaded to buy. As the buyers are unable to inspect the goods personally there is always an inherent resistance to buy these goods.

### Common Characteristics of Mail Order Retailing

**1. Easy Understanding.** The nature of the product should be easily understood from its description.

**2. Convenient Selection.** The product can be selected conveniently from different models.

**3. Immediate Use.** Goods must be capable of rendering immediate use as soon as they are delivered.

**4. Low Postal Charges.** Postal charges should be low compared to the price of the product.

**5. Not Easily Spoiled.** Goods must be of such nature that are not easily spoiled or damaged in the transit.

**6. Perennial supply.** The supply of the product is perennial.

**Procedure of Mail Order retailing**

The retailing institutions find out the addresses of the prospective buyers from telephone directories, list of car owners, voters lists etc. and send the illustrative catalogues to their addresses. This is supplemented by advertisements. The catalogues invariably contain an order form together with a stamped self-addressed envelope. The buyer has simply to put his signature in the order form mentioning the quantity required. As soon as the orders are received, the goods are packed and handed over to the post office. The goods are generally sent by V.P.P. (value payable post) and the postman collects the required amount before the goods are delivered to the buyer. The money collected is sent back to the seller through post office.

**Advantages of Mail Order Retailing**

1. Even goods not readily available in the market could be purchased through this method.
2. This business could be operated from any place where the postal facility is available.
3. No bad debts are suffered as money is collected before, the goods are delivered.
4. It widens market and helps the traders to discover untapped markets.
5. The system could be operated easily even when the demand is low.
6. Only a small amount of capital is required to undertake this business.
7. As the goods are delivered at their very doors, customers are benefited.
8. No central place is required for business.

**Disadvantages of Mail Order Retailing**

1. The buyers are unable to inspect and select goods before they are bought.
2. Even the most illustrated catalogue is incapable of giving exact idea about the product.
3. Articles required for demonstration cannot be sold.
4. After sales services is out of question.
5. No credit facilities are provided.
6. There could be delays in getting the goods.

7. Catalogues become obsolete very quickly as prices are subject to quick fluctuations.
8. The demand creating activities being costlier.
9. Higher prices are charged.
10. Sometimes the goods are damaged in transit.

**Mail Order Business in India**

In India, the Mail Order Retailing system has not made any headway. The reasons which prevent the growth of this system of retailing in the India are following :

**1. Illiteracy.** India's vast population suffers from illiteracy.

**2. Seeing Before Buying.** The general mentality of the Indian customers is to see the goods before purchasing them. This mentality is obviously the greatest obstacle in the way of this system.

**3. Low Standard of Living.** The standard of living of the people is very low.

**4. No Daily Supplies.** Majority of people buy their requirements on daily basis and this is not possible under this system.

**5. Non-Availability of Credit Facility.** This is another reason for the unpopularity of this system.

**6. No Business Ethics.** Indian traders do not observe any business ethics. Cheating is very common. It loses the faith of the public in such type of business.

**Mail Order Retailing**

The system is becoming popular in the case of books and periodicals. In U.S.A. Sears Rose Buck is the largest mail order house which actually controls the lion's share in retail business there.

## HIRE PURCHASE

In this type of retail selling, the seller agrees to sell the goods on the condition that the buyer shall pay the purchase price in fixed number of instalments. The article is not legally sold out but is only hired by the buyer. He cannot become the owner until the final instalment is paid. Till then, he will only be a mere possessor of the article and in default, the product will be seized by the seller. As the amounts paid so far by the buyer will be treated as mere hire charges, hence the name is hire-purchase.

**Instalment Selling**

Instalment selling is basically the same as Hire Purchase but with certain legal differences. Unlike the hire purchaser, the instalment buyer gets legal as well as physical possession over the products. The seller cannot repossess the article and can claim for price if instalments are defaulted. This system is also called as "Deffered Payment System." The articles are invariably delivered only after a few instalments have been paid. It enables the consumers of average means to own capital goods. The system provides large markets for the products of manufacturers. In the present day context the luxury articles such as refrigerators, cars, scooters, TV sets, etc. could only be marketed with such credit facilities provided to consumers. However, all goods cannot be traded under this system. The products traded under the system must possess the following characteristics :

1. Durability.
2. Stability.
3. Profitability.
4. Possibility of standardisation.
5. High unit value.
6. Possibility of after sale service.

**Advantages of Hire Purchase Retailing**

**1. Articles Beyond Capacity.** The consumers could get articles of such nature as are normally beyond their capacities.

**2. High Standard of Living.** It increase the standard of living.

**3. Use to Small Investors.** Small manufacturers could use the opportunity to get plants and machinery. They could be put to use and payments arranged from the income arising out of their productive use.

**4. Double Advantage.** Persons of surplus means could also use this system. While they could get the article, the money retained could be profitably invested elsewhere.

**Disadvantages of Hire Purchase Retailing**

**1. High Prices.** The prices are high due to the inclusion of interest for the deferred period.

**2. Loss in Default.** The default not only makes one lose the product but also the payments made.

**3. More Default.** It attracts customers who cannot possess such article normally so the chances of default are great.

**4. Legal problems.** It involves disputes and legal problems. This creates delay in effecting sales.

**5. Difficult Contact.** The manufacturers often find it difficult to call on customers frequently.

In India this system is a widely accepted form of retailing in towns and cities. It is a popular form of retailing in the case of durable and costly articles. Hire Purchase Act has been passed for proper controlling of these trade activities.

## CO-OPERATIVE RETAILING

**1. Retailers' Cooperatives.** Severe criticism against wholesalers and various kinds of middlemen led to a new type of retailing. In U.S.A. Retailing Cooperatives have become important distributors of convenience goods. In India however the system is not found. In the case of food items the Government agencies are playing a dominant role and the retailers are virtually absent.

**2. Consumers' Cooperatives.** It is a retail business owned and operated by ultimate consumers who purchase and distribute goods and services primarily to the members. The earliest known consumers' cooperative was started in Scotland. The modern form is traced the Rochdale Society of Equitable Pioneer and English cooperatives formed in 1844. It is claimed that the potentialities of the organised cooperatives were first revealed by Raiffesen in Germany in the 1840s.

**Rochdale Principles**

**1. Open Membership.** The consumer are free to join the cooperative.

**2. Democratic Control.** Each member has only one vote irrespective of the number of shares he might hold.

**3. Cash Sale.** All sales are made at existing market rates on cash basis.

**4. Dividend.** It is assured though maximum is limited.

**5. Purchase Bonus.** Members are allowed 'purchase bonus' on the basis of their purchases.

**6. Ownership.** These principles substitute service motive for project motive, encourage sense of thrift and make more people owners.

**Advantages of Cooperative Retailing**

**1. Low Operating Cost.** Because of service motive the cost of operating is kept down. Advertisements are eliminated.

**2. Better Quality.** Better quality goods can be sold.

**3. Ornamentation.** Elimination of costly equipment and ornamentation of the shop is preferred.

**4. Location.** It need not always be located in busy places.

**5. Credits.** As credits are allowed hence no problem of bad debts arises.

**6. Affiliation.** Easy affiliation with other societies is possible, which helps in buying in bulk.

**7. Check.** It is a check on monopoly and wasteful completion.

**8. Equitable Distribution.** During product scarcity, equitable distribution is possible. Black marketing is checked.

**Disadvantages of Cooperative Retailing**

**1. Lack of Consumers Interest.** It is so because personal attention is not paid to them there.

**2. Lack of Finance.** Only poor members can contribute to the capital of the society.

**3. Absence of Experts in Management.** The men in managing committee are elected from among the members who are not experts in managements.

**4. Attitudes.** Employees show impersonal and discourteous attitudes to consumers.

**5. No Large Scale Sellings.** There is no advantage of large scale selling.

**Consumers' Cooperatives in India**

Cooperative movement in India has not been very satisfactory. The consumers' cooperatives have become active only when there is a natural or artificial scarcity of essential articles due to hoarding, profiteering, black marketing and artificial inflation. They are confined only to important towns, they fail to create confidence among the general public. Before World War II there were about 400 Consumers' Cooperative stores in the states of Madras, Bombay, and Mysore. Post-war effects gave an impetus to cooperatives movement into existence. Their number now runs into thousands. These societies however have, failed to maintain equality in distribution as well as stability in prices. They are called society of the weak and the wicked.

**Causes of Failure**

**1. Lack of Business Training.** It does not provide experience to those who are incharge of stores.

**2. No Study.** Absence of careful and thorough study of members requirements.

**3. Methods.** Defective methods of stock ordering and stock keeping.

**4. Disloyalty.** Disloyalty of the members and admission and cancellation of their membership are very frequent.

**5. Dependence.** It leads to much dependence on honorary services which suffer from incompetency.

**6. Politics.** Extension of politics into the field of cooperation has ruined the cooperative spirit.

## SUPER MARKET

M.M. Zimmermen defines a super market as "a Departmentalised retail establishment having four basic food departments-self-service, grocery, meat produce and dairy-plus other household departments and doing a maximum business. It may be entirely owner operated or have some of the departments based on a concession basis." But this definition is incomplete as Super markets are 'self-services' states. The origin of super markets dates back to 1930 when the Great depression took place. They were successful in effecting cheap prices and operated on the cash and carry principles. They generally concentrated on food and grocery items.

**Characteristic Features of a Super Market**

**1. Parking Space.** They are located at places where consumers are given facilities like parking. Some super markets are successful without providing space.... The trend however is to provide more parking space.

**2. Advertisement.** They use heavy advertisement and mass display of merchandise.

**3. Credit.** No credit facilities are offered.

**4. Self Service.** They do not employ salesmen and hence super markets are often described as self-service stores.

**Super Markets in India**

In India there is no super market as such. The name is used for most of the departmental stores organised under cooperative principle. These super markets have grocery items and all other convenience and speciality articles. They sell goods in labelled packets through the use of salesmen. They are not self-services stores. They provide packed articles labelled with price tags and stored conveniently in shelves. The customer picks up the required products and places them in a tray provided for the purpose. Then he takes the selected articles to the cashier where the articles are billed and payment is made. No bargaining is possible and no credits are allowed in super market.

**Advantages of Super Markets**

**1. Freedom.** Perfect freedom is enjoyed by the customers. No pressure selling is possible.

**2. Low Prices.** This is on account of various organisational and establishment savings.

**3. Higher Profits.** This is due to low costs and high turnover.

**4. Packing and Protection.** Goods are packed safely and kept properly to protect them for a considerable time.

**5. Quick Shopping.** Shopping time is considerably reduced.

**6. Economies.** It enjoys economies of large-scale operation.

**Disadvantages of Super Market**

**1. Costly Premises.** The large and extensive premises for super markets is not available cheaply.

**2. No Explanation.** The products which require explanation for their proper use cannot be dealt in through the super markets.

**3. No Customer Services.** Customer services are practically absent.

**4. Capital.** A huge capital is required to establish a Super Bazaar.

## ONE PRICE SHOPS

This is a retail shop concentrating on articles largely demanded by masses. Irrespective of their use and quality the articles from these shops are sold at a single price. It gives the buyers the benefit of getting any article at a fixed price. Bargaining on prices is not permitted. This type of organisation is called 'wool worth chain stores' as such stores were organised as wool worth for the first time. Usually these shops constitute a part of the fairs and exhibitions. In recent years however, one price shops have acquired permanency in location due to wide population.

## QUESTIONS FOR EXERCISE

1. Define retail trade? What are the functions of retailers? Explain the main conditions for the success of retail business.
2. What do you mean by retailer? Mention the functions and services rendered by them.
3. What are the forms of Retail Trade Organisation? Explain.
4. What do you mean by Departmental Stores? What are their characteristics? How are Departmental Stores organised? How far are they popular in India?
5. "A co-operative society is a society of the weak and the wicked." Discuss.
6. What do you understand by Multiple Shops or Chain Stores? What are their advantages and disadvantages?
7. Compare and contrast the Multiple Chain Stores with the Departmental Stores.
8. What do you mean by Mail Order Business? Describe its advantages and disadvantages.
9. Explain Hire Purchase, Instalment Selling, Co-operative Retailing, Super Market and One Price Shops.

# 10

# Cooperative Selling

A cooperative society is a voluntary organisation based on the rules : democratic ownership, equal voting right, security of group interest, service objective instead of profit making and mutual cooperation. Under the Indian Cooperative Societies Act any ten adult persons can get a cooperative society registered for a specific economic purpose. A cooperative society can be organised as : (i) Primary agricultural purchase and sale societies, (ii) Production and sale societies, (iii) Non-agricultural products purchase and sale societies, (iv) Multi-purpose cooperative societies, (v) Central marketing unions, (vi) Consumers' cooperative stores, etc.

## DEFINITION OF COOPERATIVE SOCIETY

1. International Labour Organisation. "An association of persons, usually of limited means, who have voluntarily joined together to achieve a common economic object and through the formation of a democratically controlled business organisation, making equitable contributions to the capital required and accepting fair share of risks and benefit of undertaking."

2. Culbert. "Cooperation is a form of organisation, wherein persons voluntarily associate together as human beings, on a basis of equality for the promotion of the economic interests of themselves."

## NEED FOR COOPERATIVES

The competitive nature of retail distribution makes for many varieties and frequent changes in the types of institutions and retailing methods. The new methods have replaced the old ones. The independent stores suffered and changed their ways to improve their position. Chain stores sold the goods at cheaper rates than the independent stores. Therefore, one finds independent deviced means for reducing their costs.

## FORMS OF COOPERATIVE SOCIETIES

**1. Cooperative Buying Clubs.** Independent retailers formed cooperative buying clubs to get lower merchandise costs and enable the members to meet chain store prices. Most cooperative buying clubs failed because they had no experience. Manufacturers refused to deal with them due to a wholesalers' pressure. They deal like chain stores of cash and carry. Most independents provided credit and delivery services, operated full service stores and made little use of advertising so they had to charge higher retail prices to cover their costs and to compensate for small sales volumes.

**2. Retailer-Owned Cooperatives.** These are owned and controlled by retailer stock holders who patronise them and share in any savings in proportion to their patronage. The retailer cooperatives have a ware house, carry inventories in stock and employ a manager. They render advice and assistance on retail merchandising problems like store layout and location, store operation, record systems, advertising methods and layouts and personnel policies etc.

Most of them place more emphasis on group buying than on group promotional activities. As heavy group promotion is an important key to success, the retailer owned cooperatives emphasise group promotion. Hence, their members become strong competitors of chain store outlets.

**3. Consumers' Cooperatives.** These are retail business owned and operated by ultimate consumers to purchase and distribute goods and services chiefly to the members. Rochdale Society of Equitable Pioneer were pioneers of such societies. They laid down following principles :

(i) Open Membership to all consumers.

(ii) Democratic control, one vote for a member irrespective of their holding.

(iii) Limited periodical interest on capital invested.

(iv) All sales are at market rates only.

(v) Members got patronage dividend proportionate to their purchases.

Consumers' cooperatives flourished in Europe. In America these were comparatively controlled by chains. They supply goods at fair prices. The surplus profit after the reduction of costs were distributed as dividend among the members. They collected order of the members and purchased at wholesale prices, eliminating profit of the middlemen. They also gave suggestions to retailers about premises, equipment, advertising, display, staff and accounting. They also served as bankers.

## COOPERATIVES IN INDIA

The system prevailed in India upon the pattern of U.K. where intermediaries were avoided. The consumer was protected from exploitation by traders. As the scheme was favoured by the Indian Government, cooperatives were established at all levels, with the 'National Consumers' Cooperative Federation (N.C.C.F.) at the top. Its shares were held by Central and Provincial Governments. It guided and assisted the member institutions and consumer cooperatives. Numbering fourteen these controlled about 424 wholesale Central Consumers Cooperative Stores and 150 departmental stores. Thus, the Consumers' Cooperative Movement has achieved a large dimension in India.

The position of cooperative marketing in India was not very satisfactory before First Five Year Plan (1951-1956). After 1954 cooperative marketing became an integral part of the multi-purpose societies in India. In the Second Five Year Plan 1800 and in the Third Plan 544 primary cooperative marketing societies were registered. The number of these marketing cooperatives is increasing day by day.

### Advantages of Cooperative Marketing

**1. Facility of Proper Weighing.** According to a rough estimate, by malpractice in weighing a farmer used to be deceived of 1 kg. grains in every quintal grains that he sold. Marketing societies ensure full proper weight of the product.

**2. Better Prices.** Marketing societies ensure better prices for the product because they sell when higher prices are prevailing with market. They store the grains and other products and advance money to the owner. Thus, the farmer is not compelled to sell his products just at the time of harvest when the prices are comparatively low.

**3. Better Storage Facility.** The societies provide better storage facility to farmers.

**4. Relief from Unauthorised and Illegal Deductions.** The poor farmers were deprived of the full payment of their products when they went to unregulated markets to dispose of their products. The unscrupulous grain merchants used to make several deductions in the name of charity, donations and subscriptions. The cooperative societies have given them much relief from such illegal deductions.

**5. Elimination of Middlemen.** Cooperative marketing societies have done away with the long claw of intermediaries who were parasites on the hard labour of the poor cultivators.

**6. Loan Facility.** These societies provide facility for loans on the basis of the products of the cultivators.

**7. Collective Bargaining.** The farmers also reap the benefit of collective bargaining and better prices through the cooperative marketing societies.

**8. Provision for Grading.** These societies arrange grading facilities so that the price secured is generally high.

## CONSUMERS COOPERATIVE SOCIETY

In India the consumers cooperatives are becoming quite popular as the traders adopt anti-social practices and resort to hoarding, black marketing, profiteering and creating artificial scarcities. Today, poor look to cooperative stores for fair price and quality goods.

Consumers' cooperative is a retail business owned and operated by ultimate consumers. It purchases and distributes goods and services chiefly to its member. The Government also help the consumers to form cooperatives and purchase the goods directly from the manufacturers. The Fifth Plan also aims at consumers' cooperative movement in India. These are most popular in retailing items of food and grocery. However, there is little motivation for consumers to organise cooperatives in non-food fields. Consumers' cooperatives have been most successful in some countries like Holland, Denmark and Belgium.

### Characteristics of Consumers' Cooperative Societies

**1. Voluntary Membership.** Any person who is willing to abide by the rule of the society can become its member.

**2. Purchase in Bulk.** The consumers' cooperatives generally purchase goods in bulk which is always economical. Thus they are able to arrange goods comparatively at low rate.

**3. No Credit.** These societies sell only on cash basis. Hence there is no fear of bad debts.

**4. Distribution of Profit.** The profit made by the cooperatives is distributed among the members in the proportion of their purchases.

**5. Democratic Organisation.** Each member has one vote irrespective of the fact how many shares he holds. Thus the aim of the cooperative consumers societies is not making profit but getting quality goods at reasonable prices.

**Advantages of Consumers Cooperatives**

**1. Quality Goods.** The members are able to get quality goods at reasonable prices. There is no need of bargaining.

**2. Cash sales.** The articles are sold on cash basis. Therefore, there is no need of having complicated accounts and fear of bad debts.

**3. No Exploitation.** There cannot be any exploitation of consumers by the wholesalers and intermediaries.

**4. Social Service.** The societies foster feelings of cooperation, mutual help and brotherhood.

**5. Location.** There is no need for centrally located building for consumers cooperatives.

**Disadvantages of Consumers Cooperatives**

**1. Loose Management.** Consumers' cooperative societies are run by employees who are quite untrained, inexperienced and free from personal interest. Thus proper functioning is not possible due to loose management.

**2. Fraudulent Behaviour.** The cooperative societies are managed and controlled by a managing committee consisting of members duly elected by and among the members who generally misappropriate cash and goods in their own interest.

**3. Limited Scope.** As only members of the consumers' cooperative stores can be the consumers of the store, outsiders are invariably not permitted to purchase from such markets. Thus, these societies have limited scope for dealings.

**4. No Cooperative Feeling.** In consumers cooperatives the cooperative feeling depreciates with the increase in the number of members. It has now become a general practice to allege the members of managing committee of misappropriating cash and stores by manipulating the accounts. Unfortunately, the allegations are often true.

The above drawbacks have shaken the faith of the public in consumer cooperatives. Therefore their progress in India has remained very unsatisfactory.

## QUESTIONS FOR EXERCISE

1. Define Cooperative Society. What are the fundamental reasons behind its establishment?
2. Write a short note on Consumers' Cooperative Society.

# 11

# THE SALES ORGANISATION

## VALUE OF SALES ORGANISATION

**1. Achievement of Qualitative and Quantitative Objectives.** As the sales organisation must achieve both qualitative and quantitative personal-selling objectives, effective sales executives insist upon sound organisation. The organisation must achieve qualitative objectives concerning personal-selling's expected contributions to achievement of overall company objectives. It must attain the quantitative personal-selling objectives including objectives related to "profit" such as keeping selling expenses within certain limits and to "competitive position".

**2. Attainment of Short Term and Long Term Objectives.** Achieving short-run quantitative personal-selling objectives precedes attainment of the long-run qualitative personal-selling objectives. An effective sales executive looks upon the sales organisation both with respect to the "here and now" and to the "future." Recognizing that sales organisation makes its major contribution in the present and the near term, the effective sales executive builds both sales-mindedness and profit-mindedness into the sales organisation.

**3. Cooperative Endeavour and Human Relationships.** A sales organisation is both an orienting point for cooperative endeavor and a structure of human relationships. It is a group of individuals striving jointly to reach qualitative and quantitative objectives and bearing informal and formal relations to one another. In a sales organisation individual members cooperate to attain ends. It is not an end in itself but rather the vehicle by which individuals achieve given ends. Its existence implies the existence of patterns of relationships among subgroups and individuals established for purposes of facilitating accomplishment of the group's aims.

**4. Losses Due to Organisational Defects.** Lack of attention given to sales organisation during the early existence of a company results into many losses. When setting up a business, management is more concerned with financing and non-marketing problems. Executives of new enterprises most often consider organisation questions relating to non-marketing activities. Alterations in the sales organisation are frequently neglected or postponed, while products are improved, production quantities increased, new products added, production processes developed and the manufacturing organisation is adapted to changed situations.

**5. Vehicle of Personal Selling.** In many companies sales organisations evolve without regard for changing conditions. Designed when the company was new the basic setup remains, despite change in selling style and size of sales force. As the sales organisation is the vehicle through which personal-selling strategy is implemented, a well-designed sales organisation accomplishes more and more economically, than does one that is an artifact.

## THE IDEAL SALES ORGANISATION

The sales organisation should be adjusted to anticipate changing situations. Shifts in marketing, in competition and in other business factors call for changes in the sales organisation. The ideal sales organisation has a built-in adaptability allowing it to respond appropriately in fluid and diverse marketing environments.

Wasted motion and duplication of effort would be eliminated, friction would be minimized and cooperation maximized in the ideally organized sales department. Executive effort expended on sales organisation should not go exclusively to questions of design of the "formal" organisation plan because, how an organisation works is more important than how it is supposed to function. Sales management should direct its main organisational efforts toward the "informal" organisation. Through intelligent leadership and related "human relations" talents, the skilled manager moves both individuals and informal groups along lines that facilitate achievement of the purposes of formal organisation.

## OBJECTIVES OF SALES ORGANISATION

**1. To delegate Authority.** While a business expands and marketing and selling activities multiply and become increasingly complex, it is difficult to fix responsibility for performance of all necessary activities, particularly when executives are reluctant to delegate authority. Reorganisation of the sales department seeks to facilitate assignment of responsibility and delegation of authority, which often requires reshaping the structure so that it is easier for specialists to develop. In specialisation, division of labour is the chief means through which the processes of organisation and reorganisation are effected. As tasks grow in number and complexity, they are broken down into manageable units and are assigned to specialized personnel involving fixing responsibility for specific tasks with specific individuals. The assignments made are called "delegations of authority", which is conducive to the development of specialists.

**2. To assure Performance of Activities.** As a sales organisation grows and specialisation increases, it is increasingly important to perform all necessary activities. When jobs are highly specialized, the organisational plan may not provide for supervision of all activities. Essential tasks may not be performed, because they are not assigned to specific individuals.

In a small company executives are in close contact with users of the product. As a company grows marketing channels lengthen, and the marketing area expands geographically. Now, the top executives become farther and farther removed from the customers. They begin to lose their informal contacts with customers. As these are highly important, responsibility for maintaining them should be assigned to an executive specializing in customer relations.

**3. To achieve Coordination.** Good organisation achieves coordination. As individuals vary in competence, potential and effectiveness, forceful executives may prevent a basically sound organisation from functioning smoothly. Through assumption of authority, failure to delegate it or both, their positions are magnified out of all proportion of their importance. The total accomplishments of the organisation are less than they could have been if, great advantage had been taken of the synergistic effect in which the sum of a combination effort exceeds the efforts of the same individuals working alone. By getting people to pull together as a team rather than as an assortment of individuals collectively the organisation accomplishes more than its members could achieve independently.

**4. To motivate for Team Work.** Motivating individuals to work together towards common objectives is important in achieving coordination. Individual goals are subordinated to organisational goals. Through indoctrination and training programmes, group meetings, supervision and guidance, and two-way communications, different activities are kept in proper relation to one another so that the greatest organisational effectiveness is realized.

**5. To create Coordinating Sales Departments.** The management must guard against a tendency of each to search for ways to justify his or her own existence as specialists emerge in a growing sales organisation. Technical nomenclatures lead to increasing communications difficulties with other specialists and a reduction in overall organisational effectiveness. Top sales executives should concern themselves continually with orchestration of effort. Sales departments should be divided into small, freely communicating, face-to-face groups to decrease the possibility of uncoordinated proliferation.

**6. To define Authority.** Sales executives should know the kind of their line, staff, as functional. All executives should understand the nature of their authority with respect to each aspect of the operation; otherwise, friction develops. For instance where staff executives attempt to exercise line authority, they are headed for trouble with the line executives whose authority is usurped.

(i) *Nature of Authority* :

(a) Line authority carries the power to require execution of orders by those lower in the organisational hierarchy.

(b) Staff authority is the power to suggest the method for implementation of an order.

(c) Functional authority enables specialists in particular areas to enforce their directives within a specific and limited field.

(ii) *Functions of Authority* :

(a) Line executives make decisions on the need, place and time of action over a wide range of matters.

(b) Staff executives advise line executives about methods but have no formal power to require or enforce the execution of their recommendations.

(c) Functional executives are specialists. Experts in some aspect of the business who assist executives holding general line authority. Such specialists advise on new product introduction by issuing orders, mainly on routine technical problems, directly to lower organisational levels.

**7. To harmonize Orders and Directives.** A sales organisation receives directions from several sources. A salesperson may get instructions on merchandising the advertising from an advertising specialist, director or administrator information from a marketing research technician and general supervision and direction from the district sales manager. The real problem is harmonizing orders and directives from different sources. A smoothly operating sales organisation has built-in ways of achieving harmony, such as continuing coordination of the work of different executives and free-flowing communications systems.

**8. To economize on Executive Time.** Additional subordinates are added as a sales department's operations and activities increase in complexity and number. Higher-ranking sales executives delegate more authority. There is more effective use of specialisation. Higher executives devote less time to operations and more to planning. This helps in achieving economies in the use of executive time. Top sales executives do not concern themselves personally with all the sales department's problems and activities. Routine or technical ones are left to capable and well-trained subordinates.

**9. To widen Span of Control.** Sales executives must devote more attention and more time, to coordinating their efforts. Subordinates may not work in harmony and discharge assignments in line with expectations unless the executive is an effective coordinator.

The need for effective coordination limits the number of subordinates who report directly to certain executives. This limit is the "span of control". It is not possible to specify the proper number of subordinates because the greater the abilities of the coordinator and of those reporting to him or her, the larger the number that can be effectively coordinated. Lower-level sales executives, those with sales people reporting directly to them have a wider span of control than higher executives as they devote much time to planning and policy formulation and little to administrative and operating details. Besides the relative abilities of the coordinator and the subordinates, one must consider the nature and importance of the coordinator's other duties, other factors are taken into account in deciding optimum span of control for a particular position. The span of control is widened: (1) with improvements in the efficiency and reliability of the communications system; (2) when subordinates perform routine, similar or repetitive tasks, and (3) when subordinates are concentrated at the same location as the executive.

## STEPS IN SALES ORGANISATION

A sales organisation is not built entirely from scratch. Some structure usually exists. Thus most problems of sales organisation are problems of reorganisation. While sales organisation exists the goal is to make it more effective. However, the sales executive should approach the organisational problems, as though a completely new organisation were being built. Following are five major steps in setting up a sales organisation :

1. Defining the objectives.
2. Determination of activities and their volume of performance.
3. Grouping activities into "positions."
4. Assignment of personnel to positions.
5. Provision for coordination and control.

**1. Defining the Objectives.** Top management defines the long term objectives for the company. From these are derived the general or long term objectives for the sales department. General objectives constitute top management's vision of the company at some future time. For instance, top management may want the firm to achieve industry leadership, develop a reputation for outstanding technical research, diversify its product, provide excellent service to customers, furnish investors with a generous return and establish an image of public responsibility. From these, sales management determines the implications for the sales department and articulates a set of qualitative personal-selling objectives from which are derived quantitative personal-selling objectives. Three of the sales department's general objectives—may be summed up in three words : sales, profits and growth.

(a) ***Qualitative Objectives*** : For instance, survival is the most basic qualitative objective of any enterprise as well as of its sales department.

(i) *Sales* : Among other things, this requires a continuing flow of sales revenue securing a given level of sales volume as an important sales department quantitative objective.

(ii) *Profits* : Again, survival also requires profits. Therefore, a second qualitative personal-selling objective is to produce profits, not only by making profitable sales but by controlling departmental costs and expenses.

(iii) *Growth* : Furthermore, survival requires growth in both sales and profits; otherwise, in a growing economy the company is destined to fall behind competitors or even risk being forced out of business. Therefore, a third qualitative personal-selling objective is to realize long-term growth in sales profits.

(b) ***Quantitative Objectives.*** White qualitative personal-selling are indispensable for long-range planning, quantitative personal-selling objectives are required as operating guideposts. The qualitative personal-selling objectives such as "to increase our market share of the hand-held calculator business to 20 per cent by the end of the current year" and "to secure four wholesalers in India and one in Bangla Desh to introduce our vest-pocket calculators in those markets next year." When assigned definite goals people in the sales department, as those elsewhere, work more effectively, with less wasted time, effort and money. The sales department as a whole operates more smoothly. Its activities are more purposeful, when it has specific quantitative objectives.

While the qualitative objectives form the basis for the general policies governing long-term performance of the sales department, the quantitative objectives are the foundations from which to develop day-to-day operating sales policies and programs. Therefore, thorough examination, even a restatement of the qualitative and quantitative goals of the sales department, is necessary in setting up a sales organisation.

**2. Determination of Activities and Their Volume of Performance.** The recognition that activities are being organized is fundamental to sound organisational design. After determining all necessary activities and estimating their volume of performance it is possible to answer such questions as: What executive positions are required? What should be their relationships to other positions? What should be the duties and responsibilities of persons who fill these positions?

Determining the necessary activities and their volume of, performance requires analysis of the sales department's qualitative and quantitative objectives. It discloses which activities must be performed in what volume. Although individual sales executives think that their operations are different, most differences are more apparent than real. Almost every sales department carries on the same general activities. Differences among departments are those of detail, of relative emphasis placed upon individual activity and in volume of performance.

**3. Grouping Activities into Positions**. Now, the activities identified as necessary are allocated to different positions. Activities are aimed at achieving certain objectives. The company provides the raw material from which job descriptions are complied in terms of reporting relationships, job objectives, duties and responsibilities and performance measures.

Activities are classified and grouped to assign closely related task to the same position. Each position should contain a sufficient number of tasks as well as a sufficient vocation to provide for job challenge, interest, and involvement. In very large organisations, where extreme specialisation is practiced, a position comprises only a single activity. For administrative economy most position holders are made responsible for a number of diversified, although related, activities.

Certain activities are of crucial importance to success of the sales department. For example, in a highly competitive field, product merchandising and pricing are assigned to positions high up in the organisational structure. Activities of lesser importance are assigned to lower-level jobs.

Groups of related jobs are brought together to form departmental subdivisions when a large number of positions is being set up. A number of intermediate-level have to be coordinated by the top sales executive. However, the planner should guard building too many levels into the department. The smallest number of administrative levels is that which permits the organisation both of perform its activities and to operate smoothly.

**4. Assignment of Personnel to Positions**. Assignment of personnel to the positions brings up the question of whether to recruit special individuals to fill the positions or modify the positions to fit the capabilities of available personnel. On the one hand, some position requirements are so general that many individuals possess the necessary qualifications or can acquire though training. On the other hand, some individuals possess such unique talents and abilities that it is prudent and profitable to modify the job specifications to fit them. However, Planners prefer to have individuals grow into particular jobs rather than to have jobs grow up around individuals.

**5. Provision for coordination and Control.** Sales executives with line authority require means to control their subordinates and to coordinate their efforts. They should not be overburdened with detailed and undelegated responsibilities and have insufficient time for coordination. They should not have too many subordinates reporting directly to them as it weakens the quality of control and prevents the discharge of other duties. Thus, consideration must be given to the span of executive control.

Control and coordination is obtainable through both informal and formal means. Strong leaders control and coordinate the efforts of their subordinates on an informal basis, through sheer force of personality coupled with unusual abilities to attract and hold the loyalty of followers. They make minimal use of formal instruments of control and coordination. But all sales executives can improve their effectiveness through formal instruments of control.

**6. Control Instruments.**

*(i) Written Job Description* : Written job description is the most important formal instrument of organisational control. It sets forth for each job: reporting relationships, job objectives, duties and responsibilities and performance measurements. Its most critical section is that of setting forth the job objectives. Many planners argue that the job objective section should be emphasized and, the person who holds the job should be allowed to determine how to achieve these objectives. This encourages position holders to use their own initiative and makes it clear that they are to achieve stated job objective even if that requires performing duties and responsibilities beyond those contained in job description. However, there is merit in detailing duties and responsibilities and in defining the measures for evaluating the position holder's performance.

Good job descriptions provide clear pictures of the job holder's roles in the sales organisation. Written job descriptions are used in employee selection processes and in matching job specifications with applicants' qualifications. Job specifications form the basis for training where recruits cannot be found with all desired qualifications. Position holders can use their job descriptions as yardsticks against which to appraise their own performances.

(ii) *Organisational Chart* : An organisational chart shows formal relations among different positions. It delineates formal relations. Though it rarely provides a true picture of how the organisation actually works, its availability enables members of a sales department to learn the nature of their formal relations with others, to know with whom they are expected to cooperate, and to clarify their formal roles.

(iii) *Organisational Manual* : It is an extension of the organisational chart containing charts for both the company and the departments, write-ups of job descriptions and specifications and summaries of major company and departmental objectives and policies. It brings together a great deal of information. It helps its users to learn and understand the nature of their responsibilities, authorities and relations with others.

## BASIC TYPES OF SALES ORGANISATIONAL STRUCTURES

A sales department based on sound practices has features of one or more of four basic types: line, line and staff, functional and committee. Structural form is based on the grouping of activities into positions and the charting of relationships of positions. Linc and line and staff are the most common, while structural, functional and committee organisations are rare. Most sales departments have hybrid organisational structures, with variations to adjust for personalities and to fit specific operating conditions.

As the sales department's structure evolves from the needs of the business, different companies have different sales organisations, because no two have identical needs. The customers, the marketing channels, the company size, the product or product line, the practices of competitors and the personalities and abilities of the personnel affect the organisational structure of the sales department. So numerous are the factors influencing the structure of individual sales departments that it is impractical to draw generalisations about the many possible "mixed" types. Organisational planners should know the chief features of each type and its respective merits and limitations.

**1. Line Sales Organisation**. The oldest and simplest sales organisational structure, it is widely used in smaller firms and in firms with small numbers of selling personnel in companies that cover a limited geographic area or sell a narrow product line. In it, the chain of command runs from the top sales executives down through subordinates. All executives exercise line authority. Each subordinate is responsible only to one person on the next higher level. Responsibility is fixed. Those charged with it make decisions and take action. Lines of authority run vertically through the structure. All persons on any one organisational level are independent of all others on that level.

The line sales organisation is used in companies where all sales personnel report directly to the chief sales executive. This executive is preoccupied with active supervision and seldom has much time to devote to planning or to work with other top executives. The line sales organisation is also used where more than two levels of authority are present.

Following Figure 11.1 shows a fairly large sales department organised on the line basis. While the sales manager reports to the general manager, assistant sales managers report to the sales manager and salespeople report to assistant managers. There is no cross-communication between persons on the same level. Contacts between persons on the same level are indirect and are effected through the next higher level. The assistant sales manager of Division 1 confers with the assistant sales manager of Division 2 through the sales manager. Similarly contacts by personnel with the office staff flow up through the organisation to the sales manager and back down through the assistant sales manager-in-charge of the office to the office staff.

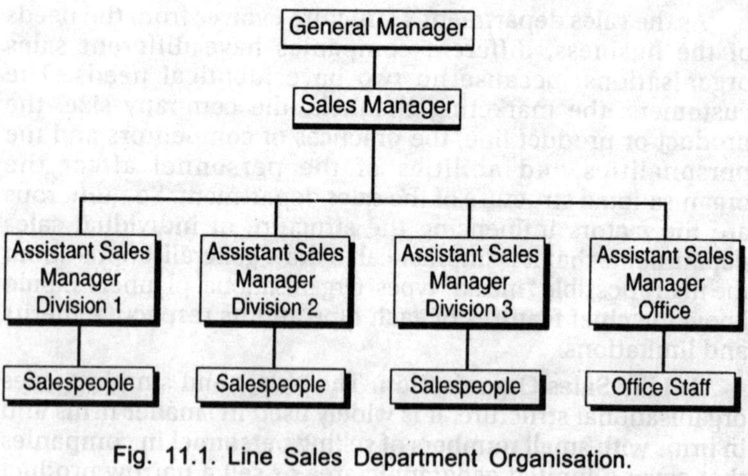


Fig. 11.1. Line Sales Department Organisation.

**Advantages**

(i) *Basic Simplicity* : The simplicity makes it easy for executives to develop close relations with salespersons.

(ii) *Less Problems* : Problems of discipline and control are less, each department member reports to only superior. Lines of authority and responsibility are clear and logical and it is difficult for individuals to shift or evade responsibilities.

(iii) *Saving Time* : Definite placement of authority and responsibility saves time in making policy changes, in deciding new plans, and in converting plans into action.

(iv) *Strong Leaders* : Executives who come up through a line organisation are frequently strong leaders.

(v) *Low Expenses* : As the typical line sales department has few organisational levels, administrative expenses are low.

**Disadvantages**

*(i) Too Much Importance of Department Head* : As there are no subordinates with specialised skills and knowledge, the head needs outstanding ability and rare qualifications and should be well versed in all phases of sales management. Even if the head is an all-around expert, there is insufficient time for policymaking and planning. Rigidity of the line structure requires that a great deal of attention be given to direction of sales operations. The head has to make decisions and take action without benefit of planning. Under such conditions, results are often disappointing.

(ii) *In Appropriate for Growing Concerns* : The line organisational structure is inappropriate for rapidly growing concerns and for those with large sales staffs. As the department grows, new layers of executives must be added to retain control. Orders and directions must be passed down through a growing series of administrative levels. As directions become more and more distorted and garbed at each succeeding organisational level, managerial effectiveness becomes impaired and results are less predictable.

(iii) *Difficult to Maintain Morale* : As growth proceeds, earlier advantages of close relations among executives and salespeople are sacrificed and maintaining morale becomes difficult.

(iv) *Difficult Replacements* : Man executives do not have the talents needed to manage a large-scale line sales department effectively. Line organisation offers little opportunity for subordinates to acquire these skills. Sound organisational practice requires that trained understudies be ready to step into the shoes of their superiors. However, chief sales executives in line sales organisations fail to groom their own replacements.

**2. Line and Staff Sales Organisation.** It is often found in large and medium-sized firms, employing substantial numbers of sales personnel and selling diversified product lines over wide geographic areas. It provides the top sales executive with a group of specialists — experts in dealer and distributor relations, sales analysis, sales organisation, sales personnel, sales planning, sales promotion, sales training, service, traffic, and warehousing and similar fields. These help to conserve the top sales executives time and free them from excessively detailed work. They make it possible for their chiefs to concentrate their efforts where they have the most skill. Staff specialists assist in increasing overall effectiveness of the department. By delegating problems involving considerable study or detailed analysis to staff executives the top sales executive has more time for planning and for dealing with higher-priority matters.

As staff sales executives do not have authority to issue orders or directives, their recommendations are submitted to the top sales executives, who transmit necessary instructions to the line organisation. Sometimes staff members may be authorised to deal directly with line executives regarding execution of plans and implementation of policies developed by the staff and approved by management. Although acting on behalf of line sales executives in these instances, staff members assume joint responsibility for results. This departure from the normal procedure speeds the translation of staff plans into line action.

Following Figure 11.2 illustrates the line and staff sales organisation. The general sales manager, the advertising manager and the manager of marketing research report to the vice-president in charge of marketing. Six subordinates report to the general sales manager, but only one, the assistant general sales manager, is a line executive. Four of the five staff executives have responsibilities in specialised fields; the fifth, the assistant to the general sales manager, is given more general assignments.

There is difference between the ***assistant to*** and ***assistant***. The ***assistant to*** is a staff executive who is given a broader operating area than those staff specialists with more descriptive titles. In contrast, the ***assistant*** has general line authority delegated by the superior. The assistant general sales manager is an understudy of the general sales manager who performs assignments of a line nature in the name of the superior. The assistant to the general sales manager carries part of the general administrative load that would otherwise be borne by the general sales manager.

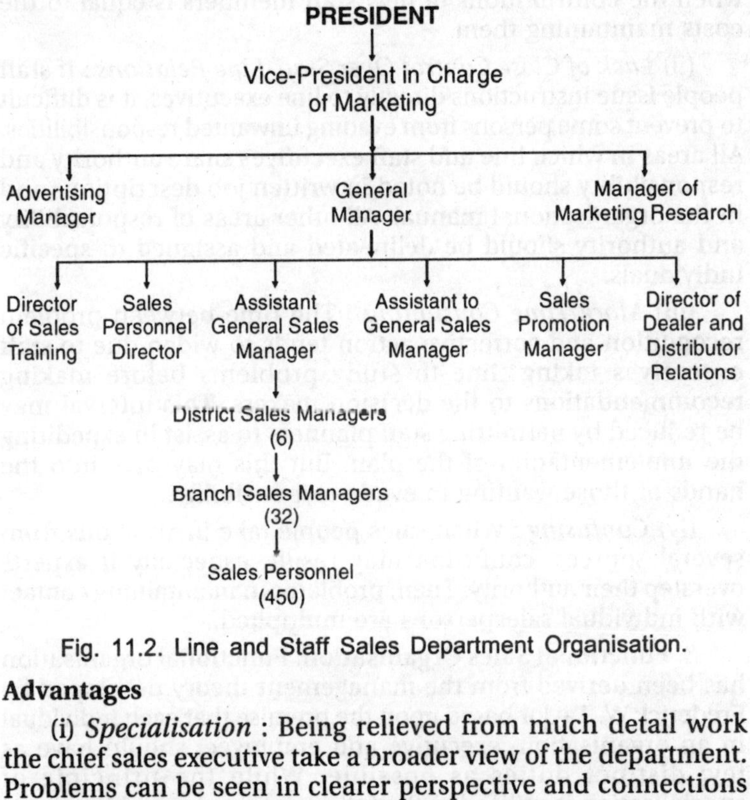


Fig. 11.2. Line and Staff Sales Department Organisation.

## Advantages

(i) *Specialisation* : Being relieved from much detail work the chief sales executive take a broader view of the department. Problems can be seen in clearer perspective and connections between apparently unrelated problems are brought into focus. A pool of experts provides advice and assistance in specialised fields. Planning activities are subdivided and apportioned to staff members and decisions and policies rest on a sounder base than in the line organisation.

(ii) *Better Control and Coordination* : The top sales executive can concentrate on control and coordination of subordinates. As staff members assume much of the burden of solving problems in their areas, the top sales executive can devote more attention to the human aspects of administration.

**Disadvantages**

(i) *Specialisation* : Coordination of the work of the staff specialists becomes costly. Other administrative expenses also increase, unless the number of staff executives is kept in line with departmental needs. The staff should be expanded only when the contributions of new staff members is equal to the costs maintaining them.

(ii) *Lack of Close Control Over Staff-Line Relations* : If staff people issue instructions directly to line executives, it is difficult to prevent some persons from evading unwanted responsibilities. All areas in which line and staff executives share authority and responsibility should be noted in written job descriptions and in the organisational manual. All other areas of responsibility and authority should be delineated and assigned to specific individuals.

(iii) *More Time Consuming* : The time between problem recognition and corrective action tends to widen due to staff executives taking time to study problems before making recommendations to the decision makers. This interval may be reduced by permitting staff planners to assist in expediting the implementation of the plan. But this may play into the hands of those wanting to evade responsibility.

(iv) *Confusing* : When sales people take instructions from several sources, confusion may result, especially if experts overstep their authority. Then, problems in maintaining contact with individual salespersons are multiplied.

**3. Functional Sales Organisation.** Functional organisation has been derived from the management theory developed by Frederick W. Taylor based upon the premise that each individual in an organisation, executive and employee, should have as few distinct duties as possible. While the principle of specialisation is utilised to the fullest extent, duty assignments and delegations of authority are made according to function. Functional organisation is used principally in highly centralised departments such as manufacturing. It is little used in departments that are by nature decentralised such as the sales departments.

In the functional sales department, sales-people receive instructions from several executives but on different aspects of their work. Provision for coordinating the functional executives is made only at the top of the structure. Executives at lower levels do not have coordinating responsibilities. All specialists in a functional organisation have functional authority. Instructions and even policies, can be put into effect with or without prior approval of the top-level coordinating executive.

Figure 11.3 shows functional sales organisational structure. The coordinating executive is the director of sales administration. All executives on the next level are specialists. Sales personnel receive instructions from six different executives.

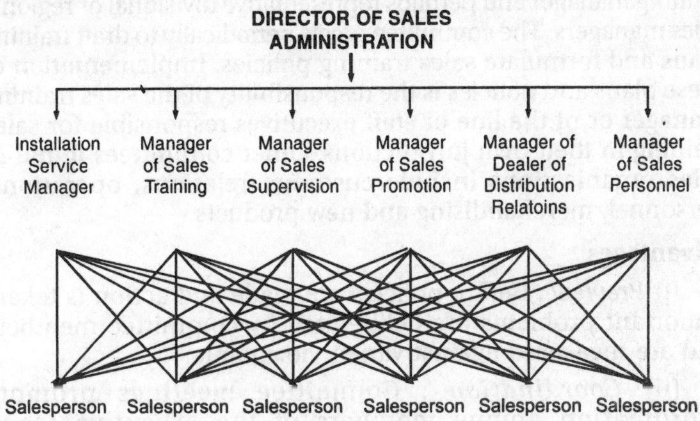


Fig. 11.3. Functional Type of Sales Organisation

**Advantages**

(i) *Improved Performance* : Specialised activities are assigned to experts, whose guidance helps in increasing the effectiveness of the sales force. The sheer size of the sales force in many large firms makes the highly centralised sales operations of a functional organisation impractical.

(ii) *Coordination* : In the functional model a lone official coordinates the specialists. Most large firms need more administrative levels when the marketing area is extensive, when the product line is wide or when large number of selling personnel are required.

**Disadvantages**

(i) *Inappropriate* : In its pure form functional organisation for the sales department is inappropriate.

(ii) *Impractical* : The practicality of functional organisation for the sales department is questionable. Small and medium-sized firms do not find it feasible, or financially viable to utilise the high degree of division of labour. Certain characteristics of functional organisation cause it to be rejected even by most large firms.

**4. Committee Sales Organisation.** The committee is a method of organising the executive group for planning and policy formulation while leaving actual operations to individual executives. Many firms have a sales training committee comprised of the general sales manager, his or her assistants, the sales training manager and perhaps representative divisional or regional sales managers. The committee meets periodically to draft training plans and formulate sales training policies. Implementation of these plans and policies is the responsibility of the sales training manager or of the line or staff executives responsible for sales training in their own jurisdictions. Other committees found in sales organisations include customer relations, operations, personnel, merchandising and new products.

**Advantages**

(i) *Preview* : Before policies are made and action is taken, important problems are deliberated by committee members and are measured against varied viewpoints.

(ii) *Coordination* : Committee meetings promote coordination among members of the executive team. Cooperation is likely to be better than under any other organisation plan. Committees provide focal points for discussion and for the making of suggestions.

**Precautions**

(i) Many companies prohibit committees from making decisions or formulating policies. No committee should develop into a vehicle for the evasion of responsibility.

(ii) The agenda must be planned and controlled to avoid wasting time of executives net directly interested in the topics considered.

(iii) If the chairperson keeps the discussion focused upon the subject at hand the tendency for committees to consume large amounts of time is counteracted.

(iv) Chairpersons should guide discussions within specified bounds, but they should not force their opinions on others.

## FIELD ORGANISATION OF THE SALES DEPARTMENT

Every growing company faces the necessity for establishing a field sales organisation. When a company is young, the sales manager personally supervises field selling operations. Only a few salespeople are employed. The sales force travels out of the home office. The marketing area is small. As more salespersons are added, it becomes difficult to supervise and control them. To make growth in sales volume parallel to the sales force, either the same marketing area must be worked more intensively or new areas must be penetrated. Both alternatives require supervision and control of field sales personnel.

The filed organisation consists of all employees of the department who work away from the home office. All outside salespeople are included such as travelling sales supervisors, branch and district managers, and clerical employees in branch and district offices. Also included are service, repair, and sales promotion personnel. These are not concerned directly with increasing the effectiveness of field selling operations.

**Objectives**

1. To facilitate the task.
2. To improve the chances that salespeople will achieve their goals.

**Influences**

(i) *The Makeup* : The makeup of the field organisation is influenced by the organisational philosophy of the management. Companies that consider centralisation desirable have complex supervisory organisations. Each salesperson is subjected to close supervision — hence the need for a considerable force of supervisors. Firms that believe in decentralisation, in contrast, permit individuals in the field to operate more on their own.

(ii) *The Size* : (a) The larger the firm, assuming similar sales-related marketing policies, the greater the required number of salespeople, supervisors and regional, branch and district managers.

(b) The relative emphasis placed on personal selling in the marketing programme affects the size of the field organisation. For example, the firm selling directly to retailers, ultimate consumers or industrial users commits itself to the performance of a sizable personal selling task and it requires a field organisation of commensurate size. In contrast, companies using wholesalers find that their field organisations can be correspondingly smaller, since parts of the personal selling and other tasks are transferred to these middlemen.

(c) Other factors affecting the size of the field organisation include desired frequency of sales calls, number of customers and prospects and geographical spread of sales counts.

## DISTINCTIONS IN CENTRALISATION AND DECENTRALISATION

**1. Meaning.** In the centralised sales organisation all activities are administered from a central headquarter. The central sales office has full responsibility for recruiting, selecting, training, compensating, supervising, motivating, controlling and evaluating the sales force. In a decentralised organisation, on the other hand, all these activities are handled by field sales executives. In a decentralised sales organisation there is decentralisation in management of various selling tasks and in performance of certain important personnel management activities. For example, branch or district sales offices may do the recruiting, selecting, motivating and supervising; the central headquarters may handle training, compensating and evaluating and the branches and the central headquarters may share responsibility, in proportions varying with the marketing situation and management philosophy, for other aspects of sales force management. However, it is rare for sales force management to be 100 per cent centralised or decentralised. Management's appraisal of relative costs and effectiveness results in some aspects being centralised and others decentralised.

**2. Use.** Smaller companies having few sales people and confining their operations to a small geographical area, keeping the unit of sales high, the sales call frequency low and the caliber of salespersons relatively high, incline toward centralised sales force management. Manufacturing firms relying almost entirely upon specialised wholesale middlemen for marketing of their products needing only minimum sales forces, tend toward centralisation. Local wholesalers with restricted sales areas having small sales forces are highly centralised by the nature of their operations. While the principal factor determining centralisation is a small size of sales force, other marketing factors also move a company in this direction.

High decentralisation in sales force management is found mainly among companies with large sales forces. A manufacturing firm distributing a wide line of consumer products over a vast market area and selling directly to varied retailers is likely to have considerable decentralisation. Wherever marketing conditions require large sales forces, decentralisation is more attractive than centralisation.

As a company grows, there is a strong pull in the direction of sales force decentralisation even though it requires at least one more level of sales management and the maintenance of branch and district offices (or both). With growth, the advantages of decentralised sales force management increasingly outweigh the higher costs.

**Advantages of Decentralisation**

**1. Sales Volume.** More intensive cultivation of the market and consequently a higher sales volume to absorb the higher fixed costs.

**2. Control and Supervision.** More effective control, improved supervision and increased sales productivity resulting from the addition of at least one intermediate level of sales executives and from reduction of geographical separations of executives and sales personnel.

**3. Customer Service.** Improved customer service stemming from effective control of sales personnel.

**4. Costs of Territorial Break in Time.** Reduced need for and costs of territorial "break-in" time, since more salepersons are recruited from the areas to which they are assigned.

**5. Improved Sales force Morale.** This is because there are more frequent contacts with executives, reductions in travel time and fewer nights away from home.

**6. Lower Travel Expenses.** This is because salespeople are dispatched from decentralised points and fewer field trips by home office sales executives are required.

**7. A "built-in" Management Development Program.** This is because branch and district offices provide realistic training and serve as proving grounds for future high-level sales executives.

## TYPES OF LINE AUTHORITY

Line authority and responsibility become excessively burdensome for the top sales executive as marketing operations expand. When there is an increasing number of people to supervise, the first remedial step taken is to add a general line assistant, such as an assistant general sales manager. As the burden of line administrative work grows, it is necessary to provide additional assistants who are given line responsibilities narrower than those of the assistant general sales manager. Their assignments cover a limited area of operations although they work with a variety of matters. Tasks of line administration are subdivided among these new assistants (1) by geographic area, (2) by products, or (3) by customers or marketing channels.

**1. Geographic Division.** Geographic division is usually made first into regions or divisions. These may or may not be broken down further into districts or branches. The large firm is likely to subdivide line authority geographically particularly if the characteristics of large numbers of customers vary by geographic location, if different selling problems are encountered in different areas or if certain products are more strongly demanded in some regions than in others. As more customers are added and as wider area is cultivated, the size of the sales task increases enormously, there is an even more compelling reason for dividing line authority geographically. Setting up geographic divisions the sales task comes down to manageable proportions. Secondary line executives are delegated authority to conduct sales operations within smaller areas when centralised administration becomes too great a burden for the top sales executives.

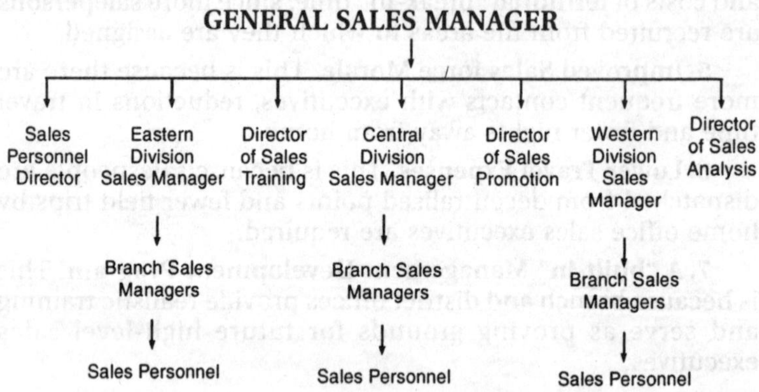


Fig. 11.4. Line Authority Geographically.

**Advantages**

(i) Local problems are handled speedily.

(ii) Many questions of importance to customers can be answered by executives personally acquainted with local conditions.

(iii) Shortening the lines of communication makes possible closer supervision of salespeople, which, in turn, helps in improving customer service.

(iv) Local markets can be cultivated intensively and tactics of local competitors can be met and countered in the field.

**Disadvantages**

(i) As this system calls for multiple offices, administrative expenses increase.

(ii) The top executive faces coordinating several regional operations. Conflicting policies may develop in different regions unless this coordination is effective.

**2. Product Division**. In product division of line authority the sales task is split among subordinate line executives, each of whom directs sales operations for part of the product line. More than one sales force may be required when authority is so divided. As some company's product lines are too wide to be distributed economically by a single sales force, while others sell both highly and non-technical products, some salespeople need specialised training and some do not. Economics of a single sales force are reduced or eliminated in still others because different products are marketed to different types of customers.

In figure 11.5, the customary line and staff organisation has been retained while in Figure 11.6, the primary division is on the basis of products and each product manager has his own staff of specialists. The use of separate staffs, shown in Figure 11.6 is unusual. Due to the expenses incurred in maintaining duplicate staffs, most companies, after mergers, gradually change the organisation to its basic line and staff form shown in Figure 11.5.

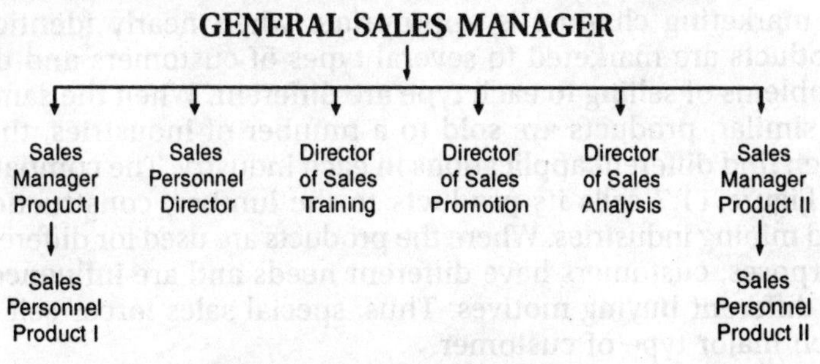


Fig. 11.5 Line Authority Subdivided by Products, but Retaining Basic Line and Staff Form.

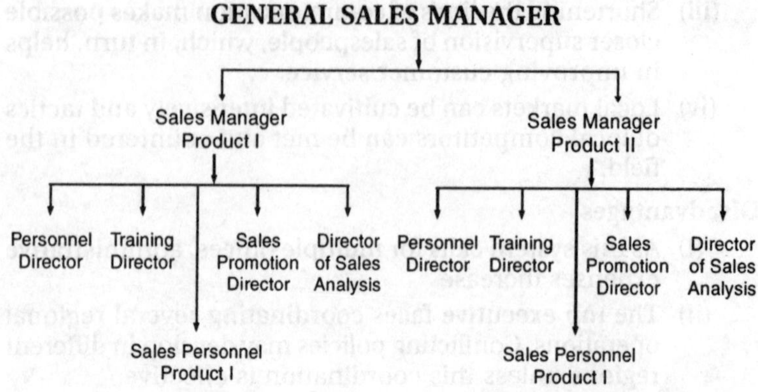


Fig. 11.6. Line Authority Subdivided by Products Utilizing Duplicate Staffs.

The products type of sales organisation should be used where the benefits of product specialisation outweigh the additional expenses. If they do not, it is wiser to organise the sales force on some other basis. Gains associated with specialised salespersons, who concentrate on selling specific products, must be outweighed against increased expenses. Maintaining more than one sales force results in higher administrative and travel expenses. Some times two company sales personnel selling different products make calls on the same customers. Although specialised salespeople may give more "push" to individual products, many customers object to multiple calls from the same company. For companies selling broadly diversified lines, reaching different markets with different products and encountering unique selling problems for the various products, the benefits of specialised sales force are greatest.

**3. Customer (or Marketing Channel) Division.** Customer or marketing channel is appropriate when nearly identical products are marketed to several types of customers and the problems of selling to each type are different. When the same, or similar, products are sold to a number of industries, they often find different applications in each industry. The company in Figure 11.7 sells its products to the lumber, construction and mining industries. Where the products are used for different purposes, customers have different needs and are influenced by different buying motives. Thus, special sales forces sell to each major type of customer.

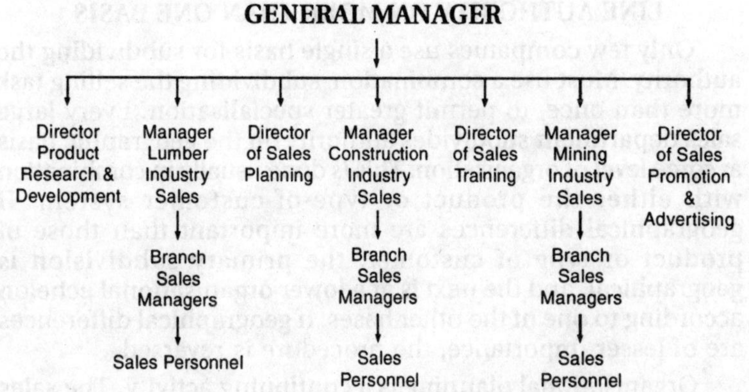


Fig. 11.7. Line Authority Subdivided by Type of Customer.

Companies in the consumer-goods field, pattern their sales organisation after the marketing channels. Although ultimate consumers may be substantially a like, they must be frequently reached in different ways. Problems of distributing to chain stores are often those of selling to independent wholesalers and retailers. Specialised sale training programmes are often required. In such cases the problems of selling vary more with the marketing channel than they do with the product or geographical location. Therefore, line authority is subdivided according to marketing channels.

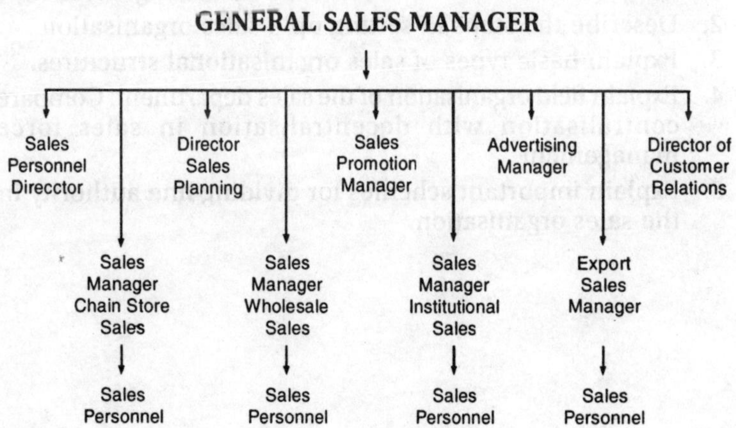


Fig. 11.8. Sales Department with Line Authority Subdivided by Marketing Channel.

## LINE AUTHORITY ON MORE THAN ONE BASIS

Only few companies use a single basis for subdividing the authority. Most use a combination, subdividing the selling task more than once, to permit greater specialisation. Every large sales department subdivides authority on the geographic basis at some level of organisation. This is done usually in combination with either the product or type-of-customer system. If geographical differences are more important than those of product or type of customer, the primary subdivision is geographical, and the next is at a lower organisational echelon according to one of the other bases. If geographical differences are of lesser importance, the procedure is reversed.

Organisational planning is a continuing activity. The sales department structure should be adjusted to changing marketing needs. Today there is less emphasis on securing order and more attention is paid to control of costs and expenses and the realisation of net profits. Therefore, an increasing number of sales organisations are structured more logically. Selling activities are performed with less waste effort, while total effectiveness of the sales effort is enhanced resulting in significant benefits to the firms achieving them and to their customers.

## QUESTIONS FOR EXERCISE

1. Discuss the value and objectives of sales organisation.
2. Describe the steps in setting up a sales organisation.
3. Explain basic types of sales organisational structures.
4. Explain field organisation of the sales department. Compare centralisation with decentralisation in sales force management.
5. Explain important schemes for dividing line authority in the sales organisation.

# 12

# MARKETING STRATEGY IN PERSONAL-SELLING

## THE COMPETITIVE SETTING

The competitive setting for a company is beyond the control of management. A company's competitive posture is shaped by (1) the competitive setting, (2) overall marketing strategy and (3) the effectiveness of strategy implementation. The management influences the company's competitive posture by making key decision on products, distribution, pricing and promotion. Unifying these key decisions into an overall marketing strategy provides the plan for the required kind of posture.

The personal-selling objectives are achieved through personal-selling strategy. Sales-related marketing policies guide key decisions in personal-selling strategy on the kind and size of required sales force. While most companies field a single sales force made up on one kind of salesperson, multi product companies utilize different sizes of sales forces to sell individual product lines. Other companies sell the same or similar products to different market segments through separate kinds and sizes of sales force. The decision on kind of salesperson defines the role that sales personnel play in their contacts with customers and prospects. The decision on sales force size dictates the deployment of sales personnel and the frequencies and intensities of their contacts with customers and prospects. The extent to which overall personal-selling objectives are achieved is effectiveness with which these roles are played by the sales force.

Realisation of the planned competitive posture depends on effective implementation of marketing strategy. It means the successful conversion of marketing plans into realities. Implementation of marketing strategy has short and long-run aspects. With its planning orientation marketing management concentrates on the long-run aspects. Short-run accomplishments add up to long-run achievement. Marketing management depends upon sales management to lead the personal sales force to achieve personal-selling objectives and to produce "bottom-line" results in terms of sales volume, profits and growth.

## TYPES OF COMPETITIVE SETTINGS

Individual companies operate in different competitive settings. Industries differ as to maturity and the number of competitors. Economists identify four basic kinds of competitive settings: (1) pure competition, (2) monopolistic competition, (3) oligopolistic competition, and (4) no direct competition. There are various components of overall marketing strategy with different levels of importance in each competitive setting. The importance of the personal-selling component is significant for sales management.

### 1. Pure Competition

According to economists, pure competition is a market setting with large numbers of buyers and sellers, none of which is powerful enough to control or to influence the prevailing market price. Economists assume that (1) relative to the market no single buyer or seller is so large that it can appreciably affect the product's total demand or supply; (2) buyers are indifferent as to which sellers they buy from as all sellers' products are identical; (3) there is no artificial restraint on price fixing or administering of prices of individual companies, trade association, labour unions or others and (4) all buyers are always informed about all sellers' prices.

These assumptions do not represent the "real world" in an industry. The economists wrongly assume that sellers and buyers are in direct contact. In the real world there are no industries operating under pure competition.

### 2. Monopolistic Competition

(i) *Modern Competitive Setting* : Most modern marketers operate in monopolistic competition settings. It means that some or all of the assumptions of pure competition are wrong. Monopolistic competition requires a large number of sellers of a generic kind of product. Each seller's brand is in some way differentiated from every other brand. Furthermore, under monopolistic competition, it is easy for additional competitors to enter the market. Retailers enter as private-label competitors.

This is the competitive setting of many products during late phases of their market growth.

(ii) *Brand Differentiation* : Every seller's brand of product can be differentiated from competing brands. Consumers are convinced that different brands of "identical" products are not exactly alike. It provides individual marketers opportunities to build brand preferences among buyers to control a share of the market. Most consumers are not fully informed about the offerings of competing sellers.

Sellers differentiate their "market offerings" through individualizing one or several components of overall marketing strategy:

1. Unique packaging may differentiate the product.

2. An unusual distribution method may differentiate the product's distribution.

3. The pricing gimmicks, such as "cents-off" pricing and list pricing may differentiate the product's pricing.

4. The main kind of sellers differentiation of products in the market-growth and market-maturity is through promotional strategy.

5. Advertising differentiates the brand in the minds of final buyers and stimulates selective demand.

6. Personal selling cures and maintains the desired distribution intensity and middlemen provide the needed "push".

Characterized by monopolistic competition, competitive settings provide marketing opportunities. These require skill in planning and implementing overall strategy:

1. The key element in the overall marketing strategy for these products is the ability to differentiate the product.

2. Appropriate promotion is the *critical element in implementing* such an overall marketing strategy.

3. Advertising relates market messages to final buyers.

4. Personal selling services the distribution network and stimulates promotional efforts by the middlemen.

**3. Oligopolistic Competition**

In the United States and other developed countries, most marketers today operate under oligopolistic competition. It is a competitive setting where the number of competitors is so small that they are individually identified and known to each other. It is difficult for new competitors to enter the market. Each competitor is a large organization having a large market share that changes in its overall marketing strategy having direct repercussions on the others. Each weighs the possible reactions of each of its competitors in formulating and implementing its own overall marketing strategy. Oligopolistic competition develops in marketing products during a late phase of their growth or during an early phase of their market maturity.

Oligopolies exist in such industries as automobiles, appliances, personal computers, soaps and detergents, and shoes in the consumer-goods field and in data-processing equipment, steel, aluminium, textile machinery, and machine tools in the industrial-goods field. While the successful firms keep on growing, the less successful fail or disappear, for example, the soap and auto industries have been reduced from numerous competitors to a small group.

Oligopoly produces the most aggressive competition. While few large companies dominate the industry, the competitive moves of any one affects the entire market. If a competitor introduces a new variation of a basic product, the other competitors must respond appropriately and almost instantaneously. Thus, competitors' actions are watched closely. Marketing changes by one firm are matched or otherwise countered. Changes in a competitor's product, its distribution, its promotion are imitated, improved upon or otherwise countered by competitors rapidly as counter-offensives. Price changes by individual industry members are often matched by others almost immediately. Industry-wide price adjustments are made quickly.

Under oligopolistic competition personal selling strategy plays important roles in building and maintaining dealer cooperation, in servicing the distribution network and in gathering information on competitors activities. The promotional strategy involves both advertising and personal selling. Both play highly critical roles in the successful implementation of overall marketing strategy.

**Status of Monopolist and Innovative Marketer**

1. Both the monopolist and the company marketing of a radically new and different product in its market-pioneering life-cycle stage have indirect competitors.

2. Both vie with sellers in other industries for the same prospects, interest and buying decisions.

3. Both must initiate and stimulate primary demand through promotional personal selling and advertising strategies.

4. Both need distribution strategies providing for marketing channels.

5. Both require a pricing strategy.

6. Both the monopolist and the innovating marketer seek to integrate their individual product, distribution, promotion including personal selling, and advertising and pricing strategies into overall marketing strategies consistent with their long-term goals keeping all elements of overall strategy "in balance".

## FACTORS INFLUENCING PERSONAL-SELLING STRATEGY

### 1. Impact of Qualitative Objectives

(i) *Personal Selling Objectives* : Varying with the kind of competitive setting the qualitative personal-selling objectives concerned with the nature of the contribution made by personal selling important are in achieving long-term company objectives. These influence both the nature of the sales job and the size of the sales force. A company expecting its salespeople to do the entire selling job needs a different kind of sales staff, than a company that expects its salespeople only to "service" existing accounts backed with heavy advertising and other promotion. Long term qualitative objectives are carried over from one operating period to another. When qualitative objectives change, there are changes in the nature of the sales job and in the size of the sales force.

(ii) *Quantitative Objectives* : The quantitative personal-selling objectives varying with the kind of competitive setting are short term and adjusted from one operating period to another. Companies regard the sales volume objective as the most critical in all competitive settings. Most companies benefit from assigning other types of quantitative personal-selling objectives in all competitive settings. For instance, a company directs that sales volume be obtained in ways that contribute to profit objectives. Companies assign still other quantitative objectives in monopolistic and oligopolistic competitive settings including ones specifying the securing and/or retaining of a certain market share.

Like the qualitative personal-selling objectives, quantitative personal-selling objectives influence both the nature of the sales job and sales force size. A company that increases its sales volume objective significantly either expects its sales force to perform differently or increases the size of the sales force or does both. Being short term and changing from one period to the next, the quantitative personal-selling objectives make impact more upon the size of the sales force than upon the nature of the sales job. In all competitive settings and in nearly all companies, changing the nature of the sales job is a rarer event which usually flows from changes in key *qualitative* personal-selling objectives.

**2. Sales-Related Marketing Policies.** Sales-related marketing policies are the guidelines for both qualitative and quantitative personal-selling objectives, providing guidance on what to sell (product policies) and to whom to sell (distribution policies). These shape the fundamental nature of a company. There are important determinants of the kind of sales personnel and their total number. Pricing policies also have an important impact on the kind of sales staff. Salespeople have to persuade target buyers to accept the company's products at the prices asked. Like personal-selling objectives, sales-related marketing policies vary with the competitive setting. They must be attuned to a company's particular situation particularly under conditions of monopolistic or oligopolistic competition.

**3. The Kind of Sales Personnel.** The kind of sales personnel, one key decision on personal-selling strategy, requires consideration of qualitative personal-selling objectives.

(i) What contribution toward the company's long-term overall objectives should be expected from those performing selling jobs?

(ii) What should be the duties and responsibilities of these individuals?

(iii) How should their job performance be measured?

Management must face up to these questions when it decides the kinds of sales personnel it requires.

About the kind of sales personnel best fitted to serve its needs, each company has some degree of distinctiveness. Each company deals with a unique set of marketing factors, such as the strengths and weaknesses of what it sells, the motivations and buying practices of whom it sells to, its pricing strategy and the relative strengths and weaknesses of competitors. Different selling jobs require different levels of selling and non-selling abilities, training and technical and other knowledge.

For example, the bottler's driver-salesperson doing route selling has a considerably different job from that of the salesperson who sells complex industrial installations.

In determining the kind of sales personnel, the job objectives, the duties and responsibilities and the performance measures are expected of them. Knowing the particular job means knowing the particular job for the particular salesperson. Different salespersons in the same company generally have quite different jobs. Knowing the particular job helps management in fitting the job to the person and the person to the job.

**4. Product Market Analysis.** No one can sell all kinds of products to all kinds of customers. While a salesperson sells a single product to many kinds of customers, another salesperson sells a wide line of products to a single kind of customers. However, most salespeople have to sell some products to some kinds of customers. Selling jobs are therefore put into three classifications: (1) product specialists, (2) market specialists and (3) combinations of product and market specialization.

Sales job analysis requires definition of the nature of product-market interactions. Companies using product-market grids construct them showing finer details of product-market interactions. This demands thorough analysis and classification of markets and products.

In Figure 12.1, the "boxes" indicate the different customers who might be sold the different products. Some boxes are blacked in, others left empty as management decides which customers should be sold which products. This answers the question whether sales personnel should be product specialists, market specialists or a combination.

(i) *Product Specialization* : It is indicated when the product is highly technical requiring salesperson to advise on uses and applications.

(ii) *Market Specialization* : It is called for when the product is non-technical but different kinds of customers have unique buying problems, require special sales approaches or need special service.

(iii) *Consideration* : In many cases, analysis reveals that sales personnel need both considerable knowledge of more than a single company product line and their applications as well as skills in dealing with more than one kind of customer.

The type and amount of specialization require consideration of both the interdependence dimension and the expertise dimension. As shown in figure, the four possible combinations of these two dimensions results in four different kinds of selling roles.

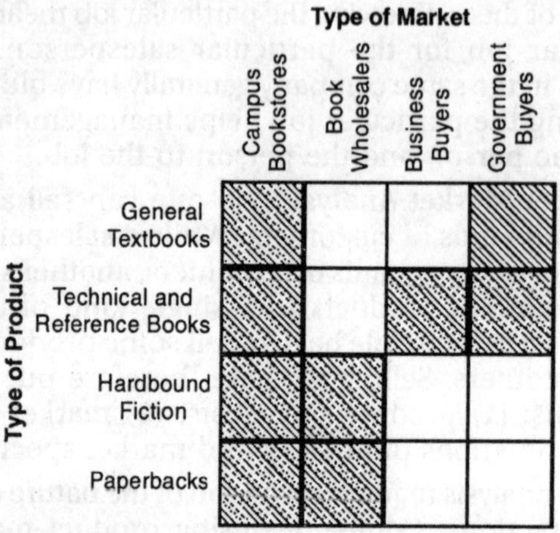


Fig. 12.1. Product-Market Grid for a Book Publishing Company

(i) *Dominant Interdependence* :

(a) ***Between Customers*** : It is between customers rather than between products, that sales personnel should be specialists. When the needed dominant expertise is in product technologies they should be product specialists. When the needed dominant expertise is in customers, applications. They should be customer specialists needing the support of market managers who provide the needed prospect expertise through their specialization in application in particular industries.

(b) ***Between Products*** : If the dominant interdependence is between products, the selling organization needs staffing by full-line salespersons.

(ii) *Product Technologies* : Salespersons sell the full line to all kinds of prospects and are supported by product managers who provide the needed product expertise if product technologies require the most expertise.

(iii) *Customers Applications* : The customers, applications require the most expertise; salespersons sell the full line to particular kinds of prospects.

## OTHER MARKETING ELEMENTS

If most customers are large, salespeople need different talents than if most customers are small. The geographical location of a territory has bearing on the best type of salesperson, particularly where local prejudice favours "natives" as opposed to "outsiders."

| Dominant Interdependence / Dominant Expertise | Between Customers | Between Products |
|---|---|---|
| Product Technologies Applications | Product Specialists | Full-Line Salespersons (supported by Product Managers) |
| Customer Applications | Customer Specialists (Supported by Market Managers) | Full-Line Salespersons supported by Kind of Customer |

Fig. 12.2. Types and Amounts of Specialization in Selling Organizations

## ORDER TAKER *VS.* GETTER

The role that a company expects its sales personnel to play in securing orders determines the kind of sales staff required. In some situations all salespeople seek orders aggressively. In others they only take orders coming their way. The relative emphasis on order taking and order getting varies in different selling environments. As product has been strongly pre-sold to consumers and retailers reorder automatically, the driver-salesperson for a soft drink bottling company is primarily an order taker. On the contrary, the encyclopedia salesperson calling on householders most often functions as an order getter.

Salespersons may be either active or passive forces in securing orders depending on whether promotional strategy places major reliance on personal selling or advertising. If the promotional strategy of a manufacturer is to rely heavily upon advertising to attract business and build demand, marketing channels include several layers of middlemen. The role of the manufacturer's salespersons is that of order taker primarily and order getter incidentally. Marketing channels contain a minimum number of layers of middlemen and the salesperson's role is chiefly order getting when advertising is used mainly to back up personal selling.

Both in consumer goods and industrial marketing, there are cases in which the salesperson plays only a minor indirect role in securing orders, his major role being concerned with other matters. In consumer-goods marketing his major role is to assist middlemen in making sales to their customers while orders from customers result indirectly, rather than directly. In industrial-goods marketing, the "sales engineer" plays two major roles.

1. Advisor to middlemen and customers on technical product features and applications and

2. Design consultant to middlemen and industrial users on installations or processes incorporating the manufacturer's products. As the result of playing their major roles as advisors and design consultants, sales engineers also secure orders indirectly.

## BASIC SELLING STYLES

**1. Trade Selling**. In it, the salesperson develops and maintains long-term relations with a stable group of customers. This is low-key selling, with little or no pressure. The job is dull and routine. This selling style predominates in marketing food and apparel and in wholesaling. It applies primarily to products that have well-established markets. Advertising and other forms of promotion are more vital to overall marketing strategy. The salesperson has to help customers build up their volume through providing promotional assistance. For a line of breakfast cereals he devotes much time to promotional work with retailers and wholesalers taking inventory, refilling shelves, suggesting reorders and setting up displays.

**2. Missionary Selling.** There the salesperson's main objective is to increase the company's sales volume by assisting customers with their selling efforts. He is only incidentally concerned with securing orders, since orders result from his primary public relations and promotional efforts with indirect customers. His job is to persuade indirect customers to buy from the company's direct customers. For a pharmaceutical manufacturer he calls on the retail druggist to acquaint him or her with a new product and to urge the druggist to stock it. Thus he seeks to persuade pharmacists to buy from drug wholesalers who are the direct customers. In some situations, he may call on individuals and institutions who do not buy the product themselves but who influence its purchase. An example is the medical "detailer" who calls on doctors and hospitals to acquaint them with new drugs. Like trade selling this style of selling is low key. It does not require high-level technical training or ability.

**3. Technical Selling.** In this style the salesperson deals primarily with the company's established accounts. His main objective is to increase the volume of purchase by providing technical advice and assistance. He performs advisory functions similar to those of the missionary salesperson. In addition, he sells direct to industrial users and other buyers. He devotes considerable time to acquainting industrial users with technical product characteristics and applications. He helps them in designing installations or processes that incorporate the company's products. The ability to identify, analyse and solve customer's problems is important.

He often specializes either by products or markets. In selling large made-to-order installations such as steam turbines and electric generators, he works with only one item in the product line. Such technical salespeople specialize in servicing industrial accounts or government procurement agencies.

**4. New-Business Selling.** It this selling style, the salesperson's main job is to find and obtain new customers to convert prospects into customers. Specializing in new-business selling, he should be unusually creative and ingenious and possess a high degree of resourcefulness. Most firms, however, expect their regular sales staff to do new-business selling also. As it is rare for the same individual to possess both needed sets of talents and because there is a tendency for salespeople to neglect new-business selling in favour of servicing established accounts, some experts advocate the specialization of sales personnel into two separate groups, one to concentrate on retaining existing accounts and the other to focus on converting prospects into customers.

## METHODS OF DETERMINING THE SIZE OF THE SALES FORCE

Having determined the type of salesperson that best fits the company's needs, management determines how many are required to meet the sales volume and profit objectives. Opportunities for sales and profits go unexploited if the company has too few salespersons. If it has too many salespersons, excessive expenditure for personal-selling reduces net profits. Thus, it is difficult to determine the exact number of salespersons that a particular company should have. Following three basic approaches each providing needed insights on the "right size" of sales force arė used in approximating this number: (1) the workload method, (2) the sales potential method and (3) the incremental method.

**1. Workload Method.** It is based on the assumption that all sales personnel should shoulder equal workloads. Management first estimates the total workload involved in covering the company's entire market and then divides by the workload that an individual salesperson should be able to handle. Companies applying this approach assume the interactions of three major factors — customers size, sales volume potential, and travel load — to determine the total workload involved in covering the entire market.

Following six steps are applied in the workload approach:

(i) *Classifying Customers, both Present and Prospective, into Volume Potential Categories* : Assuming that there are 880 present and prospective customers they are classified by sales volume potential as

| | |
|---|---|
| Class A, large | 150 accounts |
| Class B, medium | 220 |
| Class C, small | 510 |

(ii) *Deciding on the Length of Time per Sales call and Desired Call Frequencies on Each Class* : Assuming that both present and prospective customers require the same amount of time per sales call and the same call frequencies per year, the size is calculated as follows:

| | |
|---|---|
| Class A: 60 minutes/call × 52 calls/year | = 52 hours/year |
| Class B: 30 minutes/call × 24 calls/year | = 12 hours/year |
| Class C: 15 minutes/call × 12 calls/year | = 3 hours/year |

(iii) *Calculating the Total Workload involved in Covering the Entire Market* : This calculation is follows:

| | |
|---|---|
| Class A: 150 accounts × 52 hours/year | = 7,800 hours |
| Class B: 220 accounts × 12 hours/year | = 2,640 hours |
| Class C: 510 accounts × 3 hours/year | = 1,530 hours |
| Total | 11,970 hours |

(iv) *Determining the Total Work Time Available per Salesperson* : If management decides that salespeople should work 40 hours per week, 48 weeks per year then each salespersons has available:

40 hours/week × 48 weeks = 1,920 hours/year

(v) *Dividing the Total Work Available Per Salesperson by Task.* Assuming that management specifies that sales personnel should apportion their time as follows:

| | | |
|---|---|---|
| Selling tasks | 45% | 864 hours |
| Non-selling tasks | 30% | 576 hours |
| Travelling | 25% | 480 hours |
| | 100% | 1,920 hours |

(vi) *Calculating the Total Number of Salespeople Needed* : Dividing the total market workload by the total selling time available per salesperson:

$$\frac{11{,}970 \text{ Hours}}{864 \text{ Hours}} = 14 \text{ Salespeople needed}$$

Easy to understand and easy to apply, the workload approach is attractive to practicing sales executives.

**Disadvantages**

(i) *Disregards Profit as an Explicit Consideration* : Though management can take profit criteria into consideration in determining lengths and frequencies of sales calls, but the optimum length and frequency of any particular sales call depends upon many factors other than account size, such as the gross margin on the product mix purchased by an account, the expenses incurred in servicing an account and an account's likely responses to changed levels of selling effort.

(ii) *Assumption of Equality* : The workload approach is based on the inherent assumption that not only should all sales personnel have the same work load but they all can and will utilize their time with equal efficiency. Some salespersons accomplish more in a shorter time than others can although a relation exists between the amount of time spent on calling on an account and the size of the order received.

(iii) *Value of Quality* : The quality of time invested in a sales call is as important as the "quantity of time spent on a sales call."

**2. Sales Potential Method.** The method is based on the assumption that performance of the set of activities contained in the job description represents one sales personnel unit. A particular salesperson may represent either more or less than one sales personnel unit. If the individual's performance is excellent, he may do the job of more than one unit. If his performance is below par, he or she may do less. If management expects all company sales personnel to perform as specified in the job description, then the number of salespersons required equals the number of units of sales personnel required. As sales job descriptions are constructed on management's assumption they describe what the average salesperson with average performance will accomplish. Hence, one can estimate the number of dollars of sales volume that each salesperson should produce. Dividing this amount into forecasted sales volume and allowing for sales force turnover results in an estimate of the number of salepeople needed as per the following equation:

$$N = \frac{S}{P} + T\left(\frac{S}{P}\right)$$

This reduces to

$$N = \frac{S}{P} + (1 + T)$$

Where

N = number of sales personnel units

S = forecasted sales volume

P = estimated sales productivity of one sales personnel unit

T = allowance for rate of sales force turnover

Consider a firm with forecasted sales of $1 million, estimated sales productivity per sales personnel unit of $100,000 and an estimated annual rate of sales force turnover of 10 per cent. Inserting these figures in the equation, we have

$$N = \frac{\$1{,}000{,}000}{\$1{,}00{,}000} \times 1.10$$

N = 11 sales personnel units

**Disadvantages**

(i) Though this is a simplified model for determining the size of a sales force, it does not include the lead times required for seeking out, hiring and training salespeople to the desired level of sales productivity. Actual planning models have built-in lead and lag relations to allow for such requirements. If two months of full-time training are required to bring a new salesperson up to the desired productivity, recruiting must lead actual need for the new salesperson by two months. The assumption that sales potentials are identical in all territories is similar to the assumption that the number of sales personnel units required is the same as the number of salespersons needed. Where this assumption does not hold, the model should be adjusted accordingly.

(ii) With the factor being estimated (*N, S, P, T*) the company's difficulties in making estimates for this model vary. The crucial estimate of the sales productivity of one unit of sales strength relies heavily on the accuracy and completeness of the sales job description. It depends also on management's appraisal of what reasonably may be expected of those who fill the position. Estimation of the sales force turnover rate depends on review of previous experience and anticipation of such changes as retirements and promotions. Both the estimates for unit sales productivity and the sales force turnover rate require management to have some means of evaluating the efficiency of individual salespersons and of determining the probabilities that individuals will remain with or leave the sales force during the planning period.

(iii) In many situations, the magnitude of the sales forecast is itself influenced by the planned size of the sales force. As it takes time to add significant numbers to the sales force, a realistic sales forecast must take into account the number of salespersons expected to be at management's disposal during the planning period.

(iv) In a new and rapidly growing company, potential sales volume often depends chiefly on the number and ability of its sales. Management may derive the sales forecast by multiplying the estimated sales productivity of its average salesperson by the number it has, can expect to keep and can recruit and train during the planning period. The procedure reverses itself as a company expands distribution geographically and its growth rate slows down. Now the number of sales personnel units required is determined by making the sales forecast first and dividing it by the expected sales productivity of an individual salesperson, making adjustment for anticipated sales force turnover, lead times for recruiting and training and other relevant factors.

**3. Incremental Method.** This is the best approach to determine sales force size. It is based on the proposition that net profits will increase when additional sales personnel are added if the incremental sales revenues exceed the incremental costs incurred. One needs two important items of information : incremental revenue and incremental costs to apply this method.

**Disadvantages**

(i) Most difficult to apply, this method requires, first, that the company develop a sales response function to use in approximating (in terms of sales volume) the market's behaviour in relation to alternative levels of personal-selling effort. For the response function to be useful in setting the size of the sales force, sales volume must be sensitive to changes in the number of sales personnel. Not many companies have the research sophistication required for development of sales response functions, but some apply the basic concept.

(ii) It is doubtful that this method is appropriate where personal-selling is not the primary means of making sales. This is in cases where other forms of promotion, such as advertising, have stronger influences on sales volume than does personal-selling effort.

(iii) According to T.R. Wotruba: "It fails to account possible competitive reactions as well as for the long-term 'investment' effect personal-selling effort."

## INDIVIDUALIZING SELLING STRATEGIES TO CUSTOMERS

The appropriateness of personal-selling strategy is tested when particular salespeople interact with particular customers. From the composite of all such interactions evolves the company's achievement of its personal-selling objectives. Management makes its first key decision on personal-selling strategy when it determines the kind of salesperson needed. It makes its second key decision when it determines the size of the company sales force. But after the desired number of the desired kind of sales personnel have been recruited, trained and assigned to the field, each salesperson must individualize his or her own dealings with each customer. His job is to influence customer behaviour in ways that both benefit the customer and contribute to the achievement of the company's personal-selling objectives.

The extent of the salesperson's success depends on the outcome of interactions with the customers. Whenever he comes into contact with a customer, he says certain things, does certain things and behaves and reacts in certain ways to what the customer says and does. What he says and does and how he behaves and reacts to the customers' behaviour should, and generally does, vary from one sales call to the next.

**Value of Selling Skill**

(i) *Pre-Planning*: The variation in the salesperson's approach to each customer, is a matter of selling skill, which is a function of both how good is his pre-planning of each sales call has been and also his performance on the call itself. In pre-planning, he analyses a great deal of information about the customer and the nature of its business. What are its key objectives and problems? Who in the customer's organization makes and influences buying decisions and what are their aspirations, needs, motives, fears, anxieties, drives and the like? What rival sales personnel from what companies compete for the account's orders and what are they like?

(ii) *Selling Goals* : After analyzing these and similar items of information, he sets definite goals to accomplish on each call.

(iii) *Selling Strategy* : Next, he plots the selling strategy to use on each successive call in an effort to achieve these definite goals, that is, what the salesperson plans to do and when.

(iv) *Sales Calls* : How does he make the scheduled sales calls? If all goes according to plan, the salesperson achieves the goals set for each call and thus contributes to the achievement of the company's overall personal-selling objectives.

How effectively salespeople perform their assigned tasks is closely related to sales management's effectiveness in providing them with instruction on sales techniques.

## QUESTIONS FOR EXERCISE

1. Explain types of competitive setting in which a modern company has to carry on personal selling.

2. Explain various factors influencing personal sales strategy.
3. Analyse the salesperson's role in securing orders and describe kinds of basic selling styles.
4. Explain methods of determining the size of the sales force.
5. How do sales persons individualise selling strategies to customers.

# 13

# SALES AND OTHER DEPARTMENTS

As coordinating the activities of all departments is necessary for making maximum progress toward overall company objectives, it is top management's responsibility. In addition to implementing top management's directives, department heads harmonize their activities so that the tasks of all departments are accomplished effectively. Each understands the functions of other departments. Each is responsible for coordinating his or her department's activities to contribute to company success. While the primary responsibility of top sales executive is to manage the sales department, he knows the operations of other departments. He understands how other departments influence and are influenced by the sales department. A change in one department often has repercussions in others.

## FUNCTIONS OF SALES DEPARTMENT

**1. Supply of Products.** The sales department in a company spearheads the organization's effort to supply customers with ever-increasing quantities of products at profitable prices. It makes the company's reputation rest upon a sound foundation.

**2. Intra-Company Relations.** Company success is affected by the dealings and associations of the sales department with customers and the public. Its relations with other departments influence the company's reputation with the public. Individual sales personnel, as well as the entire department may add to or detract from the company reputation. They must remain alert to their responsibilities for maintaining good relations.

**3. Public Relations.** Sales executives frequently have additional responsibility for public relations because they have close relations with external public Sales executives handle the public relations programme as it pertains to the sales department. They consider the probable public relations, impact when planning and administering department programmes. They maintain satisfactory relations with all those with whom they or their subordinates come into contact.

## COORDINATING METHODS

### 1. Formal

(i) *Grouping Allied Activities under a High-Ranking Executive* : In most companies, chief marketing executives have reporting directly to them the heads of departments performing marketing activities, such as sales, advertising, marketing research, and service. Thus, marketing executives coordinate the operations of departments under them.

(ii) *Coordination through the General Administrative Officers* : The president, executive vice-president or general manager coordinates the operations of all company departments, not just those performing closely related tasks. This method is most widely used in companies having only a small number of departments.

(iii) *Committees* : The third method is to use policy, planning and coordinating committees made up of representatives of concerned departments. Though this appears the weakest method, as no one executive has responsibility for coordination but it often works out quite satisfactorily in practice.

### 2. Informal

Department heads may solve an interdepartmental problem informally while it is still being thrashed out through formal mechanisms. More important than formal coordination, informal coordination is preferred in most companies. Solutions are developed that may or may not be formally adopted later by a coordinating body. Unexpected problems with important interdepartmental implications should be handled with minimum delay, because prolonging their solution is to risk costly friction. Informal solutions are often accepted as tentative and subject to modification after review by the formal coordinating mechanism. The top sales executive maintains satisfactory relations with heads of other departments to arrive informally at workable solutions to problems affecting the sales department. All think of themselves as members of the same team, cooperating in the effort to reach company objectives.

Informal coordinating procedures are more important than formal methods, particularly where frequent communication is required. A study of four companies by R.C. Anderson and

E.W. Cundiff revealed that a large amount of communication took place informally among executives responsible for marketing-related activities. Informal coordination was partly through voluntary exchange of informational copies of correspondence, but largely through informal, non-periodic exchanges of information occurring when executives met, by chance or arrangement, in their offices, or over coffee or meals. This study revealed that one individual or occasionally more than one, served as a communication centre for exchanges of information on each important decision area. In almost every exchange of information that took place with respect to their interest area, acting as "centres," these executives were either receivers or senders. All executives assumed the responsibility for providing a continuous flow of information regarding their areas to everyone in the company who they felt might need or could use the information. The top sales and advertising executives served jointly as communication centres for all activities that create demand, including personal selling, advertising, merchandising, sales promotion, and packaging.

**Problems in Informal Communication**

1. Marketing personnel must be made aware of the need for coordination. The traditional lack of close coordination among marketing-related activities makes this a difficult challenge.

2. Marketing personnel must be given the opportunity to understand the role and responsibilities of other marketing jobs and to know the people holding these jobs. This is especially important when personnel responsible for marketing decision areas report to different superiors.

3. Marketing management must establish a climate that encourages a continuous and free exchange of ideas and information.

The operations of departments performing related marketing activities and of others, such as production, personnel, finance and data processing, where influences are indirect, influence and are influenced by sales department operations.

## MARKETING ACTIVITIES REQUIRING COORDINATION

### 1. Sales and Advertising

(i) Both these departments work toward the same objective though they use different approaches, *i.e.*, stimulation of demand. While personal selling techniques belong to the sales department, non-personal selling techniques belong to advertising department. Both selling efforts need skillful blending to achieve an "optimum promotional mix", a coordination of plans and efforts. Sales forces are planned and directed along lines increasing advertising's impact. Advertising is geared to help sales people at the time of need. Sales department helps the advertising department in selecting themes and media, in preparing schedules and in securing dealers' support for cooperative advertising programmes. Advertising department helps it in furnishing sales aids for the sales force and for dealers and by providing sales leads. Advertising conserves the sales force's time. Prospects pre-sold through advertising are easier to convert into customers. Proper timing and coordination of advertising and personal selling are essential. Promotional programmes need skilful administration by executives understanding both types of selling.

(ii) As both sales and advertising departments work toward the same goals, formal coordination is best achieved by having both department heads report to the same high-ranking executive, such as the marketing vice-president. However, most coordination between these two department is on an informal day-to-day basis, frequent interactions of department heads and subordinates, because so many matters are of joint interest and so many require frequent communications.

**2. Sales and Marketing Information**

(i) In order to obtain maximum returns per rupee spent for marketing information, the sales department must work in close cooperation with the departments producing marketing information. Sometimes this information is provided by marketing research. However, in companies with sophisticated marketing information systems, marketing research is only one of the subsystems providing information inputs. Marketing information systems assist the sales department by gathering data needed for analyzing sales problems, assisting in determining sales potentials and setting quotas, measuring the effectiveness of the sales effort, and assisting with sales tests. On the other hand, the sales department provides many of the raw statistics and other information to the information system needed for sales, marketing analysis and forecasting. Salespeople are often made available to marketing research for field interviewing.

(ii) In sophisticated marketing information systems and marketing research, the sales department works more closely with information personnel. Close cooperation becomes even more critical when sales and information personnel jointly address themselves.

(iii) The sales department provides the marketing information system with definitions of its information needs called "outputs" and the information it has available the "inputs". The data-processing unit may or may not combine the sales department's own information inputs with inputs from elsewhere. Continuing formal and informal cooperation and communications are of the highest importance both in designing and operating a management information system.

(iv) From the sales department's standpoint, it is important to bill customers correctly and promptly. Automation of order processing results in improvements in customer service. It produces as by-products data needed for making rapid changes in sales and production plans and for inventory control.

Sales volume and profit reports are used to measure the performance of the sales force. Computers turn out these reports quickly, frequently and in great detail. Sales executives call for "exception reports" which highlight things requiring attention. Details are held in reserve until the executive requests them. Exception reports include sales personnel failing to achieve quotas; sales activities exceeding budgeted expenses; territories in which the company is losing competitive position; customers with declining purchases and product lines having slow sales movement, declining profit margins or both.

(v) The distribution systems of many companies provide customers with automatic ordering procedures. This makes it convenient for customers to reorder and speed up order processing, both improving relations with customers. The continuing need for developmental selling for keeping in close touch with customers' problems shows that the salesperson's role has only changed, not eliminated. Automatic reordering procedures are spreading. Sales executives work with data-processing specialists both in setting them up and in monitoring their operations, adjusting them to meet changing customer requirements.

(vi) As there is room for improved coordination and cooperation between the sales department and the information function, sales executives are in continuing need to maintain close relations with information and computer specialists. The greatest opportunity lies in the development of closer informal relationships among personnel at all levels. Both marketing information and sales department heads generally report to the same superior.

**3. Sales and Service**

(i) Cooperation and close contact of the sales and service departments are essential in companies manufacturing products requiring installation and repair services. Technical advice on the installation of new product is a powerful selling argument. There are implications for the service department in a salesperson's promises to buyers. In many industries, the recommendations of service personnel often influence buyers' decisions. Service personnel act in a sales-making capacity in selling vacuum sweepers and other household appliances.

(ii) Provisions for formal coordination are built into the organizational structure where service is important in sales strategy. The organization should provide for bridging the gap between the home office and the fields when both sales and service departments are decentralized. Sales and service relate usually by locating sales and service personnel in the same field offices. Regional managers are responsible for both activities. Under both centralized and decentralized organisational plans, sales and service functions are coordinated at the department head level. Most often both these heads report to the chief marketing executive. The need for continuous cooperation between sales service means that between personnel on lower organizational levels, the great bulk of coordinating is informal.

**4. Sales and Physical Distribution**

(i) Most firms believe that all business operations should be geared toward serving customers at a profit, which requires the maintenance of favourable relations between sales volume and costs of various kinds, including physical distribution costs.

(ii) Physical distribution activities such as proper packing, accurate freight-rate quotations and promptness in delivery are important in securing sales volume. If costs of performing these activities are not kept under control, sales volume yields less profit. Sales policies are coordinated with the capabilities of the physical distribution operation and its costs.

(iii) According to W.M. Stewart, the benefits of effective coordination with physical distribution help to generate the following additional sales volume and profit :

(a) *Minimize Out-of-Stock Occurrences* : It helps to reduce sales lost because of outs and helps raise the level of customer satisfaction.

(b) *Reduce Customers' Inventory Requirements* : If a company develops a more responsive distribution system than competitors, its customers obtain an economic advantage by doing business with it. This is a strong selling point.

(c) *Solidify Relations with Customers* : This is through integrating company delivery facilities with customers receiving facilities, consignment of stocks to customers, and similar devices.

(d) *Allow Greater Concentration on Demand Creation* : Development of a well-organized physical distribution activity, in which a separate administrative group is set up to plan and operate the distribution system, can free marketing and sales personnel, allowing them to concentrate more on their basic responsibility — demand creation. In many companies this has led to an increased number of warehouses and a consequent reduction in total distribution costs.

(iv) If the heads of both operations report to a common superior, such as the marketing vice-president, the most effective formal coordination of sales and physical distribution results. There should be informal coordination of sales and physical distribution personnel, at all levels, on a day-to-day basis.

Sales people and their counterparts in the physical distribution department should communicate directly and frequently. This will ensure efficient processing of customers' orders.

## DEPARTMENTS REQUIRING COORDINATION

### 1. Production Department

**1. Coordination of Sales and Production.** Formerly production was started only after orders were on hand although some products, such as defence materials for the Armed Forces are manufactured to specifications established by buyers. Today most production is in anticipation of future sales. Most products today are manufactured according to specifications set within the company itself.

**2. Coordination in Planning and Operations.** Joint consultations are required in planning when deciding the products to manufacture the quantities to produce, the production schedule, inventories and packaging. Changes in plans must be worked out jointly by sales and production personnel if the sales estimate may prove in error, or the sales department may accept rush orders, necessitating reshuffling of production schedules, addition of extra shifts or payment of overtime wages. Output may not conform to planned quantities because of labour difficulties, material shortages, adverse weather conditions and the like.

**3. Coordination of Sales Estimates and Production.** Sales estimates, prepared by or with the assistance of sales executives are needed for efficient planning of production. The sales department has a reservoir of market knowledge invaluable to production executives seeking more efficient utilization of plant facilities. Sales executives keep production executives informed of changes in market demand for different products. This increases the chances of attaining optimum production level. Sales executives recommend elimination of slow sellers, addition of promising new products and changes in product specifications. The sales department gives its appraisals from the standpoints of price and potential volume for all products present and proposed.

**4. Coordination of Information.** The production department helps the sales department. It provides detailed technical information on products. It assists in training salespersons in product information. In drafting promotional plans, sales executives draw upon production executives know-how on such matters as manufacturing costs at different output levels, limitations of production facilities and the practicality of building given characteristics into products. The production department helps in stimulating sales personnel to greater efforts by relaying information on unused plant capacity and work-in-process to the sales department. The same information is useful for detecting the need to change the sales emphasis given to different products.

**5. Various Methods for Achieving Interdepartmental Coordination.** (a) If the company has a separate merchandising department, top management delegates to it the authority to coordinate many sales and production activities through staff channels. (b) In other companies, merchandising committees with representatives from both sales and production obtain formal coordination. Close informal contacts between personnel at many levels are important in handling many complex problems arising in the course of operations with minimum expenditure of executive time.

**2. Research and Development Department**

Research and development (R&D) is organized as a separate staff department. In smaller and more conservative firms, responsibility for R&D may be placed in the marketing or production department. Research and development work consists of scientific and engineering efforts to develop new products and to improve established products. R&D is related to merchandising, that is, structuring the product line and adjusting product features to fit customers' wants, which is of prime concern to the sales department as well as to the production department. Synchronization is required of research and development, sales and production departments — all of which are involved in product innovation as engineering and design characteristics affect the salability of products.

**1. New Product Departments.** These are charged with responsibility for developing new products through coordination of R&D, production and sales marketing personnel.

**2. New Product Managers.** It includes one-person units responsible for developing new products through coordinating R&D production and sales and marketing personnel.

**3. New Product Project Management Team.** It is composed of persons home-based in other departments brought together to work on a new product.

**4. Product Development Committee**. It is similar to (3), but with a permanent existence and dealing with continuing problems of innovation relating to a given product group.

Coordination should take place at *lower* organizational levels whether main reliance is placed upon formal or informal mechanisms. As department heads find it difficult to keep abreast of the multitude of rapidly changing factors which must be considered in the day-to-day process of developing new products, specialists supply the detailed knowledge of markets and technologies that enables them to make the frequent decisions innovation requires.

**3. Personnel Department**

Most personnel department are ill-equipped to service sales personnel due to the unique problems in managing employees located away from company offices and facilities. Sales departments handle nearly all their own personnel problems while the personnel department acts mainly in an advisory capacity. Specialists in job analysis, recruiting, selecting, training, and motivation often are consulted by sales executives. The personnel department performs some routine personnel work, such as maintaining records or personal data. Both the departments cooperate in formulating policies on pensions, vacations, sick leaves, safety, health checks and similar matters. Besides significant informal coordination there is formal coordination through top management.

**4. Finance Department**

**1. Interdepartmental Activities**. By furnishing sales estimates for the company budget, by developing the sales department's budget, and by assisting in control of selling cost, the sales department assists the finance department. The finance department assists the sales department by providing rapid credit checks on prospective accounts, keeping sales people informed of customer's credit standings, helping locate prospective accounts and providing credit information on candidates for sales positions. Sometimes salespersons represent the finance department in making collections and securing credit information. These interdepartmental activities require good communications, consistent policies and close working relationships. Most organisational plans provide for formal coordination through budget and executive committees.

**2. Coordination in Credit Policy**

(a) In a mutual effort to overcome the natural conflict of interest in credit policy, coordination of sales and finance takes place informally by personal contact. Length of the credit period, size and nature of discounts, relative liberality in granting credit — all can be instrumental in persuading prospects to buy.

(b) Good reasons exist for keeping control over credit policy and its implementation away from the sales department. Some sales executives and many salespeople are more interested in obtaining orders than in collecting amounts due, resulting in a tendency to grant credit to below-average risks. Salespersons also shy away from making collections, especially from slow-paying accounts, for fear of antagonizing customers.

(c) But there is a need for tact in credit negotiations, both by salespeople and by credit personnel. When a customer's credit must be shut off, both tact and coordination are required to avoid buck-passing and resultant loss of goodwill. Wanting to increase sales, the sales department favours liberalizing credit policies, whereas the credit department favours tightening them wanting to control credit losses. Close coordination and communication are required to balance these inclinations to serve the best interests of the whole company.

## 5. Accounting Department

Formerly the sales department relied upon the accounting department to bill customers, handle the department's payroll computation and disbursement problems and provide data for sales analysis and marketing cost analysis. Now the performance of these functions has shifted away from the accounting department, which may retain primary responsibility or even the centralized data-processing unit under its jurisdiction. To handle data-processing and analysis functions for all or nearly all departments more companies have set up such units sometimes called "computer centres".

## 6. Purchasing Department

(i) Sales department provides purchasing department with sales estimates so that adequate stocks of raw materials, fabricating parts and other items can be procured in advance of scheduled production runs. Sometimes these data are furnished through an intermediary such as the production department or data-processing unit.

(ii) The purchasing department informs the sales department, again sometimes through an intermediary, for material surpluses and shortages, so that sales emphasis can be changed with regard to products made from these materials.

(iii) Data on sales department needs are furnished by the purchasing department so that purchases can be made on advantageous terms.

(iv) In companies where reciprocity is approved policy, the two departments coordinate their efforts, buying as much as possible from customers and selling as much as possible to suppliers. Coordination is achieved formally through top management and informally through personal contacts.

**7. Public Relations Department**

Public relations department is consulted on any contemplated moves that might have public relations repercussions. The sales department assists public relations personnel by relaying information, secured through its contacts with various publics, that has public relations significance. Relations between the two departments are normally informal and with frequent personal contacts. Formal coordination is the responsibility of top management.

**8. Legal Department**

Legislation regulating and affecting marketing activities makes effective coordination of the sales and legal departments imperative. Every sales department activity can have legal implications. Sales executives require legal advice on contracts with sales personnel, pricing, relations with competitors and trade associations, salesperson recruiting policy and practice and disputes with customers. Sales executives and legal officers are in continuing communication to avoid costly litigation and unfavourable publicity. While interdepartmental coordination on legal matters is informal, formal coordination of the sales and legal departments is achieved through top management.

## EXTERNAL RELATIONS

The sales department has important contacts with final buyers, industry and trade associations, governmental agencies, educational institutions and the press.

### 1. Final Buyer Relations

**1. Importance.** Final buyers are the most important public that any marketer strives to please. The competitive free enterprise system is based on the premise that customers' wants must be satisfied. Individual companies prosper when their products contribute to this end. Manufacturers and their products are on trial with the final buyer public. The trial goes on each and everyday. Satisfaction or the lack of it is recorded daily in sales order books patterns and at the nations' checkout counters.

**2. Research.** Buyer attitudes and behaviour patterns are not easily changed. Manufacturers have a competitive edge when they know the reasons for them. Research among final buyer groups gathers the information required for planning ways to alter their attitudes and behaviour. It measures progress toward overcoming prejudices. It determines prejudices against competitors and their products. It detects the need for product improvement. It evaluates middlemen's prestige.

**3. Responsibility.** Responsibility for good final buyer relations rests with other departments also besides the sales department. For example, if the production department makes products that do not meet final buyers' expectations, unsatisfactory final buyer relations result. Personnel policies are part of the consumer relations programme in consumer goods fields, since employees are often customers and have contact with other customers. Dividend and other financial policies affect consumer relations, since stockholders and their friends may be customers. Final buyer relations are influenced by the seller's purchasing policies and procedures when suppliers of industrial products are also customers. Middlemen at all distribution levels mould final buyer attitudes toward manufacturers and their products. While the sales department plays a key role, the effort of all departments need skilful blending with those of middlemen.

**4. Basic Product Service Policies.** Sales department personnel play major roles in formulating basic product service policies and in implementing them. These policies affect final buyer attitudes as well the ease with which initial sales are made. For example, if products fail to perform adjustments, refunds, repairs, or replacements should follow. Instruction booklets should be clear and complete. Final buyer's requests for service or information should be answered without delay, all employees in contact with final buyers should be courteous, friendly and competent in their jobs.

**2. Industry Relations**

**1. Two Objectives of Trade Association.** Two objectives of trade association are of special interest to sales executives : (i) to interpret the industry and its problems to outside publics, and (ii) to encourage member companies to act in the public interest. Activities directed toward the first objective include trade association advertising, furnishing expert witnesses for legislative hearings and disseminating industry news. Activities directed toward the second objective include studies of attitudes and opinions of final buyers toward the industry and counselling on public relations problems.

**2. Other Functions**

(a) Some associations serve as clearing houses for industry production and sales statistics useful to individual companies for planning and controlling their activities.

(b) Others sponsor employee-training programmes; conduct management development programmes; arrange for or conduct cooperative research; serve as vehicles for reaching the educational, governmental and press publics and provide consulting services.

(c) Some coordinate advertising and other promotion is aimed to simulate primary demand.

(d) Finally, some associations plan, organize and direct industry-wide trade conventions attended by manufacturers, middlemen and sometimes even final buyers.

**3. Contacts with Competitors and Other Business Executives through Professional and Service Organizations.** Chambers of commerce, manufacturers' associations, the American Marketing Association, all furnish sales executives with excellent opportunities to exchange ideas. Participation in local business clubs and service groups is worthwhile. Most sales executives find it advantageous, professionally and personally, to maintain as many contacts as time permits.

**4. Common Courtesy.** Sales executives as well as sales personnel should refrain from making disparaging remarks about competitors and their products. They should play up the strengths of one's own company and its products.

**5. Controversial Conduct.** Many practices are controversial — considered ethical by some, unethical by others. Among these are hiring sales personnel away from competitors, persuading suppliers not to sell to competitors, cutting prices in the hope of driving competitors out of business and paying distributors' or dealers' employees to push the company brand.

### 3. Government Relations

**1. Impact of Government Rules and Regulations.** Government lays down the rules and regulations affecting the sales department, which are continuously modified with shifts in judicial and administrative interpretations. In USA, effective sales executives are familiar with such basic pieces of legislations as Robinson Patman Act; Civil Rights Act; Age Discrimination Act; Wool Products Labelling Act : and Food, Drug and Cosmetic Act. They keep abreast of judicial and administrative interpretations of such laws. To protect company and industry interests, they cooperate with and appear as witnesses before legislative committees investigating or holding hearings on industry problems and practices.

**2. Impact on Markets.** Federal and state governments affect the size of the market for many products through changing tax laws and rates. Over the past half-century, the effect has been to change the shape of the income distribution curve. Lower economic groups have had their disposable personal incomes raised and higher groups have had theirs lowered. Most consumer incomes have been rising and fewer people are in the extremely high- and low-income groups. The average consumer has more disposable income, which has made possible significant expansions in the markets for many products.

**3. Impact on Credit.** Government influences sales department operations by controlling credit. In USA the federal government has powers to expand or contract credit and thus to affect business conditions and the ease with which sales are made through the Federal Reserve System and the Treasury Department. Changes in the relative availability of credit expand or contract the market for such "big-ticket items" as automobiles, consumer durables and housing. Credit policy of the federal government, is of considerable interest to sales executives in many fields.

**4. Buying by the Government.** Governmental units are large buyers. During wars and other periods of national emergency, governmental purchases swell the sales of a long list of items. During peacetime, governmental purchases account for important shares of total sales for paper, office equipment and furnishings, automotive equipment and supplies, laboratory equipment and supplies and computers and data processing equipment. The Armed Forces are important customers for foodstuffs, optical goods, photographic equipment and supplies, clothing, chemicals, arms and munitions, aircraft, aerospace items and communications equipment. Government contracts often lie behind the purchases made by contractors working for federal, state and local governmental units. Government business is so important to many companies that specialized staffs are formed to negotiate and administer government contracts. Sales executives have a stake in their performance although these staffs may not be wholly under the sales department's jurisdiction.

**5. Impact of Government Income.** The government provides income for millions of consumers such as government employees and other millions who receive income from governmental sources, including retired government employees, social security recipients, holders of government securities and disabled war veterans. The Medicare and Medicaid programmes have brought additional widespread benefits and a major impact on sales of drugs, pharmaceuticals and other health care products.

**6. Impact of Government Agencies.** Many governmental agencies provide services or engage in activities that affect the sales executive. Federal and state governments compile and distribute statistical and other information useful for sales planning. Federal agencies help in promoting standardization of product characteristics. The Federal Trade Commission encourages the development of voluntary trade and competitive practice regulations. The federal government USA has taken up the cause of small companies, helping them through the Small Business Administration. Other governmental agencies protect legitimate business enterprises from commercial shysters and racketeers such as smugglers and bootleggers. Through tariff laws and other import regulations, domestic firms find relief and protection from overseas competitors.

**7. Role of Sales Executives.** Sales executives assist in implementing government relations programmes. They expedite the gathering of data needed by governmental statistical agencies. They ensure that the communication lines from the sales department to governmental agencies are open and clear. They lend their support to governmental units seeking appropriations for purposes of gathering information of interest and use to business.

**4. Educational Relations**

**1. Impact of School.** Future members of significant publics, including the final buyer public, receive their first, and usually most lasting, impressions of the business system and individual companies during their years in school. Schools serve as training grounds for future dealers, distribution, sales personnel and sales executives. The schools are important customers for many products. There are both future and present payoffs in having good relations with educational institutions.

**2. Education of Sales Executives.** The educational world provides many services to sales executives. Collegiate schools of business, research bureaus and institutes and individual instructions conduct studies on relevant problems and make the results available. The expertise of scholars is brought to bear on problems of direct interest to sales executives, such as application of computer techniques to the design of sales territories and analysis of sales performance. Evening schools and extension divisions provide opportunities for developing sales department personnel. Many universities offer management development programmes, providing occasions for sales executives to blend their own experiential knowledge with the thinking of scholars.

**3. Impact of Sales Executives on Educational Programmes.** They assist in collecting and preparing teaching materials. They recommend that their companies award scholarships, fellowships and grants-in-aid to educators. They serve as guest speakers in such courses as marketing, sales management and consumer behaviour. Some companies provide summer internships for educators. Others work with educational specialists in developing case materials and new research techniques. Company publicity is welcomed by the educational public, but the company preparing it should guard against making it overly commercial. Effective sales executives accept their responsibilities as public-spirited citizens by seeking to improve the educational system.

**5. Press Relations**

**1. Impact of Publicity**. The press consists of writers and editors of newspapers, magazines, trade journals, news services, radio and television stations and other media. Unfavourable media comments about a company, its policies, products or personnel damage a company's reputation and impede its selling efforts. Bad publicity makes it difficult to make sales and increases the cost of those made. Good publicity makes it possible to obtain sales at less expense.

**2. Impact of Good Press Relations.** Good press relations help in obtaining good publicity. Press publicity should be planned as part of the promotional programme. Planned press release complement or supplement other elements, such as personal selling and advertising. Skill in handling press relations and basic appropriateness of the publicity plan are the factors causing publicity to be good, bad or indifferent.

**3. Simple Rules for Managing Press Relations**

(a) All stories given to the press should have news value. A story has news value if it has human interest, or concerns a subject of interest to the audience reached. Newsworthy stories originating in the sales department relate to the introduction of new products and improvements, new models, promotional plans, additions to the sale staff, promotions of sales personnel and retirements.

(c) Presenting the press with copy that amounts to advertising which the press calls space grabbing is a sure road to poor relations. Press publicity is not unpaid advertising.

**4. Avoidance of Pleasure, Influence or Threats to Discontinue Advertising.** If a news story is likely to present the company or its product in an unfavourable light, it is better to provide reporters the pertinent details than to ask that the story be suppressed. If interviews are on controversial subjects, or involve material that might be misunderstood, reporters are handed statements covering the situation; in other circumstances, prepared press releases are avoided.

**5. Open Door Policy**. Building and maintaining good press relations is a matter of the sales executive's exercise of good judgment. Effective sales executives maintain an open-policy with press representatives. All are treated fairly and courteously. Favourable publicity generated by preferential treatment to some is offset by bad relations incurred with others. The effective sales executive compliments reporters and editors responsible for well-written stories.

## QUESTIONS FOR EXERCISE

1. What are the functions of sales department in a company? How does it achieve interdepartmental relations and coordination?
2. Describe the marketing activities to which coordination of personal selling is required in a company.
3. Which departments of a company require coordination of the personal selling?
4. To which external publics, the sales department has contacts? Explain the nature and form of these external relations.

# 14

# The Sales Manager

Like those of other line executives, the sales manager is to make decisions and to see to it that others carry them out. However, his job is more action-oriented and less planning-oriented. They are concerned about planning but their plans cover rather short periods and have near-term personal-selling objectives and how to attain them. Their main concern is the "present" — the "here and now". Their plans typically are near to the action point.

## QUALIFICATIONS OF SALES MANAGERS

**1. Experiential and Other Knowledge.** This base provides a "feel" for problems and possible solutions.

**2. Keen Awareness of Company and Sales Department Goals.** They must recognize the key features distinguishing the sort of company that top management is trying to build. They must visualize the nature and type of contributions the sales department can make toward realizing that future "company image".

**3. Ability to Conceptualize Problems.** They need the ability to conceptualize problem situations in areas where they have the main decision-making responsibility and in those where they contribute to decisions that have implications in other marketing areas and/or in other parts of the business.

## SALES MANAGERS' DECISIONS

**1. Impact.** The decisions of the sales managers may not effect only the sales department. They may have significant implications elsewhere in the organization.

**2. Abilities.** In performing their jobs, sales managers must know how to analyze information, how to combine its significance with their own experiential knowledge and judgement and their willingness to accept a certain amount of risk, how to apply imagination in searching for alternative solutions to problems, how to predict the likely outcomes of different alternatives and how to choose that alternative with the highest payoff.

## NATURE OF SALES MANAGEMENT POSITIONS

The requirements of the sales managers' job vary from company to company and from position to position within companies. However, certain responsibilities are typically assigned to them in different companies. Some companies have formulated concise statements of duties, activities, and responsibilities of sales managers, district sales managers, product managers and other sales or marketing executives. These are known as job or position descriptions. Following are the typical job descriptions for the jobs manager and district sales manager.

## GENERAL SALES MANAGER

**1. Reporting Relationship.** He reports to the vice-president of marketing.

**2. Job Objective.** To secure maximum volume of dollar sales through the effective development and execution of sales programmes and sales policies for all products sold by the division.

**3. Duties and Responsibilities**

(i) *Sales Programme* : He takes the initiative in establishing short and long-range sales goals of the division and in collaboration with other marketing executives, sets sales, profit, growth, market share, and other goals.

He arranges for the development of detailed sales programmes designed to improve competitive positions, reduce selling and other distribution expenses and reach established sales goals.

He reviews and approves sales policies, sales strategies and pricing policies (to the extent that they impact upon sales goals) for all products to ensure that short-term operations are in accord with long-term profitability and do not jeopardize other phases of the company's operations.

(ii) *Organization* : He establishes an effective plan of organization and methods of controlling the activities of members of the sales organization, that will provide sufficient time for carrying out the full line of departmental responsibilities.

He provides leadership both to immediate subordinates and all levels of the sales organization in establishing a sound basis for each individual's self-development and in making certain that rewards are in line with responsibilities and performance.

(iii) *Sales Force Management* : He identifies promising sources for the recruitment of new sales personnel and sets standards for selection of the most promising recruits. He provides for the training of new personnel so as to achieve high-level performance in the shortest possible time. At the same time, the sales manager provides for the training of veteran sales personnel, so as to improve their performance levels and to prepare them for possible promotion. He ensures that there is an adequate supply of sales executive talent for replacements up, through and including the sales manager's own position.

He ensures that sales personnel are properly motivated, so as to achieve optimum sales performance.

He establishes a system of sales supervision that controls waste and inefficiency and points sales efforts into the most profitable channels.

(iv) *Internal and External Relations* : He develops effective working relations with other department heads and the general manager so that significant sales developments can be translated into appropriate course of action.

He develops and maintains relationships with key accounts that provide maximum long-term participation in their available business.

He develops and maintains effective working relationships with sales, training and other key personnel in the employ of customers to ensure that cooperation is beneficial to both parties.

(v) *Communications* : He establishes a system of communications with other sales personnel that keeps them informed of overall departmental sales objectives, results and problems and keeps the sales manager informed of their needs and problems.

He establishes a system of communications with other sales personnel that keeps them informed of overall departmental sales objectives, results and problems and keeps the sales manager informed of their needs and problems.

(vi) *Control* : He consults with the production manager so that production rates and inventories are geared as closely as possible to actual sales needs.

He reviews and approves sales and expense budgets and evaluates periodically the performance of all sales activities in relation to budget and sales goals and takes such corrective actions as are required.

He delegates authority and develops control records and performance standards to permit a proper balance of time spent on the various activities in this job description.

(vii) *Performance Criteria* : His performance is considered satisfactory when :

(a) The department's dollar and unit sales are equal to or exceed the quantities budgeted.

(b) The profit contribution of the sales department is in the line with plan.

(c) The details of sales plans are in writing and are acceptable to marketing management.

(d) The turnover rate of sales personnel is maintained at a level regarded as satisfactory by marketing management.

## DISTRICT SALES MANAGER

**1. Reporting Relationship.** He reports to the sales manager.

**2. Job Objectives.** To secure maximum dollar sales of the company's products in the sales district in accordance with established sales policies and sales programmes, within the limits of the sales budget.

**3. Duties and Responsibilities.** He is responsible for the effective deployment of selling efforts and the maintenance of good trade relations in the assigned district. In working toward achievement of the primary job objective, the district sales manager is expected to be concerned with :

(i) *Supervision of Sales Personnel* : He evaluates the sales opportunities in the district and assigns territories that have equitable workloads and that permit minimum travel costs, so as to secure maximum dollar sales at minimum cost.

He directs, assists and supervises sales personnel in maintaining and improving the company's competitive position and in handling special sales or competitive problems.

He rates sales personnel in the performance of all their duties and at least annually discusses these ratings with them to direct their attention toward areas where improvement is needed.

He advises the sales manager on important personnel problems.

He evaluates the sales personnel's strategies for key accounts, helping each to the strategy for all assigned accounts and to develop new accounts.

(ii) *Control* : He forecasts short-term sales of the district and works with sales personnel in estimating future sales in their territories so that accurate sales budgets and sales quotas can be developed.

He prepares a periodic progress report on industry condition, forward plans and the progress made toward sales objectives.

He reports on significant sales or competitive development that may affect the company's future.

(iii) *Administration* : He is responsible for the efficient administration of the district office operations and warehouse and stock facilities in accord with established policies and procedures.

He develops effective working relations with technical personnel, other district managers and home office personnel so as to take full advantage of their help to achieve sales goals, reduce costs and effectively carry out sales programmes.

(iv) *Communications* : He studies and analyzes the plans, programmes and policies originating in the home office and interprets them to the sales staff so that these plans, programmes and policies can be coordinated in the district's activities.

He communicates to the sales manager and top administration any information about customers and markets or about personnel that should be of interest to them.

He maintains membership in professional organizations whose activities are of interest and concern to the division so as to promote better customer relations and develop intelligence sources.

(v) *Performance Criteria* : His performance is considered satisfactory when

(a) The district's dollar and unit sales are equal to or exceed the quantities budgeted.

(b) The district's total expenses are no higher than the amounts budgeted.

(c) The profit contribution of the district office and warehouse and stock facilities is in line with plan.

(d) The turnover rate of district sales personnel is maintained at a level regarded as satisfactory by the (general) sales manager.

## FUNCTIONS OF GENERAL SALES MANAGER

Some sales managers get promoted into their positions due to their previous performances as salespersons. Outstanding salespersons have an inside track when sales executive jobs are being filled because it is believed that outstanding salespersons will be outstanding sales managers. This is wrong since much beyond those required of salespeople, the sales manager's job demands administrative skills. Personal-selling experience is useful as sales manager manages people who do personal selling. However, personal-selling manager is different from managers with outstanding personal-selling performance. Sometimes an outstanding salesperson fails in a sales manager's job.

**1. The Operating Functions.** These include sales force management, handling relationships with personnel in other company departments and with the trade middlemen and/or customers communicating and coordinating with other marketing managers and reporting to some superior executives such as the marketing vice-president. Besides, in some companies to keep a "hand in" and to keep abreast of current selling problems and conditions the sales managers sell some accounts personally.

**2. The Planning Functions.** These include those connected with the sales programme, the sales organization and its control. The sales manager sets personal-selling goals, develops sales programmes designed to achieve these goals, formulates sales policies and personal-selling strategies and puts together plans for their implementation. While sales programmes are put into effect through the sales organization, the sales manager designs and shapes the sales organization, staffs it, develops the skills of those who are part of it, and provides leadership to it. The sales manager is responsible for achievement of sales departmental goals which require controls over selling activities, sales volume, selling expenses, and the like.

## GOVERNING FACTORS

The managers lay relative emphasis on the operating and planning functions. This varies with (1) the type of products, (2) the size of company, and (3) the type of supervisory organization. Sales managers at all organizational levels devote more time and attention to sales force management than they do to any other single activity.

**1. The Type of Products**. Sales manager's significance attached to operating and planning functions varies with the product. If the product is a consumer good, he attaches the greatest importance to planning functions: development of sales programmes, coordination of personal selling with advertising and building and maintaining relationships with dealers and customers. If the product is an industrial good, he attaches the greatest importance to the operating functions — managing and directing the sales force, making calls with salespeople and selling personal accounts. As compared to their counterparts in industrial goods companies, consumer-goods sales managers spend more time on planning and less on operating.

**2. Size of the Company**. The sales manager's time devoted to planning and operating functions is influenced by the size of the sales organization. In small companies he spends less time on planning and more on operating. As the size of the company increases, he devotes more time to planning and less to operating.

**3. Type of Supervisory Organisation**. Sales managers distribute their time and effort according to type of supervisory organization. If he supervises the field sales force directly, he or she spends most of the time on operating functions. If he supervises the field sales force through subordinate sales executives, more attention is devoted to planning and less to operating. Sales managers having high-caliber subordinates are more willing to delegate most of the performance of the operating functions to them and have more time left for planning.

## OBJECTIVES OF EFFECTIVE SALES MANAGER

**1. To define the Position's Exact Functions and Duties in Relation to the Goals the Company should expect to attain.** Sales managers calculate what is entailed in their responsibilities. They draw up their own descriptions consistent with the responsibilities assigned by higher management whether or not the company provides them with a job description. Revisions are necessary whenever changes occur in the assigned responsibilities or in company goals.

**2. To select and Train Capable Subordinates and Willingness to delegate Sufficient Authority to enable them to carry out Assigned Tasks with Minimum Supervision.** Effective executives select high-caliber subordinates and provide them with authority to make decisions. Decisions are made by subordinates within existing policy limits. The superior decides when an exception falling outside these limits occurs. The more capable the subordinates, the wider are policy limits and the more the superior's time is free for planning.

**3. To utilize Time Efficiently.** The time of sales manager is valuable. He budgets it and uses it carefully. He allocates working time to tasks yielding the greatest return. He arrives at an optimum division between office work and field supervision. As excessive work time and too little leisure reduce efficiency, successful sales managers balance leisure time activities such as community service and professional meetings against personal social activities, recreation and self-improvement.

**4. To allocate Sufficient Time for Thinking and Planning.** Able administrator makes his contributions through thinking and planning. He knows how and is willing to think. He recognizes that reviewing past performances is a prerequisite to planning. He strives to gain new insight that will bring problems into better focus. He shields from routine tasks and interruptions. He sometimes retreats to places where surroundings are conducive to thinking and planning.

**5. To exercise Skilled Leadership.** Skilled leadership is important in dealing with subordinates and with everyone else. A competent manager develops and improves his skills in dealing with people. Although he relies to a certain extent on an intuitive grasp of leadership skills, he depends far more on careful study of motivational factors and shrewd analysis of the ever-changing patterns of unsatisfied needs among those with whom he works.

## RELATIONS WITH TOP MANAGEMENT

**1. Personal Goals.** In initiative and personal drive, effective sales manager is well above average. Realizing his potential, however, depends largely upon his relations with top management. He should seek to get ahead, for personal goals are as vital to him as the objectives he sets for the sales department. If he is to achieve these goals he must know where he is going, but the top management must be kept abreast of his progress.

**2. Harmony with Company Objectives.** Effective sales manager plans and implements his own self-development programmes and sets definite career goals. He harmonizes his own goals with those of the organization, for maximum progress of individual and company. Whenever he and the company cease to move toward mutually compatible goals, friction causes both to fall short and either the two sets of goals must be reconciled, or he should leave the firm. Sometimes, he unilaterally reconciles such goal conflicts usually by adjusting personnel goals to fit those of the organization. Often he reconciles them through interaction with company top management.

**3. Not Indispensable.** He accepts responsibility for all activities related to his position but he avoids becoming indispensable. Indispensability is undesirable for both the manager and the company. For the sales managers it means blocking opportunities for promotion; for the company it means that too much is being staked on one individual. In order to avoid becoming indispensable, one must practise and advocate delegation of authority. Effective sales managers place high priority on training their own replacements. Junior sales managers are well advised to learn and master the duties and responsibilities of the positions immediately above theirs. While promotions come to those prepared for them, preparation consists of setting definite career goals and adhering to programmes of continuing self-development.

**4. Not Much Help Sought.** Effective sales manager is highly qualified as problem-solver and decision-maker. He guards against taking too many of his problems to top management. As asking for help in deciding problems is asking for closer supervision and less authority, competent sales managers do not require a close watch over their activities.

**5. Keeps Top Management Informed.** Effective sales managers keep top management informed of important decisions and the department's plans and accomplishments. He transmits all ordinary reports promptly and special reports when appropriate. He exercises restraint in reporting his own activities but he ensures that his superiors have all the information required to evaluate his personal effectiveness. His reports ensure that top management knows in broad outline the problems encountered in selling the company's products, the ways they are handled and the results accomplished.

**6. No Insistence.** Effective sales manager pays attention to the manner in which he communicates with top management. He does not hesitate to give his superiors the benefit of thinking, but he is willing to modify preconceived ideas unless matters of high principle are involved.

**7. Having Great Idea.** When the sales manager has a great idea, is absolutely sure of it and top management is unconvinced, he must play the role of super-salesperson and "sell" to those with the authority to decide. When the facts do not speak for themselves and when those in authority fail to grasp their full significance, he should bring to bear his or her full powers of persuasion like any competent executive.

**8. Listens and Learns.** Effective sales manager listens and learns. He keeps a dated record of important conversations. He refrains from voluntarily discussing the personal competence of fellow executives. He avoids relaying rumours. He controls his executive contacts and never misses scheduled engagements without reason. Following rules of conduct, he experiences little difficulty in winning top management's confidence and respect.

## RELATIONS WITH PRODUCT MANAGEMENT

Product planning and the formulation of product policies require numerous decisions because periodically each product needs appraising in terms of its profitability and its ability to fulfil buyers' wants. Decisions are made on whether each should be retained, changed or improved or dropped from the line. Other decisions are made on adding new products and on changes in product design and other features. Still others decisions concern product quality, services rendered in connection with sales and packaging.

Product decisions are often the shared responsibility of marketing, production research and development and financial executives, operating as a product committee. Sales managers provide inputs for these decisions. His contact with the market through subordinates and sales personnel provides him with feedback about product performance and acceptance generally not available from other sources.

## RELATIONS WITH PROMOTION MANAGEMENT

**1. Coordination.** While chief marketing manager sets promotional policies, sales manager participates in their formulation. His knowledge of the market and his control over personal-selling activity make him a key source of information. He occupies a strategic position in implementing promotional plans. Sales personnel transmit sales messages to prospects but for securing the use of point-of-purchase display and coordinate dealer efforts with advertising programmes. Because of their key roles in making and implementing promotional policies, sales managers must closely coordinate with other executives in the formulation and implementation of the promotional programme.

**2. Keeping Selling Costs Down.** At one or more points in the marketing channel, every product relies on personal selling as a promotional method. Personal selling's effectiveness depends on the use of personal contact in conveying the sales message to prospective buyers. In terms of cost per sales message transmitted, personal selling is the most expensive promotional method. Therefore, the proportion of personal selling must be limited in the promotional mix. The sales managers should keep selling costs down.

**3. Advertisement Campaigns.** The sales manager ensures that salespeople know current advertising campaigns and get briefing on specific advertising appeals, enabling them to adapt their selling approaches in ways that enhance the total promotional impact. They should know which media are scheduled to carry advertisements for which products and the timing of each ad's appearance. Advertising personnel need access to the sales manager who is an important source of information about customers, their needs, behaviour and motives.

**4. Promotional Methods.** Sales manager plays similar roles regarding other promotional methods. Decisions of these methods in the promotional mix are normally made by the chief marketing executive or by other specialists. The sales manager secures coordinative efforts by the sales force to ensure that each promotional activity obtains optimum results, besides serving as an important source of information.

## RELATIONS WITH PRICING MANAGEMENT

**1. Pricing Decisions.** Both the chief marketing manager, executive and the sales manager occupy influential positions in top management councils when major decisions on pricing policy are required. They generally have much clearer ideas of the prices final buyers are willing to pay as the sales manager has close and continuing contacts with the market and the marketing manager has access to pricing information gathered and interpreted by the marketing research staff.

**2. Pricing Policies.** Price policies should be formulated and prices should be set by a group of executives though these two executives are well qualified to speak with authority on pricing matters. Each affected department should be represented as pricing policy-making is an interdepartmental activity. Representatives of the marketing department as well as of production cost accounting, credit, advertising, legal and public relations should be included in the policy-making group. Pricing policies should result from the cooperative action of the group rather than from compromises among its members.

**3. Implementation.** Now implementation of pricing policy is the responsibility of the sales manager. While the pricing committee might adopt suggested list prices, the sales manager is responsible for informing distributors and dealers and obtaining their conformance. Responsibility for administering prices should be assigned to him, because the sales department has the closest relationship with the market.

## RELATIONS WITH DISTRIBUTION MANAGEMENT

Distribution policies determine the breadth and complexity of the sales department's organization and functions. Both geographically and as to the classes of customers, selection of a marketing channel or channels sets the pattern for sales force operations. Therefore, it is also necessary to determine the number of outlets for the product at each distribution level. This affects the size and nature of the manufacturer's sales organization and the scope of its activities. The marketing management determines policies on the amount and extent of cooperation it desires with members of the distributive network. It also influences the size of the sales force, the nature of the salesperson's job, the need for sales supervision, and the like. Sales manager plays key role in providing information needed for formulation of distribution policies as they are responsible for their implementation.

## QUESTIONS FOR EXERCISE

1. Explain the status, qualifications and abilities of sales manager and analyse the nature of sales management decisions.
2. Describe the functions and qualities of the sales manager.
3. Explain the relations of sales manager with other members of the organization.

# 15

# The Sales Force Management

Managing the sales force involves the implementation of personal-selling strategy as the two key personal-selling strategic decisions are on selling style(s) and sales force size. These decisions are based on planning how to achieve the sales volume and related company goals. The decisions on selling style(s) determine the range and nature of activities required for personnel management of the sales force. The decision on sales force size determines the magnitude of these activities. It is the sales manager's responsibility to implement these strategic decisions.

## SALES FORCE INTERFACES

Levitt writes 'the difference between marketing and selling is more than semantic'. Selling focuses on the needs of the seller, marketing on the needs of the buyer. Among the four "P"s Product, Price, Promotion, Place, selling comes under promotion alongwith advertising, personal selling, direct marketing and sales promotion. The sales force must interact with other departments within an organization and between different organizations, shown below :

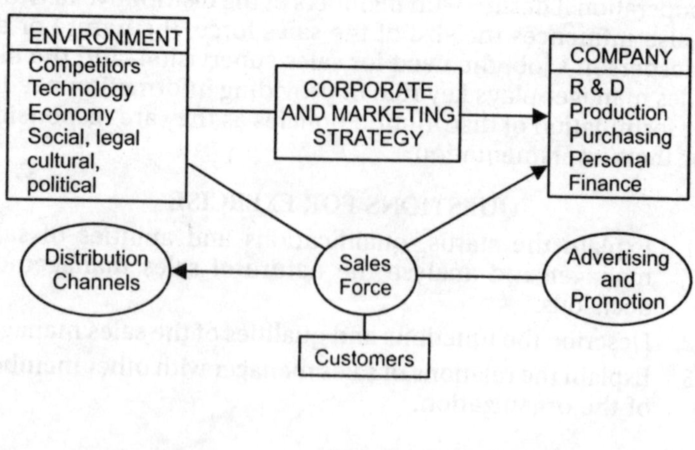

Several marketing aspects can be crucial to the role of sales force and to individual sales persons effectiveness. Sales management devises sales policies to achieve the firm's sales, marketing and corporate goals. Many factors, outside the control of the firm, effect the goals *e.g.*, competitors, technology, economy and social, cultural and legal factors. The sales force has to coordinate with other departments like production, purchasing, personnel and finance. Sales force also has relationship with distribution channels, advertising and finally customers.

## STRATEGIC DECISIONS

**1. Type of Personnel Management**. Sales force management is a type of personnel management which focuses upon sales, production, office and workers. Both consider the same set of problems need though each problem varies in nature and importance.

**2. Less Supervision**. It is impractical to exercise close and constant supervision over sales personnel as that which one can do in case of production and office workers. As sales personnel work away from their coworkers and immediate superiors, it is difficult to develop a spirit of identity with and loyalty to the company and to weld them into a unified team.

**3. More Freedom.** Sales personnel are given freer rein than are production or office workers. They are relied upon as individuals to plan and control their own activities. They visit the home office only infrequently. The centralized direction of their activities is carried on mainly by phone and mail. The salesperson's job provides limited opportunity for face-to-face contact and supervision. Therefore, personnel are often referred to as "account administrators" or "territory managers."

**4. Motivation Problems.** The salesperson is often away from home and family for extended periods. His selling success or failure depends upon prospects' and customers' actions and reactions. Disheartening order turndowns and rebuffs from customers require him to repress normal responses and a natural tendency to become discouraged. These conditions accentuate the need for him to pay continual attention to motivational factors.

**5. Activities.** Steps in sales force management are the same as those in general personnel management. As shown in Figure 25.1, sales force management work starts with job analysis determining the job objectives, the component duties and responsibilities, performance criteria and reporting relationships. The job analysis provides written job description used in deriving the necessary job specifications of the employee. Finding of qualified job applicants requires decisions on recruiting sources and methods. Those meeting the job specifications are selected from the applicants. Applicants undergo initial training after hiring. Throughout their entire careers with the company, they receive continuing training through diverse delivery systems. Compensation plans are designed to provide appropriate levels and methods of compensation.

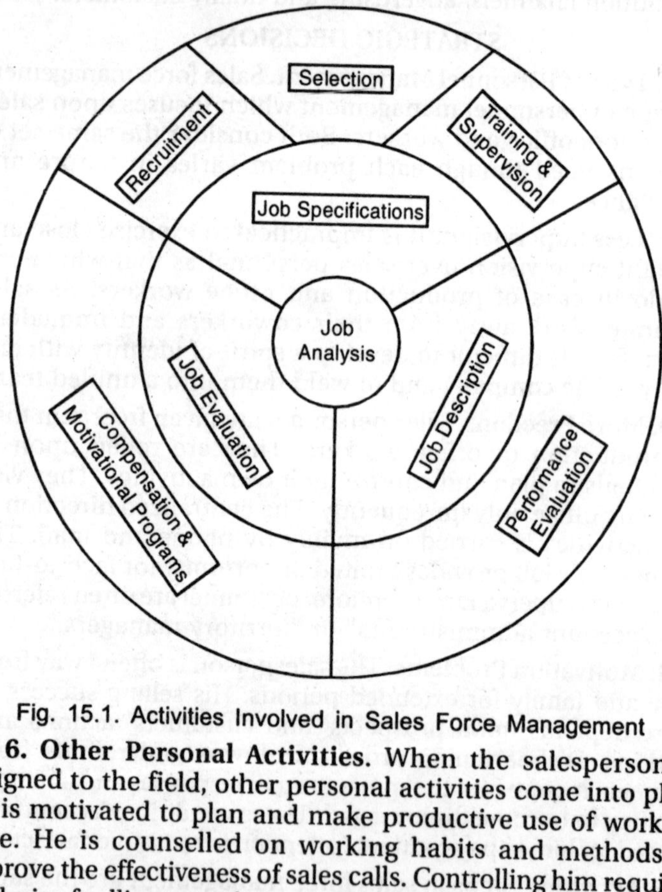


Fig. 15.1. Activities Involved in Sales Force Management

**6. Other Personal Activities.** When the salesperson is assigned to the field, other personal activities come into play. He is motivated to plan and make productive use of working time. He is counselled on working habits and methods to improve the effectiveness of sales calls. Controlling him requires analysis of selling records and evaluations of sales performance.

**7. Management System.** Sales person management activities form a system, whose faulty execution results in complications. Supervision problems become greater, motivating and controlling salespersons is more difficult and the run over of sales personnel is accelerated if recruiting and selecting are sloppy and training tasks are magnified. Potentially good people fail to reach high productivity, the compensation system does not work as planned, supervision is ineffective, and there is excessive personnel turnover. Similar "bundles" of difficulty arise in case of ineffective performance of other activities in the sales force management system if training is inadequate.

## ECONOMIES OF EFFECTIVE SALES FORCE MANAGEMENT

There are economies in effective sales force management. Suppose a company has ten salespersons, each making five calls per day, a total of fifty per day for the company. Assume that four calls out of five result in sales and that the average sale amounts to Rs. 500. If through more effective management, each salesperson increases the number of calls to six per day, the company's daily total becomes sixty (an increase of ten) and eight more sales per day are made (8 × Rs. 500 = Rs. 4,000). This is equivalent to adding two new salespeople at the old call rate. If sales personnel are paid wholly or partially on a commission basis, their incomes are now higher and morale should be improved. As some selling costs are related to the number of sales people, the company's average cost per call should be reduced.

### Types of Expenses

There are two types of expenses of maintaining a sales force.

1. **Fixed**. The fixed expenses are identical for all sales personnel regardless of their productivity. These include sales salaries, travelling, equipment autos, sales folios, sales manuals and so forth and advertising used to assist the sales force.

2. **Variable.** The variable expenses are the highest for the least productive sales personnel. Variable expenses include sales commissions, training, motivating, supervising and controlling — these expenses are lower per unit of product sold for productive salespersons than for unproductive salespersons. Thus, when a company incurs variable expenses for maintaining its sales force, it receives its highest return from the most productive sales personnel. Total expenses per unit of product sold vary inversely with the productivity of the salesperson.

## MEASURING QUALITY OF SALES FORCE

A measure of the quality of sales force management is the rate of sales personnel turnover. It is the ratio of separations per 100 sales-people. For example, a company employing a sales force of 250 persons and having twenty separations during the year has a rate of turnover of 8 per cent.

A convenient formula for calculating the rate of sales personnel turnover is rate of personnel turnover (expressed as a percentage) :

$$= \frac{\text{Number of Separations}}{\text{Average Total Sales Force}} \times 100$$

**1. Total Expenses.** The turnover rate influences the total expenses of sales force management. Costs of recruiting, advertising, fees to employment agencies, and so forth often run to more than Rs. 500 per recruit. Interviewing costs are high, because companies interview several applicants for each selection. If an interview by an executive takes two hours, an executive's time is worth Rs. 25 per hour, and thirty people are considered for each vacancy, total interviewing costs amount to Rs. 1,500 per person hired. The costs of travel and time used for preparatory and follow-up training easily run to Rs. 10,000 per person.

Some expenses are not readily calculated. For example, new recruits do not produce as much as experienced sales personnel and the ratio of selling expenses to sales for a new person is likely to be excessive for at least the first year. A conservative estimate of the excess is Rs. 3,500 per new salesperson during the first year, and in some companies this excess is higher because it takes longer for a salesperson to get fully into stride.

The expenses of sales personnel turnover can account for a significant drain on profits. In a company with a sales force of 400 and an annual turnover rate of 25 per cent, if the costs of replacing a single salesperson come to Rs. 10,000, the annual costs of turnover total Rs. 1 million — and this is only out-of-pocket cost. Other costs are increased expenses for supervision and motivation, lost business, decline in customer goodwill from mistakes of inexperienced salespersons, and miscellaneous expenses associated with taking on people who do not succeed. Few accounting systems measure the impact on profit of excessive sales personnel turnover. But profits are lower because inexperienced salespeople are assigned where turnover has occurred. Profits are not realized from sales not consummated.

**2. Uses of Turnover.** All turnover is not bad, even though it seems costly. Most salespeople who leave a company have less than three years of service. If a person is unsuccessful, and is likely to leave, it is desirable to turn him out immediately. The earlier the unsuccessful person leaves, the better off is the company both in terms of costs and effect upon other sales personnel. Too low a rate of turnover may indicate that the sales force is overloaded with veterans who do not produce as much as new personnel may do. The entire system of sales force management needs overhauling. A sales force with no turnover may be growing stale, prospective new salespeople are not being attracted and older ones are lingering on because of management laxity. Hence some turnover is desirable.

**3. Age Distribution.** The age distribution among sales personnel should be analyzed for its impact on sales force turnover. It is desirable to spread salespersons' ages over a wide range. Otherwise, the productivity curves for all rise together, all reaching their peaks and declining together, and all reaching retirement at the same time. Under these circumstances, it is necessary to recruit an entire sales force almost at once, at considerable loss in market coverage and customer relations. Before evaluating the turnover rate, companies should establish an average length of service, which management considers desirable. If the average length of service should be twenty years, then the personnel turnover rate should be 5 per cent — one-twentieth of the sales force should be replaced each year. As even the best selection procedure is far from perfect, the actual turnover rate would run higher than 5 per cent. Some people do not take sales jobs with the intention of keeping them forever. A sales job is often the springboard to higher positions and a company using its sales force as a source of managerial talent anticipates higher turnover.

**4. Value of Awareness.** For planning the operation of service functions, awareness of the current turnover rate is necessary. In planning recruiting, selection and training programmes the personnel turnover rate is important. For example, a company with a turnover rate of 25 per cent is replacing its sales force every four years. It must organize its service functions to handle an annual volume of new recruits equivalent to one-fourth of its sales force. The costs and extent of the recruitment, selection and training programmes largely depend upon the amount of turnover.

**5. Causes of Turnover.** The personnel turnover rate is analyzed periodically to determine the causes. Analysis often uncovers areas where improvement is needed. An exit interview between the departing salesperson and a line executive or a personnel consultant provides an opportunity to identify conditions contributing to personnel turnover, which enables management to modify or correct conditions within its control.

Management should take corrective action when the causes are concentrated on the controllable list, particularly when turnover traces to reasons 1 through 7. Turnover resulting from reason 8 sometimes is unavoidable and that resulting from 9 and 10 is usually desirable. Managerial action may be called for, even in the cases of some reasons appearing on the "not controllable" list. Only reasons 2, 3 and 6 may be regarded as completely unavoidable.

**Chart 15.1**

**Causes of Turnover of Sales Personnel**

| Caused by Actions Controllable by Company | Caused by Actions Not Controllable by Company |
|---|---|
| 1. Poor recruiting | 1. Retirement |
| 2. Improper selection and assignment | 2. Death |
| 3. Training deficiencies | 3. Illness or physical disability |
| 4. Inadequate supervision and motivation | 4. Personal and marital difficulties |
| 5. Breakdown in communications | 5. Dislike for the job—travel, type of work, working conditions, etc. |
| 6. Unsatisfactory performance — customers complaints, etc. | 6. Military duty |
| 7. Discharged for cause, *e.g.*, alcoholism, conviction of a felony, dishonesty, etc. | 7. Better position elsewhere |
| 8. Cutbacks in personnel | |
| 9. Transfer to another department | |
| 10. Promotion to a higher position | |

## INVOLVEMENT OF SALES EXECUTIVES

### Roles of Different Levels of Executives

At all organizational levels, sales force management is a concern of sales executives. Successful performance by sales personnel is the single most important responsibility for some sales executives. Sales supervisors devote the bulk of their energies to managing the sales force. Others spend less time on managing salespersons' activities though concerned with their effectiveness. Middle-level sales executives manage lower echelon sales executives who, in turn, manage the sales force. Other middle-level sales executives specialize either in some aspect of sales force management or in a phase of marketing that affects the salesperson's job.

### Role of Top Executive

The chief sales executive has general responsibility for managing subordinate sales executives and through them for managing the sales personnel as well as the management of other sales and marketing activities. As sales executives move to and through middle management levels, they retain their concern for management of the sales force. However, pressures cause them to ration their efforts among a growing set of responsibilities. Retaining concern for sales force management, they participate increasingly in long-range planning and forecasting the product line, setting prices, planning promotional programmes and managing marketing channels and physical distribution. However, sales executives should never forget that their own job's existence is to contribute to the effectiveness of the sales force.

### Need for the Proper Setting

Programmes for effective sales force management need installing in a favourable setting. Market exploration should provide the management knowledge of market and sales potentials, identities and locations of customers and prospects, the individual in customers' organization who influence buying decision and the methods for reaching them. Product uses and applications must have been identified and different selling appeals evaluated. Now, the management is prepared to draft and implement appropriate programmes for effective sales force management.

## GUIDE LINES IN USA

In USA two agencies, the Equal Employment Opportunity Commission (EEOC) and the Office of Federal Contract

Compliance (OFCC), assist employers in implementing non-discriminatory personnel policies. The guide lines issued by the EEOC apply to all employers of twenty-five persons or more; those of the OFCC apply to firms with one hundred or more employees that contract with the federal government.

Both the EEOC and OFCC concern themselves with a broad range of personnel policies. Their regulations limit the use of ability tests to measure eligibility for hiring, transferring, promotion, training, and referral or retention. They apply to all formal, scored, quantified, or standardized techniques used to assess job suitability, including specific qualifying or disqualifying personal history or background requirements, specific educational or work history requirements, scored interviews, biographical information blanks, interviewers' rating scales, scored application forms and the like. These agencies require an employer using such techniques to have evidence of each technique's validity. This must consist of empirical data demonstrating that the technique is predictive of or significantly correlated with important elements of work behaviour that comprise or are relevant to the job or jobs for which candidates are being evaluated. Federal regulations require that employers using personnel administration techniques of this type for purposes of selecting from among candidates for a position or in making decisions on transfers, promotion, training, or dismissals must be prepared to prove that the techniques are used in a manner that does not discriminate on the basis of race, colour, religion, sex, or national origin.

## GUIDE LINES IN INDIA

Article 24 of our Constitution prohibits employment of children below the age of 14 years in any factory or mine or any hazardous employment. Similar prohibition is imposed by the Child Labour (Prohibition and Regulation) Act of 1986. Despite all this, India has the notoriety of having the world's largest child labour population. There are varying estimates of the number of children at work in the country. According to the 43rd Round of the National Sample Survey, over 170 lakh children are working as labourers in the country. An unofficial estimate puts this figure at 440 lakh. According to W.H.O., one out of every four working children in the world is in India.

Child labour in India is generally found employed in match and fireworks industry, stone quarrying, slate-pencil making industry, precious stone polishing industry, glass industry, calendar and label printing industry, tin and aluminium containers, carpet industry, automobile workshops and small dhabas. All these industries are mostly located in Uttar Pradesh, Tamil Nadu, Madhya Pradesh, Andhra Pradesh and Gujarat.

In a recent field study of child labour in Sivakasi (Tamil Nadu) carried out by the International Confederation of Free Trade Unions (ICFTU), it has been revealed that children are brought to factories from the nearby villages by agents. Working conditions in the factories are very poor. Children often complain of headaches and back pain and catch T.B. and skin diseases. Managers employing children either register their age as being above 14 or do not register them at all. When honest inspectors report child labour at a factory, the prosecution often fails. This is because the Child Labour Act stipulates that a worker's age may be assessed only by a registered and approved doctor—not an inspector.

The ICFTU study team concludes its report highlighting the imperative need for the government to specify, under Sec. 18 of the Child Labour Act, the competent authority to issue birth certificates and make it a mandatory obligation on the employers to keep lists of employees containing their dates of birth based on approved birth certificates and their dates of employment.

The Central Government has set up a National Child Labour Elimination Authority (NCLEA) to launch a programme to withdraw all children from hazardous industries by the year A.D. 2000 in a phased manner. The number of such children is estimated to be 20 lakh. The programme assumes that no fresh child labour will be allowed to enter these hazardous industries in future.

The government is also considering a proposal to amend the Child Act to make it obligatory to pay equal wages to adults and children. This will remove the existing pecuniary incentive to employ child labour.

## JOB ANALYSIS

Job analysis is assembling and analyzing factual information on specific jobs. It is the basis for professional personnel management. It provides the data required for preparing written job description used to derive job specifications. The two derivatives of job analysis, the job description and job specification, provide factual foundations for making decisions on hiring, transfers, promotion, training and dismissals.

### Sales Job Analysis

In modern sales force management, sales job analysis is the critical first step. It is the foundation for enlightened personnel management. It has risen in importance since the law brought pressure on sales executives to justify decisions on hiring, transfers, promotion, training and dismissals. Sales executives are now concerned with making objective personnel decisions based on facts.

Sales job analysis requires systematic collection and study of information on particular sales jobs, such as that of territorial salesperson. It determines the job's objectives and what the person holding the job should do to reach them. It answers questions like: To whom does this person report? Who reports to this person? What products does this person sell? What information should this person gather? What reports should this person make and to whom? In addition it elicits details on specific duties and responsibilities, relations with customers, relations with other sales department and company personnel, and the like. Its outcome is a detailed picture of the role(s) that the salesperson plays. These include four basic selling styles: trade, missionary, technical, and new business. The salesperson's job in a particular company, in most cases, combines two or more of these basic styles.

### Sales Job Description

A sales job description is an organized factual statement covering (1) the reporting relationship of a particular job to other jobs, (2) the job objectives, (3) duties and responsibilities, and (4) job performance criteria. It tells to whom the sales job-holder reports, what has to be done, how it is done, and why in addition it describes the standards against which performance is measured.

## PROCEDURE FOR SALES JOB ANALYSIS

Four main steps are identifiable in procedure for sales job analysis and preparation of written job description used in well-managed companies: (1) assembly of factual information about the job, (2) analysis of the information, (3) writing of the job description and (4) as required, repeat the process.

### 1. Assembling Factual Information about the Job

(i) Clarifying reporting relationships by questioning salespersons and those to whom they report.

(ii) Preparing a questionnaire for sales personnel, asking them to list the job objectives, together with the major duties and what is involved in performing them, in doing the job effectively.

(iii) Prior to receipt of the completed questionnaires having sales executives and other executives interested in sales activities write down their conceptions of the salesperson's job objectives, the salesperson's responsibilities and the duties they feel the salesperson should and should not perform.

(iv) Surveying customers to find out what they believe should and should not be the functions of a company salesperson.

**2. Analyzing the Information Gathered**

(i) Tabulating the information received.

(ii) Reconciling differences revealed by the three viewpoints, write a concise statement of job objectives and prepare a detailed list of duties that sales personnel are to perform.

(iii) Classifying the duties into major responsibility, such as sales, service, territory management, sales promotion, executive, and goodwill duties.

**3. Writing the Job Description**

(i) Putting the reporting relationships in writing.

(ii) Adding the concise statement of job objectives.

(iii) Inserting the detailed information on duties and responsibilities.

(iv) Developing a written statement of job performance measures.

4. As required, repeating the first three steps when changes in markets, customer's requirements, products, competition, the economic climate, and so forth require a review of job objectives, job duties and responsibilities, and/or performance measures.

A checklist of activities and sub-activities generally accepted as comprising salespersons' jobs is an alternative approach to developing the "job duties and responsibilities". One checklist, originally put together for the U.S. Small Business Administration, is shown in Chart 15.2. This approach is helpful in preparing tentative descriptions of newly created sales jobs.

**Chart 15.2**
**Checklist for Compiling "Duties and Responsibilities" Section of a Sales Job Description**

**Sales**

Make regular calls.
Sell the line; demonstrate.
Handle questions and objections.
Check stock; discover possible product uses.
Interpret sales points of the line to the customer.
Estimate customer's potential needs.
Emphasize quality.
Explain company policy on price, delivery and credit.
Get the order.

**Service**

Install the product or display.
Report product weaknesses, complaints.
Handle adjustments, returns, and allowances.
Handle requests for credit.
Handle special orders.
Establish priorities, if any.
Analyze local conditions for customers.

**Territory Management**

Arrange route for best coverage.
Balance effort with customer against the potential volume.
Maintain sales portfolios, samples, kits and so forth.

**Sales Promotion**

Develop new prospects and accounts.
Distribute home office literature, catalogues and the like.
Make calls with customer's salespeople.
Train personnel of wholesalers, jobbers and so on.
Present survey reports, layouts and proposals.

**Executive**

Each night make daily work plan for the next day.
Organize field activity for minimum travel and maximum calls.
Prepare and submit special reports on trends, competition.

Prepare and submit statistical data requested by home office.

Investigate lost sales reason for loss.

Prepare reports on development, trends, new objectives met and new ideas on meeting objectives.

Attend sales meetings.

Build a prospect list.

Collect overdue accounts; report on faulty accounts.

Collect credit information.

**Goodwill**

Counsel customers on their problems.

Maintain loyalty and respect for the company.

Attend local sales meetings held for customers.

---

## PREPARATION OF SALES JOB SPECIFICATIONS

Compared to preparing a complete and accurate sales job specification, preparing a complete and accurate sales job description is simple. It includes the "duties and responsibilities" portion of the job description focused upon to determine the qualifications that an individual needs to perform the job satisfactorily. If the job description states that the salesperson is to train dealers' sales personnel then the salesperson must be qualified to conduct such training. What should the salesperson know about the products, their uses, and the dealers' customers, about dealers' operating methods and problems and about training methods and will this require the salesperson to have a certain kind of education and/or special experience? In the job description similar sets of questions must be answered about each of the duties and responsibilities.

Sales management decides which qualifications all new recruits should possess, and which should be provided through training. A company specifying somewhat higher entrance qualifications than another can expect that its training programme will have to accomplish less.

Sales job specifications should set forth the required personality characteristics, which the salesperson must bring to the job, since sales training programmes are not effective instruments for personality development. These include certain traits: empathy and the ability to get along well with others; integrity and character; and in terms of a sensible self-perspective. There is an optimum level of motivation for each job. Some sales jobs require their holders to be routine order-takers only, but others serve as providing grounds for future managers.

Job specifications may stipulate minimum requirements with respect to education and product or technical knowledge. The importance of these requirements varies widely. Some selling jobs demand the detailed technical training offered only by colleges of engineering; others require only average ability to read, write and do simple arithmetic and there are all gradations in between. Graduation from an educational institution is tangible evidence that the job candidate has a certain level of ability.

Job specifications provide recruiters with a device for the conservation of time and energy — the set of minimum requirements to use in weeding out unqualified applicants. This usually takes the form of a list of negative factors, the presence of any of which automatically disqualifies an applicant. A set of minimum requirements or preliminary screening standards, should be prepared only after a company analyzes its dismissals and should reflect the main reasons why a company's sales personnel fail. Companies must be prepared to prove that each minimum requirement is significantly related to successful job performance and does not result in discrimination on the basis of race, colour, religion, sex, age, or national origin.

Many companies do not formalize sales job specifications. Instead, sales executives and others interviewing prospective employees are provided with written sales job descriptions. Each interviewer has a set of desired qualifications in his or her mind. Instead of a single set of qualifications for the sales job, there are as many as there are users of the written job description.

## QUESTIONS FOR EXERCISE

1. Describe the characteristics of sales force management.
2. What are the economies of sales force management? How do you measure its quality?
3. Discusses the involvement of sales executives in sales force management. Analyse the role of law in it.
4. Explain the process of job analysis in sales force recruitment.

# 16

# Training in Sales

Formerly sales managers believed that good sales personnel are born not made. Newly recruited sales personnel were given product descriptions, a territory and an order book with instruction to "go out and sell!" Admittedly there were and are some born or natural salespeople, but most recruits become productive sales personnel after appropriate initial training. Continuing sales training improves job performances for both born and made sales personnel. Therefore, modern sales executives are convinced that sales training contributes to sales job performance. They regard training as a supplement to experience.

## TYPES OF SALES TRAINING PROGRAMMES

The most comprehensive and longest sales training programme is the training programme for newly recruited sales personnel. More intensive and shorter programmes on specialized topics, as well as periodic refresher courses are presented for experienced sales personnel. Many companies offer sales training programmes for the sales personnel of their distributors and/or dealers. Some programmes are designed to develop individuals as sales trainers or as junior-level sales executives. Each type of programme serves a different purpose and its content reflects that purpose.

## BUILDING SALES TRAINING PROGRAMMES

Building a sales training programme requires five major decisions defining training aims, identifying initial training needs, identifying continuing training needs, deciding training content and selecting training methods.

## THE CONTENTS OF TRAINING PROGRAMME

**For New Recruits.** Product knowledge, selling skills, sales administration, company information, customer knowledge and market knowledge. For existing staff—selling skills, new product information, sales administration, market/customer information and company policy.

Following are myths about salesmen :

(1) Salesmen are born not made.

(2) Salesmen must be good talkers.

(3) Selling is a matter of knowing right tricks.

(4) A good salesmen can sell any thing—even ice to Eskimos.

(5) People don't want to buy, but have to be conned.

## STEPS IN TRAINING PROGRAMME

**1. Defining Training Aims.** Defining the general aim of training is not sufficient. General aims are translated into specific aims phrased in operational terms. We must identify what must be done to achieve increased productivity. Defining specific aims (the A in A-C-M-E-E) is the first step in planning sales training programme. Defining specific aim begins with a review of general aims and the means currently employed to attain them. The process can be completed only when sales management perceives the *training needs* from which specific training aims derive directly.

**2. Identifying Initial Training Needs.** Determining the need for an initial sales training programme requires analysis of job specifications, individual trainee's background and experience, and sales-related marketing policies.

(i) *Job Specifications* : The job specifications detail the qualifications needed to perform the job. At the time of hiring, few people possess all these qualifications. The set of job specifications needs scrutinizing for clues to the points on which new personnel are most likely to need training. Other questions related to job performance are: How should sales people apportion their time? Which duties require the greatest proportion of time? Which are neglected? Why? Which selling approaches are most effective? Answers to these questions help in identifying specific training needs of newly recruited sales personnel.

(ii) *Trainee's Background and Experience* : Each individual enters an initial seals training programme with a unique educational background and experience record. The nature and amount of needed training depends on the gap between the qualifications in the job specifications and those a trainee already has. As it is not practical to adjust training precisely to individual differences time and money are saved by putting all recruits through identical programmes. Where training mechanisms are highly flexible, information about trainees' qualifications makes possible some tailoring of programmes to individuals, increasing both trainee satisfaction and programme efficiency. Determining recruits' real training needs is essential to developing initial training programmes of optimum benefit to company and trainee alike.

(iii) *Sales-Related Marketing Policies* : Sales-related marketing policies must be analyzed to determine initial sales training needs. Differences in products and markets mean differences in selling practices and policies. These point to needed differences in training programmes. For example, selling a line of machine tools required emphasis on product information and customer applications, whereas selling simple, non-technical products demands emphasis on sales techniques. Differences in promotion, price, marketing channel, and physical distribution have implications for initial sales training. In the case of promotion, sales training should prepare sales personnel to handle considerable promotional work. If advertising is used extensively to supplement the sales force's efforts, new sales personnel should learn how to coordinate their activities with advertising.

**3. Identifying Continuing Training Needs**. Identification of specific training needs of experienced sales personnel is necessary to determine the specific aims for a continuing sales training programme. Basic changes in products and market create needs for training, as do changes in company sales-related marketing policies, procedures, and organization. But sales personnel change, in some respects for the worse, even though products and markets change little and company policies, protrudes, and organizations remain stable.

Sales management must know a great deal about how sales personnel perform to identify training and, in turn, to define specific aims. To gain this knowledge salespersons' reports are scrutinized for symptoms of needed training. Sales records are inspected to uncover performance weaknesses. Sales personnel are observed personally toward detecting deficiencies. Details contained in the sales job description are compared with the qualifications possessed by individual sales personnel.

**4. Deciding Training Content**. Both in initial and continuing programme, the content (the C in A-C-M-E-E) of a sales training programme derives from the specific aims that management formulates. Compared to continuing programmes, initial sales training programmes are broader in scope and coverage. They provide instruction covering all important aspects of performance of the salesperson's job, while continuing programmes concentrate on specific aspects of the job.

An initial sales training programme must cover all key aspects of the salesperson's job. Its content varies from company to company due to differences in products, markets, company policies, trainees' ability, and experience, organizational size, and training philosophies. No two programmes are alike. However, different companies cover the same general topics despite variations. Every initial sales training programme devotes sometime to each of four main areas: product data, sales technique, markets, and company information.

(i) *Product Data* : Product knowledge is basic to a sales person's self-confidence and enthusiastic job performance. Product training is basic to any initial sales training programme. Companies with technical products devote more than half their programmes to product training. However, in many situations new sales personnel require only minimal product training, to know enough about the products, their uses, and applications.

Trainees receive instruction on customers' problems and requirements. They learn how company products can solve these problems and meet these requirements. Training provides them with full appreciation for buyer's viewpoints. New salespersons learn how to relate company products to the fulfilment of customers' requirements.

Many companies include a period of initial sales training at the factory, where trainees observe and study the products during manufacturing and testing. They work alongside factory personnel getting thorough product knowledge and increased confidence in demonstrating products to customers.

Sales people should know the important characteristics of competitors' product, their uses and applications. Thus, informed they can structure sales presentations to emphasize superior features of the company's products.

(ii) *Sales Technique* : Most new sales personnel need instruction in sales techniques. This is reflected both in company sales training programmes and in industry-wide programmes offered by such groups as the National Association of Food

Manufacturers and the National Association of Machine Tool Builders.

(iii) *Markets* : The new salesperson must know the customers, their locations, the particular products in which they are interested, their buying habits and motives, and their financial condition. He must know why and how they buy. As market is always changing, so training in this area should be continuous, the content changing with market changes.

(iv) *Company Information* : Training programme should include coverage of all sales-related marketing policies and the reasoning behind them. For instance, to answer customer's questions, the salesperson must know company's pricing as well as policies relating to product services, spare parts and repairs, credit extension and customer relations. He must know recording and submitting customers' orders for processing and delivery, preparing expense and other reports, handling inquiries, following up on customers' requests and so forth. The initial sales training programme must provide the needed instruction and the sales department's personnel policies. It should include selection procedures, training programmes, compensation and incentive systems, advancement requirements and opportunities, savings and retirement plans, medical and insurance plans, and the like. This information contributes to employee morale and job effectiveness.

(v) *Customer Knowledge* : Contributing to the building of morale is "general company information" concerning the company's history, its importance in the industry and economy, and its relations with stockholders, unions, competitors, government and other groups. This bolsters the recruits' confidence in its products. He must get formal training on general company information.

**5. Selecting Training Methods.** The planners select training methods (the M in A-C-M-E-E) from a wide variety but the programme content often limits those that are appropriate. The training method almost certainly will be the lecture, supplemented perhaps, with visual aids', the content is a new policy on vacations and holidays. It is important to select those training methods that most effectively convey the desired content.

## TYPES OF TRAINING METHODS

**1. The Lecture.** This ancient instructional method is used extensively in sales training. Trainees mainly watch and listen.

The lecture features passive, rather than active, trainee participation. It emphasizes teaching more than learning. If the lecturer is able and enthusiastic, a lecture can be effective using examples, demonstrations, and visual aids. Compared to other training methods, the lecture is economical.

Many professional business teachers and sales trainers regard lecturing as the least effective group instructional method because the average trainee can immediately recall less than 10 per cent of what he or she hears in a lecture using visual aids. No lecturer has any immediate or objective means for gauging the effectiveness of a lecture because of the absence of immediate participant feedback. He must rely on a personal appraisal of its reception or on volunteered comments by participants.

However, initial sales training is brief, lecturing may be the only way to cover the desired content, and handle instruction when the training group is too large to permit constructive audience participation. Given longer training periods and smaller training groups, lecturing is most appropriate for introductory and orientation sessions and for providing summaries of major topics taught through methods such as case discussion and role playing. It is used in continuing sales training programmes for providing new information about the company, its policies, products, markets and selling programmes.

Learning in lecture method is improved through a multimedia approach. The room is equipped with two to six projectors and screens. The entire lecture is projected visually on succeeding screens across the front of the room. Further support is provided by projecting illustrations, charts and graphs and through sound effects.

**2. The Personal Conference**. In this method the trainer and trainee jointly analyze problems, such as effective use of selling time, route planning and call scheduling, and handling unusual selling problems. Personal conferences are held in offices, restaurants, bars, motel rooms, and elsewhere. The curbstone-conference takes place immediately after the trainee has called upon a customer or prospect accompanied by the trainer. The personal conference is an unstructured and informal method varying with the personalities of the trainer and the trainee and the topics discussed.

**3. Demonstrations**. These are appropriate for conveying information on new products and selling techniques.

Demonstrating how a new product works and its uses is much more effective than lecturing on the same material. It is more effective than lecturing in initial sales training. Used with other methods it enlivens an otherwise dull lecture and reinforces the interchange.

**4. Role Playing.** In it the trainees act out parts in contrived problem situations. Its session begins with the trainer describing the situation and the different personalities involved. The trainer provides needed props, then designates trainees to play the salesperson, prospect and other characters. Each plays his or her assigned role. Afterward, they appraise each player's effectiveness and suggest how the performance of each might have been improved.

In another version of this method, a training group is given information on a buyer's objection to a particular product and then is asked to extemporize a solution. Thus a "sweat session" provides individual trainees a chance to apply what they have learned. Post-mortem critiques afford opportunities to reinforce what has been learned through participating in, or viewing, the role playing.

In role playing those playing roles must become actively and emotionally identified with the characters they portray; audience interest must be maintained throughout, even though spontaneous reactions are suppressed. This tendency may be overcome with repeated use of the method. Problems can be minimized by briefing trainees on what is and is not presumable. The group is limited to no more than ten or twelve. The trainer exercises discipline and control throughout. Role-playing assignments are realistic. This training method provides realistic practice in applying what has been learned in other training or by experience. It is flexible and adapts to extreme diversity in role-playing situations. It lends to training new personnel, experienced salespeople, or even mixed groups. Other benefits include the following:

(i) Trainees learn to accept criticism from others, and the group soon recognizes that sound suggestions benefit everyone.

(ii) When a trainee criticizes another's performance, that individual has an incentive not to perform similarly later.

(iii) Role players practise interposition through participating in the appraisal of their own performances. Videotaping makes self-criticism even more beneficial and objective.

(iv) The freewheeling nature of role playing is conducive to generating new ideas and approaches. Defects inherent in stereotyped solutions become apparent.

(v) In role-playing sessions for mixed groups, junior people have a chance to learn valuable tricks and experienced personnel are kept alert as a matter of personal pride.

(vi) Role players gain acting experience, which may help later in handling difficult selling situations.

**5. Case Discussion**. Originated by business educators as a partial substitute for learning by experience, this method is widely used in sales training. Write-ups of selling and other problems encountered on the job provide the bases for group discussion. Sometimes long and complex cases are assigned in advance and participants come prepared to the session. However, generally the cases used are short and trainees are given ten to fifteen minutes to read them before group discussion starts. Each case describes a real selling problem or is developed around a situation sufficiently real to stimulate emotional involvement by the trainees.

Trainees discussing a case should identify the issue(s), marshal the relevant facts, devise specific alternatives and choose the one most appropriate. Most trainers believe that securing a thorough grasp of the problem situation is more essential to learning than the rapid production of solutions. To derive maximum benefit from case discussion, each session should conclude with the drawing of generalizations on lessons learned.

**6. Impromptu Discussion**. Also called a sales seminar or buzz session, it begins with the trainer, group leader or some member of the sales force making a brief oral presentation on an everyday problem. General give-and-take discussion follows. Group members gain an understanding of many problems acquired only through long personal experience. Many complexities and implications are revealed to all. Trainees learn a valuable lesson in which fixed selling rules and principles are often less important than analysis and handling of specific situations. Impromptu group discussion improves the salesperson's ability to handle problems. It differs from lecturing. The discussion leader assumes a less dominant role than the lecturer. Trainees are active than passive participants. Learning receives more emphasis than teaching. The atmosphere is informal and relaxed. Impromptu discussions are being increasingly used in training programmes for experienced sales personnel.

An effective leader or moderator is essential in the impromptu discussion, otherwise it drifts into extraneous subjects or becomes sterile. The discussion leader must command the trainees' respect, be skilled in dealing with people, and well informed. The room arrangement helps in generating discussion as all trainees can see each other and someone draws conclusions at the close of the discussion.

In impromptu discussion most companies schedule sessions for at least a half-day or more commonly for a full day. The impromptu discussion is an effective training method to maximize trainee learning of specific points in depth.

**7. Gaming.** Also known as simulation, this method somewhat resembles role playing, uses highly structured contrived situations, based on reality, in which players assume decision-making roles through successive rounds of play. The players receive information feedback. Trainees play the roles of decision makers in customer's organizations, using data ordinarily available to make decisions on the timing and size of orders, managing sales forces and advertising efforts and so on. The results of these decisions then are calculated by referees using computers and are fed back for the plays to use in the next round of decisions.

Preparation of a game requires research to dig out the needed facts and their incorporation into a game model, development of detailed instructions for players and referees, and the writing of a computer programme. Expertness and substantial investments in time and money are required. Once prepared, a game may be used in many training programmes.

**Advantages**

1. Participants learn easily due to men involvement.

2. Players develop skill in identifying key factors influencing decisions.

3. Games lend themselves readily to demonstrations of the uses and value of analytical techniques.

4. Games, with their built-in information feedback features, are effective in emphasizing the dynamic nature of problem situations and their interrelationships.

**Limitations**

1. Some minimum time, usually three or four hours, is required for playing to generate sufficient decision "rounds" to provide the desired learning experience.

2. Since game designs are based on ordinary decision-making processes, their rules often prevent payoffs on unusual or novel approaches.

3. Players may learn somethings that are not so, a limitation applying especially to poorly designed games.

**8. On-the-Job Training.** Also called the coach-and-pupil method, this method combines telling, showing, practising, and evaluating. The coach begins by describing particular selling situations, explaining various techniques and approaches that might be used effectively. Accompanied by the pupil, he makes actual sales calls, discussing each with the trainee afterward. Under his supervision the trainee makes sales calls, each one being followed by discussion and appraisal. Gradually, the trainee works more and more on his or her own, but with continuing coaching.

**Advantages**

Given a qualified coach, the trainee starts off on the right foot, using appropriate selling techniques. Early deficiencies are corrected before they harden into habits. However, the trainee learns the coach's bad habits. On-the-job training is an important part of most initial sales training programmes. It is the most effective way for learning a job. It is appropriate for developing trainees' skills in making sales presentations, answering objections and closing sales. It provides expertly supervised practice.

**Limitations**

Many seasoned sales people, otherwise qualified for coaching are unwilling to spend the necessary time and effort, particularly when personnel are paid commissions on sales. The problem of recruiting coaches is resolved through paying bonuses for each person coached, or "overriding" commissions on pupils' sales.

**9. Programmed Learning.** It breaks down subject matter into numbered instructional units called frames incorporated into a book or microfilmed for use with a teaching machine. Each frame contains an explanation of a specific point, plus a question or problem for the trainee to use in testing his or her understanding. Trainees check answers by referring to another designated frame. If the answer is correct, he is directed to new material; if it is incorrect, additional explanation is provided and he is retested on the point before going on to new materials and moves through them at his own speed. Companies using programmed instruction regard formal examinations as necessary incentives for the trainees.

**Limitations**

Because of difficulties in preparing appropriate programmed instructional materials, this method is not used for training in sales techniques and market information. Its preparation requires expert skills and thorough grounding in the psychology of learning.

**10. Correspondence Courses.** This method is used in both initial and continuing sales training. In the insurance field it is used to acquaint new salespeople with industry fundamentals and to instruct in basic sales techniques. Companies with highly technical products and small but widely deployed sales forces use this method to acquaint experienced salespeople with new product developments and applications. It is also used to train non-company sales personnel, such as distributors' salespersons, to improve their knowledge of the manufacturer's product line and selling techniques.

**Advantages**

It is most appropriate as an interim training method when trainees are scattered geographically but are assembled periodically for lectures, seminars, role playing, and other instruction. Initial sales training might be by correspondence courses begun at different times and places; continuing, or follow-up, training might come later through group methods at a central location. Preparing a standardized correspondence course covering technical product data, general company information, selling techniques and markets presents few difficulties other than those of choosing, organizing and writing up the material. In many companies, particularly in the insurance field, institutional materials are also taped for cassette players.

**Limitations**

Successful use of the correspondence method requires administrative skill and motivation of trainees to complete assignments on schedule. Enrollees engaged in full-time work require that correspondence lessons be done after hours. Few have sufficient self-discipline to study without direct supervision. It is necessary to provide regular examinations, prizes for completing work on time, or other incentives. As method does not answer enrollees' questions, hence, successful users arrange for periodic face-to-face discussions. Similar problems are met in processing completed assignments, evaluating work and correcting errors. Correspondence instruction is a useful supplement to other sales training methods despite these administrative problems.

Of the above-mentioned ten training methods, lecturing, role playing, case discussion, impromptu discussion and gaming are group methods, the personal conference, on-the-job training, programmed learning and correspondence course are individual methods and the demonstration is either a group or an individual method, depending on whether the audience is a group or an individual.

## PHILOSOPHIES OF SALES TRAINING

Differentiated by the nature of the behavioural change they seek to bring about in trainees, there are two philosophies of sales training.

**1. The Conditioned-Response Philosophy.** It seeks to train sales personnel so that they will respond in standardized or programmed ways. In a conditioned-response sales force, all individuals react in the same way to any given situation, while in an insight-response sales force, each person reacts in an individualized way.

**2. The Insight-Response Philosophy.** It seeks to develop trainees' insight and analytical skills so that they respond appropriately, and in their own individualized ways.

### Determining Factors

**1. Predominant Selling Style.** The choice of appropriate philosophy depends partly upon the predominant selling style the company expects its sales personnel to apply. The conditioned-response philosophy is a natural choice if predominant selling style is either trade or missionary. Both the caliber of the persons in customers' organizations on whom calls are made and selling styles are low key, not requiring high-level technical training or ability, and programmed responses both conserve time and suffice for handling most situations. If the predominant selling style is either technical or new business, the insight-response philosophy is a natural choice. Both of these selling styles are characterized by endless nonworking situations, requiring either unusual knowledge or creativity and ingenuity. Appropriate responses need tailoring to highly individualized situations.

**2. Caliber of Sales Person.** If the management regards the sales force as a source of future executive talent, the insight-response philosophy is the more appropriate choice. Here the desired calibre of sales personnel is considerably higher than that required for performing rather routine job activities. The higher the calibre of sales personnel, the less likely they are to take kindly to conditioned-response training.

**3. Calibre of Customers.** Similarly, the calibre of the persons in customer's organization upon whom calls are made influences the choice of training philosophy. If these are low-level people in low-level positions, conditioned-response training is the better choice. But if personnel in customers' organizations are high-level people in high-level jobs, insight-response training is the necessary choice.

How does sales training philosophy affect programme planning, execution and evaluation ? Since aims will differ significantly, as will content and methods, planning is influenced. Training a new salesperson to sell house wares door to door (a field where sales personnel turnover rates are high) is most economically done according to conditioned-response philosophy—programmed responses to situations recurring with great frequency. Training a new salesperson to sell house wares to high-ranking buyers in supermarket chains, in contrast, calls for insight-response training. Thus, the aims are different, which, in turn, cause differences in training content and methods. The major portion of the execution phase (that is, the who, when and where) influenced is the who—who will be the trainees—insight-response philosophy, requires trainees of higher-calibre than is true of conditioned-response philosophy. The part of execution consisting of the preparation of instructional materials and training aids is strongly affected—the conditioned-response philosophy requiring materials and aids designed to facilitate memorizing programmed responses while insight-response philosophy puts more emphasis upon materials and aids conducive to development of analytical skills and internalizing of responses.

The conditioned-response philosophy simplifies evaluation, if it consists mainly of determining the extent of accomplishment of training aims. Have the trainees learned the standardized responses? Among the ways of determining this are through written or oral tests, observing sales personnel on the job and quizzing customers. By contrast, measuring the acquisition of insight and analytical skills (the general aim of insight-response philosophy) cannot be done precisely but are judgment evaluations. The results of conditioned-response training are measured objectively, those of insight-response training are appraised subjectively. For instance, a multiple choice test suffices to measure conditioned-response training, while an essay test is required to measure insight-response training.

## ORGANIZATION OF SALES TRAINING

The execution step of A-C-M-E-E (the first E) requires four key organizational decisions: (1) identifying the trainees, (2) identifying trainers, (3) identifying the training time and (4) identifying the training site.

**1. Identifying Trainees.** It is more complex for continuing than for initial sales training programmes. When it firms up sales job descriptions and hires sales job applicants, a company identifies the trainees for its initial sales training programme. In continuing sales training programmes prescribed for all personnel in some companies, the general practice is to select trainers according to some criterion from the following: (i) reward for good performance, (ii) punishment for poor performance, (iii) convenience (of trainee and trainer), and (iv) seniority (the greater the seniority, the greater the opportunity for added training). Those selected for continuing training should be aware of the criterion used.

**2. Identifying Trainers**

(i) *Initial Sales Training*: Initial sales training is both a line function and a staff function. Responsibility for initial training is assigned to the top sales executive in line function. Responsibility for initial training is given to the personnel director and sales management has an advisory role in a staff function. Actually both executives should participate in initial sales training—the sales executives because of selling expertise and the personnel director because of training expertise.

If much initial training of new sales personnel parallels that for other new employees, cost considerations cause the personnel director to have primary responsibility. The sales executive has primary responsibility if little of the initial sales training parallels other new employee training.

(ii) *Continuing Sales Training* : Responsibility for continuing sales training resides with the top sales executive who decides introduction of new products, adoption of revised sales policies, perfection of improved selling techniques, and similar developments call for training. He recognizes the need and design and executes appropriate sales training programmes. Sales training is a never-ending process. The sales executive has continuing responsibility regardless of who is responsible for initial training.

(iii) *Sales Training Staff* : Top sales executives usually delegate sales training performance to subordinates such as a sales training director, reporting to the top sales executive. The director conducts and coordinates training. On a decentralized (and usually part-time) basis this is done by regional and district sales managers. In smaller organizations while some top sales executives handle some training themselves, in most cases, they rely upon assistant sales managers or district managers, to do the training. Companies without sales training directors have full-time or part-time sales trainers, or both. The large sales organization makes efficient use of a full-time sales training director and sometimes even a full-time staff. The small organization must rely on executives to train in addition to other duties. Due to specialized knowledge requirements, companies generally train their own sales trainers rather than recruiting outsiders.

(iv) *Training the Sales Trainers* : As no training programme is more effective than the people conducting it, many companies have a training programme for sales trainers by identifying the subjects that trainers should know thoroughly; the company and its policies, the products, the customers and their problems, the salesperson's job, and sales techniques. If not experienced sales people trainers are given field selling experience. Subjects presented formally are handled by personnel already skilled as trainers, using the instructional techniques.

Besides having expert specialized knowledge, sales trainers must be effective teachers. Stressing the theory and mechanics of teaching (and learning) throughout their period of preparation, trainers are required to master and learn how to apply them effectively, preferably through doing practice training themselves.

They also learn to plan and organize teaching materials for clear and effective presentation. More formal training does not prepare an individual for effective teaching. It requires a well-planned and well-executed programme for sales trainers. However, sales trainers generally develop their own teaching skills.

(v) *Outside Experts* : Many companies hire outside experts to conduct sales training programmes, generally relating to sales techniques. Outside training consultants present sessions on sales techniques such as prospecting, selling by telephone, or basic ways to meet objections and achieve high effectiveness. They are true professionals charging substantial fees, but when spread over several participants these fees are reasonable enough. As the outside experts are under pressure to put on a good show, they provide something out of the ordinary, helping to maximize programme benefits.

**3. Identifying Training Period.**

(i) *Timing Group versus Individual Training* : About the proper timing of group and individual training, sales executives contend that newly recruited trainees should receive formal group training before starting to sell. Some, however, assign trainees to selling jobs before sending them on to sale schools. In support of this view, three things can be said: (1) new personnel prove that they can sell before money is spent on their training; (2) new persons are not always, not even usually, hired in groups large enough to justify immediate formal training and (3) on-the-job experience furnishes needed learning motivation and makes initial training more meaningful. This position is inappropriate when highly technical products are sold to sophisticated buyers. In such cases, product training is best through formal group instruction at the outset of trainees' careers.

In case of large numbers of new personnel, group training is the way to train at the lowest cost per person. However, in planning the curriculum and the sales school, management determines the content that should be taught in the field. Group training is more effective when supplemented by individualized field training. There must be an integration of product data, company information, market information, and the theoretical and practical fundamentals of selling. Practical training in sales technique is best handled individually in the field conducted in the field office or in the trainee's home. On-the-job training features personal conferences of the trainer and trainee and demonstrations. But in many companies, trainees in the field are enrolled in correspondence and programmed learning courses. On-the-job training is supervised by a supervisor in person with trainees participating in correspondence and programmed learning courses by mail, phone, or cassette correspondence.

(ii) *Timing Initial Sales Training Programmes* : Timing of initial sales training depends upon the number of new personnel each year which, in turn, depends upon the size of the sales force, sales personnel turnover, and management's plans for changing sales force size. In case of a large number of new personnel, comprehensive highly structured programmes are scheduled several times a year, dates being set after consideration of recruiting quotas and deadlines. When the number is small, initial training programmes are infrequent.

The optimum number of trainees who are effectively trained, in an initial sales training programme depends upon training aims, content, methods, and the amount and availability of training talent. Individualized training is indicated in some situations. Although it is expensive per individual trained, its timing can be flexible, depending only upon availability of trainees and trainers. In most situations, limitations of training funds and talent dictate training recruits in groups, programmes being scheduled whenever the backlog of untrained people approximates the optimum. Groups smaller than twelve to fifteen involve inordinately high costs, while those larger than thirty to forty incur heavy losses in training effectiveness.

(iii) *Timing Continuing Sales Training Programmes* : Effective sales management believes that training and learning must be continuous. New information must be assimilated and older concepts modified in the light of new developments. New products, new refinements of selling techniques, new product applications and uses, new customer problems, new selling aids, new selling suggestions require that each salesperson's training continues as long as he or she is on the job. Sales personnel are kept abreast of new developments informally through field distribution of information bulletins. But a formal retraining programme is scheduled when new development are unusually important or imply a need for substantial changes in sales person's attitude and behaviour patterns. Many companies integrate retraining programmes into a series of sales meetings or a single sales convention.

All salespersons in any sales force do not have deficiencies that are correctable through training. The practical and economical solutions of the weaknesses are on-the-job coaching. If several people are weak in the same area(s), it is both practical and economical to use group instructional methods in an organized formal programme.

Regular scheduling of retraining programmes is advisable even when sales management has no clear indication of the need. A survey of nearly 500 purchasing agents revealed that 60 per cent felt that the majority of sales people calling on them either had never learned or had forgotten how to sell. It also implied that continuing training provided sales personnel with more adequate product information and taught them how to present it in terms of user benefits.

Sales personnel are eager to improve selling techniques. They feel entitled to explanations of policy changes. They want to learn how to tie in more closely with advertising programmes. They are eager to learn about new products, model and design improvements, and market shifts. Continuing sales training programmes are designed and "sold" as a means of helping salespeople do their jobs more effectively. Salespeople are motivated when it is demonstrated that training results in more take-home pay and increased job satisfaction. When they see that these benefits are obtainable through the continuing sales training programme, its chances of successful execution are enhanced.

**4. Identifying Training Site**. Some companies hold initial sales training programmes at the central offices. Others conduct separate programmes at branch offices. The centralized programme generally provides better product training, while higher costs are incurred in bringing trainees to the central point. In many companies because central location is a necessity, the small number of trainees does not justify decentralized initial training. Large companies by contrast, have the option of decentralized initial training. They train new salespeople near their future territories. They acquaint them early with field selling problems. As decentralized products training often requires the substitution of motion pictures, slides and working models, it becomes less realistic, less interesting and less effective than centralized training. Unless supervised by higher management decentralised programme tends to be poor. The trainers, who have other responsibilities and regard training as a sideline often turn in the poor teaching performances. Initial sales-training programmes should be at central locations except in a company with a vast pool of administrative and training skills.

Short retraining programmes for seasoned sales personnel are held either at centralized or decentralized points. If retraining programmes coincide with sales conventions, they are held nationally at convention headquarters otherwise they are held regionally, on a decentralized basis.

## INSTRUCTIONAL MATERIALS AND TRAINING AIDS

Successful execution of sales training programmes depends on the instructional materials and training aids which vary not only for different companies but for programmes with different aims and methods.

**1. Manuals.** Often known as workbooks, manuals are used in most group type sales training programmes. They contain outlines or summaries of the main presentations, related reading materials, statements of learning objectives for each session, orienting questions or thought provokers, cases and problems, plus directions for sessions involving role playing or gaming. Some include concise statements of selling, pricing, training of sales personnel, and other policies as well as details on company systems and procedures. Others contain information on the products and their applications. Distribution should be observed in selecting items for inclusion. Manuals are deigned to serve as study guides during training and as references later. Many are in loose-leaf form to facilitate additions and changes.

**2. Other Printed Materials.** These include company bulletins, sales and product handbooks, information bulletins, standard texts, technical and trade books and industry and general business magazines and journals. Company publications are used chiefly to furnish field sales personnel with up-to-date and needed information. Keeping field sales personnel informed is also the reason for subscribing to industry and general business magazines. Text, technical, and trade books supplement workbook materials.

**3. Training Aids.** A training aid is an auxiliary device capable of transmission of sight and/or sound stimuli.

(i) *Blackboard* : The most used and indispensable is the black-board which is used to illustrate points, summarize discussions and the like, adding visual to vocal appeal. Modern substitutes for the blackboard such as the Vue-Graph projector, transparency roll and screen offer improvements by making it possible for the trainer to face the class even while his or her writing appears on a screen and conserving time through using prepared diagrams, charts, statistical tables, and so on. There is no substitute for a blackboard. Nothing is free of possible mechanical or power failure. Blackboard and chalk should be available for standby use and to illustrate and explain points that arise in informal discussion even when main reliance is placed upon some mechanically operated device.

(ii) *The Motion-Picture Projector and Film* : These are effective for training to explain complex situations. Nothing short of actual demonstration is as effective as a movie in conveying technical information on installation and operation of new machine tool models. Since cameramen, actors, a director and special sets are needed, substantial costs are incurred in producing training films. In deciding whether to produce tailor-made films, management appraises their probable effectiveness against the cost. While most sales training films seek to convey information on products and their applications, some aim to refine sales techniques. Sales training films of varying quality, most relating to sales techniques are available commercially for the firms with limited funds. Whether company-produced or commercially produced, training film should be previewed before use.

The motion picture's effectiveness is achieved at lower cost with still pictures projected from slides or filmstrips. *A* sound disk presents a commentary together with automatically timed changes in still pictures. The trainer makes comments varying the change interval between pictures with a remote-control device. Many companies produce their own slides and filmstrips. Commercially produced items are available for purchase or rental.

(iii) *Tape-Recording and Playback Equipment* : Ideal for training in sales techniques, actual or simulated sales presentations are taped and played back for individual or group appraisal. Miniature, sometimes concealable cassette-type recorders make it easy for salespersons to tape their own sales interviews and play them back later. Thus, they gain greater objectivity in appraising their own effectiveness and in finding ways to improve performance. Larger recorders are used in formal training programmes to tape group discussions and role-playing sessions. The tapes are played back with commentaries and appraisals by the participants and the trainer. Some trainers tape their own sessions routinely. Later playbacks help to improve teaching effectiveness and to conserve preparation time for repeat performances.

(iv) *Closed-Circuit Television* : It is used when timing is important. It is appropriate in decentralized programmes, such as those in which new product lines are introduced to salespersons or dealer personnel. Closed-circuit television is used in brief, decentralized retaining programmes on policy changes, and as a substitute for training at national sales meetings.

**4. Advance Assignments.** Many programmes require trainees to prepare assignments in advance to conserve time. These may be reading assignments chosen to provide some minimum comprehension of subjects scheduled for coverage in formal sessions. Sometimes, the assignment is to read a case and prepare a plan of action for use in scheduled session. Trainees should understand the purposes of advance assignment and receive clear and written instructions. Trainees' motivations are strengthened when opportunities for feedback are built into advance assignments. Advance assignments are used for groups as well as for individuals. In many companies, trainees are divided into groups and instructed to prepare specific individuals in the groups to play particular roles. Advance assignments consume time outside formal sessions, reducing trainees inclinations to "go out on their own" or otherwise goof off.

## EVALUATING SALES TRAINING PROGRAMMES

The second E in A-C-M-E-E, the evaluation step focuses upon measuring programme effectiveness. As sales training programme represents investments of time, money and effort, sales management expects return commensurate with the investment. Though measuring sales training effectiveness is not easy, it is possible to gauge programme effectiveness.

**1. Comparison of Aims with Results.** The starting point is to compare the programme's aims (the A in A-C-M-E-E) with the results, but the results such as improved selling performance, may not show up until months later. Management makes certain comparisons, such as the length of time new salespersons take to attain the productivity level of the experienced salesperson, the performance against standards of trained and untrained sales personnel, and the respective training histories of the best and worst performers. Some companies plot each salesperson's sales records on a before-and-after training basis, generally converting them to market share percentage.

However, territorial sales volumes are influenced not only by personal selling but by advertising, competitors' activities, economic fluctuations, and similar factors. No known analytical technique exists for precise isolation of the influence of these factors.

**2. Written Tests.** Some companies use written tests on a before-and-after training basis to determine how much trainees have learned. This is appropriate for measuring improvements in amount and depth of product knowledge. However, it reveals little about the trainee's ability to apply this in the field.

**3. Observation.** Other firms send observers to work with sales personnel who have completed training programmes and to report the extent to which trainees are applying what was taught in programmes.

**4. Customer's Reaction.** Other companies solicit customers for their reactions to a salesperson's performance after training. None of these approaches produces precise evaluative data. They only provide indications as to whether results are positive or not.

## COMPARATIVE ADVANTAGES

To obtain insight for improving the effectiveness of future programmes, management measures the effectiveness of training programmes both while they are in progress and upon completion. Tests and examinations measure trainee retention of materials presented most appropriately when trainees are to memorize certain information, as product specifications and applications. There is little value in using tests and examinations for evaluating training in sales techniques. Performance in role playing assignments is a better approach. In some companies trainers rate each trainees' performance in role playing, panels and other discussion. Though these are subjective ratings, but they provide learning incentives. The practice of requiring to rate each trainers' performance, either in each session or in the total programme may stimulate trainers to improve their effectiveness. Many sales executives, however, argue that trainees are in no position to judge the trainers' effectiveness unit they gain additional field experience. Comment sheet similar to Chart

16.1 is used in numerous sales training programmes. Many companies also ask trainees to evaluate training programmes after they return to their territories.

**Chart 16.1**

**Form for Trainee Rating of Sales Training Session**

A brief, candid review of this training session will help you evaluate what you have learned and help us in our efforts to improve the programme. Please answer all questions. Do not sign your name; the results are anonymous.

Place an X where appropriate to describe your reactions to each of the following:

| | |
|---|---|
| 1. Material covered | Exciting............... Dull |
| 2. Instruction | Excellent............. Poor |
| 3. Worthwhileness of material | Great.................. Little |
| 4. Completeness of coverage | Very Complete.... Totally Inadequate |

5. How might the session have been improved ?

________________________________________

________________________________________

________________________________________

## QUESTIONS FOR EXERCISE

1. Elaborate and discuss the elements, stages, or decisions involved in a sales training programme.
2. What are the two philosophies of sales training? Which factors determine them?
3. Discuss the key organizational decisions for organization of sales training.
4. Identify instructional materials and training aids in sales training.
5. Write short note on evaluating sales training programmes.

# 17

# Remuneration of Sales Personnel

## MONEY AS MOTIVATOR

Money has limited potential as a motivator. In Maslow's hierarchy, it loses motivating power once an individual satisfies physiological needs and most safety and security needs, retaining only declining residual motivating power in fulfilling esteem and self-actualization needs, insofar as a larger income can fulfil them. In Herzberg's motivation-hygiene model, money is a hygiene factor, contributing to the prevention of job dissatisfaction but otherwise not motivating at all.

## SALES COMPENSATION PLANS

### Nature

**1. Motivational Roles.** An essential part of the total programme for motivating sales personnel, a sales compensation plan has three motivational roles: (i) To provide a living wage, (ii) To adjust pay levels to performance, thereby relating job performance and rewards (in line with expectancy motivation theory) and (iii) To provide a mechanism for demonstrating the congruency between attaining company goals and individual goals also in line with expectancy theory.

**2. Attractive Returns.** A properly designed sales compensation plan fits a company's special needs and problems. From it flows attractive returns for both the company and its sales personnel. While sales and growth goals are reached at low cost, profits are satisfactory. Sales personnel receive high pay as a reward for effective job performance and team spirit is high.

**3. Aids to Effective Motivation.** Sales compensation plans are aids to effective motivation. No plan can be the entire motivational programme. A compensation plan should not conflict with what may be important motives such as to conform, to be like others, to belong to be liked by one's peers. The basic appropriateness of a compensation plan depends on the way it is implemented and administered. Sometimes, a fundamentally poor compensation plan works satisfactorily when a skilled executive administers it.

**4. Revision of Plans**. In established companies, sales executives concern themselves mainly with revising plans already in effect. Most changes are instituted to bring the plan and marketing objectives into closer alignment. For example, an adjustment in compensation may be required as additional sales effort is needed for the factory to operate at optimum capacity. This could mean paying bonuses on sales and the quota, paying additional compensation for larger orders or for securing new accounts, or revising commission rate schedules.

**5. Rare Major Changes**. Major changes in the compensation plan are rare. Sales personnel resist sweeping changes, particularly when this requires them to alter accustomed ways of doing things. For instance, many individuals have difficulty in adjusting their living and spending habits when a firm switches from paying straight salaries to straight commissions.

**6. Implementation of Far-reaching Change**. Whether a change should be made in one step or in many depends upon the particular situation, and no easy generalization is possible. Careful orientation is a must as explanation of impending changes is important.

**7. Conditions of Total Overhauling**. There are two situations where total overhauling of compensation plans are in order :

(i) One is the company whose sales force already has low morale because of the current compensation plan. If the plan is at the root of the morale problem, drastic change is appropriate.

(ii) A second situation calling for a complete revamping of the sales compensation plan occurs when a company is anticipating the cultivation of new and different markets. The problems in both these situations are like those in the newly organized company, which musk build its sales compensation plan from scratch. In both cases management must consider many factors, the nature and number of which vary with the company and the situation. Usually it includes the types of customers, the marketing channels, characteristics of the products, intensity of competition, extent of the market, and complexity of the selling task.

**Requirements**

1. It provides a living wage, preferably in the form of a secure income. Individuals worried about money matters do not concentrate on doing their jobs well.

2. It fits with the rest of the motivational programme and does not conflict with other motivational factors, such as the intangible feeling of belonging to the sales team.

3. It does not penalize sales personnel because of factors beyond their control. Within the limits of seniority and other special circumstances, sales personnel receive equal pay for equal performance.

4. It is easy for sales personnel to understand. They are able to calculate their own earnings.

5. It adjusts pay to changes in performance.

6. It helps in attaining the objectives of the sales organization.

## STEPS IN SALES COMPENSATION PLAN

### 1. Defining the Sales Job

(i) *Re-examination of the Nature of the Sales Job* : Up-to-date written job descriptions are logical. If jobs descriptions are outdated, inaccurate, or incomplete, then a revision is in order. If there are no written sales job descriptions, they are prepared.

(ii) *Consideration of Company Operations* : Other aspects of company operations should be considered in relation to their impact upon the sales job. Sales department objectives are analyzed, sales volume objectives are translated into what is expected of the sales personnel, as a group and individually. The impact of sales-related marketing policies such as distribution policies, credit policies, price policies and other policies which affect the salesperson's job are determined. Current and proposed advertising and sales promotional programmes must assist in clarifying the nature of the salesperson's goals, duties and activities.

### 2. Consideration of the Company's Job Evaluation Method

Most large and many smaller companies use job evaluation systems to determine the relative value of individual jobs. Job evaluation procedure is an orderly approach based on judgment. Without considering the ability or personality of individuals who do the work, it focuses on the jobs to arrive at fair compensation relationships among jobs.

There are four job evaluation methods. Two are non-quantitative: simple ranking and classification or grading. The other two are quantitative : the point system and the factor-comparison method.

(i) *Simple Ranking* : It is widely used by small businesses. In it an executive committee sorts job descriptions in the order of worth without considering the individuals currently in the jobs or their compensation levels. No attempt is made to determine critical factors inherent in the jobs. Only overall appraisals are made of the relative worth of different jobs.

(ii) *Classification or Grading* : It utilizes a system of grades and grade descriptions, against which individual jobs are compared. Sometimes called classes, the grades are described in terms of job responsibility, skills required, supervision given and received, exposure to unfavourable and hazardous working conditions and similar characteristics. Job descriptions are classified into appropriate grades by an executive committee or personnel specialists by comparing job descriptions with grade descriptions. All jobs within a grade are treated alike with respect to base compensation.

(iii) *Point System* : It is the most widely used job evaluation method, which involves establishing and defining the factors common to most jobs that represent the chief elements of value inherent in all jobs. While the specific factors chosen differ from one company to another, they generally include mental and physical skills, responsibility, supervision given and received, personality requirements, and minimum education required. Each factor is assigned a minimum and maximum number of points. Different ranges are associated in line with the relative importance of the factors. Now appraised factor scores are combined into a total point value. Finally, bands of points are decided upon making the different compensation classes. Less arbitrary judgment is required than under the classification method. The use of point values makes it possible to determine the gap or distance, between job classes.

(iv) *Factor-Comparison Method* : Resembling the point system it is more complex, utilizing a scheme of ranking and cross-comparisons to minimize error from faulty judgement. It employs selected factors and evaluation scales. No upper limit exists to the valuation that can be assigned to any one factor. Typical of similar jobs throughout the company, a selected number of key jobs are then evaluated, factor by factor, by arranging them in rank order, from highest to lowest for each factor. As a check against this judgmental evaluation, the compensation rupees actually paid for each job are allocated to the factors which automatically establishes the relationship among jobs for each factor. The judgment ranking and the ranking by allocation of compensation are compared and differences are reconciled or else the jobs are removed from the key list. Additional jobs are evaluated and their monetary values for each factor interpolated into the scale on the basis of the dollar amounts assigned to the several factors making up key jobs. This procedure is repeated until all jobs are evaluated.

(v) *Job Evaluation and Sales Positions* : Job evaluation is inescapable in organizational life. Informal job evaluation exists in firms not using formal job evaluation. Sales executives oppose using formal job evaluations to determine the compensation levels of sales personnel, contending that compensation levels for sales personnel are more closely related to external supply-and-demand factors than to conditions inside the company. Sales personnel enjoy greater job mobility than most other employees and are in everyday contact with potential employers.

If a company has a formal job evaluation programme including the jobs of sales personnel, there should be sales department representation on the committee that arrives at quantitative evaluations. If the job evaluation programme does not cover sales personnel programme or the company does not use formal job evaluation, the sales executive should establish the value of sales jobs relative to other company jobs. This will assure that the monetary attractiveness of sales positions is no less than for comparable jobs elsewhere in the company. If the sales executive knows the relative differences between sales jobs and other company jobs, he or she is preparing for the day when sales positions are regarded as appropriate for inclusion in formal jobs evaluation programmes.

**3. Consideration of Compensation Patterns in Community and Industry**

It is important to consider prevailing compensation patterns in the community and industry because compensation levels for sales personnel are related to external supply-and-demand factors.

A company-wide formal job evaluation programme should take into account the current rates for sales positions in the community and industry. A programme for setting compensation of sales personnel is sound only if it considers the relation of external compensation practices to those of the company. Effective sales executives maintain constant vigilance against the possibility that the pay of sales personnel gets out of line with that paid for similar jobs in the community or industry.

**4. Determining Compensation level**

(i) *Evacuation of Sales Force* : Although the compensation level might be set through individual bargaining or on an arbitrary judgment basis, neither expedient is recommended. Management should ascertain whether the calibre of the present sales force measures up to what the company would like to have. It should determine the market value of sales personnel of the desired grade. It should weigh the worth of individual persons through estimating the sales and profit rupees that would be lost if particular sales people resigned.

(ii) *The Compensation Amount the Company can Afford to Pay* : It is excellent practice to plot each cost estimate on a break-even style chart. When the several plots are compared with the company's cost goals, the sales volume needed to break-even at each compensation level is revealed. The compensation levels for individual salespeople under the proposed plan also should be plotted in break-even style.

In some firms, company-wide formal job evaluation programmes are used to set compensation level for sales positions. It serves as a check on the compensation levels prescribed through job evaluations. When the job evaluation programme is sound, there should be few, if any, discrepancies. Any discrepancies should be reconciled.

(iii) *Over Compensation* : Sometimes two companies operate under similar selling conditions but with different sales compensation levels. Sales personnel in one company earn more than those who do essentially the same work in another company. Relatively speaking, the first group of salespeople is over compensated. Sometimes management does not know the true worth of individual sales personnel. Management regards some sales personnel as indispensable, or managerial inertia prevents adjustment of the compensation level to changed selling conditions. In still other cases, sales managers are biased in favour of high compensation for selling jobs.

**(5) Provision for Various Compensation Elements**

A sales compensation plan has four basic elements :

(i) A fixed element, either a salary or a drawing account, to provide some stability of income;

(ii) a variable element, for example, a commission bonus or profit-sharing arrangement to serve as an incentive;

(iii) an element covering the fringe or "plus factor", such as paid vacations, sickness and accident benefits, life insurance, pensions and the like and

(iv) an element providing for reimbursement of expenses or payment of expenses allowances. Management selects the combination of elements that best fits the selling situation. Most companies split the fixed and variable elements on a 60:40 to an 80:20 basis.

## COMPENSATION PLAN TO MEET COMPANY NEEDS

Though a sales compensation plan is no panacea for marketing ills, it is often possible to construct a plan that increases marketing effectiveness. Despite the existence of other managerial alternatives, it may be possible to adjust the compensation plan to stimulate the selling of better balanced orders. Variable commission rates might be set on different products, with the higher rates applying to neglected products.

If a firm might have a "small-order" problem, it is possible to design compensation plans that encourage sales personnel to write larger orders. Commission rates can be graduated so that high rates apply to larger orders. Such a revised compensation plan must be supplemented with a customer classification and call scheduling system, enabling management to vary call frequency with account size.

If a company wants to obtain more displays or local advertising by retailers, the presence or absence of point-of-purchase displays can spell the difference between marketing success or failure. Securing retail displays is a task that sales personnel may neglect, if they are paid commission based on sales volume. An incentive payment for obtaining retail displays is often incorporated in the compensation plan to overcome this tendency.

Incentive plans may assist in securing new customers and new business, improving the quality of salespeople's reports, controlling expenses of handling complaints and adjustments, eliminating price shading by the sales staff, reducing travelling and other expenses, and making collections and gathering credit information. However, repeated tampering with the sales compensation plan frequently results in complex and difficult-to-administer plans.

## STEPS IN REVISION OF COMPENSATION PLAN

**1. Consult the Present Sales Force.** The management should consult the present sales personnel because many grievances have roots in the compensation plan. It should encourage sales personnel to articulate their likes and dislikes about the current plan and to suggest changes in it. Criticisms and suggestions are appraised relative to the plan or plans under consideration. The management compares the caliber of the present sales force with that of the people whom it would like to have. As nearly every sales force has some people of the desired caliber, more weight can be attached to their opinions than to those of others.

**2. Reduce Tentative Plan to Writing and Pretest It.** The tentative plan is put in writing for clarification and to eliminate inconsistencies. The amount of testing required depends upon how much the new plan differs from the one in use. The greater the difference, the more thorough is the pretesting. Pretests are mathematical and usually computerized. Past payrolls for a year or two are reworked to check operation of the proposed plan against experience under the old system. Analysts compare what happened with what would have happened had the new plan been in effect. Calculations are made for periods representative of average, good, and poor business.

Utilizing sales forecast data, new and old plans are applied to future periods. The plan is tested for the sales force as a group and for individuals faced with unique selling conditions. Analysis reveals whether the plan permits earning in line with the desired compensation level. If deficiencies show up, weaknesses may be traced to the way territorial assignments have been made or to inaccuracies in sales forecasts, budgets or quotas.

Several territories representative of different sets of selling conditions are selected to conduct a pilot test. The proposed plan is applied in each one long enough to detect how it works under current conditions. Pilot tests are invaluable for spotting possible sources of trouble and other deficiencies.

**3. Revise the Plan.** Now, the plan is revised to eliminate deficiencies. If alterations are extensive, the revised plan goes through further pretests and perhaps another pilot test. But if changes are only minor, further testing is not necessary.

**4. Implement the Plan.** When the new plan is implemented, it is explained to sales personnel convincing them of its basic fairness and logic. The sales personnel are told what the management hopes to accomplish through the new plan and how this is to be done. All sales personnel should receive copies of the new plan, together with written examples of the method used for calculating earnings. If the plan is complex, special training sessions are held teaching sales personnel how to compute their own earnings. If sales personnel do not understand the total plan or some of its features, they may presume that the company is taking unfair advantage of them. Inadequate understanding of the sales compensation plan is often a cause of low morale. No effort should be spared to make certain that everyone on the sales force fully comprehends the compensation plan and its workings.

**5. Provide for Follow-up.** Provisions for follow-up are made. Need for further adjustments is detected from periodic check-ups. These provide evidence of the plan's accomplishments. These also uncover weaknesses needing correction.

## TYPES OF COMPENSATION PLANS

Disregarding the "fringe benefit" and "expense reimbursement" elements, there are only three basic types of compensation plans : straight salary, straight commission, and a combination of salary and variable elements.

**1. Straight-Salary Plan.** It is the simplest compensation plan in which the salespersons receives fixed sums at regular intervals usually each week or month but sometimes every two weeks representing total payments for their services. A recent study by Executive Compensation Service, Inc., shows that under 17.5 per cent of all selling organizations use straight-salary and these are industrial-goods companies rather than consumer-goods companies. Firms formerly using the straight-salary have tended to combine a basic salary with a variable element thus switching to combination plans.

**Conditions of Suitability.** However, the straight-salary plan is the logical compensation plan when the selling job requires extensive missionary or educational work, when sales people service the product or give technical and engineering advice to prospects or users or when salespeople do considerable sales promotion work. It is worthy of serious consideration if non-selling tasks bulk large in the sales persons total time expenditure. It is commonly used for compensating salespeople heavily engaged in trade selling in which selling amounts to mere order-taking. It abounds in the wholesale and manufacturing fields, where consumer necessities are distributed directly to retailers. It is used for paying driver-salespersons selling liquor and beverages, milk and bread, and similarly distributed products.

**Advantages**

(i) From Management's Standpoints

(a) The straight-salary plan provides strong financial control over sales personnel and management can direct their activities along the most productive lines.

(b) Component tasks making up salespersons jobs can be recast with minimum opposition from those affected. Thus, there is flexibility in adjusting field sales work to changed selling situations.

(c) If sales personnel prepare detailed reports, follow-up leads, or perform other time-consuming tasks, they cooperate more fully.

(d) Because of their basic simplicity and compared with straight-commission plans, accounting costs are lower in straight-salary plans which are economical to administer.

(ii) For Sales Personnel

(a) Stability of income provides freedom from financial uncertainties inherent in other plans.

(b) Sales personnel are relieved of much of the burden of planning their own activities.

(c) Because of its basic simplicity, sales personnel have no difficulty in understanding straight-salary plans.

**Disadvantages**

(i) Since there are no direct monetary incentives, many salespeople do only an *average* rather than an outstanding job.

(ii) They pass up opportunities for increased business, unit management becomes aware of them and orders the required actions.

(iii) There is a tendency to under-compensate productive salespeople and to over-compensate poor performers.

(iv) If pay inequities exist for long, the turnover rate rises and it is often the most productive people who leave first, resulting in increased costs for recruiting, selecting and training.

(v) As arguments occur on pay adjustments for ability, rising living costs, and length of service, problems are encountered in maintaining morale.

(vi) As the selling expense is fixed, it is difficult to adjust to changing conditions.

(vii) During business upturns, there is difficulty in securing the company's share of rising industry volume, because salaried salespeople are not disposed to exceed previous sales records by any large amount.

(viii) As in administering a straight-salary plan, individual sales personnel are paid according to their relative performance, the difficulty lies in measuring performance. Management needs to define "performance" and the meanings of good, average, and poor performances. When management has these definitions and develops methods for performance measurements, it can set individual salaries fairly and intelligently.

In the absence of well-defined quantitative performance standards, the sales job description, if up to date and complete, is the place to start in appraising job performances of sales personnel.

All sales personnel need rating not on their achievement of sales and cost goals and on their performance of each assigned duty. The total evaluation of an individual is a composite of the several ratings, weighted according to relative importance. Persons rated as average are paid average salaries. Salaries of below-average and above-average sales personnel are scaled to reflect the extent to which their performances vary from the average. Each individual's performance is regularly reviewed. Upward adjustments are made for those showing improvements. Downward adjustments are made for those with deteriorating performances.

**2. Straight-Commission Plan.** It is based on the theory that individual sales personnel should be paid according to productivity. It is assumed that as sales volume is the best productivity measure, it can be used as the sole measure.

In its purest form, this plan is almost as simple as the straight-salary plan. However, many commission systems develop into complex arrangements. As sales volume rises to different levels, some provide progressive or regressive changes in commission rates. Others provide for differential commission rates for sales of different products, to different categories of customers or during given selling seasons. These refinements make straight-commission plans more complex than straight-salary plans.

**Types**

(i) Straight-commission with sales personnel paying their own expenses. Advances may or may not be made against earned commissions.

(ii) Straight-commission with the company paying expenses, with or without advances against earned commissions.

Today no more than 6 or 7 per cent of all companics use such plan. It is used in situations where non-selling duties are relatively unimportant and management emphasizes order getting. It is common in the clothing, textile and shoe industries and in drug and hardware wholesaling. Firms selling intangibles, such as insurance and investment securities and manufacturers of furniture, office equipment and business machines frequently use this plan.

**Advantages**

(i) It provides maximum direct monetary incentive for the salesperson to strive for high-level volume. The star salesperson is paid more than he or she would be under most salary plans and low producers are not likely to be over-compensated. When a commission system is first installed, the sales personnel turnover rate accelerates, but usually the exodus is among the low producers. Those remaining work longer and harder with more income to show for their efforts.

(ii) It provides a means for cost control as all direct selling expenses, except for travelling and miscellaneous expenses fluctuate directly with sales volume changes and sales compensation becomes virtually an all variable expense.

(iii) It is characterized by great flexibility. By revising commission rates applying to different products, it is possible to stimulate sales personnel to emphasize those with the highest gross margins.

**Disadvantages**

(i) It provides little financial control over salespeople's activities.

(ii) Salespersons often feel that they are discharging their full responsibilities by continuing to send in customer's orders. They are careless about transmitting reports, consider individual accounts private property, shade prices to make sales and may use high-pressure tactics with consequent loss of customer goodwill.

(iii) Unless differential commission rates are used, sales personnel push the easiest-to-sell low-margin items and neglect harder-to-sell high-margin items. Seeking to correct this through using differential commission rates, management increases record-keeping expenses.

(iv) The costs of checking and auditing salespeople's reports and of calculating payrolls are higher than under the straight-salary method.

(v) Some salespersons' efficiency may decline because of income uncertainties. If a sales force has many financially worried salespeople, management may have to invest considerable time, effort and money to buoy up their spirits.

**Implementation**

(i) *Determining Commission Base* : Implementation of a straight-commission system requires determining commission base strongly influenced by company selling policies and problems.

(a) If obtaining volume is the main concern, then total sales is the base.

(b) If sales personnel make collections on sales, commissions are based on collections.

(c) If a firm has excessive order cancellations, commissions can be based upon shipments, billings, or payments.

(d) To control price cutting by sales personnel, some companies base commission on gross margins.

(e) Other companies use net profits as the base, seeking

simultaneously to control price cutting, selling expense and net profit.

(ii) *Drawing Accounts* : In drawing account method, the company establishes separate accounts for each salesperson, to which commissions are credited and against which periodic withdrawals are made. It resembles salaries since customarily individual sales personnel are allowed to overdraw against future earnings. If sales personnel become greatly overdrawn, they may lose incentive to produce, because earned commissions are used to reduce the indebtedness. Some sales personnel become discouraged with the prospects of paying back overdrawn account and quit the company. To forestall this, some firms use "guaranteed" drawing account plans, which do not require the paying back of overdrawals. Sales executives in these firms are conservative in setting the size of guaranteed drawing accounts, for they are in effect combination of salary and commission plans. Drawing account plans generally include a provision that covers the possibility of overdrafts.

**3. Combinations of Salary-and-Incentive Plan.** Most sales compensation plans are combinations of salary and commission plans, developed as attempts to capture the advantages and offset the disadvantages of both the salary and commission systems. In the straight-salary method, the sales executives lack a financial means for stimulating the sales force to greater effort. In the straight-commission system, the executive has weak financial control over non-selling activities. By a judicious blending of both basic plans, management seeks both control and motivation though actual results depend upon management's skills in designing and administering the plan.

**Advantages**

(i) Sales personnel have both the security of stable incomes and the stimulus of direct financial incentive.

(ii) Management has both financial control over sales activities and the apparatus to motivate sales efforts.

(iii) As selling costs are composed of fixed and variable elements; greater flexibility for adjustment to changing conditions exists than under the commission method.

(iv) There are beneficial effects upon sales force morale.

(v) Disagreements on pay increases and territorial changes are less violent than under a straight-commission plan.

(vi) If salespeople realize that the company shares their financial risks, a cooperative spirit develops between them and the company.

**Disadvantages**

(i) Clerical costs are higher than for either a salary or a commission system.

(ii) More records are maintained and in greater detail.

(iii) There are risks that the plan will become complicated and that sales personnel will not understand it.

## BONUSES

**Meaning**

A bonus is an amount paid for accomplishing a specific sales task. Bonuses are paid for reaching a sales quota, performing promotional activities, obtaining new accounts, following up leads, setting up displays, or carrying out other assigned tasks. The bonus is an additional financial reward to the salespersons for achieving results beyond a predetermined minimum.

**Types**

Bonuses always appear with one of three main sales compensation methods :

(i) If used with the straight-salary, the plan resembles the combination.

(ii) If used with the straight-commission, the result is a commission plan to which an element of managerial control and direction has been added.

(iii) If used with the combination of salary and commission plan, the bonus becomes a portion of the incentive income that is calculated differently from the commission.

**Administrative Actions**

(i) The bonus conditions require thorough explanation as all sales personnel must understand them.

(ii) The necessary records must be set up and maintained.

(iii) Procedures are needed for keeping sales personnel abreast of their current standings relative to the goals.

(iv) Any bonus misunderstandings or grievances arising should be dealt with fairly and tactfully.

## FRINGE BENEFITS

**Kinds.** Fringe benefits do not bear direct relationships to job performance. Fringe benefits are such as payments for social security premiums, unemployment compensation, and worker's compensation. They range from 25 to 40 per cent of the total sales compensation package. Some are required by federal and state laws. Others, the company provides to be competitive

TABLE 17.1

**Fringe Benefits Offered by U.S. Companies**

| | |
|---|---|
| ***Time*** | Country clubs |
| Holidays | Professional association |
| Vacations | ***Miscellaneous*** |
| Sick leave | Automobile |
| Personal leave | Use of vacation spot |
| Sabbaticals | Parking |
| Pregnancy leave | Dry-cleaning and laundry |
| ***Retirement Programmes*** | Lunches (all or part) |
| Social security (mandatory) | Secretarial services |
| Pension plan | Employee stock purchase plan |
| Profit sharing | Company-provided housing |
| Salary reduction plans | Legal services |
| ***Insurance and medical*** | Financial counseling |
| Physical examinations | Tuition for continuing education programmes |
| Medical payments and reimbursements | Financial support for dependents' education |
| Hospitalization insurance | Credit unions |
| Dental insurance | Discounts for purchases of company products |
| Disability insurance | Childcare payments |
| Life insurance | Matching funds to charities and schools |
| Travel insurance | Company social events |
| Accident insurance | Company sport tournaments |
| Worker's compensation (mandatory) | Retirement counselling |
| Unemployment insurance (mandatory) | Career counselling |
| Cancer insurance | Payment of moving expenses |
| Psychotherapy expense | |
| ***Organization dues*** | |
| Trade association | |
| Civic clubs | |

with other companies in the industry or community to furnish reasons for employees to remain in the company's service and to comply with what employees expect as fringe benefits.

**Nature.** Like monetary benefits, fringe benefits are not motivating factors. In the Maslow hierarchy they contribute to fulfillment of safety and security needs, although some such as payment of country club dues contribute to fulfilment of esteem and other higher-order needs. Since fringe benefits do not vary with job performance, they help to prevent job dissatisfaction but do not add to job satisfaction.

**Cafeteria Approach.** Many companies offer a "cafeteria" approach to fringc benefits. The company offers a core of basic benefits including the benefits required by law plus other traditional benefits, including paid vacations, medical disability, and death benefits and a retirement programme. Employees then use credits based on age, pay, family status, and years of company service to obtain optional benefits not included in the core. This lets employees select those benefits that best fit their needs. As needs for benefits change, employees are given opportunities to change their selection of benefits that best fit their needs. As needs for benefits change, employees are given opportunities to change their selection of benefits that best fit their needs. As needs for benefits change, employees are given opportunities to change their selections. Companies using the cafeteria approach have "awareness" aimed at making employees aware of the benefits available.

## THE WORK LOAD APPROACH

The number of salesmen requires may be calculated on the basis of work load. The formula for calculating the number of salesmen is as follows:

$$\text{No. of salesmen} = \frac{\text{Number of Customers} \times \text{Call Frequency}}{\text{Average weekly call rate} \times \text{Number of working weeks per year}}$$

The number of customers must be grouped according to the value of goods bought and potential for the future. The total work load for the year is given by number of customers multiplied by call frequency for each category of customers. The number of weeks must not include holidays illness and training period etc.

## QUESTIONS FOR EXERCISE

1. Is money a motivator? Discuss the nature and requirements of a sales compensation plan.
2. Explain the steps in devising a sales compensation plan.
3. How is compensation plan used to meet in company needs? What steps should be taken in devising the plan?
4. Describe various types of compensation plans.
5. Write short note on use of bonuses and fringe benefits.

# 18
# MOTIVATION BY SALES MANAGEMENT

Motivation is goal-directed behaviour fulfilling certain needs or desires. Needs suggest a lack of something that reaching the goal could satisfy. Desires suggest positive ardour and strength of feeling. The complex of needs and desires stemming from within leads individuals to act so as to satisfy them. As applied to sales personnel, motivation is the amount of effort the salesperson desires to expend on the activities associated with the sales job, such as calling on potential accounts, planning sales presentation, and filling out reports. Expending effort on each activity lead the sales job to some level of achievement on total sales volume, profitability, sales to new accounts, quota attainment and the like.

## MOTIVATIONAL HELP FROM MANAGEMENT

Sales personnel require motivational help from management as individuals and as group members to reach and maintain acceptable performance levels. As individuals, they are targets for personalized motivational efforts by their superiors. As members of the sales force, they are targets for sales management efforts aimed toward welding them into an effective selling team. Following four aspects of the salesperson's job affect the quality of its performance. Each is an important reason why sales personnel require additional motivation.

**1. Inherent Nature of the Sales Job.** The inherent nature of the sales job is the first reason that additional motivation is required. Although varying from one company to the next, sales jobs are alike in certain respects :

(i) Every sales job is a succession of ups and downs, a series of experiences resulting in alternating feelings of exhilaration and depression. During course of a day's work, salespersons interact with many pleasant and courteous people, while others are unpleasant and rude and are difficult to deal with.

(ii) When aggressive competing sales personnel view for the same business and they meet numerous turndowns they are frustrated.

(iii) They spend not only working time but considerable after-hours time away from home, causing them to miss attractive parts of family life.

These conditions cause salespersons to become discouraged, to achieve low performance levels, or even to seek non-selling positions.

**2. Salesperson's Boundary Position.** Occupying "boundary position" in the company, the sales person must try to satisfy the expectations of people both with the company and in customer organizations. He has linkage with four groups : (i) sales management, (ii) the company organization that handles order fulfilment, (iii) the customers, and (iv) other company sales personnel.

**3. Role Conflicts.** Role conflicts traceable to the salesperson's linkage with groups that have divergent interests is another reason why additional motivation is required. Each group imposes certain behavioural expectations on the salesperson. In playing these different roles, the salesperson faces following role conflicts :

(i) *Conflict of Identification* : It is out of multi-group membership. As the salesperson works with the customer, he identifies with the customer rather than the company. On returning to the company, he drops identification with the customer and identifies with the company.

(ii) *Advocacy Conflict* : It arises when the salesperson identifies with the customer and advocates the customer's position to other groups in the company organization. It may be important and may be encouraged by the sales management group, but the advocator is in difficult position.

(iii) *Dual Role Conflict* : This is conflict in the salesperson's usual role as an advocate for both the customer and the company and the salesperson's pecuniary interest as an entrepreneur. As an entrepreneur paid directly or indirectly on the basis of sales volume, he has an interest in selling as much as possible in the shortest time. However, he may uncover facts overlooked or unknown to the customer, indicating that difficulties in the customer's organization limit the product's usefulness. If the salesperson tells the customer about these conditions, he risks losing the sale and the income that goes with it.

Nothing can be done to reduce the role conflicts of sales personnel. Experienced sales personnel perceive significantly less role conflict than do those with less experience. His perceptions of and ability to cope with role conflict are influenced not only by experience but by the effectiveness of sales training. Those who become experienced sales personnel may cope better with role conflicts than those leaving the sales organization earlier. So improving sales training effectiveness and revising selection criteria are two means to reduce the impact of role conflict on sales force morale.

**4. Tendency toward Apathy**. Salespeople require additional motivation to maintain continuing enthusiasm to generate renewed interest in their work. The sales personnel who cover the same territory and virtually the same customers year after year lose interest and enthusiasm. Gradually, their sales calls degenerate into routine order-taking. Knowing the customers so well, they believe that good salesmanship is no longer necessary. They do forget that friendship in no way obviates the necessity for creative selling and that most customers do not sell themselves on new products and applications. When a competing salesperson calls on the same account and uses effective sales techniques, he gets an order.

**5. Maintaining a Feeling of Group Identity**. Working alone the salesperson finds it difficult to develop and maintain a feeling of group identity with other company salespeople. Team spirit is weak. Thus, the contagious enthusiasm, so much conducive to improving the entire group's performance, does not develop.

If through providing added motivation, sales management succeeds in developing and maintaining team spirit, individual sales personnel strive to meet group performance standards. Those who consider themselves members of the sales team do not want to appear poor performers in the eyes of their colleagues. Effective sales management must work continuously to achieve and maintain the kind of working atmosphere in which all members of the sales force feel they are participating in a cooperative endeavour.

## THEORIES OF GRATIFICATION AND MOTIVATION

All human activity, including the salesperson's job behaviour, is directed toward satisfying certain needs that is, reaching certain goals. As individuals seek to fulfil different sets of needs in different ways, patterns of individual behaviour differ. Because of the differing motivational patterns and amounts and types of efforts they exert in performing their jobs, some salespersons are more successful than others.

Their behaviour depends upon the nature of their fulfilled and unfulfilled needs modified by their environmental and social backgrounds. There is a tension to satisfy any need and any specific action is motivated to remove the tension which is under consciousness. Any action taken is for the purpose of reducing these tensions fulfilling a need or needs to reach a goal or goals.

**1. Maslow's Hierarchy of Needs**

**1. Primary Needs.** Primary needs are the inborn or physiological needs for food, water, rest, sleep, air to breathe, sex, and so on, the fulfilment of which are basic to life itself. Until primary needs are satisfied, other needs have little motivational influence.

**2. Secondary Needs.** These arise from an individual's interaction with the environment. These are not inborn but develop with maturity. These include those for safety and security, belongingness and social relations and self-esteem and self-respect.

Based on the notion that an individual seeks to fulfil personal needs according to some hierarchy of importance, A. H. Maslow, a psychologist, developed a theory of motivation. He suggests that after an individual gratifies basic physiological needs, he or she proceeds to strive to fulfil safety and security needs, then belongingness and social relations needs, and so on. The individual's level of aspiration rises as needs on higher levels are satisfied. Every salesperson does not establish the order of priority of need fulfilment suggested by Maslow. Some sales personnel appear to assign earlier priority to filling the esteem need for self-respect than they do to filling the need for social relations within a group.

Salespersons' motives for working vary according to the nature and potency of the unsatisfied portion of their individual hierarchies of needs. However, some of the salespeople's needs are filled off the job. One salesperson works because of the need for money to feed a family; another because the job is seen as a means for gaining esteem of others; still another because of a need to achieve self-actualization, through job performance to the maximum of one's abilities.

For knowing the make-up of the unsatisfied portion of a salesperson's hierarchy of needs at a particular time, sales management could determine the best incentives. If management can harmonize the individual's goals with those of the organization, then individual behaviour is channelled along lines aimed at achieving both sets of goals. For a salesperson worried about providing for a child's education, an important individual goal is to obtain money to remove the uncertainty. If management sees how giving the salesperson an opportunity to earn more money will also further the attainment of organizational goals, then offering the salesperson the chance to earn more money for obtaining larger orders is a powerful incentive.

Once the individual has gratified physiological needs and most safety and security needs, the money loses its power as an incentive. Other incentives become increasingly effective, for example, a chance for promotion, which is one way to fulfil esteem and self-respect needs. The farther up in the hierarchy an individual's unfulfilled needs are pushed the promise of more money becomes a weaker incentive. The power a larger income retains is related to unfulfilled esteem and self-actualization needs and the extent to which income can gratify them. The threat of receiving a lower income, a negative incentive, endangers the fulfilled part of an individual's need structure and money continues to have power as an incentive to the extent that this threat exists. Whereas motives are internal to the individual, incentives are external. Sales management influences the behavioural patterns of sales personnel indirectly through the incentives it offers.

**2. Motivation-Hygiene Theory**

Frederick Herzberg and his co-researchers developed the motivation-hygiene theory, according to which the factors leading to motivation and job satisfaction are not the same as those leading to apathy and job dissatisfaction. Job dissatisfaction is not the opposite of job satisfaction. Here two separate groups of needs are involved, one related to job satisfaction and the other to job dissatisfaction. While most needs have potentials for influencing both the relief of job dissatisfaction and the increase of job satisfaction, each need serves predominately either a hygiene or motivator purpose.

(i) *Hygiene Factor* : Hygiene needs relate to the working environment, compensation, fringe benefits, type of supervision, and other factors extrinsic to the job factors. Deficiencies in fulfilling the hygiene needs cause job dissatisfaction. Fulfilling the hygiene needs does not lead to job satisfaction, but to the achievement of a neutral point known as the "fair day's work" point at which the individual is ripe for influence by the motivation factors, ones intrinsic to the job itself.

(ii) *Motivation Factors* : These factors reflect needs for personal growth, including achievement, recognition, nature of the job itself, responsibility and opportunities for advancement. The motivation factors represent needs that, when fulfilled, lead to job satisfaction.

Figure 18.1 shows the considered similarity of the Maslow and Herzberg models. Herzberg's division of the need hierarchy into two factors—hygiene and motivational—implies that for most sales personnel, only Maslow's higher-order needs (esteem and self-actualization) are primary motivators. Yet even these people must satisfy the lower-order (hygiene) needs for maintenance of their job satisfaction.

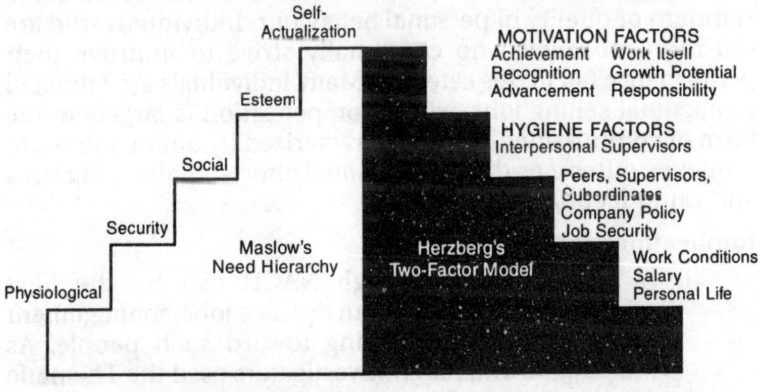


Fig. 18.1. The Maslow and Herzberg Models Compared.

## Implications

Motivation-hygiene theory has two important implications for sales management :

(i) The management must see that the job provides the conditions that prevent job dissatisfaction and get a fair day's work from the salesperson. The management must provide an acceptable working environment, fair compensation, adequate benefits, fair and reasonable supervision, and job security.

(ii) To motivate performance beyond that of a fair day's work, the management must provide opportunities for achievement, recognition, responsibility and advancement.

### 3. Achievement — Motivation Theory

**High Need for Achievement.** In association with other researchers. David McClelland developed achievement — motivation theory according to which if a person spends considerable time thinking about doing his or her job better, accomplishing something unusual and important, or advancing his or her career, that individual has a high need for achievement (NACH). Those who have high need for achievement :

(i) like problem situations in which they take personal responsibility for finding solutions (ones in which the possibilities of reaching them are reasonable),

(ii) tend to set attainable achievement goals and

(iii) want feedback on how they are doing.

In practical terms, NACH is a motivation to exceed some standard of quality in personal behaviour. Individuals who are self-motivated and who continually strive to improve their performance fall in this category. Many individuals are attracted to personal selling jobs, where compensation is largely in the form of commissions — jobs characterized by opportunities to influence outcomes through personal efforts, challenging risks and rapid feedback of results.

### Implications for Management

(i) If individuals with high NACH can be the best performers in the company's sales jobs, management might target its recruiting toward such people. As McClelland and his co-investigators used the Thematic Apperception Test (TAT) in their research on achievement, so management might consider including the TAT in the sales selection system to make certain that the sales job environment is one in which high achievers flourish.

(ii) As NACH drives individuals to act from an internally induced stimulus, people with high NACH are self-starters. They require little external incentive to succeed and constantly challenge themselves to improve their own performances. Such people require the management only to provide the right kind of job environment. The conditions that individuals high in NACH seek in their jobs, helps to explain and predict the behaviour of sales personnel.

**4. Expectancy Model**

This model, developed by Vroom, conceptualizes motivation as a process governing choices of behavioural activity because the strength of a tendency to act in a certain way depends upon the strength of an expectation that the act will be followed by a given outcome and that outcome is attractive to the individual. An individual's desire to produce at a given time depends on his specific goals and perception of the relative worth of performance alternatives as paths to attainment of those goals.

Figure 18.2 shows an expectancy model, based on Vroom strength of an individual's motivation to behave in a certain way he depends upon how strongly he believes that these efforts will achieve the desired performance patterns. If he achieves the desired performance, then how strongly he does believe that the organization's rewards/punishment will be appropriate for that kind of performance, and to what extent will this satisfy his needs?

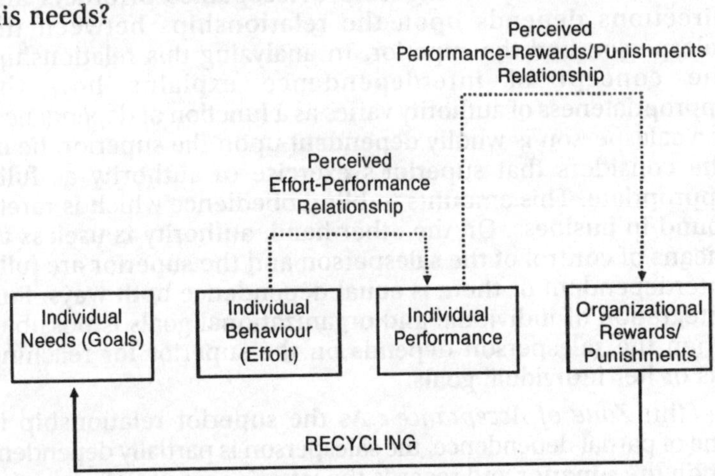


Fig. 18.2. An Expectancy Model of Motivation

The expectancy model raises motivational issues about sales management. Sales management must recognize that this model is concerned with expectations. Besides sales management's support in developing the skills that lead to improved performance, sales personnel need counselling to view their own competencies realistically.

## FACTORS IN MOTIVATION AND SUPERVISION

### 1. Interdependence

(i) *Meaning* : According to traditional theory, the superior has the authority to require that the salesperson takes action and the salesperson is obligated to carry out the superior's orders. This theory assumes that authority can be equated with power. In a formal organizational plan, each salesperson reports to someone higher up in the structure such as sales supervisor, district sales manager, or the chief sales executive. However, practical sales managers know that issuing an order to a salesperson or suggesting how he or she should act does not necessarily mean that henceforth the salesperson will change. As long as they are clearly stated and apply to simple tasks that are done quickly, there is little problem in having orders and directions put into effect. However, if orders and directions require significant permanent modification in the salesperson's behaviour his acceptance of the desired change is unpredictable.

(ii) *Analysis of Relationship* : Acceptance of orders and directions depends upon the relationships between the salesperson and the superior. In analyzing this relationship, the concept of interdependence explains how the appropriateness of authority varies as a function of dependence. If a salesperson is wholly dependent upon the superior, he or she considers that superior's exercise of authority as fully appropriate. This amounts to blind obedience which is rarely found in business. On the other hand, authority is useless as means of control of the salesperson and the superior are fully interdependent or there is equal dependence both ways. Full integration of individual and organizational goals is possible, when the salesperson depends on the superior for reaching his or her individual goals.

(iii) *Zone of Acceptance* : As the superior relationship is one of partial dependence, the salesperson is partially dependent upon the superior and regards the latter's exercise of authority as appropriate in some circumstances and not in the others; the superior is partially dependent upon the salesperson for help in reaching the organizational goals for which he or she is held responsible by higher management. Each salesperson has a "zone of acceptance", a range over which he or she accepts direction from the superior. Each superior has a similar zone over which he or she honours requests from the salesperson. Within their respective zones of acceptance, both the salesperson and the superior exhibit a "degree of acceptance" which varies from grudging acquiescence to enthusiastic cooperation according to the exact circumstances.

(iv) *Task of Sales Manager* : The sales manager should try to widen the zone and increase the degree of acceptance of each salesperson. This also means widening his or her own zone and increasing his or her own degree of acceptance. Thus effective supervision is prerequisite to improved performance. Through it, the sales manager satisfies many of the salesperson's needs. By giving due credit for good work, by convincing each salesperson of his or her job's importance, by earning the sales personnel's confidence in his or her leadership and by following other enlightened supervisory practices, he obtains fuller cooperation from them. In striving for organizational goals, sales personnel work hard to earn praise and recognition, social approval, esteem and self-respect. In effective supervision, salespeople are treated as human beings, as individuals in their own right, not as mere cogs in an impersonal industrial machine.

**2. Leadership**

(i) *Executive as Leader* : Effective sales executives who are the leaders, rather drivers, of sales personnel earn voluntary cooperation of members of the sales organization. They motivate them to reach the sales department's goals individually and as a group. Knowing the motivations, desires and ambitions of those they lead, they use this knowledge to guide them into learning and performing.

(ii) *Good Example* : The effective sales executive sets a good example. He works with the same diligence he or she expects of sales personnel. He leads his or her life as he or she expects them to lead theirs. The subordinates do emulate their superior if he a symbol of success.

(iii) *Handling Relationships* : Leadership closely related to motivation has to do with the handling of required relationships with sales personnel. Experience, maturity and common sense are necessary attributes in this area. Effective sales executives treat sales personnel fairly about assignments, promotions, and changes in pay. They commend salespeople for jobs well done. If performances are not up to par, they call the subordinate's attention privately. When discussing a salesperson's weakness, effective sales executives also refer to his strong points. Before making changes in their jobs, they consult them helping to prevent the damaging impact of rumours upon morale. Individually and collectively the sales force should be convinced that the sales executive can be depended upon to carry their case to top management. Finally, effective sales executives do not lose sight of the fact that they are managing the sales staff. They "sell" sales personnel on plans, policy changes and anything else that affects them. When sales executives apply good sales techniques in all their relationships with them, sales personnel are all the more sold on their jobs.

### 3. Communications

(i) *Meaning* : There should be good communication between each salesperson and his or her superior to avoid depressed morale and low productivity. With pent-up grievances, real or imagined, the salesperson displays both low morale and unsatisfactory performance. Like everyone else he comes up against personal problems, such as sickness in the family, inability to pay overdue bills, or marital troubles, all of which adversely affect morale and performance.

Good communications allow for free discussion of problems related to the salesperson's job because personal problems left untold, hurt job performance. The existence of good communications means freedom of self-expression. It is freedom to talk over problems, business and personal, with the superior. For the supervisor it means ease in talking with the salesperson, determine what is bothering him or her, and to provide assistance in solving problems.

(ii) *Interpersonal Contact* : An important way to communicate and to motivate sales personnel is interpersonal contact. Management uses contacts to make comprehensive evaluations of morale. Interpersonal contacts provide opportunities to financial, family or other personal worries having impacts upon job performance.

At all levels sales executives have personal contacts with the sales staff but at higher levels of sales management, contacts are confined to conventions and sales meetings. The individual salesperson's contact with management is through immediate supervisor. While supervisors have other important functions to perform, such as training, evaluation and control, they also detect personal or business problems, for motivational purposes. At all levels they reserve sometime for observing and conferring with sales personnel. District managers visit each sales person on the job in the assigned sales territory. As it is impractical for top sales executives to personally visit all territories or even all sales districts in large sales organization, there are other ways to maintain personal contact. One way is to arrange individual conferences between sales personnel and the top sales executive during regional or national meeting. The opportunity to visit with the "big boss" provides strong motivation to sales people.

(iii) *Telephone Contact* : Executive contact with the more effective salespeople is largely through written means. Many sales executives keep in touch with their subordinates not through letters, but through regular telephone calls. The sales personnel should be contacted personally or by telephone rather than by letter. When a reprimand is necessary, a face-to-face meeting is better than a letter. Personal and disciplinary problems are best handled by face to face contact. Though sometimes a carefully phrased letter can avoid misinterpretations and misunderstandings, but the executive is still well advised to follow up with personal contacts. Effective sales executives develop empathy with their subordinates. A special effort should be made to know each salesperson well and to learn what is important to each.

(iv) *Motivational Interviews* : Motivational interviews are a way to gather valuable information bit by bit. In progressive companies, sales executive sets planned "informational" goals for personal visits with sales personnel. He attempts to find out salespeople's patterns of need fulfilment and the order of priority assigned to each need. While insights are gained on individual's motivational patterns, guidance is furnished for choosing appropriate incentives. A single interview can not gather all this information. After many interviews, the executive has the information to put together a comprehensive picture.

(v) *Written Communications* : Sales personnel are kept informed through letters, announcements, bulletins and other mailed pieces. Written communications sometimes become routine and deadening. Spending hours in planning a sales meeting, one elects to appraise the motivational impact of its correspondence. Though a single letter or bulletin has no strong motivational effect yet the total impact of written communication, effectively used, can be much greater.

The effective executive writing personal letters and bulletins to salespeople avoids generalities and concentrates upon specific helpful suggestions.

To congratulate a salesperson for good work, a letter is superior to interpersonal contact and provides lasting evidence recognizing the salesperson's performance. It has prolonged beneficial effect on morale, but it does not substitute deserved promotions or compensation increases. A commendation letter is a personal expression that management recognizes and is pleased with, the salesperson's performance.

**4. Unionization of Sales Personnel**

(i) *Little Progress* : There are several reasons why unions have made little progress in organizing sales personnel :

(a) It is difficult to develop strong group identification in most sales departments because each person works alone and sees other members of the sales force infrequently. Little opportunity exists for mutual exchange of grievances.

(b) In contrast to most employee groups, salespersons think of themselves as independent operators rather than as cogs in an industrial machine.

(c) Sales personnel have some control over their workday and workweek. If they work excessive hours, it is often to add to their compensation and there are no time clocks.

(d) The prospect of higher wages has never served as a strong organizing incentive for sales personnel, as sales personnel have been made to feel that low earnings are the result of personal ineffectiveness, not of the employer's niggardliness.

(ii) *Limitations* : Unionization has made headway in industries where sales personnel are paid straight salaries, where they work together on the same premises and where the selling job is combined with that of delivery, as in the distribution of beer and soft drinks. Unions have made little progress in organizing sales personnel who sell directly to industrial users or those who make calls on middlemen. Sales personnel in these classifications, paid in whole or part according to productivity, frown upon union affiliation.

(iii) *Opposition* : Many sales executives oppose unionization chiefly because unionization affects the motivation and control of sales personnel and places limitations on management. Managerial action is circumscribed by the collective-bargaining agreements. The uses of incentive compensation are restricted.

Unions object to sales contests and other devices for motivating the sales force. Sometimes they insist that all additions to the sales force be recruited through the union. They discourage the use of quotas and other standards of performance. They demand strict system of seniority. The organizational structure of unions does not harmonize with the demands of the selling job.

## QUESTIONS FOR EXERCISE

1. Define motivation and explain reasons for motivational help from sales management.
2. How is a salesperson's behaviour influenced by need gratification and motivation? What are the implications of various themes of motivation for sales behaviour?
3. Explain important factors in effective supervision and high motivation of sales people.

# 19

# SALES FIELD, TERRITORIES, QUOTAS AND SALESMAN'S REPORT

## STEPS IN MANAGEMENT PROCESS

**1. Planning.** The management process starts when top management makes known the company's goals, and department heads, including the top sales executive, use them to derive departmental objectives. For the sales department, the next step is to formulate policies and plans to achieve these objectives.

**2. Organising.** Then, the sales management group maps out sales programmes and campaigns, determines specific methods and procedures, and takes other needed actions, including making indicated changes in the sales organization to execute the policies and implement the plans.

**3. Coordinating.** In performing these activities, sales executives coordinate the department's activities with each other and with related activities performed in other departments and by distributive outlets in the marketing channels.

**4. Controlling.** The steps are : (i) establishing performance standards, (ii) recording performances, (iii) evaluating performances against the standards and (iv) taking action.

The first three steps are static which enable sales management to measure the progress towards achieving departmental objectives. The three static steps cannot contribute maximally to sales management, despite the information they provide. The "Action" step is the dynamic facet of control. It keeps the department "on course." Sales management may decide (a) to take "no action" now, (b) to take action aimed to increase the degree of attainment of objectives, (c) to revise the policy or plan or the strategies used in their implementation to facilitate achievement of objectives, or (d) to lower or raise the objectives or the standards or criteria used for measuring their degree of attainment, to make them more realistic.

**Order of Performance**

The managerial function — planning, organizing, coordinating and controlling — are not performed in an unchanging straight-line sequence. The order of performance is circular. This is better illustrated in the controlling phase. The first step in control, the decision to set sales performance standards requires planning which means deciding where the sales department is going (that is, setting the objectives) and determining how the department is to get from where it is to where it wants to be. The initiation of control through standard setting is realistic. It does little good to set performance standards beyond the capabilities of the sales force. To reach maximum effectiveness, management must coordinate sales planning with sales efforts. More planning, organizing, and coordinating are required after sales force control is set in motion. The benefits of dynamic control are not realized unless sales management takes planning, organizing and coordinating steps.

## DETERMINANTS OF STANDARDS

**1. Standard of Important Activities.** Sales job analysis is necessary to determine job objectives, duties and responsibilities, and the like, called standards of performance. These, in turn, depend upon selling strategy. In some companies the key problem is to obtain new customers. New-business selling requires skills different from those needed in companies concerned with servicing established accounts, that is, trade selling. Setting performance standards for new-business sales personnel require different measures from those for trade-selling sales personnel. Selling strategy calls for the manufacturer's sales personnel to devote major segments of their time to training dealers' sales personnel, assisting in the planning and preparation of dealer advertising, and securing "preferred" display space in dealers' showrooms in companies relying upon dealer sales effort to push the product through the marketing channel. Performance standards are designed to measure the performance of activities that the company considers most important.

**2. Nature of Selling Job.** It is important to recognize the nature of the selling job before selecting standards of performance. The mainframe computer "salesperson," is both a management consultant and a system analyst — needing to know the decision-making approach appropriate to the particular industry or establishment buying the computer. Evaluating the job performance of a computer salesperson requires standards that measure not only skill in new-business selling but, effectiveness as a management consultant and skill as a system analyst.

**3. Marketing Knowledge.** Setting sales performance standards requires considerable market knowledge. Marketing intelligence provides evaluations of competitors' strength, weaknesses, practices and policies. One should know the total sales potential and the portion that each sales territory is capable of producing. One needs evaluations of customers and prospects from the standpoint of potential profitability for each class and size of account. One must know the selling expenses in different territories. All these items bear on the setting of performance standards.

**4. Other Factors.** In setting performance standards, sales management takes still other factors into account. Sales planning should be the best possible under the circumstances. The policies and procedures being used to carry the personal-selling portion of the marketing programme into effect should be appropriate. Adjustments should be made for the strengths and weaknesses of the individual sales personnel and for the differences in their working environments. Sales management should put together a combination of sales performance standards to fit the company's needs, its marketing situation, its selling strategy, and its sales organization.

### Relation of Performance Standards to Personal-Selling Objectives

Standards of sales performance help in measuring the progress made towards departmental objectives. Though specific objectives vary with changes in the company's marketing situation they are reconcilable with the general objectives of volume, profit and growth. The general sales volume objective is broken down into specific operating objectives in successive steps. Performance standards are established for the business as a whole and also for each salesperson. These standards are used to measure the extent of achievement of general and related specific objectives.

## KINDS OF PERFORMANCE STANDARDS

A. Quantitative Performance Standards

B. Qualitative Performance Standards

## A. Quantitative Performance Standards

**1. Meaning.** Quantitative standards define both the nature and desired levels of performance. They are used for stimulating good performance as well as for measuring it. Most companies use quantitative performance standards, whose combination varies with the company and its marketing situation. They provide descriptions of what management expects. Each person on the sales force should have definitions of the performance aspects being measured and the measurement units. These definitions help sales personnel make their activities more purposeful. Sales personnel with well-defined objectives waste little time or efforts in pursuing useless activities.

**2. Types.** The first quantitative standards that any firm should select is one that permits comparisons of sales volume performance with sales volume potential. From the sales department's standpoint, the volume objective is the most crucial and takes precedence over the profit and growth objectives. Before profits can be earned and growth achieved, it is necessary to reach a certain sales volume level. It is logical for sales management to first develop a standard to gauge sales volume performance.

**3. Objectives**

(i) *Profit* : Quantitative performance standards measure success in achieving profit which results from complex interactions of many factors. The modicum of control over profits provided through the standard for sales volume is not enough. Standards should be set to bring some or all factors affecting profit under sales management's control. Performance standards are needed for such factors as selling expenses, the sales mixture, the call frequency rate, the cost per call, and the size of order.

(ii) *Growth* : Setting quantitative performance standards to gauge progress made toward growth objective is more complex. Growth objectives are met through the natural momentum picked up as a company approaches maturity. The performances by sales personnel have impact upon growth. In an expanding economy, where the gross national product each year is larger than that in the year before, it is reasonable to expect individual sales personnel to show annual sales increases. This assumes that marketing management keeps products, prices, promotion and other marketing policies in tune with market demand and that sales management's efficiency is continuously improved. The standards needed for individual sales relate to such factors as increased sales to old accounts, sales to new accounts, calls on new prospects, sales of new products, and improvements in sales coverage effectiveness.

**4. No Single Standard.** A single quantitative standard, such as one for sales volume attainment, provides an inadequate basis for appraising an individual's total performance. Formerly, the performances of individual sales personnel were measured solely in terms of sales volume. Today sales managers have realized that it is possible to make unprofitable sales, and to make sales at the expense of future sales. In some fields, sales result only after extended periods of preliminary work, and it is misleading to appraise performance over short intervals solely on the basis of sales volume.

**5. Little Control over Many Factors.** Sales personnel have little control over many factors affecting sales volume. They are accountable for "uncontrollables" such as differences in the strength of competition, the amount of promotional support given to the sales force, the potential territorial sales volume, the relative importance of sales to national or "house" accounts, and the amount of "windfall" business secured. Management should set other quantitative performance standards besides that for sales volume. Each company selects a combination of quantitative performance standards that fit its marketing situation and selling objectives. Some times, it develops its own unique standards designed best to serve those objectives. These include the following :

(i). *Quotas* : Expressed in absolute terms and assigned to a specific marketing unit, a quota is a quantitative objective. The terms may be rupees, or units of product. The marketing unit may be a salesperson or a territory. Quotas are the most widely used quantitative standards. They specify desired levels of accomplishment for sales volume, gross margin, net profit, expenses, performance of non-selling activities, or a combination of these and similar items. When sales personnel are assigned quotas, the assumption is that management knows which objectives are realistic and attainable. Its validity depends upon the market knowledge management has and utilizes in setting quotas. The first step in setting sales volume quotas is to estimate future demand for the company's products in each sales territory. When sales volume quotas are basted upon sound sales forecasts, they are valuable performance standards. But when sales volume quotas are guesses, chosen chiefly for inspirational effect, their value as control devices is dissipated.

(ii) *Selling Expense Ratio* : Sales managers use this standard to control the relation of selling expenses to sales volume. Many factors cause selling expenses to vary with the territory. Therefore selling expense ratios should be set individually for each person on the sales force. These may be determined after analysis of expense conditions and sales volume potentials in each territory. The salesperson can affect them both by controlling expenses and by making sales.

**Limitations**

(a) The selling expense ratio does not take into account variations in the profitability of different products. A salesperson who has a favourable selling expense ratio may be responsible for disproportionately low profits.

(b) It may cause the salesperson to over-economize on selling expenses to the point where sales volume suffers.

(c) It inhibits sales personnel from exerting efforts to bolster sales volume in times of declining general business.

If national advertising, home office sales department expense, and branch managers' and supervisors' salaries and other indirect expenses are included and allocated to each territory, sales personnel are accountable for expenses over which they have no control. In most companies, only expenses incurred directly by sales personnel, and controllable by them, are considered selling expenses. About one-half of all companies use this standard including the salesperson's salary and/or incentive compensation in the computation. Other consider only selling expenses incurred directly by sales personnel in performing their jobs. Where sales personnel pay their own travelling expenses, the selling expense ratio is calculated by simply dividing his compensation by sales volume.

Selling expenses ratio standards are used more by industrial-product companies than by consumer-product companies due to differences in the selling job. As industrial-product firms place the greater emphasis on personal selling and entertainment of customers, their sales personnel incur higher costs for travel and subsistence.

(iii) *Territorial Net Profit or Gross Margin Ratio* : Target ratios of net profit or gross margin to sales for each territory focus sales personnel's attention on the needs for selling a balanced line and for considering relative profitability.

Managements using ratio as a quantitative performance standard, regard each sales territory as a separate organizational unit that should make a profit contribution. Sales personnel influence the net profit ratios by selling more volume and by reducing selling expenses. They may emphasize more profitable products and devote more time and effort to the account and prospects that are potentially the most profitable. The net profit ratio controls sales volume and expenses as well as net profit. The gross margin ratio controls sales volume and the relative profitability of the sales mixture but it does not control the expenses of obtaining and filling order.

**Limitations**

(a) The sales personnel may "high-spot" their territories, neglect the solicitation of new accounts, and overemphasize sales of high-profit or high margin products while under-emphasizing new products that may be more profitable in the long run.

(b) Both ratios are influenced by factors beyond the salesperson's control. For example, pricing policy affects both net profit and gross margin, and delivery costs, which also affect both net profit and gross margin, not only vary in different territories but are beyond the salesperson's control.

(c) Neither ratio should be used without recognition of its shortcomings.

(d) The net ratios profit presents computational problems. As allocation of indirect selling expenses to territories are arbitrary, the practice is to use contribution to profit, which takes into account only direct selling expenses identifiable with particular territories.

(e) Questions arise as to whether sales salaries and commissions should be included in calculating territorial net profit.

(iv) *Territorial Market Share* : It controls market share on a territory-by-territory basis. Management sets target market share percentages for each territory. It compares company sales to industry sales in each territory and measures the effectiveness of sales personnel in obtaining market share. By setting target market share percentages for each product and each class of customer or even for individual customers, closer control over the individual salesperson's sales mixture is obtained.

(v) *Sales Coverage Effectiveness Index* : It controls the thoroughness with which a salesperson works in the assigned territory. It consists of the ratio of the number of customers to the total prospects in a territory. Individual standards for sales coverage effectiveness are set up for each class and size of customer to apportion the salesperson's efforts more among different classification of prospects.

(vi) *Call-Frequency Ratio* : It is calculated by dividing the number of sales calls on a particular class of customers by the number of customers in that class. Management directs selling effort to those account most likely to produce profitable orders by establishing different call-frequency ratios for different classes of customers. The interval between calls should be proper — neither so short that unprofitably small orders are secured nor so long that sales are lost to competitors. Sales personnel who plan their own route and call schedules find target call frequencies helpful, because these standards provide information essential to this type of planning.

(vii) *Calls per Day* : It is desirable to set standard for the number of calls per day in consumer-product fields, where sales personnel contact large numbers of customers. Some sales personnel make too few calls per day and need help in planning their routes, in setting up appointments before making calls, or simply in starting their calls early enough in the morning and staying on the job late enough in the day. Other sales personnel make too many calls per day and need training in how to service accounts. Standards for calls per day are set individually for different territories, taking into account territorial differences as to customer density, road and traffic conditions, and competitors' practices.

(viii) *Order Call Ratio* : It measures the effectiveness of sales personnel in securing orders. Also called a "batting average," it is calculated by dividing the number of orders secured by the number of calls made. Its standards are set for each class of account. When a salesperson's order call ratio for a particular class of account varies from the standard, he needs help in working with the class of account. Sales personnel vary in their effectiveness in selling to different kinds of accounts—one person may be effective in selling to small buyers and poor in selling to large buyers, another may have just the opposite performance pattern.

(ix) *Average Cost per Call* : It is set to emphasize the importance of making profitable calls. When considerable variation exists in it on different sizes or classes of accounts, standards are set for each category of accounts. Target average cost per call standards are used to reduce the call frequency on accounts responsible for small orders.

(x) *Average Order Size* : It controls the frequency of call on different accounts. Different standards are set for different sizes and classes of customers. Management controls the salesperson's allocation of effort among different accounts and increases order size obtained, using average order size standards along with average cost per call standards. In accomplishing this objective, sales personnel have to reduce the frequency of calls on some accounts.

(xi) *Non-Selling Activities* : Some companies establish quantitative performance standards for non-selling activities such as obtaining dealer displays and cooperative advertising contracts, training distributors' personnel, and goodwill calls on distributors' customers. Appropriate standards should be set, if non-selling activities are critical features of the sales job. As quantitative standards for non-selling activities are expressed in absolute terms, they are, in reality, quotas.

(xii) *Multiple Quantitative Performance Standards* : It is a widespread practice. A form is used by a company whose sales personnel are assigned nine different quantitative standards per operating period.

**B. Qualitative Performance Criteria**

Certain aspects of job performance, such as personal effectiveness in handling customer relations problems, make the use of some qualitative criteria unavoidable. Qualitative criteria are used for appraising performance characteristics that affect sales results, especially over the long run, but whose degree of excellence can be evaluated only subjectively. Qualitative criteria defy exact definition. Many sales executives do not define the desired qualitative characteristics with any exactitude. They arrive at informal conclusions regarding the extent to which each salesperson possesses them. Other executives consider the qualitative factors formally, one method being to rate sales personnel against a detailed checklist of subjective factors such as that shown in Table 19.1.

Companies with merit-rating systems differ on the desirability of using numerical ratings. Most numerical scoring systems are in companies that rate sales personnel primarily for detecting needed adjustments in compensation. Companies that use merit rating primarily to improve and develop individual salespersons usually do not use numerical scoring systems.

Executive judgement plays the major role in the qualitative performance appraisal. Written job descriptions, up-to-date and accurate, are the logical points of departure. Based upon the job description each firm develops its own set of qualitative criteria. The manner in which these criteria are applied depends upon the needs of management.

## RECORDING ACTUAL PERFORMANCE

### Factors in Sales Control

Sales management has to measure actual performance. In this phase of control, emphasis shifts to gathering performance information. One should define information needs, determine the information sources and collect the information.

TABLE 19.1

**Form Used for Qualitative Analysis of Salesperson Performance**

**SALESPERSON PERFORMANCE ANALYSIS**

Name ............................................................ Date ......................

| | Problem | Fair | Average | Good | Superior |
|---|---|---|---|---|---|
| **Job Factors** | | | | | |
| Product Knowledge | | | | | |
| Awareness of Customer Needs | | | | | |
| Relationship with Customers | | | | | |
| Number of Sales Calls | | | | | |
| Quota Performance | | | | | |
| Service Follow-up | | | | | |
| **Personal Factors** | | | | | |
| Punctuality | | | | | |
| General Attitude | | | | | |
| Dress & Appearance | | | | | |
| Diligence | | | | | |
| Cooperation | | | | | |
| Accuracy | | | | | |
| Adaptability | | | | | |
| Reliability | | | | | |

Strongest Point ..........................................................................................

..........................................................................................

Weakest Point ..........................................................................................

..........................................................................................

Comments ..........................................................................................

..........................................................................................

Signature

**1. Information Needs.** The choice of performance standards dictates the information needed. With increasingly sophisticated management information systems, the choice of performance standards is based as much on information availability as on the desire to use certain standards. The sales performance standards in use and the availability of other information that might permit use of different or additional standards should be reviewed periodically.

**2. Determining Information Sources.** There are two basic sources of performance information : sales and expense records and reports of various sorts. Every company has a wealth of data in its internal sales and expense records, which frequently require reworking, or reprocessing, before it is useful for sales control purposes. Reclassified according to sales management's information needs, sales and expense data contribute to the determination and measurement of actual performances.

Among the reports available for sales management are those from sales personnel and the lower echelons of sales management. Companies using such quantitative performance standards as sales volume quotas and target share-of-the-market percentages require information contained in sales forecasts, which are prepared for sales management's use and for managerial planning through the enterprise.

**3. Methods of Data Collecting.** The methods of collecting data depend upon the sources. Internally generated information, such as that from the data-processing installation is provided on a routine basis, or in response to requests for special tabulations. Information obtainable only from sales personnel or field sales management personnel is gathered through formal reports. It is also obtained through personal observation—by trips to the field or through field sales supervisors.

## SALES REPORTS

1. (a) *Uses* : Field sales reports seek to provide control information. Good communications require interaction between those preparing and those receiving reports. A good field sales reporting system provides both for communication from the field to headquarters and from the headquarters to the field.

(b) *Basis for Discussion* : Field sales reports provide sales management with a basis for discussion with sales personnel on the matters on which sales people need assistance. The sales executive uses field sales reports to determine whether sales personnel are calling on and selling to the right people, and whether they are making the proper number of calls. Field sales reports also assist in determining how to secure more and larger orders. They provide the raw materials that sales management processes to gain insights on giving needed direction to field sales personnel.

(c) *Self-Improvement* : A good field sales reporting system assists sales personnel in their self-improvement programmes. Recording accomplishments in written forces individuals to check their own work and to become their own critics. Thus self-criticism is more valuable and effective than that from headquarters. It motivates sales personnel to improve coordination of their efforts with sales management's plans.

**2. Purpose**

(i) To provide information for measuring performance.

(ii) To Provide Data for Evaluating Performance. It includes details concerning accounts and prospects called upon, number of calls made, orders obtained, days worked, miles travelled, selling expenses, displays erected, cooperative advertising arrangements made, training of distributors' personnel, missionary work, and calls made with distributors' sales personnel.

(iii) To help the Salesperson Plan the Work. This includes planning itineraries, sales approaches to use with specific accounts and prospects.

(iv) To record Customers' Suggestions and Complaints and Their Reactions. This is towards new products, service policies, price changes, advertising campaigns, and so forth.

(v) To gather Information on Competitors' Activities. This is about new products, market tests, changes in promotion and changes in pricing and credit policy.

(vi) To report changes in local business and economic conditions,

(vii) To log important items of territorial information for use in case sales personnel leave the company or are reassigned.

(viii) To keep the mailing list updated for promotional and catalogue materials.

(ix) To provide information requested by marketing research, for example, data on dealers' sales and inventories of company and competitive products.

**3. Types of Sales Force Reports**

(i) *Progress or Call Report* : It is prepared individually for each call or cumulatively, covering all calls made daily or weekly. It keeps management informed of the salesperson's activities. It provides source data on the company's relative standing with individual accounts and in different territories. It records information that assists the salesperson on revisits. Usually it records not only calls and sales, but more detailed data, such as the class of customer or prospects, competitive brands handled, the strength and activities of competitors, best time to call, and "future promises."

(ii) *Expense Report* : Most companies have an expense report because most sales personnel are reimbursed for expenses and itemized expense records are required for income tax purposes. Its purpose is to control the nature and amount of salespersons' expenses. It also helps the salesperson exercise self-control over expenses. It reminds salespersons that they are under moral obligation to keep expenses in line with reported sales. Sometimes, it requires salespersons to "correlate" expenses with sales. Its details vary with the plan for reimbursing expenses.

(iii) *Sales Work Plan* : The salesperson submits a work plan giving such details as accounts and prospects to be called upon, products and other matters to be discussed, routes to be travelled, and hotels or motels for a future period, usually a week or a month. It assists the salesperson in planning and scheduling activities and informs management of the salesperson's whereabouts. It provides a basis for evaluating the salespersons' ability "to plan the work and to work the plan."

(iv) *New-Business or Potential New-Business Report* : It informs management of accounts recently obtained and prospects who may become sources of new business. It provides data for evaluating the extent and effectiveness of development work by sales personnel. It seeks to remind sales personnel that management expects them to get sales reports point the way to needed sales training, changes in customer service policies, and product improvements. It reports the reasons for the loss of the business.

(v) *Report of Complaint and/or Adjustment* : It provides information for analyzing complaints arising from a salesperson's work, complaints by class of customer, and cost of complaint adjustment. It assists management in detecting needed product improvements and changes in merchandising and service practices and policies. It is helpful for decisions on sales training programmes, selective selling, and product changes.

**4. Reports from Field Sales Management.** Field sales executives play an important part in setting sales performance standards in decentralized organizations. Branch and district sales managers and sales supervisors assist in establishing sales volume quotas for sales people who are also consulted on their own quotas. In addition, branch and district sales managers play roles in breaking down branch and district sales volume quotas to quotas for individual sales personnel, and to products or product line and/or to types of customers — occasionally, even to specific accounts. At the district level, profit and/or expense quotas are sometimes set for individual sales personnel and by product lines especially in larger companies.

(i) *District Sales Plan* : The district sales manager's planning report called a district sales plan is prepared by compiling, with or without revisions, sales work plans, and covering the work or results that each district salesperson expects to accomplish during the month, quarter, or year ahead. It breaks down dollar or unit sales volume quotas by products or product lines for each salesperson. It includes standards for number of calls, number of calls on each type of account or on individual accounts, and target number of new dealers and/or distributors. It requires the district sales manager to suggest standards for appraising his or her own performance, for example, the recruiting of a certain number of new sales personnel and the carrying out of some amount of sales training. It is subject to review and to revision by higher sales executives.

(ii) *Progress Report* : Field sales executives are responsible for reporting information on personnel performance. As they are in the most frequent contact with the sales force, they may observe individual sales personnel in the field. Consequently, they prepare "sales personnel evaluation" reports, often of the merit-rating type, which gather information on qualitative sales performances. In some companies, this is called a "progress report." It includes qualitative information on personnel performance and data comparing individual performance to quantitative standards. Progress reports are prepared either periodically or each time a district sales manager or supervisor works with a salesperson. Companies are increasingly utilizing centralized data-processing facilities for processing quantitative data. The role of the district sales office in gathering, collating, and-reporting quantitative sales performance data has declined. As no good substitute method for gathering information on qualitative aspects of personnel performance has been found, the district sales manager continues as the main unit for gathering such information.

While the salesperson's immediate superior, a sales supervisor, branch sales manager, or district sales manager is responsible for appraising his or her performance, higher sales management reviews these appraisals (a) to make certain that the appraisal form has been fixed out properly, (b) to check against personal bias or errors in judgement, and (c) to rate the rater's ability to set performance standards and to evaluate sales personnel.

**5. Number of Reports.** The minimum necessary to produce the desired information is the optimum number of reports. Holding down the number of reports is important as they are generally made out after the selling day. Report preparation places demands on free time, while the best people often have the least time. To determine whether the information is worthwhile, all reports are reviewed from time to time. The burden of proof of its need is upon its advocates. Information obtainable through other means at no higher cost should not be gathered through field sales reports. In assessing the worth of a sales report, some companies discontinue it without notice or insert intentional errors in the form, thus learning whether the report is essential and the use, if any, made of the information.

**6. Design and Format of Reports.** Each field sales report should be as short as required for its purpose. The form should provide for easy checking of or routine information items whenever possible. Sales report forms should be of conveniently portable size and shape. More and more companies have adopted IBM or similar types of cards for all reports, which facilitate analysis. Sales reports should include carbons so that the salesperson has copies. A minimum of clerical work should be required of sales personnel.

Information on field reports should be so arranged that it can easily be summarized. There should also be set routines for transferring information onto other records. To avoid needless accumulation of data, original reports should be destroyed after a short time.

**7. Detail Required in Sales Reports.** The amount of detail required in sales reports varies from firm to firm. As compared to a company with a few sales people covering a compact area, a company with many sales personnel covering a wide geographical area needs more detailed reports. The more freedom that sales personnel have to plan and schedule their activities, the greater should be the detail required in their reports. However, commission sales personnel are asked for less detail in reports than are salaried sales people; it has less power to direct their activities. The higher the caliber of sales personnel, the less is management's need for details. High-caliber people are expected to exercise self-control, thus reducing the need for detailed formal reporting.

## EVALUATION FOR SALES FORCE CONTROL

Evaluation means the comparing of actual performances with standards. It is more than a mechanical comparison. It is difficult because evaluation requires judgment. The same standards cannot be applied to all sales personnel. There are differences in individual territories, their sales potentials, the impact of competition, and the personalities of sales personnel and their customers. By setting individual performance standards for each territory, it is possible to take territorial differences into account, but it is not possible to adjust differences in the personalities of the salesperson and the clientele. Complications often develop in relating individual performances to standards when two or more salespersons work on the same account or when an account deals both with the salesperson and the home office.

Evaluation of sales personnel requires both a comparison of performance with quantitative standards and an appraisal against qualitative performance criteria.

**1. Comparison of Performance.** Sales personnel with poor performance may be making offsetting qualitative contributions. Individuals who do not reach sales quotas or keep to prescribed call schedules may be building for the future by cementing relation with distributors and dealers. Evaluation of performance of sales personnel requires judgement and deep understanding of market factors and conditions.

Performance trends, as well as the current records, are relevant to judgment entering into evaluation of sales personnel. An individual showing improvement but with still substandard performance needs encouragement. There is always the chance that something is wrong with a standard. Management should investigate whether the standard has been set too high when an individual continually fails to reach a standard.

The general procedure in scientific work is to set up tests that measure the variable under observation while taking account of the effects of other variables. It is not possible to set up such tests in the evaluation of sales personnel. Each salesperson's performance results from complex integrations of many variables of which some are beyond the control of the salesperson and management. The time element changes and so do the sales personnel, the customers, general business conditions, competitors' activities, and other variables. Some companies measure the impact of particular variables on personnel performance through careful design of experimental and control groups.

**2. Taking Action**. The comparisons of actual performance with standards point the way to needed action. If performance and standards are in alignment, the decision may be : no action needed. Otherwise, the three alternatives are : (i) adjust performance to the standards, thus increasing the degree of attainment of objectives; (ii) revise the policy and/or plan, or the strategies used for their implementation, which fit better in the achievement of objectives; or (iii) lower or raise the objectives or the standards and/criteria used in measuring their degree of attainment to make them more realistic. These actions are conditioned by the executive's judgement, experience, knowledge of the situation, and administrative skill.

## CONTROLLING THROUGH SUPERVISION

Management also controls sales personnel through supervision to improve the job performance of sales personnel. The executive with supervisory responsibilities establishes working relations with sales personnel for purposes of observing, evaluating, and reporting on performance; coercing deficiencies; clarifying responsibilities and duties; providing motivation; informing sales personnel of changes in company policy; helping to solve business and personal problems; and continuing sales training. Thus sales supervision is concerned mainly with the action phase of control action. It aims at enhancing personal contributions to the achievement of objectives.

Conditions needing supervision are :

(i) Sales personnel turnover rate excessive in a branch, district, or other organizational unit.

(ii) High turnover of accounts.

(ii) Increased complaints from customers.

(iii) Mail or phone orders increasing for no known reasons.

(iv) Low ratio of orders to sales calls.

(v) Total number of calls very low or very high.

(vi) Increasing ratio of selling expenses to sales in an organizational unit.

(viii) Low morale, as implied by negative attitude towards company, lack of enthusiasm, signs of restlessness, and job hunting.

These conditions apply to the wrong as well as to too much or too little supervision. This list is useful for appraising the effectiveness of sales supervision. Many of these conditions may have their roots in deficiencies in other phases of sales force management. Sometimes, a company upgrades the quality of its sales personnel and fails to adjust the pattern of supervision. In many companies the selling task has changed. It is now high-level, key account selling which demands independent, self-reliant, highly educated sales personnel who can and must make their own decisions. Traditional supervision and the attitudes that underlie it stifle those whom management seeks to encourage. The type of supervision should be adjusted to the type of person in the selling job. As the type of person changes, so should the type of supervision

## WHO SHOULD SUPERVISE?

Sales personnel may be supervised by home office personnel, branch or district managers, or field sales supervisors.

**1. Executive or Specialist.** Sales supervision may be either through executives or through specialists.

**2. Top Executive or Assistant.** If the sales force is small and experienced, sales supervision is generally through the top sales executive or an assistant. Control through home office supervision is minimal especially when the sales organization is small and permits the development of close relations among sales personnel and executives.

**3. Branch or District Managers.** Companies having decentralized sales organizations sometimes assign the supervision responsibility to branch or district managers, who are well prepared to supervise field sales personnel. Limitations exist on the amount of supervision that branch managers should exercise even in companies with elaborate field sales organization. The branch manager is often a local general manager more than a specialized sales executive. In this capacity he is responsible for the local conduct of all the company's affairs for managing sales personnel as well as for warehousing, extending credit and making collections, providing service, and performing other work. As he spends most of his time attending to details, it is unusual for him to devote much time to personal supervision of sales personnel. But when he has a large number of sales personnel under him, he can spend limited time mainly with each one. He mainly relies upon sales personnel to supervise themselves.

### Qualifications of Sales Supervisors

**1. Good Teacher**. They must recognize training needs, know how to train, be patient with those who have less skill, and be tactful in pointing out better ways of doing things.

**2. Understanding of Reconstitution.** As vital links in the chain of communication, they must understand the needs and problems of both and reconcile them in the field.

**3. Skilled**. They must be skilled in handling people equipped to deal with many complex situations.

**4. Selling.** Some companies expect sales supervisors to sell certain accounts personally, this being one way to motivate them to keep up-to-date on field selling techniques. Many salespersons are eager for promotions to supervisory positions, since they often are stepping stones to higher positions.

## TERRITORY MANAGEMENT

It is not always necessary to have sales territories. However, most companies may establish territories for one or more of the following reasons :

(1) To gain thorough coverage of the market.

(2) To define the sales person's responsibilities more accurately and specifically, if possible, by name.

(3) As a means of performance evaluation.

(4) To improve customer relations.

(5) To reduce selling expenses.

(6) To match selling effort to fit customer needs.

(7) To help the salesperson.

The five stage process for establishing sales territories are :

(a) Select the basic Unit.

(b) Evaluate accounts and sales potential.

(c) Analyse work load. This depends on type of selling and product, newness of product or market and market share.

(d) Design basic territories.

(e) Assign salesmen to territories.

The high proportion of time that salesmen spend travelling may be of concern. To save this time one way is to shape the visit of territories in a circle system. They should cut down social chit chat, take fewer breaks and start earlier.

To analyse any sales territory, the management should take following steps :

(a) Select one or more appropriate measures of performance such as sales or profit per salesman.

(b) Develop operational measures of factors considered to determine sales territory performance.

(c) Analyse the criteria and predictor variabe using empirical data.

(d) Determine the relationship by regression analysis.

(e) Determine performance bench marks for each territory to spot poor areas.

(f) Evaluate individual territory performance.

## QUESTIONS FOR EXERCISE

1. Describe steps involved in the management process and explain management functions concerning sales personnel.
2. What are the determinants of performance standard?

   Or

   What is the relation of performance standard to personal selling objectives? Describe performance criteria in various types of performance standards.
3. Describe method of recording actual sales performance system of field sales reports as a factor in sales control.
4. Examine evaluation as a step in sales force control. Describe control through supervision.

# 20

# MARKETING POLICIES

Having impact upon the functions and operation of the sales department, sales-related marketing policies delineate the guidelines within which the effort to reach personal-selling objectives are made. There are three major types : (1) product policies (what to sell), (2) distribution policies (to whom to sell), and (3) pricing policies.

In determining sales-related marketing policies, sales executive's roles vary from company to company. At one extreme, his role is not to determine, but to administer, policies laid down by higher management. At the other extreme, he bears sole responsibility for determining self-created marketing-policies subject to top management's approval.

The sales executive has to participate as a member of an executive group charged with responsibility for determining all marketing policies. Sales related marketing policies directly influence his job. These policies provide direction to how the company will reach personal-selling objectives, as sales executives organize the sales effort, as they manage the sales force, and as they control the sales effort. Sales related policies constitute the company-imposed marketing framework within which sales executives and their departments must operate.

## PRODUCT POLICIES — WHAT TO SELL

### Meaning

The products a company sells determine its basic nature. As its organizers visualize opportunities to make and/or market certain products, the company comes into existence. As it grows, management makes key decisions on products policies such as whether to drop old ones, whether to add new ones, whether to expand the product line or add new lines. Product policies also deal with product design and product quality as well as on product-related matters such as guarantees and services.

## POLICIES IN RELATION TO PRODUCT

Often product policies take the form of a series of short definitions or of questions arranged as a checklist. Deriving from product objectives, product policies serve as guides for making product decisions. If a product objective states that "this company desires to make and market products requiring only a minimum of service after their purchase by consumers," then product policies spell out how this objective is to be attained. If a product objective states that "this company desires to make and market only products superior to those of competitors in ways of great importance to users," then product policies define the nature of superiority from the standpoint of product users.

## TYPES OF PRODUCT LINE POLICIES

Policies on the width of a product line are classified as either short line or full line. Companies use short-line policies for some product groupings and full-line policies for others. Management decides for each product grouping whether the basis of competition should be specialization (short line) or wide selection (full line). For example, a manufacturer concentrating exclusively on a cornflakes product has a short-line policy.

**1. Short-Line Policies.** The company following a short-line policy handles all or most of the items making up a line.

**2. Full-Line Policies.** A company offering a complete or almost complete, line of breakfast cereals has a full-line policy.

The extent to which a short-line policy should be pursued is governed by the amount of risk that management is willing — to assume-the narrower the line, the greater the risk. If a firm concentrates on a single product, the rewards can be great. Product specialization enables the manufacturing division to achieve low unit costs. In turn, this may make the company almost invulnerable to price competition, even though the product is of the highest quality. But the penalty for failure is also great. If the product is displaced by substitutes introduced by competitors, the company finds itself "locked out" of the market.

The company following a short-line policy handles only part of a line. The company with a full-line policy handles all or most of the items making up a line. The extent to which a full-line policy should be followed is determined by such factors as the number of items the sales force can sell effectively, the need for after-sale service, the desires of middlemen and product users, the expenses of promotion, and the effect on production costs. In sharp contrast to the short-line policy, the wider the product line, the more the risk is spread and diversified over many products. But, while there is less penalty attached to failure of any one item, there also is less reward for the success of any item.

## FULL LINE POLICY

### Reappraisal of Items in Product Line

All items in a product line should be reappraised at regular intervals (1) to determine whether individual items are still in tune with market demand, and (2) to identify those that should be dropped from, or added to, the line. Market demand may shift, and more alert competitors may capture larger market shares if the product line is not reappraised regularly.

Sales executives should participate in product line appraisals, as they have the most intimate contact with markets. They should ensure that effective procedures are in place for receiving communications on product acceptance from the sales force. They should make this information available to those participating in product line reappraisals.

### Attention to Significant Trends

Each item in the line is compared with similar and competing items in other manufacturers' lines. With focus upon identifying strengths and weaknesses, especially as to which features of each item consumers consider desirable or undesirable, special attention is paid to significant trends in usage. These provide insights useful in constructing sales presentations and in motivating the sales force and dealer organization.

### Profitability

1. Generally, an item in the line should not be retained unless it meets standards for profitability or shows promise of meeting them. Nevertheless, other factors need to be considered before an item is dropped because of inadequate profitability.

2. Some companies cater to customers and dealers who expect a full-line offering. Dealers insist on a complete line if distribution is through exclusive agencies. Repair and replacement parts are unprofitable for many manufacturers, but most manufacturers must retain them because of needed

service on major products. Many companies find that some unprofitable products must be retained to help sell profitable products, since markets are made up of segments with unique tastes and preferences. However, subject to exceptions unprofitable products should be eliminated from the line.

3. (i) If the resources required for marketing could be used to better advantage on behalf of a product with a brighter future or in which the company has a greater investment, it is appropriate to drop a profitable product.
   (ii) An item should be dropped if it causes sales personnel to divert their efforts from more profitable items.
   (iii) Products with slow turnover rates should be discontinued if dealers place more emphasis on the better selling products in the line.
   (iv) Finally, any item not fitting logically into the line should be eliminated.

**Reappraisal for Diversification**

**1. Restriction of Growth.** Management makes reappraisals of the line to meet growth objectives, which are restricted, when the industry is dying, or when competitors succeed in making permanent inroads in a company's "natural" market. If action is long delayed in these situations, the survival of the firm itself is at stake. Often the indicated action is to add new products or even entirely new product lines.

**2. Diversification.** Some firms diversify to survive, but most diversify to expand sales or to reduce costs. A decision to shorten marketing channels causes parallel consideration on widening the line. New products are required if sales personnel are to write orders large enough to justify the higher costs of direct selling. When top management assigns the sales organization a substantially larger task than previously, one solution is to add new products. Sometimes, new products are added to stimulate the sales force or dealer organization. An addition to the line, it may help sales people to earn larger commissions and assist dealers in increasing sales and profits.

**3. Role of Sales Department.** The sales department pushes hardest for line diversification. Its intimate contact with the market enables it to keep close watch on the market acceptance of new products of other manufacturers. When the objective sales executives press for new products to hold or improve market share, any shift in customers' buying patterns may signal the need for line diversification.

**4. Circumstances of Diversification**

(i) If there are unused plant facilities or if seasonal sales fluctuations cause manufacturing irregularities.

(ii) Production department initiates the search for new products. The treasurer advocates diversification of idle funds causing financial criticism or if there is an opportunity for profitable acquisition of a firm with related products.

(iii) The purchasing department suggests new products, particularly when difficulty is experienced in procuring materials for the fabrication of existing products.

(iv) Pressure for line diversification originates in the scientific research division, when it discovers or perfects a new product.

(v) Diversification is advocated by marketing research department, when it uncovers natural additions as the result of other studies.

(vi) Either through research or by chance, uses for industrial waste materials result in additions to the line.

**Ideas for New Products**

**1. Internal source**

Product ideas coming from within the company are related to regular operations.

(i) The sales department identifies unsatisfied needs.

(ii) In its day-to-day contacts with customers and prospects, the production department develops improvements in existing products.

(iii) The research and development department turns up ideas for new products as a routine part of its activities.

**2. External Source**

Ideas from outside the company are often unique because they represent thinking undulled by close association with the established product line.

(i) A pottery company got its idea for a new display case from a museum exhibit.

(ii) One plastics manufacturer secured an idea for a film-viewing device from an unsolicited outside suggestion.

(iii) Another plastics manufacturer got an idea for a similar device from a list of needed inventions published by a bank.

(iv) A chemical company picked up an idea for an insecticide from a list of government-owned patents available for licensing.

**Criteria for Appraisal of Proposed New Products**

1. As in the reappraisal of established offerings, the key question is : Will this item (line) add to profitability?

2. Other factors include the nature and size of likely markets, competition, price policy, sales programmes and legal implications.

3. The marketing and production characteristics of a proposed product should be compared with those of the existing line. An addition should be in alignment on both the marketing and production sides.

4. These natural additions round out the line and make marketing and production efforts more efficient and more profitable. The same sales force can sell the product and reap the benefits of goodwill built up for other items in the line. The new product's seasonal sales dovetail with present sales patterns; and the product broadens the market base. It diversifies the company's business by adding new classes of customers.

## TYPES OF PRODUCT DESIGN POLICY

The two main policy decisions on product design are (1) the frequency of design change and (2) the extent to which designs should be protected from copying.

**1. Policy on Frequency of Design Change.** Frequent introduction and promotion of design changes and improvements is an important marketing factor in many industries, such as clothing, automobiles, home appliances, and office machines. Users are persuaded to replace old models with new models through design changes that make the product more attractive. In addition to weakening buyers' sales resistance, changes in design reduce the emphasis on price, assist in the stimulation of sales people and dealers, and provide new inspiration for the advertising department. However, since the successful promotion of a design change requires exceptional skill in the planning and execution of promotional programmes, a policy of changing designs frequently is not appropriate for all companies or for all types of products.

**2. Policy on Design Protection.** It is related to policy on frequency of design change. It is impractical to protect a new design in certain industries, such as in women's apparel. The rapid rate of fashion change makes legal protection impractical. Success in high-fashion fields depends upon the extent to which designs are adopted by competing firms to make the style fashionable. Design protection is practical and desirable where design changes occur less frequently, as in the home appliance, furniture, and jewelry industries. Legal protection is effected through design patents granted by the government. These patents protect a company against use of the design by others.

## PRODUCT QUALITY AND SERVICE POLICY

**1. Relationship.** Product quality and service are related for consumer durables, and most industrial goods. High-quality products require less service and low-quality products require more service. As buyers expect product performance to vary with the quality, manufacturers with high-quality products have liberal service policies. Product quality is often a matter of characteristics built into a product that the buyer is unable to judge until after the purchase. As technical features are apt to be deeply hidden, a liberal service policy helps to reduce the customers' reluctance to buy. The maintenance and improvement of product quality are important matters for the sales department. If quality deteriorates the sales department bears the brunt of customer and middleman dissatisfaction.

**2. Forms of Service Policies**

(i) The simplest merely provides for education of the buyer in the use and care of the product.

(ii) Service policies for industrial products and such consumer lines as air-conditioning and heating equipment provide for product installation, inspection and repair.

**3. Aims of Service Policy.** An appropriate service policy facilitates the making of initial sales and helps in keeping products sold, stimulating repeat sales, and building customer goodwill. There is no legitimate place for a service policy that fails to accomplish these aims.

**4. Charges For Service**

(i) Many manufacturers do not charge for service at least for a specified period after sale of the product. "Free" service may be provided either under the terms of a written guarantee or as a matter of policy.

(ii) When the buyer requests service for a considerable time after the purchase, most manufacturers charge for it.

(ii) Firms with centralized service facilities, or operating their own service stations, generally make the charge nominal, which pays part of the costs and eliminates many unreasonable demands,

(iv) Companies that depend upon dealers or distributors to provide service have less control over the charge. It may be nominal, with the manufacturer absorbing part and the user the remainder. It may be larger, and borne entirely by the user. Unless the manufacturer pays some of the cost, middlemen hesitate to assume responsibility for service.

**5. Guarantee Policy**. Guarantees, sometimes called warranties serve as sales promotional devices and as guards against abuses of the service policy. If the product does not perform as represented, the guarantor may promise to replace it, to refund the purchase price or a multiple of that price, to furnish the purchaser with a competitive product at no expense, or to remedy defects free of charge or for a small fee. When a guarantee is used for promotional purposes, its terms are liberal. When used for protection, its terms are hedged with conditions and restrictions.

A guarantee does not serve both promotional and protective purposes well. Because it includes clauses to protect the manufacturer, it is weakened as a tool for sales promotion. On the other hand, the absence of such clauses makes it less effective as a protective device. However, a promotional guarantee should not lack protective provisions, and a protective guarantee is not useless for promotional purposes. But the guarantee must emphasize one purpose, not both.

## DISTRIBUTION POLICIES

### Uses of Distribution Policies

1. Distribution policies determine the functions of the sales department.

2. They set the pattern for sales force operations, both geographically and as to the customers from whom sales personnel solicit orders.

3. They affect the size and nature of the sales organization and the scope of its activities.

4. They influence sales operations and salespersons' jobs.

**Policies on Marketing Channels**

Figure 20.1 shows the principal choices available for marketing channel(s). Manufacturers selling to the consumer market have a choice of five main channels, while those selling to the industrial market have four main options. Few manufacturers use only one marketing channel; most use two or more. Firms that sell to both the consumer and industrial market fall in this classification, as are the many who sell through both chain and independent outlets. However, the actual situation is more complex than that depicted in the diagram. For instance, the toothpaste manufacturer sells through both chain and independent outlets in the drug, grocery, variety and department store fields.

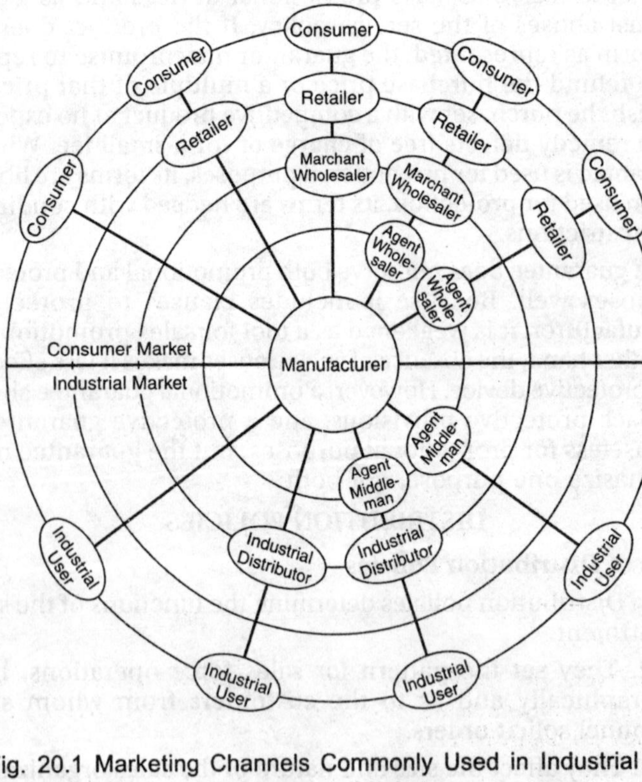


Fig. 20.1 Marketing Channels Commonly Used in Industrial and Consumer Markets

The obvious occasions for decisions on marketing channels are those following the initial organization of the enterprise, and when making additions to the product line. The desirability and appropriateness of different channel options are evaluated at this time.

At other times reappraisals are advisable even though the product line is unchanged. Shifts occur in the nature and importance of the factors that governed the original selection. New institutions appear, marketing innovations develop, characteristics of markets change, and so on. Marketing is dynamic. The effectiveness of different marketing channels is always changing. The sales executive keeps higher management apprised of changes in the factors affecting marketing channels. He points out attention to the need for policy decisions.

**Criteria of Selecting Channels**

**1. Maximum Profit**. The initial selection of marketing channels requires determining which channel, or channels, afford the opportunity for the greatest profit. Channels should be so chosen as to obtain the optimum combination of profit factors. Neither maximum sales volume, nor minimum cost, should be considered alone, the most profitable combination of both must be sought.

**2. Time Dimensions**. Management must look to the long-run effect as well as to the short term impact upon net profits. The policy makers remember all three profit factors — sales volume, costs and resultant net profits. They consider the effect of different channel options and combinations on each factor over both short and long periods.

**Sales Volume Potential**

**1. Market Analysis**. Raw data are secured from the company's own records, external sources of market statistics and field investigations. These data are analyzed. After allowances are made for the strengths of competitors, the potential sales volume of each channel option is estimated.

**2. Factors Determining Sales Potential**. The ability of sales management, the excellence of its planning, and its skill in implementing sales programmes are the most important factors influencing any channel's sales potential. Regardless of the channel chosen, the sales management functions will be performed with the same degree of managerial competence. It makes little sense to compare a well-designed and skilfully executed plan for selling through wholesalers with a poorly designed and awkwardly executed plan for selling direct to retailers.

**Comparative Distribution Costs**

**1. The Costliest Channels are the Shortest.** When a manufacturer decides to sell directly to the consumer, he assumes responsibility for the additional performance of marketing functions. As he steps up performance of selling, transportation, storage, financing and risk bearing, he incurs higher costs. If he chooses to use the door-to-door direct-selling method, he faces problems on the selection, training, supervision and general management of this class of sales personnel. If he decides to open its own retail outlets, he has problems in selecting store locations and buildings, negotiating leases, designing store fronts, obtaining equipment, arranging store layouts, managing retail personnel, conducting retail advertising, and procuring retail-minded executives. Using short channels has a higher gross margin to compensate for additional selling costs, but because it may perform these functions less efficiently than the middleman its net profits are often lower. Most middlemen carry a broader line of merchandise due to which fixed costs are spread over more products. Direct distribution leads to more intimate contact with consumers and closer control over the conditions of product sale. Selecting direct-to-consumer selling one must recognize that he will face a broad range of problems and incur additional distribution expenses. Furthermore, the shorter the channel, the more fixed is the manufacturer's selling costs. The break-even point is almost always higher when short marketing channels are used.

**2. Direct Distribution to Industrial Users.** Direct sale is more common in the industrial than in the consumer field. The costs of selling directly, even to large buyers, are still high. Direct-to-user sales personnel in the industrial market, need considerable technical education, long and expensive training and high compensation. However, when compared with that of less qualified persons selling directly to industrial users enables the manufacturer to provide special attention to each customer's needs. This more than offsets the additional expenses.

**3. Indirect Distribution.** Longer marketing channels result in lower selling costs. As middlemen perform some functions that the manufacturer would otherwise perform, it is necessary to compensate them for performing these functions.

Consequently, when a manufacturer switches from short to longer channels, its own gross margins are reduced. A reduction in selling expense more than offsets the loss in gross margin. The result of using indirect distribution is often higher profit per unit of product sold. The manufacturer also shifts a wide range of problems to the middlemen. In most situations, they operate with a lower break-even point. The disadvantages of indirect distribution are (i) greater remoteness from final consumers and (ii) less control over the conditions of product sale.

**Net Profit Possibilities**

**1. Distribution Costs.** Volume potentials are meaningful only when considered in relation to distribution costs. A channel with high sales potential may involve high distribution costs, causing low net profit. A second channel might not produce a worthwhile sales volume, even though it involves low distribution costs.

**2. Relationships among Gross Margin, Expenses and Net Profit.** High gross margins, such as those obtained through using short channels, do not always mean higher net profits. Expenses of distribution are incurred for performing marketing activities. Choosing marketing channels is a matter of determining the extent to which the manufacturer should perform these activities and the extent to which their performance should be delegated to middlemen. One should determine whether the manufacturer or the middleman can perform the particular activity most efficiently. If this rule is followed, the manufacturer's total costs of moving the product or final buyers should be lower, and profits should be higher.

## POLICIES ON DISTRIBUTION INTENSITY

**1. Value of Policy on Distribution Intensity.** At each level of distribution, decisions are made on the desired number of outlets. It is advisable to decide first upon the policy to be followed at the distribution level nearest the final buyer. Generally the same decisions must be applied at other distribution levels. Once the policy on distribution intensity is set, the sales executive has to interpret and implement it. He, his subordinates, and often even the field sales personnel must decide to use or not to use particular distributive outlets.

**2. Mass Distribution.** A company following a policy of mass distribution aims at maximum sales exposure by securing distribution through all those outlets from which final buyers might expect to purchase the product. This policy is used in distributing many consumer convenience items such as cigarettes, candy and chewing gum. These can be bought at stores, shops, variety stores, restaurants, theatre and hotel lobbies; news-stands; and from vending machines. The manufacturer using this policy needs several marketing channels. But its sales personnel cannot possibly sell directly to all retail outlets. Consequently, he must determine how large each account must be before it is sold directly. In areas where retail outlets are concentrated, the manufacturer may find that it can sell directly to all accounts, large and small. In other markets, manufacturers secure distribution through wholesalers.

**3. Selective Distribution.** It means selecting only those outlets that can best serve the manufacturer's criteria related to sizes of orders, volume of purchases, profitability, type of operation and geographical location. Directly or indirectly, selective distribution represents an attempt to make every account a contributor to net profit. Its basic procedure is to set up criteria for the selection of accounts. An account analysis helps to identify the characteristics that differentiate profitable from unprofitable accounts. A small percentage of the customers contributes a large proportion of the total net sales and profits. Usually 20 per cent of the accounts produce 80 per cent of the net sales, and even more of the net profits.

However, there are exceptions to the general rule that only profitable accounts should be retained or solicited. Some losing accounts may be retained because of long-standing relationships, others because of their future promise. If unprofitable accounts contribute to the payment of overhead expenses, they may add enough to sales volume to enable the firm to realize certain economies in manufacturing. However, savings result from the elimination of unprofitable accounts.

**4. Exclusive Agency Distribution.** Exclusive agencies are common in marketing automobiles, musical instruments, household appliances, machine tools, high quality men's and women's shoes, and branded men's clothing and furnishings. It is an extreme form of selective distribution. The manufacturer makes a written or oral agreement, with a middleman in each market area stipulating that the distribution of his product or products within that area is to be confined solely to that middleman. In return, the middleman is expected to provide more aggressive selling than under milder forms of selective distribution or under mass distribution.

**Disadvantages**

(i) In some markets, the most desirable dealers may be under agreement with another supplier, and the company may have to select a second- or third-rate dealer or open up its own outlet.

(ii) Some middlemen want no part of an exclusive agency contract, perhaps because of the history of exclusive agencies in the food field.

(iii) If exclusive distribution is used at the wholesale level, the wholesaler may not reach certain desirable outlets on the dealer level.

(iv) It is sometimes difficult to sever relations with a middleman whose performance is unsatisfactory.

(v) Some middlemen accept an exclusive agency merely to deprive a competitor of it.

**Advantages**

(i) It is easy to develop distributor enthusiasm for product and stimulate the distributor to sell it aggressively.

(ii) The manufacturer should be able to persuade exclusive outlets to stock a complete line and to service the product or handle repair and replacement parts.

(iii) Relations between sales personnel and the middlemen are likely to be of long duration, and, after the agreements have been reached, sales people can focus more on "servicing" and less on "selling."

(iv) The sales force should be able to spend more time assisting dealers in planning local promotions of the product.

(v) The sales force can be smaller and subject to more effective supervision and control.

## SALE RELATED PRICING POLICIES

In formulating pricing policies, the sales executive's role is advisory. However, all sales executives are responsible for implementing pricing policies. Field sales personnel, the company employees who most directly persuade buyers to accept the products at the prices asked, do the actual implementing of pricing policies, though responsibility for implementation lies with the sales executive. Due to their impacts upon the ease of making sales, pricing policies are of direct interest to sales executives and sales personnel. Pricing policies are of several kinds such as relative to the competition, relative to cost, relative to buyers, and policies on list pricing, and discounts, geographical pricing policies, etc.

**1. Policy on Pricing Relative to the Competition**

Products are priced relative to the competition. If competition is price-based, a company sells its products at the same price as its competitors. If there is non-price competition, the choice is one of the following three alternative policies.

(i) *Meeting the Competition* : It is the most common choice. Hoping to minimize the use of price as a competitive weapon, companies competing on a non-price basis meet competitors' prices. This price policy does not mean meeting every competitor's prices. Only the prices of important competitors who may lure customers away are met.

(ii) *Pricing above the Competition* : It is less common though appropriate in certain situations. Sometimes it conveys an impression of above-average product quality or prestige. Many buyers relate a product's quality to its price, particularly when it is difficult to judge quality before buying. A policy of pricing above the competition needs the support of strong promotion by both the manufacturer and the middlemen. The promotional support of dealers is secured by setting high list (resale) prices, which the manufacturer suggests the dealers to use in reselling the products. Middlemen pass the higher mark-ups on to final buyers in the form of higher prices. Increased support by the dealers of the manufacturer's product more than offsets the sales-depressing tendency of the higher prices and may even increase total unit sales. To compete at a price above the competition, a product must either be so differentiated that buyers believe it superior to competitors' offerings or middlemen must enthusiastically promote it. The manufacturer's sales personnel play key roles, in securing this kind of promotion from the middlemen.

(iii) *Pricing under the Competition* : Most manufacturers do not willingly price under the competition but some price under their competitors and appear to have demonstrated, that aggressive pricing increases market demand and keeps new competitors from entering the field. Sales executives dislike this alternative because it causes sales personnel to sell price more than the product.

## 2. Policy on Pricing Relative to Costs

Every company has a policy regarding the relationships between its products' prices and the underlying costs. Most companies follow a full-cost pricing policy under most circumstances. They also spell out the circumstances under which departures are permissible.

(i) *Full-cost Pricing* : Under it no sale is made at a price lower than that covering total costs, including variable costs and allocated fixed costs, because if short-run sales revenues cover short-run costs, they also cover long-run costs. Nevertheless, the price buyers are willing to pay bears little relationship to the seller's cost. Moreover, it is next to impossible to determine "real" costs especially with respect to allocating a share of fixed costs to a particular unit of product. If it were possible to determine real costs, there are times when prices on products already on hand must be cut below full cost to sell at all. One needs a policy detailing the conditions under which prices may be used that do not cover full cost.

(ii) *Promotion Pricing* : Pricing is a promotional tool, particularly in industries producing consumer non-durables. For instance, a company launching a new packaged convenience food may offer it at a "special low introductory price." Another example of the use of a low introductory price when a company invades a geographical market in which a competitor is already well entrenched. Other circumstance in which pricing is used as a promotional tool includes that in which management wishes to counter the effects of competitors' increases in promotional activity such as heavier or more effective advertising, the use of in-store demonstrators, or more frequent calls on customers by competitors' sales personnel.

(iii) *Contribution Pricing* : It means pricing at any level above the relevant incremental costs. Incremental costs are those incurred in changing the level or nature of an activity, for example, making and/or selling a larger quantity of a product. Incremental costs may be either variable or a combination of variable and fixed costs. Suppose that a seller is offered a special contract to supply a large buyer, who will not pay the going price. The buyer argues that the lower price is justified because of savings to the seller in selling time, credit costs, handling expenses, so that total sales rupees from the proposed transaction are not sufficient to cover total costs. The seller should accept the order if the resulting total sales rupees are sufficient not only to cover all incremental costs but to make a contribution to fixed costs and/or profits. After all, assuming the incremental costs are all variable, sale at a special price will not raise fixed costs, so this sale need not bear an allocated share of fixed costs to yield net profit. So long as the proposed price more than covers the out-of-pocket costs of the transaction, the excess is profit.

Three important conditions should all be present for such offers to be accepted : (a) the company already has the necessary production capacity, (b) this capacity cannot be put to a more profitable use, and (c) the portion of the output sold below full cost is destined for a different market segment. The third condition is critical to the continuance of going prices at full cost or above for the bulk of the output. The word that one account has been favoured with a lower price travels at the speed of light to all other accounts in the market area.

**3. Policy on Uniformity of Prices to Different Buyers**

In pricing to different buyers, companies choose between (i) a one-price policy, under which all similar buyers are quoted the same price and (ii) a variable-price policy, under which the price to each buyer is determined by individual bargaining. Most marketers of consumer goods adhere to a one-price policy, even though many vary prices among different classes of customers and from one geographic region to the next.

The variable-price policy is common wherever individual sales involve large sums, as in many industrial marketing situations. The bargaining power of individual buyers varies with the size of the transaction. A large buyer represents a greater potential for future business than does a small buyer, therefore, a seller may make price concessions to gain or retain the large buyer's patronage.

**Advantages**

(i) Since prices are not negotiated with individual customers, sales personnel spend only minimum time discussing price and devote maximum time to "creative selling."

(ii) There is no risk of alienating customers because of preferential prices given to others.

(iii) Laws prohibiting price discrimination make it safer legally for a marketer to apply a one-price policy than a variable-price policy.

### 4. Policy on List Pricing

Distributing through middlemen a marketer either does not suggest standardized resale (list) prices or seeks to control middlemen's resale prices through list pricing. The two most common variety of forms, list pricing takes are that of printing the price on the package or requiring sales personnel to suggest the resale price to buyers. When the marketer utilizes selective or exclusive distribution, list pricing is easiest to implement because the difficulties of enforcement of suggested list prices multiply with increases in the number of middlemen. Effective enforcement of list pricing means assigning the additional role of "resale price reporter" to sales force personnel.

### 5. Policy on Discounts

(i) *Trade Discounts* : A manufacturer selling to both wholesalers and retailers may offer different "trade discounts," to each class of customer. Under laws prohibiting price discrimination, discounts must be made available on proportionately equal terms to all similar customers. As wholesalers and retailers perform different distributive function, they are not similar customers. The law permits a manufacturer to charge a higher price to retailers than to wholesalers, even though some buyers in each class may buy in the same quantities. Policy on trade discounts depends on the importance of each class of buyer and on their relative bargaining power.

(ii) *Quantity Discounts* : These are price reductions granted for purchases in a stated quantity or quantities and are normally aimed to increase the quantities customers buy. Sellers increase sales through price reductions by passing on to buyers part of the savings that result from large purchases. These savings are considerable, for it may take little of a salesperson's time to sell a large order than to sell a small one. The same holds for order processing, order filling, billing, and transportation costs.

The firm using a quantity discount policy must keep two legal restrictions in mind : (i) the discounts must reflect actual savings and (ii) the discounts must be available on proportionately equal terms to all similar purchasers.

### 6. Geographical Pricing Policies

The farther away the customer is from the factory, the greater are the freight charges for a given size order. Irrespective of the policy the company adopts, freight differentials are reflected in price quotations. Regardless of the policy on payment of shipping charges, its administration is the sales executive's responsibility. There are three alternatives : (i) F.O.B., or "free on board" pricing, under which the customer pays the freight; (ii) delivered pricing, under which the seller pays the freight and (iii) freight absorption, a compromise between F.O.B. and delivered pricing.

(i) *F.O.B. Pricing* : The marketer using this policy quotes selling prices at the factory and buyers pay the freight charges. Each buyer adds freight to the factory price and determines total delivered cost. F.O.B. pricing results in variations in the resale price that middlemen put on the product in different areas. In consumer-goods marketing, F.O.B. pricing is used for items that are heavy or bulky relative to their value, for example, canned goods and fresh vegetables. In industrial marketing of raw materials and heavy machinery, F.O.B. pricing is also in widespread use.

(ii) *Delivered Pricing* : The marketer using this policy pays freight charges and includes them in its price quotations. The price is really an "F.O.B. destination" price, and the net return to the seller varies with the buyer's location. Delivered pricing is appropriate when freight charges account for only a small part of the product's price. It is a necessary policy when a marketer uses list prices. Standardized resale prices are likely to be obtained if middlemen pay a uniform nationwide delivered price — sometimes called a "postage stamp" price. Makers of chewing gum, candy bars, and many drug items, particularly patent medicines, use postage stamp pricing. As all middlemen pay the same price, the resale price is roughly the same throughout the entire market.

(iii) *Freight Absorption* : Under zone pricing the market is divided into zones and different prices are quoted to buyers in each zone. The manufacturer builds the freight charges into its quoted price, but it quotes different prices to buyers situated in different zones.

**7. Policy on Price Leadership**

Generally, price leaders have large market shares and price followers small market shares. In some industries there are well-established patterns of price leadership. In selling basic industrial materials, such as lumber and cement, one company is the price leader and is usually the first to raise or cut prices. Other industry members simply follow or, sometimes, fail to follow, as occasionally happens in the case of a price increase, thus causing the leader to reconsider and perhaps to cancel the announced increase. Similar patterns exist in marketing such consumer products as gasoline and bakery goods, where, usually market by market, one company serves as the price leader and others follow.

Producers know that the middlemen handling their products are sensitive to price changes; they will consider switching suppliers, in response to even minuscule price changes, up or down. Even when the marketer of a consumer product competing on a non-price basis must be alert to impending price changes, the important policy issue is whether to initiate or to follow price changes. The decision depends upon the marketer's relative market position and the image of leadership that it desires to build and maintain.

**8. Product Line Pricing Policy**

A Different items in a product line "compete" with each other. A buyer buying one member of the line does so to the exclusion of others. One decision relates to the "price space" between the prices of individual members of the line. Having the right amount of price space is critical; too little may confuse buyers, and too much leaves "gaps" into which competitors can move and make sales. Through their knowledge of the market, of buyers' motivations, and of competitors' offerings and prices, sales executives contribute major inputs to this decision.

Another important decision is concerning the pricing of the "top" (highest-priced item) and the "bottom" (lowest-priced item) in the line. Companies price the "in between" members of the line so that they account for the line as a prestige builder. As the traffic builder, the lower-priced item affects total sales far more than does the price of any other item. A price increase on it causes higher sales on other line members. The same is true for the prestige builder. A change in the price of the top of the line influences sales of other line members.

**9. Competitive Bidding Policy**

In purchasing certain products, industrial and governmental buyers solicit competitive bids from potential suppliers and award the business to the bidder offering the best proposal. Depending on which is most important to the buyer, a proposal may be selected as best for a number of reasons such as price, delivery dates, reputation for quality. In some industries, competitive bidding is the general rule and individual manufactures have no choice but to participate. In other industries, only a part of the volume is sold on this basis, and each manufacturer decides whether to participate. For example, a typewriter manufacturer who sells to industry on a uniform price basis must participate in competitive bidding if it wants orders from governmental agencies. Believing that competitive bidding reduces competition to a price basis, many manufacturers avoid bid business unless the share of the total market involved is too large to ignore.

The sales executive and the sales personnel play important roles in competitive bidding. Their close contact with the market puts them in a good position to estimate how low a particular price must be to obtain the order. The long-term relationships developed between salespersons and their customers are important in giving the company a chance to make a "second bid" in those cases where industrial buyers give favoured suppliers the chance to meet lower bids submitted by competitors. This chance does not exist in competitive bidding for government business, where closed bids are specified, that is, all bids are opened at the same time and there is no chance for high bidders to adjust their quotes downward. By persuading the purchasing agent or the value of a differentiating characteristic of the product and include this characteristic in the written specification supplied to potential bidders, an effective salesperson can often remove competition from closed government bids.

## QUESTIONS FOR EXERCISE

1. What are the functions of sales related marketing policies? Explain product policies in detail.
2. Discuss sales related distribution policies.
3. Discuss and explain sales related pricing policies.

# 21

# Market Measurement, Sales Forecasting and Sales Budget

## DEFINITION OF SALES FORECASTING

1. Allen. "Forecasting is a systematic attempt to probe the future by inference from known facts."

2. Henry Fayol. "To foresee in this context means both to assess the future and make a provision for it, that is forecasting is itself action already."

3. American Marketing Association. Sales forecasting is, "an estimate of sales in dollars or physical units for a specified future period under a proposed marketing plan or programme and under an assumed set of economic and other forces outside the unit for which the forecast is made. The forecast may be for a specified item of merchandise or for an entire line."

4. Philip Kotler. "The company sales forecast is the expected level of company sales based on a chosen marketing plan and assumed environmental condition."

5. Condiff and Still. "Sales forecast is an estimate of sales during a specified future period, which estimate is tied to a proposed marketing plan and which assumes a particular set of uncontrollable and competitive forces."

6. Anderson. "A forecast is nothing more than an estimate of a future condition."

7. C.E. Sultan. "Business forecasting is the calculation of probable events to provide against the future. It, therefore, involves a look ahead in business and idea of predetermination of events and then financial implications as in the case of budgeting."

## OBJECTIVES OF SALES FORECASTING

### 1. The Short-Run Objectives

(i) *To Formulate Suitable Production Policy* : The first object of the short-run sales forecasting is to formulate a suitable production policy so that problems of under-production or over-production might not arise and production may be made according to the demand forecast.

(ii) *To Make Provision for Regular Supply of Raw Material* : The second objective is to make provision for the regular supply of raw material for the production on the basis of estimated sales during a short period.

(iii) *To Achieve Best Utilisation of Machines* : One of the important objectives of sales forecasting is to make the best utilisation of the available machines so that in case of increase in demand there should not be any shortage of production and in case of decrease in demand the machines should not remain idle.

(iv) *To Determine Appropriate Price Policy* : Sales forecast has an important bearing on production policy which in its turn influences the production-costs which again affect the organisation's price policy. Therefore to determine an appropriate price policy is an important objective of sales forecasting.

(v) *To Arrange Regular Availability of Labour* : One of the objectives of sales forecasting is also to arrange for trained personnel and non-technical workers so that the organisation might not experience any shortage of personnel and at the same time they do not remain idle when the production is curtailed.

(vi) *To Forecast Short-term Financial Requirements* : The financial requirements of the organisation depend on the level of sales and production volume. On the basis of sales, forecasting of short term requirements and arrangements can be made accordingly much in advance.

(vii) *To Set the Sales Target and Establish Controls and Incentives* : Sales forecasts help in setting the sales target for different market segments on the basis of which control can be exercised on the personnel engaged in the work and necessary incentives can also be provided for implementing the programmes and achieving the targets of sales, etc.

**2. Long-Run Objectives**

(i) *To Estimate Cash Inflows* : Cash inflows from sales can be well estimated through sales forecasting by determining the cash and credit sale ratio. It can also help planning for credit policy of the organisation.

(ii) *To Determine Dividend Policy* : The profits can also be forecasted on the basis of gross profit ratio on sale and dividend policy can be determined.

(iii) *To Plan Plant Capacity* : A long run objective of sales forecasting is to plan plant capacity in accordance with the demand. If the estimates of the sales forecast reveal that the plant capacity will fall short of meeting the future demand then decision in regard to increase in the production capacity of the present plant or setting up of new plant can be made.

(iv) *To Achieve Man power Planning* : Another long run objective of sales forecasting is planning for manpower so that production work might not suffer in the long-run.

(v) *To Plan Long-run Production* : Long-run production planning also depends upon sales forecasting. In the long-run product has to be adjusted to the market demand and other condition.

*(vi) To Forecast Long-run Financial Requirements* : Sales forecasting also determines the long-run financial requirements of the organisation for working capital as well as for capital expenditure.

(vi) *To Achieve Budgetary Control over Expenditures* : In forecasting the sales, all the activities are to be forecasted for which purpose budget is to be prepared for the income and expenditure of the organisation. The budgeting figures for income and expenditure are then compared with the actual performance and any variation is removed. Thus budgetary control over expenditures is possible.

## IMPORTANCE OF SALES FORECASTING

According to John D. Luth, A good sales forecast is undoubtedly the most important single planning tool. It is the basis of fund budgeting; all budgeting starts with the sales forecast. Financial planning for working capital requirements, plant expansion and other needs are based on anticipated sales. Scheduling of all production resources and facilities such as setting manpower needs, purchasing raw material requirements and determining the rate of production output depends upon the sales forecast. It is essential to review the sales forecasts periodically. Manufacturing concerns give great importance sales forecasting. They base their production on the expectation of future demand. On the basis of correct forecast, the producer adjusts his production to the market demand and adjusts the productive capacity of the plant. Thus, production policy and price policy all depend on accurate sales forecasting. It influences all the activities of the organisation such as production and distribution, for the success and achievements of the overall objectives of the organisation. Sales forecasting is equally important in the field of organising personnel management. The main users of sales forecasting are departments of production, distribution, purchasing, finance, personnel, marketing and R&D.

Thus, the importance of sales forecasting may be seen in (i) importance in promotion; (ii) basis of planning; (iii) correctness of management decisions; (iv) status of effective control; (v) incentive to cooperation and coordination; (vi) it facilitates the estimation of future needs of business; (vii) it is the basis of succession business; (viii) singleness of purpose which helps the management in achieving the overall goals of the organisation.

## ROLE OF SALES FORECASTING

**1. Base for Marketing Planning.** No marketing plan can be made dependable and strong unless it is based firmly on sales forecasting. If the marketing manager has no idea about the future expected sales, he cannot decide about correct marketing programme and various production activities. Therefore, sales forecasting is the base for marketing planning.

**2. Discovery of Marketing Opportunities.** Sales forecasting helps in discovering new marketing opportunities. The possibilities of tending new markets encourage the personnel of the marketing department to take more and more interest in their work.

**3. Reduction of Marketing Risks.** Sales forecasting throws light on the future marketing risks. The marketing manager can guard himself against such risks on the basis of sales forecasting. He can face the challenges of new situations in a better way. He can modify and make necessary changes in the marketing programme and thus reduce the chances of loss.

**4. Help in Control.** Sales forecast reveals the weak areas where more control and intensive attention are required.

## FACTORS AFFECTING SALES FORECASTING

**1. General Business Conditions.** While making sales forecast the marketer should give due consideration to the general conditions of the economy, growth of population, distribution of income and wealth, general customs, government policy, fashion and seasonal fluctuations, etc. during the future period.

**2. Conditions within the Industry.** The marketing manager cannot expect to win over the whole potential for his company. He has to be satisfied with a share of this potential. The ratio of the company's sale is only a part of this potential. While making sales forecast, the forecaster should keep in view the changes going on in the total demand of the product, the number of other units engaged in the industry and their sales, research potentials and product development, etc.

**3. Changed Market Situations.** The marketing manager should always be alive to the various factors which bring about changes in the market demand. A change in the total market demand is bound to reflect the demand for the company's product. In making sales forecast, the market behaviour in the past should be analysed and evaluated properly. Future market conditions should also be analysed.

**4. Conditions within the Company.** Internal changes within the company in the coming future in price structure, distribution channel, sale promotion measures, product or other marketing policies of the company also affect future sales. Therefore, it is necessary to anticipate the extent to which such measures may affect the future sales. As such factors are well within the controls of the company, therefore sales forecast may take them into consideration.

**5. Factors Affecting Export Trade.** Such factors include export and import controls imposed by the government, export conditions, export-import policy, export finance, new agreements, etc. If the company is engaged in the export trade, the marketing manager must consider the various factors in forecasting the export sale because such factors greatly influence the export trade.

## LIMITATIONS OF SALES FORECASTING

**1. Changes in Consumer's Needs, Tastes, Fashion, etc.** Introduction of new fashion product is seldom accurate. Future sales depend on the reception by the market. If it becomes popular, sales will be enormous, otherwise it be the reverse, in the face of the ever-changing tastes, fashions and styles.

**2. Lack of Data Regarding History.** There is no past sales history for new products. Guesswork proves limitation to the accuracy of forecast.

**3. Anticipatory Growth Element.** As it is difficult to maintain a rapid rate of growth over an extended period of time, the market manager must estimate the probable rate of growth and consider it while preparing the sales forecast for his company.

**4. Psychological Factors.** The consumer attitude can change suddenly from confidence to apprehensiveness about the future. A rumour of war, for example, would create a fantastic demand for motor car tyres and tubes.

## BASIC RULES OF SALES FORECASTING

*Rule 1*—Distinguish between hard and soft data. Hard data are facts which can be objectively assessed *e.g.*, past sales. Soft data can be subjectively assessed.

*Rule 2*—Use as few variables as possible and distinguish between dependent and independent variables. Dependent variables are like sales, and independent variables like price, advertising and sales activity.

*Rule 3*—Use general economic and industry indicators that have proved most reliable.

*Rule 4*—Identify appropriate time relationship, particularly lag effects.

*Rule 5*—Do not use variables which cannot themselves be forecasted.

## STEPS IN THE PROCESS OF SALES FORECASTING

**1. Determination of the Objectives.** The objectives of sales forecasting should be determined first of all. Certain points in this regard should be very clear before taking up the forecasting task such as, short-term or long-term period of forecasting; area for sales forecasting (whole country or a specific area for a specific product); unit of sale for forecasting in quantities or value and the time, labour and money to be employed on forecasting. These points are determined taking into account the objectives of sales forecasting.

**2. Subdivision of the Task of Forecasting.** The second step in making the sales forecast is to subdivide the forecasting programme into homogeneous groups according to product, area, activities or customers. The total sales forecast of the company is the sum-total of the sales forecast of all the groups.

**3. Determination of the Relative Importance of Factors.** Having subdivided the task of forecasting, the relative importance should be determined so that due weight may be given to different factors affecting sales forecasts.

**4. Selection of Method.** The method is to be selected by the appropriate authority taking into account all the relevant situations, purposes of forecasting and the degree of accuracy required.

**5. Collection and Analysis of Data.** By applying the appropriate method, the necessary data for the forecast are collected, tabulated, analysed and cross-checked. The data are interpreted by applying statistical techniques to draw necessary deductions. Therefore, it may be called the preliminary sales forecast which forms the basis of final sales forecast.

**6. Study of Correlation between Sales Forecast and Sales Promotion Plans.** Making the forecast reliable, the sales promotion plans such as advertising policy, personal selling and other policies should be reviewed with reference to the sales forecasts. A study of correlation between sales forecast and sales promotions plans should be made in order to establish their role in promoting the sales in the past.

**7. Study of Competitor's Activities.** As the volume of sale of a company is largely affected by the activities of competitors, therefore, the efficient marketer must study the competitors' activities, policies, programmes and strategies and their effects on the market. Marketer should guess their behaviour and adjust his own forecasting results accordingly.

**8. Preparation of Final Sales Forecasts.** Taking the sales promotion plans and competitors' activities into stock, the preliminary sales forecasts results are converted into final sales forecast results relating to the products and territories involved. The aggregate of sales forecasts of different products, or territories or customers or activities may form the sales forecasts of the company.

**9. Evaluation.** The figures for final sales forecasts are the basis for the operations of the company in the next period. The actual sales performance in the coming period should be reviewed and evaluated from time to time. The evaluation work may be made monthly, quarterly, half-yearly or yearly. The forecast figures may be revised in the light of difficulties experienced during the course of actual operations.

**10. Adjustment.** On the expiry of forecasts period, the actual sales and forecasted sales should be compared and causes of variation be found out which would help the marketer improve the next period sales forecast figures.

## METHODS OF SALES FORECASTING

A. William J. Stanton has mentioned the following two types of techniques for sales forecasting :

**1. Build-up Techniques**

(i) Past sales and trend analysis

(ii) Executive judgement

(iii) Sales force composite

(iv) Analysis of market factors

**2. Statistical and Quantitative Methods**

(i) Direct derivation method

(ii) Correlation analysis technique

B. Philip Kotler has explained the following methods :

**1. Methods based on "What People Say?"**

(i) Survey of buyers' intentions

(ii) Composites of sales force opinions

(iii) Experts' opinions

**2. Methods based on "What People Do?"**

(i) Market test Method.

**3. Methods based on "What People Have Done?"**

(i) Classical time-series analysis

(ii) Statistical demand analysis

C. According to Bill Donaldson

**1. Market research and Consumer Surveys**

**2. Consensus method**—executives or experts or sales force opinion.

**3. Objective techniques**

(a) Time Series

(b) Casual methods like linear equation

$$Y = a + bx$$

## 1. EXECUTIVE JUDGMENT METHOD

It is a process of combining and averaging or evaluating the opinions and views of top executives. Opinions are sought from the executives of marketing, finance and other divisions of the company and forecasts are made.

(i) The process is easy and simple. Speedy forecast can be done.

(ii) There is no need of collecting elaborate statistics for the forecasts because forecasts are based on the experiences of experts of different departments.

(iii) It permits pooling of specialised viewpoint.

(iv) It is the only feasible means of forecasting in the absence of adequate data.

(v) It is economical also.

**Disadvantages**

(i) It has no factual basis so it is inferior method.

(ii) It disperses responsibility for accurate forecasting. Moreover accuracy cannot be claimed.

(iii) It utilises costly executive time.

### 2. SALES FORCE COMPOSITE METHOD

In this method, views of the salesmen and sales executives are utilised for the different segments. There are many variations. The combined view of the sales force as to future sales expectations may be secured and careful scrutiny many be made at successive executive levels for the future sales estimate submitted by the individual salesmen. An alternative way is to rely upon the knowledge of company's sales executives in preparing the sales forecasts.

**Advantages**

(i) The advantage of specialised knowledge of persons who are close to the market, can be obtained.

(ii) It imposes greater confidence in sales force.

(iii) It places the responsibility for the forecasts on those who are expected to produce results.

(iv) Market segmentation can be developed on the basis of products, territory, customer or salesmen.

(v) It provides greater stability through magnitude of sample.

**Disadvantages**

(i) Being unduly optimistic or pessimistic salesmen are poor estimators. So, accuracy of forecasts is always doubtful.

(ii) Salesmen are not aware of the broad economic patterns and therefore cannot forecast long term trends.

(iii) The salemen's time for their primary job selling is curtailed.

(iv) Salesmen can intentionally underestimate the demand if sales quota are to be fixed on the basis of this information.

## 3. THE USER'S EXPECTATION METHOD

In this method, actual users of the product are contacted and asked to submit the estimated quantities of the product they expect to purchase in a given future period. Total sales forecast of the product is estimated by combining such responses. From this, an estimate is made for the demand which can be filled by the company preparing the forecast.

**Advantages**

(i) Sales forecast is based on direct information from the actual users whose buying action will really decide the future demand.

(ii) It proceeds from a subjective feeling of the market and of the thinking behind the buying intention of the actual users.

(iii) This method is more appropriate for sales forecasting in cases where new product is to be introduced without any previous sales record or the number of customers are limited.

(iv) It is most suitable for short-run forecasting.

**Disadvantages**

(i) It is not practicable when consumers are numerous.

(ii) User's estimates are mainly based on expectations which may change later on.

(iii) It is not fit for long-term forecasting.

## 4. EXPERTS' OPINIONS

In this method the organisation collects opinions from the outsider specialists in the field such as opinions given in the newspapers and journals, wholesalers and distributors, agencies or professional experts. Forecasts can be done by analysis of these opinions and making deductions for the companies' sales.

**Advantages**

(i) Forecasts can be made easily and speedily.

(ii) Different experts' ideas and opinions are taken into consideration for forecasting and they may be evaluated.

(iii) It is suitable where past record of sales is not available or a new product is to be introduced.

(iv) It is economical because the expenses for seeking the opinions of experts are much less than that of the actual survey.

**Disadvantages**

(i) Market segmentation on the basis of product, territory or customers is not possible.

(ii) The reliability of forecasting is always doubtful because forecasting is based on opinions and suggestions and not on the facts.

## 5. MARKET TEST METHOD

It is most appropriate when product is quite new in the market or good estimators are not available or buyers do not prepare their purchase plan. Thus, under this method, the seller sells the product in a part of the market for sometimes and makes the assessment of sales for the full market on the basis of results of test sales.

**Advantages**

(i) It is best for introducing the product in the market.

(ii) Any defect in the product may also come in the light and it may be removed immediately to make the product successful in the market.

(iii) Sales forecasts are based on actual results. Hence forecasts are more reliable.

**Disadvantages**

(i) It takes a long time to test the market.

(ii) The sales forecasts data are projected on the basis of results of a part of the market. As all the parts of the market are not homogeneous, forecasts may not be reliable.

## 6. STATISTICAL AND QUANTITATIVE METHODS

(i) *The Trend Method* : The statistical methods commonly used are trend and cycle projection and mathematical approaches including moving average correlation analysis. The relationship is often expressed as a mathematical formula or model. With the help of the formula, trend is projected and the sales forecasts are made assuming that the same trend would continue in the future.

The trend method can be used for both linear and non-linear relationship. The basic assumption in this method is that factors which had been responsible for the past movements will also play an important role in the future. Where steady progress was noticed in the movement of the product over a considerable period of time, it may be felt reasonable to project the past trend into future. Before projecting the trend, one must be aware of causes about the applicability of the assumption.

(ii) *The Regression Technique* : Here an attempt is made to estimate a statistical series of dependable variables through fixed relationship by using another variable called the independent variable to which the first is related instead of using regularly spaced time intervals. In this sense, part data are also used by the regression techniques. Under this method, like trend method, a curve is drawn with the help of correlationship between the dependent and independent variables. The methods used are either the least squares or the graphical correlation method. Sales forecast is made on the basis of economic indicators. For example, the demand for paper will increase with the increase in the number of students. Number of students is an indicator for the demand of paper. This method is based on the presumption that the one variable affects the other dependable variables.

**Advantages of Statistical and Quantitative Methods**

(i) They help to describe in measurable objective terms, the factors and their relationship with the course of sales.

(ii) The degree of reliability is indicated.

(iii) These methods force the forecaster to quantify assumptions underlying his estimates and thus enable a checking of results by managements.

(iv) They force the forecaster to consider the major factors influencing sales.

**Disadvantages**

(i) These methods correlate sales to indicators which are themselves generally estimates.

(ii) Such techniques rely largely on statistical methods and do not rely much on personal skill and experience.

(iii) They involve complicated statistical methods.

(iv) They require considerable technical skill and experience for it to be effective.

## WHAT IS SALES BUDGET?

Sales budget is an important part of the general budget of the company. It is the basic budget because it affects the budgets for other departments such as production budget, cash budget, personnel budget, etc. Sales budget shows the estimated amount of sales in a specified future period normally a year. It must indicate both the quantities expected to be sold as well as the receipts anticipated from such sales.

It is only after preparing the sales budget, that production capacity and inflows and outflows of cash are anticipated, expenses on various heads are estimated and cost data are considered. The accuracy of sales forecasts is the main basis for the accuracy and reliability of other budgets.

Sales budget is prepared by the marketing manager or sales manager on the basis of figures collected through one of the various methods of sales forecasts with the help of market researchers, regional managers, branch managers and salesmen.

Presenting sales forecast is not the sales budget. The necessary adjustment in respect of the following should also be made in the figure of sales forecasts :

(i) Opening stock of saleable items of the product.

(ii) Sales orders, outstanding at the beginning of the budget period.

(iii) Estimated volume of production during the budget period.

(iv) Estimate quantity of saleable product at the end of the period.

Thus, sales budget serves as a measuring device to inform management as to how far the company is making the desired progress towards the achievement of the predetermined objectives. It serves as a control device presenting the standard against which actual performance can be measured and a control mechanism for the sales volume and the distribution cost. Sales budget can be prepared area-wise, product-wise, customer-wise, and sales representative-wise. It offers a better control on sales.

## FACTORS IN PREPARING SALES BUDGET

**1. Internal Factors.** These refer to those factors which relate to the internal situations of the concern and are in most cases within the control of executives. Such factors include :

(i) Sales-volume of the last year and sale-trend.
(ii) Long-term sale-trend of different products of the concern.
(iii) Profitability of different products.
(iv) Production capacity of the concern.
(v) Plant development programme.
(v) Possibility of fluctuation in future production.
(vii) Seasonal changes in company-products.
(viii) Advertisement and other sales-promotion measures.
(ix) Selling and distribution systems.
(x) Market research and product development possibilities.
(xi) Price policy — its effects on product demand.
(xii) Level of efficiency of salesmen.
(xiii) Sales-orders outstanding at the beginning of the budget period.

**2. External Factors.** These are such factors which occur outside the concern and are to a great extent uncontrollable. Such factors are :

(i) General trend of industrial activities in the country.
(ii) Business, industrial, economic and taxation policies of the government.
(iii) Change in population.
(iv) National and international trade conditions such as business cycles, monopolistic tendencies, monetary policy, etc.
(v) Purchasing power of the general public — income, national production and employment positions are to be studied.
(vi) Standard of living of the masses — purchasing habits, fashions, ways of living, etc.
(vii) Competition position — in relation to price, product, etc.
(viii) Market conditions of the market segment for the product.

## FORECASTING IN INDIAN CONTEXT

As compared to the advanced countries, forecasting by business enterprises in India is practically unknown. Functioning in an economy insulated from foreign competition and boosted up under the impact of price inflation due to excessive demand and money expansion, the Indian business enterprises have operated for long in a "seller's market" where demand exceeded supply. However, during the recent years the situation has materially changed, though this cannot be described as a complete transformation. There has been a marked shift towards market mechanism and the market forces can be as much helpful as devastating. Consumer resistance has developed with the result that a large number of consumer goods industries find it difficult to maintain their regular levels of sales. Prize competitions, special discounts, gift coupons, etc. have been employed to push up sales. For example, the recession that originated in the engineering industries spread its tentacles to consumer goods industries. Contrary to the popular belief that the economy was slowly reviving, the recession widened and deepened. At no other time was there a greater need for forecasting. Business enterprises should seriously undertake the exercises in forecasting their sales. Reverting to competitive mechanism is not easy after enjoying buoyant conditions for more than a decade. The transitory period has already posed a number of problems. It is imperative that business enterprises should take to forecasting and evolve their production programmes on its basis.

For example, in recent years, the motor car industry in India has found itself to be priced out of the market. The prices kept shooting up until customer resistance overtook the industry. Instead of waiting list, a car can now be secured from off the shelf. The same thing also happened with the television industry. There was a slump in the sales after an initial boom. Here the government came to the rescue of the industry. An excise cut was offered by the government in its budget whereby the basic price of the set did not exceed Rs. 1,800 as the excise duty payable was reduced from 20 per cent to 5 per cent. Accordingly a large number of manufacturers immediately pegged their price at Rs. 1,800 and charged extra for glass screen, antenna, etc. Other factors which helped the industry was a cut in the price of picture tube by about Rs. 190. The Electronics Corporation of India, the prime supplier of sets to Greater Bombay found its sets selling about 1,000 sets per month with bookings around 1,400 to 1,500 a day, while formerly it was barely selling 500 to 600 sets a month.

Thus sales forecasting helps in determining what is likely to happen in the future. It can give indicators of direction in which efforts could be made to improve the situation before it hits the industry or unit concerned.

## QUESTIONS FOR EXERCISE

1. Define sales forecasting. Discuss its objects and importance
   Or
2. Write a short note on sales forecasting.
3. Discuss the role of sales forecasting in marketing planning
   Or
4. Explain in brief the factors affecting the sales forecasting
   Or
5. Explain the limitations of sales forecasting Or
6. Assess the role of forecasting in the Indian context.
7. Explain in brief the major steps in the process of sales forecasting.
8. Explain different methods of sales forecasting. Discuss their merits and demerits Or
9. It is said that the investigator can build his forecast on the basis of what people say, what people do, and what people have done. Discuss and analyse the various methods of forecasting demand.

# 22

# Psychology of Sales

Both buying and selling are modes of behaviour and since all forms of behaviour obey certain rules, it is possible to discover the laws applicable in this case and to control buying and selling. Since he is human being, the buyer is influenced by psychological laws. Hence, if the seller knows what he should do to awaken a specific response in the buyer he can do his job much better. The situation of buying and selling consists of the buyer, the seller and the material to be sold. While it is desirable that the seller's behaviour should be psychologically tangible, it must be kept in mind that it is easy to sell goods which the buyer requires and demands. Therefore, it is better to manufacture goods which satisfy the buyer's demands and fulfil his requirements. Human beings have a variety of psychological and physical needs. Physical needs include hunger, thirst, the need to maintain an even body temperature, sleep, sex desire, etc. Among psychological needs are ambition, sex instinct and other individual requirements, in addition to more social needs such as the desire to win social prestige or to attract the attention of others towards oneself. Nowadays the manufacturer turns his attention to these needs of his prospective customers and tries to make his products conform to the requirements of the customer. If he succeeds in this, he finds little if any difficulty in selling them.

## VARIOUS STEPS IN SELLING

The manufacturer's task does not end with the manufacture of an article because the customer must be aware of a particular article that he needs and also of the place where he can procure it. In addition, conveying this information to the customer will not suffice because others offer similar or even identical products which are marketed by many other manufactures and are available in the market. The customer is attracted to one such product but not towards another. The answer to this lies in advertisement. Advertisement is the science of attracting the attention of the people since it informs the customer about the goods available and the distinctive qualities of each. This is the first stage in selling. In the second stage the manufacturer aims at interesting the customer in his own product. If interest is lacking, the customer does not buy the product, but if it is present, he can at least be induced to inspect and examine it. Once interest is established, the desire to buy follows. But the act of buying occurs only after the individual has examined the article. The confidence that the customer would get on first-hand examination of the article is created by the manufacturer through advertisement, his own credit and through the gift of the gab, the ability to talk and to convince the customer. If the article is dependable, the customer decides to purchase it. The seller convinces him and removes his doubts, and finally the customer's decision to buy is translated into action. After the actual purchase, if the customer is satisfied with the performance of the article, he talks of it to other people and, if need be, returns to buy it a second time. This mental satisfaction is an essential step in the process of selling.

## METHODS OF SALES DIALOGUE

The process of going from step to step as mentioned above, in the business of selling, is facilitated by psychological laws. People who pay heed to psychological laws and apply them in practice find it easier to sell their product. People who do not, face considerable difficulty in selling. In order to encourage the customer to move these five steps, the seller has to talk to him. The method and the nature of his sales interview or sales talk change with any change in the seller, the customer or the product being sold. For this reason it is not possible to be a successful salesman merely by reading books. Nevertheless, it is possible to formulate a rudimentary pattern for sales dialogues in most conditions. The work has been done very successfully in recent years by psychological research. Laboratory experiments have been conducted to determine the validity of the various prevalent methods of sales dialogue. The more prevalent methods of sales dialogue include exhibition through use, verbal description, lengthy inducements to buy, brief inducements of a similar nature, serious lecturing or free and informal approach. A brief description of these methods now follows :

**1. Practical Demonstration.** Most people have seen the salesmen actually operating a new article in his shop in order to attract the customer. Most manufacturers try to arrange such practical and operational exhibitions of their products in shops, markets and exhibitions. When the customer sees the article in actual use, he is more easily satisfied about its utility and efficiency. But this method cannot be applied to the selling of all objects. For example, it is not possible to display objects concerned with feelings, in the way. Hence, for such commodities other methods are applied.

**2. Verbal Description.** The shopkeeper or the salesman uses the method of verbal description either when a practical demonstration is not possible or the salesman describes the article, its qualities and its utility in many ways so that the buyer may be convinced. It is desirable that the description should be psychological. And even if there is an element of deception in this description it should be mentioned in such a way that the buyer does not suspect it.

**3. Entreaty to Buy after Mentioning Facts.** In this method the salesman starts by mentioning facts about the article he wants to sell and then requests, begs or entreats the customer to buy it. This entreaty to buy is made in many ways. Some people talk enthusiastically but seriously about the merits of the article in question. Some salesmen adopt a very rude manner while others assume a friendly manner to win confidence of the customer. Such salesmen try to convince each customer, that they are concerned only with the customer's welfare and that their aim is not to earn money but to serve the customer by fulfilling his demands. They create the impression that their objective in selling is to provide satisfaction to the customer.

The advantages and disadvantages of each of the above selling methods can be understood by comparing them. One experienced salesman adopted each of these sales techniques so that they could be evaluated by forty students. The results obtained were entertaining. It was seen that the method of practical demonstration was better than verbal description. A factual description was found better than a simple entreaty or request to buy. It is self-evident that a friendly manner during the sales talk was better than the blunt or rude manner. But the enthusiastic and the very serious and grave descriptions were found to be equally effective.

## PSYCHOLOGICAL FACTORS IN SALES

In the field of sales, the psychological importance of motivation, research, analysis of concepts, development of the methods of introducing goods, improvement in questions, evaluation of verbal reactions, consumption, effective advertisement of indirect evidence, the evaluation, its effect, group information, etc., has been discovered. Besides, efforts have been made to discover, through research, the effect produced on consumers by particular forms of behaviour. Considerable data have been collected on this subject by circulating questionnaires through post. Although many researches involve the use of questionnaires it has been found that only those consumers care to reply to the questionnaire who are especially interested in a particular product. But in order to encourage the other consumers some incentives can also be provided. Sometimes the consumer's opinion has been obtained through interview in a personal meeting or over a telephone. In research of this kind it is necessary to keep in mind the fact that many consumers do not provide valid information because every individual does not have a uniform capacity to evaluate things. Some people can arrive at a more objective evaluation than others. Then memory also plays an important part in this. Some people can recall facts heard a long time ago while the majority of people forget them rapidly. Generally, a thing seen can be remembered for a longer time than a thing heard. For this reason in some cases practical demonstration proves more valuable than a verbal description. Suggestion plays an important part in selling and for that reason it is extensively used in marketing.

The power of suggestion works in the case of fashion also. Certain goods sell because they are fashionable. Sometimes fashion is artificially created, and it can be made so powerful that certain goods and articles come to imply status and become status symbols. In such a case people are willing to pay a very high price for such things. The sex instinct is exploited frequently in advertisement campaigns. In advertising products to be used by men and women, the advertiser often displays nude and semi-nude figures of beautiful women. In addition to the sales talk of the salesmen, the commodity itself should be useful and attractive. If an article is to remain on the market for a long time it should have some inherent utility but in order to attract attention, it must also be attractive. For this reason, these days considerable attention is paid to the packing of commodities. The packing should be so attractive that the customer's attention should be diverted towards it as soon as he enters the shop. He should want to pick it up and touch.

This end is achieved by making bottles of various attractive shapes and by making the containers more colourful. The labels and the words on the outside of boxes and bottles also play an important part in attracting the customer. As far as possible, the description should mention all the qualities of the product containing some suggestion for the customer which induces him to buy it. Nowadays the customer is induced to buy things because articles of daily use are offered to him in the form of free gifts along with the things he buys. Most of the successful manufacturers conduct research to find out ways and means of advertising their goods in such a way that they should be able to sell more than their competitors.

## FUNDAMENTALS OF SUCCESSFUL SELLING

According to Whitehead, salesmanship "is the art of so presenting an offering that the prospect appreciates the need for it and that a mutually satisfactory sale follows....It is the method of arriving at a common point of view with the prospect in regard to the desirability of some article, service or idea." This definition provides the following essential elements of successful selling :

1. Salesman's skill,
2. The selling goods,
3. The prospect to whom the sale is to be made and
4. Bringing the sales effort to a satisfactory close.

All the above elements are interrelated. The salesman must be able to speak properly and explain his proposition. Thus he will make first impression favourably. He must know the features and the selling points of the goods which he has to sell. This knowledge will help him to convince the prospect and induce him to take favourable decision. Besides the perusal skill, knowledge of goods, knowledge of the psychology of the customers, he must also know how and when to use them.

**1. Salesman's Skill in Presenting his Proposition.** First of all a salesman must have the capacity to speak. He must know how to express his ideas pleasingly, logically and convincingly. He should have a command over language. He should know how to speak two /three languages as it is by speech that he endears himself to others. His arguments should not be advanced emphatically like a lawyer in the court. His should not be loud. His voice most be restrained. Even if he differs, the difference must be conveyed sweetly such as "May I take a different view" or "Let us agree that you are correct," "May be you are right" or "This matter may need further examination." Never say, "You are wrong sir." The salesman should behave like an artist who knows how to use brush. He must be honest. He should not misrepresent or exaggerate facts. Good behaviour and manners lead to large sales. Customers respond to good behaviour with regard and respect. When the salesman speaks earnestly and courteously they listen with attention. When the customer points out defects he should never get angry. He remembers that the customer is always right. While carrying on sales talks he must be intelligent, imaginative and wise. Experience shall make him wise and save him from repeating mistakes. Sales proposition must be presented wisely and skilfully when sales of large amount are involved.

A good salesman must enjoy sound health. Unhealthy or weak person can never become a successful salesman. He has no patience with customers and is irritated soon. A healthy, smiling, cheerful salesman listens carefully and patiently and succeeds in bringing the other man around to his views.

By improving the qualities and increasing the knowledge essential for the purpose, persons make themselves good salesman. Salesmen are not born but made. Though some salesmen are gifted with certain qualities, many qualities can also be acquired with effort. Qualities like patience can be developed by habit. Vocabulary can be improved by study. Talking can be refined by hearing the sales talks of expert salesmen. Good health can be maintained by regular exercise. Good manners can be learnt.

**2. Goods for Sale**

(i) *Variety of Goods* : Goods vary widely. There are agriculture goods, individual machines, luxury goods, conference goods, staples entering into world trade and so on. In the service also they differ from each other. The salesmen should know the history of the organization he represents. Manufacturing companies of long standing have well known directors and technicians. Their very names carry conviction with the customers because the quality of goods cannot be inferior.

(ii) *Facts and Methods of Manufacture* : The salesmen should know the facts and methods of manufacture. The durability and worth of an article depend upon the materials of which it is made. Dealing in wrist-watch the salesman must know the number of jewels in the watch. If he sells pens, he must know the metal point in the nib of a fountain pen, or the power of the lens he must know in the camera. His mention of these product features makes the sale talk impressive and convincing. He may easily achieve confidence of the customers.

(iii) *Advantages* : The salesman should get well familiar with the advantages of the product. He must specifically mention these advantages. He should vividly enumerate the multiple benefits that may be acquired. While selling silver wares and utensils he should emphasize that they are not only beautiful to look at but an investment at the same time. They add to the owner's social prestige. In this way additional advantages must be pointed out.

(iv) *Comparative Merits over Similar Goods* : Nearly all the consumer goods have got substitutes. The salesman must point out the superiority of his goods and the shortcoming of the competing goods. Complete information can clear most of the doubts in the minds of the customers. His knowledge about the goods should be complete. Simply saying high quality, best, excellent, etc. would not do. He should be able of justify these remarks.

(v) *Relevant Information Relating to Goods* : All relevant information about transport, freights, octroi duty and packing methods must be given to the customer. How to fix aerials, antenna, earthing, utility of inside and outside aerials should be explained while selling radios. etc.

(vi) *Selling Points* : Selling points are facts incremental in overcoming sales resistance which a product meets in the markets. There are specific reasons which cause people to demand one particular product in preference to others. These are to be gathered by the salesman from the features of goods. The example in case of fruits and vegetables, the points are freshness, weight, vitamin content, food value, price, taste, flavour, preservation, etc. In case of mechanical goods, the main points to be understood are size, price, shape, portability, durability, non-rusting quality, noiseless operation, quick reparability, economy of space, etc.

(vii) *Sources of Information* : Among the various sources of information are books, pamphlets and sales literature, observation of the products, technical journals, exhibition, display room and manufacturing centres. The salesmen must always be alert and keen to gather all possible importance about the product from the various sources. Some companies publish guides and pamphlets to give detailed information about their products.

## UNDERSTANDING CUSTOMER'S PSYCHOLOGY

A salesman must improve his skill of presenting his proposition by understanding his own products. These will go a long way for making a successful sale. He should also understand the psychology of customers, their buying motives, their temperaments and behaviour. In the competitive world of multiple substitutes, the consumer is regarded as sovereign. He has a wide choice to choose and buy. A successful salesman must understand his psychology. A slight indifference, disrespect or overhearing attitude towards the customers may permanently lose them and embitter them. That is why one salesman loses a sale in spite of his better product standing, while another makes more than the usual sales due to correct approach and understanding of the psychology of a customer.

## PSYCHOLOGY OF THE PROSPECT

As the science of human behaviour "psychology" seeks to understand the working of the mind, the way human beings behave and the nature of their thoughts, feelings, desires and interests. The salesman is supposed to know the customer's mind : What things appeal to him and what pleases and displeases him. The more the salesman understands the psychology of the prospect, the more he is able to know his buying behaviour.

The salesman knows consumer behaviour through the related areas of recognition, recall and habitual response. He has to look at the total experience of the individual and consider learning as a process in which total functions are changed and rearranged to make them more useful to the individual. Particular external stimuli do not always activate predictable responses. Motives and other internal factors also affect responses.

**The Basic Factors Influencing Learning.** In his *Learning Theory and Symbolic Processes,* O. Mowers has called Repetition, Motivation, Conditioning, Relationship and organisation retention and for getting as factors that influence learning.

(i) *Repetition* : It is required for the progressive modification of psychological functions and must come with attention, interest and aim. Advertisers bent upon repetition only waste their efforts and money.

(ii) *Motivation* : Activity in harmony with one's motives is satisfying and pleasing while other activity is annoying. Thus motivation is helpful to the salesman to prepare advertising and sales presentations.

(iii) *Conditioning* : Conditioning is the way of learning how new response to a particular stimulus is developed. The conditioned response established a temporary behaviour pattern and at times, it disappears. Research shows that all persons do not repoud equally well to conditioning, nor are their responses generally predictable.

(iv) *Relationship and Organising* : These also facilitate learning. If a thing is presented in a familiar setting, learning effectiveness is increased. Sales message should relate the products to the consumer's needs and lay the groundwork for buying.

(v) *Retention and Forgetting of Learned Information* : Retention is the impression left on the buyer. Forgetting is the negative retention. Messages should be spaced closely together to fortify the learning process.

## PSYCHOLOGICAL TESTS OF BUYING BEHAVIOUR

Psychological tests have shown that buying behaviour is always directed towards and satisfaction of certain basis needs. Actions are modified by the particular environmental and social background in which persons happen to be placed. The motivation comes from the tension made to satisfy the basic needs that come from within consciousness. The action taken by the person reduces tension.

### Basic Needs

Maslow has described basic needs in the following way :

**1. Physiological Needs.** These needs refer to hunger, thirst and sleep, as the most basic needs. They need first priority. Other needs have no importance unless these basic needs are first satisfied.

**2. Safety Needs.** These needs come for economic and social security while physical security is not much needed.

**3. Belongingness and Love Needs.** The affectionate relations with individuals and a social place are of much importance. If these are not fulfilled, it results in maladjustments.

**4. Esteem Needs.** Persons crave for self-honour. Its fulfilment leads to self-confidence and usefulness. If it is not afforded, there is feeling of inferiority and helplessness.

**5. Need for Self Actualization.** It is to get the maximum of one's capabilities. Its fulfilment depends upon prior fulfilment of basic needs.

**6. Desire to Know and Understand.** This means the process of searching for meaning in the things around us.

**7. Aesthetic Needs.** The need for beauty is very strong among those who have fulfilled the basic needs.

Marketing success of an article depends on its ability to satisfy several needs at once. A departmental store dealing with furniture, refrigerators and other domestic goods advised people to buy the goods on instalments. They asked the buying persons to give one-fourth of their price at once and the rest in balanced instalments of 1/10 of price for 12 months. They did not know if they will earn the profits but they liked the popularity and sales of their goods through advertisements and publicity of the goods. Every month their salesman approached the customers on specified dates and took the amount. The defaulters were required to pay the interest on the instalment. After one year, the firm developed its business to such an extent that it had to start several branches throughout the province.

## BUYING MOTIVES

The salesman should know the different buying motives of different persons and take their full advantage in selling goods. Following are chief buying motives :

(i) *Desire for Good Health* : Desire for good health is so strong in some persons that in the name of keeping better health, the salesman may sell food products, dry fruits, chocolates, fruit preparations, biscuits, etc. referring to their nutritive value. He can also sell sports goods for children reminding people that such goods are for children to play and preserve health.

(ii) *Pride, Vanity and Love for Administration* : People take pride in having better things than others. They expect to be admired for their liberal spending. Experienced salesmen understand these instincts and play upon them in their customer's mind and sell costly and novel things, beautiful and rare articles. When salesmen compliment customers on their aesthetic sense, the latter may buy more.

Taking advantage of the robe of sensual satisfactions, salesmen can sell soft-bedded furniture, soft shoes, smooth things to such customers who derive pleasure by touch. Scented oils, perfumes, sweet smelling things, etc. can be easily sold to customers who derive pleasure from smell.

**Recognition of Buying Motives**

While some buying motives can be quickly and easily grasped, others can be understood as the sales talk goes on. The following are the main things for grasping buying motives of the customers :

**1. The Nature of Article asked for.** If a customer insists on cheaper products and goes on haggling, he/her motive may be a wish to buy economically. If one looks for children's things, the motive may be affection. If rare and curious things are enquired for, the motive may be "curiosity".

**2. Nature of Question Asked.** "Will you please give 5 tablets of Aspirin, 10 of Codopyrin and 1 tube of Burnol?" These words are indicative of the motive of precaution. The salesman in addition may sell Glycodin Vaska, laxatives and other popular medicines by proper suggestions and information.

**3. Long Acquaintance with the Customer.** Long acquaintance with customers reveals the nature of their whims, favour, preferences, character, moods, etc. Their motives can be easily deduced from these.

**4. Dress and Demeanour.** Paying capacity is some times indicated by dress and demeanours.

**5 Behaviour.** The customers' behaviour gives sufficient indications about their buying motives. By understanding these motives, a salesman can make suitable appeals so that a prospect may be inducted to give his consent to the deal. Sometimes customer may not give any clue of his consent to the deal. Salesman must silently study the idiosyncrasies, tastes, feelings of the customers they have to deal with and then adapt himself as the situation requires. This goes a long way in achieving the salesman's purpose.

**6. Psychological Classification of Buyers.** The National Salesman's Training Association of the U.S.A. has grouped buying people into the following main types — indifferent, sluggish, reserved nervous, impatient, discreat, curious, affable, business-like, enthusiastic, communicative, intuitive impulsive, ambitious, conservative, over-cautious, pessimistic, pretended, dissipative, reflective, logical, methodical, emotional, extravagant, etc.

## TYPES OF CUSTOMERS

According to Professor Alfred Gross, "The appearance of an individual or his place of business, his attitude and expressions as the salesman speaks to him, and the actions of people around him help to build a picture of the prospect." Actions are the results of thoughts. Whatever movements the customers make provide an index to the working of the customers' minds.

**1. Friendly Customer**. The salesman meets no opposition from a friendly customer. The customer listens and responds and inspires hope in the mind of the salesman. He will not argue or contradict the salesman's statement. This does not mean that he purchases things easily. His friendliness does not mean that the salesman should make short-cut towards booking an order. The salesman must give him the same attention and facts as he would give to any other customer.

**2. Shy and Timid Customer**. A shy and timid customer cannot take any decision independently. He lacks confidence in his own discretion and judgement. He should be taken in confidence and advised to the best course possible. He can easily be persuaded to make purchases. Once he is assured, he readily acts on the advice of the salesman. He can also be a permanent customer. However, the salesman should be very careful not to give him chance for any misunderstanding. He should give him an impression that he is a friend of the customer and not a highway robber.

**3. The Impulsive Customer**. An impulsive customer takes decision very quickly without much thinking and analyzing or without any sense of proportion and importance. He wants quick action and less talk. The salesman should be quick enough to identify such type of customers and act accordingly.

**4. The Undecided Customers**. An undecided customer is also at a loss to take any decision. Indecisive he is always weighing pros and cons of things and not in a position to eliminate the unimportant details and narrow down his thinking process. He can easily be recognized by fleeting and undecided glances, puzzled and doubtful gestures. The salesman should avoid to mention disadvantages of products. He should mention only the bright side of a thing. This will relieve the undecided customer of the great strain of confusion in his mind and make it easy for him to arrive at a decision. The salesman has simply to suggest the decision in a disguised way.

**5. The Deliberate Customer**. This type of customer is stubborn and sometimes aggressive. He takes delight in finding out some flaw and advancing an argument. He does not listen to any explanations. He is not always logical. He is likely to be emotional. The salesman must be cautious in dealing with him. He should not enter into any discussion which is of no use. He should not try to contradict such a customer. The customer will insist on examining the article from all angles and take a lot of time to do that. He will try the salesman's patience till he is fully convinced of the utility of the article.

**6. The Silent Customer**. A silent and calm customer is very trying. Outwardly be seems to he impressed by the talk of the salesman, but inwardly he keeps on thinking and brooding in his own mind. His silence is sometimes very embarrassing. But the salesman should not get impatient. He should wait till the customer has decided either way. He should not allow the customer's silence to deter him.

**7. The Snobbish Customer**. A snobbish customer looks down upon other persons. He has a very high sense of himself. He can be easily satisfied and elated by a little praise and flattery. If the salesman pretends to recognize his importance, it is very easy to deal with him.

**8. Suspicious Customer**. A suspicious customer does not believe either in the quality of the product or in the sincerity of the salesman. He regards all salesmen as swindlers and out to exploit the innocent people. He has a very poor opinion about the salesman. He scoffs and laughs at his so-called fixed price of first grade articles. He is incredulous of even human goodness. The salesman should not find fault with such a suspecting prospect. A suspicious customer is not silent. He speaks out his mind sufficiently. One good feature of this class of doubting customers is that once their confidence is won, they continue to buy from the same shop.

**9. Important Customer**. An important customer expects the salesman to attend to him without delay. He is restless at the least delay and complains loudly about how long he has to wait. However, he is a nice man if he is understood. He does not like bargaining. He either takes goods at the price told or walks away unsatisfied. The best way of handling such a customer is to attend to him as quickly as possible.

**10. Rude and Sarcastic Customer**. As is clear by the title, this type of customer is rude, malingered, offensive, impudent and even vulgar. His rudeness is not directed towards anyone in particular but towards the world in general. He means no offence to the salesman. He is under some mental strain which causes him to utter some rude words unconsciously. The salesman should never feel insulted. He should keep up a quiet attitude and be courteous.

**11. Price-minded Customer**. Price rather than the quality is the main consideration with most of the customers. This is because of the general poverty in India. The skill of the salesman lies in convincing the customer that because of its quality and durability, costly material would be of greater service and cheaper in the long run.

**12. The Grouse and Sore Head**. These customers complain about the whole world and about the salesman' goods too. They are the sort of persons who have lost all interest in life and want the other people to share their sorrow and discontent. A sympathetic attitude towards these customers will win them, ultimately.

**13. Prattling Customer**. Always talking he simply wants to exhibit his talent. Everything that he sees inspires him. His talks soon becomes boring. He will go on accusing Government policy and the inability of the ministers to bring down the price level. The best way to dealing with him is to try to cut short the conversation by putting some question and breaking the content of his talk. The bill must be prepared and the things handed over. The salesman need not make any attempt to explain details as the customer is least interested in them.

**14. Women Customers.** The woman customers are generally talkative. They think that the chances of being deceived will be less in company. The difficulty with them is that they do not decide quickly and do not mind time. They like to bargain. They act more by intuition and taste than by deep study and scrutiny. They prefer to visit the shops where they find themselves more comfortable. The salesman must not hurry women to decide quickly as it is not possible for them to do so because they like to see as many things as possible before they decide. He must answer the various questions they like to ask. He must agree to their comments first. He may later on explain them away. Women want price concessions. If these are given, they become good customers and patronise the shop. They also recommend it to other women friends. Greetings at the time the women step in and leave the shop will create a favourable impression on their minds.

## QUESTIONS FOR EXERCISE

1. Explain the use of psychology in selling.
2. What are the fundamentals of successful selling? Discuss the importance of understanding customer's psychology.
3. Explain the importance of understanding customer's psychology for successful selling of products.
4. How do the psychological tests show that buying behaviour of persons is directed towards the satisfaction of certain basic needs?
5. Describe different types of customers generally met by the salesman. What should be his approach to different types of customers?

# 23

# TECHNIQUES OF SELLING

The techniques employed in selling process are very much dependent upon two factors :

(a) The type of product or service and

(b) The type of customer.

Different technique will be called for if the salesman is travelling to meet his customers in their places of work. When the customer visits a showroom, he has to tell about the product's importance to the customer in terms of time and place. If a salesman calls at a house at 10 A.M. to sell cleaning materials, while the lady of the house is busy with her cooking, the salesman is an interruption of work which she considers more important at that time. At 5 P.M. the woman goes shopping and may be prepared to visit several stores and spend time at each place selecting the same type of products which she refused in the morning.

Thus, the product time and place are important considerations to both buyer and seller. The Fig. 23.1 shows this.

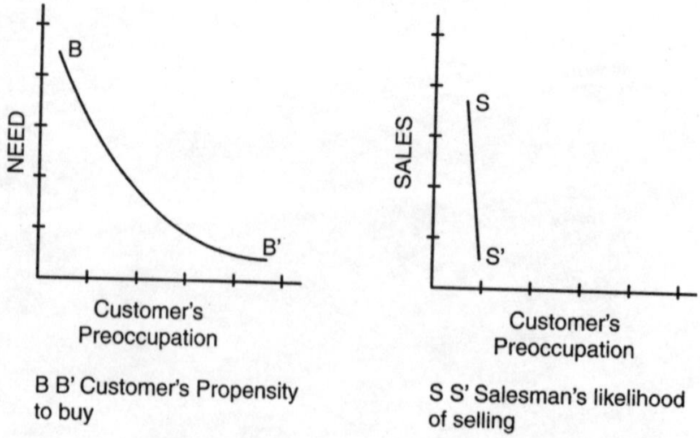


Fig. 23.1. Effect of Customer's Preoccupation on Sales

Following assumptions can be drawn from the curves :

1. The customer is most likely to buy when the needs are highest and preoccupation is lowest. The converse is also true.

2. The salesman's likelihood of selling is greatest when the customer's preoccupation is lowest, but it will rapidly diminish as preoccupation grows.

3. This tendency will hold true in most circumstances as greater the level of preoccupation the lower is the level of immediate need.

4. Elasticity of demand does not influence the general assumptions because the degree of elasticity is implict in the level of preoccupation.

5. The greatest influence on the customer to lower the level of pre-occupation at a given time will be the ability of the salesman to stimulate the level of immediate need. If he is to succeed in doing this, he has to give consideration to following points :

(i) When is the best time to see my customer?

(ii) Where is the best place to see my customer?

(iii) What is the best product to show my customer?

All the subsequent steps in the selling process will be negated if inadequate attention is given to these fundamental points.

## THE SELLING PROCESS

### Fundamental Elements

The objective of the selling process is to persuade customers to buy products that will give them satisfaction. Following are four elements in the process fundamental to all other factors :

1. The company and its policies,
2. The customer,
3. The products and service and
4. The salesman.

It is the prime responsibility of sales management to ensure that the sales force has an appreciation and clear understanding of these four major elements in the selling process before they embark upon the subsequent steps.

### The Subsequent Steps

1. Approach and greeting,
2. Determining the customer's needs,

3. Effective presentation of the products,
4. Counting objections,
5. Closing the sale and
6. Developing goodwill after sale.

In some forms of selling, one can interpose an additional step of suggestive selling of related products between (5) and (6). For example, toothbrush to a man who has brought tooth powder or matching fall to a saree to the lady who has purchased a saree. As the objective of the selling process is the satisfaction of a specific need or the winning of a substantial order, this additional step may be avoided.

## THE MENTAL PROCESSES IN A SALE

Accomplishing a sale is not a spontaneous single event. It is a transition from one state to another in which the buyer progresses from a state of having little, or no knowledge of the product to a state in which he decides to buy the product. Following are seven mental stages in the process of making a sale : (1) interest aroused, (2) knowledge increased, (3) adjustment to needs, (4) application to suitability, (5) desire to process, (6) consideration of cost and (7) decision to buy.

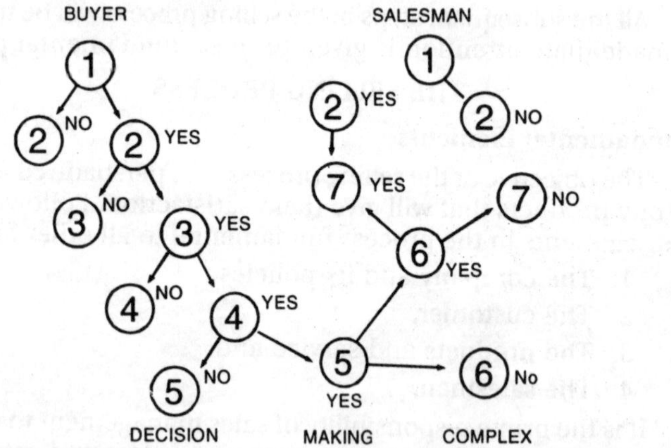


Fig. 23.2. Decision Making Complex

| Buyer | Salesman |
|---|---|
| 1. Interest? 2. More knowledge? | (Worth Continuing?) |
| 3. Adjustment to need? 4. Suitable? | S = Sale. |
| 5. Desirable? 6. Justify cost? 7. Buy? | |

**1. Interest aroused.** Fig. 23.2 assumes that a customer has a higher propensity to buy when he has a low preoccupation level. Hence the salesman's first task is to arouse the interest of his customer. Until this has been achieved, the customer will not give all his attention to the salesman's proposition.

**2. Knowledge increased.** If the salesman has accomplished stage (one) the consumer is receptive to further information and wishes for further knowledge of the product.

**3. Adjustment to needs.** While a customer may find a salesman's product information interesting, the sale will not be accomplished unless it can be shown that the product fulfils his needs.

**4. Appreciation of suitability.** Following the adjustment to needs, the customer will consider whether the product is suitable to solve his particular problem.

**5. Desire to possess.** If the customer has been successfully taken through the preceding stages, the desire to possess arises naturally and leads to purchase.

**6. Consideration of cost.** If the setting process has been conducted sensibly, the customer wishes to consider whether he can afford to buy the product he desires.

**7. Decision to buy.** The decision to buy should gradually become larger in the customer's thoughts until the right moment for the decision is arrived. The salesman's knowledge and skill lie in making this stage as natural as possible. The mental stages in the selling process are important to the successful conclusion of a sale, but they exist only within the wider context of the selling interview.

## PHYSICAL PROCESS IN SALES

**1. Approach to customer.** Approach means meeting the customer. All that leads to this meeting is called the "Approach." The salesman should be careful to make his first impression favourable. He should be neatly dressed, courteous and friendly in his behaviour and tactful and sincere in his talk. He should know how to get along with all sorts of people.

**2. Getting an Appointment.** Approach consists of two aspects, viz. the meeting and the interview. Meetings with important personalities and businessmen are usually arranged through private secretaries or receptionists. Though subordinates, they are equally important and capable of influencing the entry and meeting of the salesman if not the final sales. The salesman's attitude towards these intermediaries should be courteous and friendly. Busy men generally dislike to be interrupted by visitors and particularly by salesmen. Interview with such persons is, therefore, a very delicate affair. Permission to seek interview can be sought through—telephone, business card, introductory letter, etc.

**3. Interview with the Customer.** Creation of the right environment is essential for the salesman. When the company's salesman and the customer meet, they exchange views, information, opinions. Both the seller and the buyer alter the relationship between them. The manner in which this is brought about is illustrated in Fig. 23.2. From this may be understood the complex claim of decision making. For the seller, it is a simple consideration of continuing or not but the buyer, the seven mental stages are expressed as decisions. Therefore, the mental stages form an essential part of the whole process of the sales interview. The sales interview is a more complex process. One may identify fifteen steps in the typical sales interview.

*Steps in a typical sales interview*

1. Opening
   - (i) Exchange of courtesies
   - (ii) Salesman's opening
   - (iii) Interest aroused
   - (iv) Interest developed
2. Body
   - (v) Commencement of selling proper
   - (vi) Demonstration :
     - (a) Presentation of product
     - (b) Explanation of selling points
     - (c) Operation of product by salesman
     - (d) Operation of product by customer
   - (vii) Discussion of Price
   - (viii) Counting of objections
3. Close
   - (ix) Commencement of close
   - (x) Persuasion and trial close
   - (xi) Decision making
   - (xii) Order taken
   - (xiii) Completion of details
4. Departure
   - (xiv) Closing courtesies
   - (xv) Departure

## IMPORTANT CLUES

1. The opening remarks in the exchange of courtesies begin the selling process. The customer may well draw conclusions about the salesman from his first words. Whether the conclusion is favourable or unfavourable, permanent or temporary will be decisive.

For example, a man from Meerut called on a customer at Dehradun during a period of prolonged bad weather. The salesperson in an attempt to be jolly began : 'Good morning, Sir, I always knew Dehradun was wet but you must be enjoying this...." The results were a foregone conclusion.

2. A little prior knowledge can also help. Does your customer play cricket or fond of poetry or interested in astrology or astronomy, Asian Games, etc.?

3. The ability to use his eyes will help the salesman. On entering a customer's office, the successful salesman can look around the room at opening a glance and learn about his customer. The, remarks should succeed in getting the customer's agreement at the outset. For example, "It's rather wet...." "It's nice morning." "The flowers on your desk are magnificent...." If the customer is pleased at the outset he may be inclined to go on further.

4. Seek to guide and control the interview at all times and be prepared to be guided by circumstances. There should be a certain amount of marwevnring for advantage in the beginning while the younger salesman frequently makes the error of plunging into the sale too quickly.

5. Frequently the sales are lost because the salesman is over eager and fails to ensure that his customer's interest is aroused before he begins the real selling.

6. It is important to get the customer's point of view as early as possible. His interest must be developed into enthusiasm. To achieve this, the salesman must be enthusiastic about his products as enthusiasm is infectious and the salesman who can involve the customer from the outset will succeed.

7. Assuming that interest has been aroused, the salesman reaches the point to commence the selling proper. Whether or not a sale is accomplished depends upon what the salesman says and does. Sometime should be spent in developing product knowledge. By combining experience and sound presales

preparation, the salesman will assess selling points arrange them in the best sequence.

8. If the product can be demonstrated, a sequence should be selected leading the buyer to the point at which he is prepared and keen for a demonstration sales talks. The sales talks should be standardised but standardisation should concern facts and not become a parrot fashion talk. At the beginning of the selling process one shall endeavour to inspire confidence by the following :

(i) Sincerity of manner as conveyed by voice and bearing;
(ii) capitalizing the good name of the firm and its prestige;
(iii) product knowledge and by
(iv) basing selling techniques upon sound customer investigation.

**9. Demonstration.** The demonstration will have two effects :

(i) It will show the customer the performance of the product and
(ii) It will show the customer that the product is as good as the salesman says it is.

To ensure maximum effectiveness, the demonstration should be practised frequently. New techniques and experience should be incorporated where possible. The demonstration must be effective and informative. The customer should be told what is happening at every stage. Many salesmen are unsure of themselves when it comes to the demonstration. They work too fast. One should learn to develop the demonstration so that natural pauses give effect, and allow the customer to digest what he has seen and ask questions if has wishes. The salesman should always remember that the customer has not seen the product earlier.

**10. Finding the Customer's Needs.** On certain occasions the demonstration may be less specific. Determining the customer's needs and presenting the merchantise may sometimes be two aspects of the same operation. Among commercial travellers, the presentation is the means by which the customer finds the products he need. A demonstration involves the following to be effective :

(i) Knowledge of location of products, in bag or showcase;
(ii) Sensible selection of what is to be demonstrated;
(iii) Careful selection of selling points;

(iv) Correct display of product and
(v) Effective presentation.

## RELATIONSHIP SELLING

One of the factors of concern to sales management is to try to understand what happens when sales person and prospect meet. Various models of interaction process can be found. Stiden's (1967) compact model attempts to describe behavioural changes as a result of direction and orientation initiated by the sales person. Plank and Dempsey (1980) say that buyer-seller dyad is effected by : (a) Characteristics of both buyers and sellers; (b) Antecedents of seller and buyer behaviour; (c) The process itself including content, form of communication; and (d) The customer-sale person relationship. The model given by Weitz (1981) suggests that these are three groups of variables impinging on the effectiveness of selling behaviours : (1) The customer's buying task. A buyer may be PHILES (who loves the supplier), PROMISCUOUS (who are indifferent to the supplier) and HOBES (who are hostile to the supplier); (2) The sales person resources; and (3) Sales person-customer relationship. The relationship ladder may be business (doing right things), commercial (doing things right) and personal (putting people first).

Selling nowadays is no longer about selling to customers but about doing business with customers. There is a need to view buyers and sellers in new and different ways. Markcting

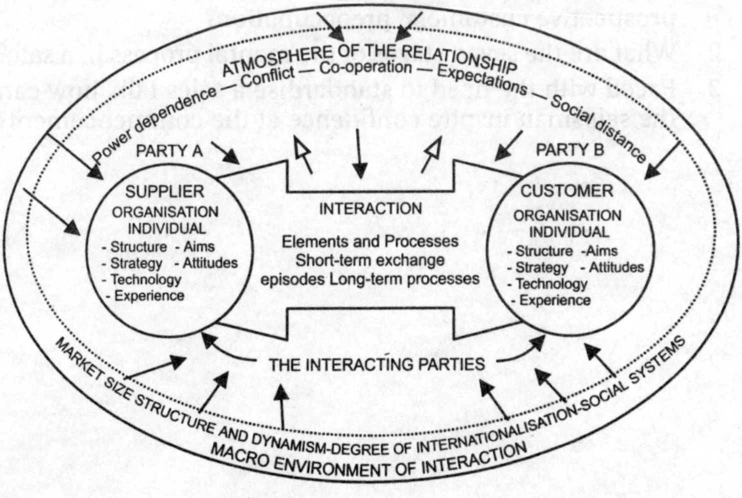

is not a management activity only but the relationships between buyers and sellers are to be viewed in terms of processes, participants, environment and atmosphere. There is now a dissatisfcation with the concept of 4 Ps.

## PUBLIC RELATIONS

Public relations cover a wider field than selling or marketing. Public relations can't be easily defined. Public relations is the deliberate, planned and sustained effort to establish mutual understanding between an organization and the public. It is a tangible activity. Public relations exist sometimes, even if the organization likes it or not. The public includes the community, employees, government, distributors, consumers and opinion leaders.

Public relations is not a free advertising. In order to make it effective Public Relations should :

1. Set specific objectives.
2. Integrate public relations as a function of the organization.
3. Select proper personnel for public relations department.

The general objectives of public relations may be to attract sales inquiries, attract investors/customers/employers, open market, solve union problems, reward for recognition and get in touch with government and non-government agencies.

## QUESTIONS FOR EXERCISE

1. How can the salesman succeed in overcoming the prospective customers' preoccupation?
2. What are the seven stages of the mental process in a sale?
3. Faced with the need to standardise a sales talk, how can the salesman inspire confidence at the commencement?

# 24

# Sales Talks

When the salesman and the prospect meet, a sales dialogue follows. A sale is effected or lost on the outcome of this dialogue. It very important what a salesman should speak in a sales interview. A creative sale cannot be made without making a talk. Such occasions are rare when sale takes place without any talk. The sales talk must be thoroughly planned and complete to the minutes detail. It must not be too lengthy nor too short. At no time it should become embarrassing. Presence of mind is of the utmost importance as despite all preparations one cannot anticipate all the contingencies of a sales interview.

## ADVANTAGES OF PLANNED TALKS

Some salesmen do not bother to plan their talk. They prefer to depend on the spur of the moment but over confidence does not always pay. Every minute spent with the prospect must be packed with selling ammunition. Advanced planning of the sales talk is absolutely necessary for success in selling. A well planned talk offers the salesman following benefits :

1. It helps the new salesman to overcome nervousness and tension.

2. It helps him to give to the prospect a fuller and more sensible sales presentation. The salesman should plan sales talk logical, believable and complete. He must take into account the type of customer, his buying motive and his temperament. He must forcast objections and prepare to answer them.

3. It saves the time of the prospect and also of the salesman.

4. It helps the salesman to sell more. He not only sells but also gets the respect of prospects.

## ESSENTIALS OF SALES TALKS

**1. Pre-planning.** Planned sales talks may be either the standard, memorised presentation or the outlined presentation.

A beginner will find the standard memorised presentation more helpful. But as he gains experience he can switch over to the outlined presentation which gives him more freedom to make it flexible and lively.

**2. Freedom from Show or Self-Esteem.** Whatever may be the qualification, wealth and position of the salesman he must speak with his customer with utmost courtesy and regard. The whole talk must be carried on in a friendly spirit. There should not be an iota of self-importance in it.

**3. Confidence.** A sales talk iota must be made with absolute self-confidence. If the salesman has no confidence in his ability, he cannot build up a sales talk.

**4. Humanitarian.** A sales talk must be characterised by a humanitarian feeling. A salesman must feel that when he sells bad or defective things he is simply wasting the time and money of the customer. If there are defects he may point them out and offer some discount. If they are not material he must explain it that way. The customer must not think the salesman is selfish and callous.

**5. Emphasising utility aspect of articles.** A sales talk must dwell on the service and utility aspects of things rather than price. Usually high prices scare persons. Hence the sales talks should magnify the utility aspect and make the customer feel the enjoyment the possession of the thing will provide him. The salesman should create a picture of enjoyment that the customer might feel that he need not worry about the price.

**6. Pleasant.** A sales talk should not be a boring affair but a pleasant dialogue. The salesman should allow the other party to participate in the talk.

**7. Just and Fair.** The sales talk should be characterised with justice, balance, fairness and integrity. It not aim at exploiting the customer. There should be no mispresentation or suppression of facts.

**8. Without Pressure.** A sales talk should not exercise pressure but invite demand. Salesmen who exercise high pressure salesmanship only cause resentment and develop uncompromising attitude in the customer.

**9. Well Planned.** Good sales talks are well planned and prepared for the occasion. In sales involving lakhs of rupees such as sales of property, buildings, plants, shares and stocks, the salesman should collect all particulars with prior preparation.

**10. Psychological.** A good creative sales talk is a process with a right beginning, a right development and a right closing. Understanding the psychology of the prospect, it is developed on right lines. The salesman should know how to arouse the interest and create desire among the prospects. He should be fully prepared and mentally alert to answer objections and close the deal. If all the time he says "I have no knowledge of this thing, I shall consult the head office, I shall tell you after consultation, etc." he will only cut a sorry figure before the purchaser.

## AWAKENING INTEREST

Sales talk must be commenced, continued and completed with an understanding of the psychology of the customer. The salesman should have the object of awakening interest in the mind of the prospects in what he has for sale so that the interest so aroused may be followed by a desire to buy.

By the term 'awakening interest' is meant getting a person interested in an article or proposition. The extent to which interest can be awakened in a thing depends upon the article as well as the efforts of the salesman. A unique article will itself arouse the interest of persons and they are tempted to look at it. The interest can also be aroused by the salesman by his effective and forceful sales talk as follows.

1. Tactfully introducing his proposition and commencing his sales talk. The first few sentences are always significant. If a proposition is wrongly stated it is very difficult to fit in into the right gear. If the salesman stars well and intelligently, the prospects unconsciously listens to him attentively. The object of opening talk should, therefore, be to get the attention of the prospect fixed on the sales talk at once.

2. Developing his proposition with the correct graph of the buying motives of the customer. This can be achieved by introducing the proposition by way of any of the following methods :

(i) *Offering something useful* : The person addressed wants to know how he is going to gain by the salesman's proposition and hence pays attention to what he says. For example — "Good morning Sir, I am Raju of A B C Co.; I have come to show you a device which if used will double your profits.... May I show it to you?" The listener cannot but answer in the affirmative.

(ii) *Making an Enquiry* : An enquiry does not upset the prospect. He keeps at ease feeling that the inquirer is not asking him for a favour of buying. For a example — "Madam, will you be just kind enough to let me know whether any member of your family is interested in reading our journal 'Sure success guidance in competitive Examinations'." There may be educated persons aspiring for high posts in every house, they naturally enter into talk.

(iii) *Just Supplying a Piece of Information* : A salesman can commence his talk by giving same useful information. For example, "Sir, my company has employed expert electronic engineers to provide instantaneous home repair service of electronic gadgets like washing machine, refrigerator, fan, cooler, Television, tape recorder, typewriter, etc. Will you mind if I fix this card to the switchboard so that the moment you need our service you many just drop a postcard at the address printed on it or ring us to send our man?" No sensible person will raise any objection to such an innocent request. When you are just asking for permission, the lady of the house might be reminded of the trouble she was experiencing the day before with her washing machine. She would be prompted to talk further with the salesman.

(iv) *Distributing Samples* : It is a common and popular way to begin a sales talk by giving samples.

(v) *By mentioning the name of some known person to the prospect* : The salesman can open his talk thus, "Sir, I am coming to you being asked by your friend Mr. Gupta of Meerut to see you." The mention of the very name makes the prospect listen attentively to the salesman just to what his friend had said.

The above forms of introducing a proposition are suggested by way of illustration. The list is in no way exhaustive. An ingenious salesman may think of any number of such methods. By his moves he must draw in the prospect to begin to speak with him. Then he should try to transform this initial interest into an intentional interest.

## BUYING MOTIVES

Just as power causes a machine to move so also motives induce persons to act. Motives are drives or urges or promptings responsible for human behaviour. Buying motives are those which urge persons to buy things. For example, affection for children may urge people to buy toys and other things that children want. Patriotism or love of Swadeshi motivates persons for buying goods made in the country though they may be far inferior in quality and dearer in comparison with imported goods. Desire for good health, self-preservation, pride, variety, love, sensual satisfaction are some important buying motives which a good salesman must learn to recongnise and utilise in his sales talk. An experienced salesman can sense these motives at once in the prospect by his dress, demeanour and the manner of his conversation.

Having a prospect before him, the salesman must try to grasp which of the buying motives work uppermost in the buyer's mind and cautiously touch on them. The interest once aroused may culminate in a purchase subsequently.

## HANDLING OBJECTIONS FROM PROSPECTS

As the salesman carries on the sales talk, he thinks he has created the desire. But the prospect is still undecided. Customers rarely concede without raising objections. An objection expresses disapproval of an action. Objections must be met tactfully and to the full satisfaction of the customers. Objections may arise due to ignorance, fear, misunderstanding, incompleteness in the sales story, wrong demonstration, unsatisfactory part performance, etc. In every case the salesman must accept it as a challenge in a sportive mood. Only beginners and inexperienced salesmen dislike objections. A seasoned salesman always welcomes objections and answers them to the satisfaction of the prospect. Following are the common ways of expressing objection :

### Ways of Expressing Objections

**1. Remaining Undecided.** While the prospect listens patiently to the sales talks, he still remains unmoved. He remains in a state of indecision. He feels as if he can reply neither in the affirmative nor in the negative.

**2. Advancing False Pleas.** The prospect does not remain a silent listener but speaks out. He advances some plea or excuse as if he is trying to get out. He may feel that the salesman is putting unnecessary pressure. To him the quality of the prospect may look inferior. But he has not the boldness to tell openly his mind and displease the salesman. He feels shy to open his mind.

**3. Frankly disclosing genuine objection.** The prospect may clearly come out to state his genuine objections. He intends neither offending nor evading the salesman. His objection may be to the price, or the quality of the goods. He simply says, "Thank you gentleman, I am sorry I don't want the thing. Your terms of sales are not acceptable to me."

**Precautions in Handling Objections**

1. The customer's objections surely mean one thing and that the customer is taking interest in the article. Whatever the nature of objections, they can best be met by establishing their invalidity by furnishing hard facts and figures.

2. It is sometimes advisable to ignore the objection if the salesman has reason to believe that the objection is not serious one. A serious objection will be repeated by the customer and he will insist on an answer. The salesman can then proceed to meet the same.

3. Any genuine objection raised by the customer should not be brushed aside. It means an insult to the customer. However trivial it may appear, one must look to the customer's point of view. Nobody would like to have his opinion underrated. The salesman must regard the customer the sovereign and neglecting his opinion is a deadly offence. Therefore, he must be as much interested in receiving the objections and in removing the same as he is in receiving sales.

4. The salesman must not enter into a battle of wits.

**Ways of Handling Objections**

Objections when classified fall into a set of more or less standard types. There are two kinds of objections : true and false. True objections must be taken seriously. False objections are mere excuses and have to be brushed off. They take the form of lame excuses or pretexts and are prompted by the desire to escape without displeasing the salesman. In such cases, the salesman must humorously explain them away. There are four standard ways to meet objections.

**1. Denial.** An objection believed to be mistaken one be denied flatly.

**2. "Yes-but".** In the "yes-but, method" the salesman should admit the fault but should immediately show him other compensating advantages. A salesman may admit that the article he sells is a bit. Costlier than any other article of the same type. But he should convince the customer that his article is far durable and therefore more economical in the long run.

**3. Boomerang.** The 'Boomerang' method is one in which the objection is turned into a reason for buying. When vague and meaningless objections are raised just to rid of the salesman or to irritate or ridicule him, the salesman should ask questions defining the exact objection. He will soon find that most of them melt away like snow in the hot sun.

**4. Ignore.** Objections can be ignored if they are not repeated. Sometimes it happens that the customer puts the objection only casually and without any seriousness attached to it. If the customer is serious about the objections, he repeats them. The salesman should then treat it as a serious objection and meet it effectively. Objections should be treated as opportunities for further explanation.

**5. Meeting Objections.** Meeting objections correctly and effectively, constitutes the most difficult part of the selling process. Many objections can be easily anticipated and countered in the presentations but the unexpected can also occur. The experienced salesman will have the knowledge and ability to deal with the general and specific objections. He also knows to ignore mere excuses. Following are some general guidance and rules dealing with objections :

(i) Do not argue with the customer.
(ii) Anticipate objections.
(iii) Counter objections firmly and completely.
(iv) Inspire confidence.
(v) Do not condemn competitors.
(vi) Answer objections as soon as they are raised. The prospect is thinking about his objection and expects on immediate answer. If the answer is postponed, he may try to memorise it and pay only half-hearted attention to the rest of the sales story.
(vii) Postpone answers to objections. When price objection is raised too early in the interview or the objection will be met automatically in the rest of sales story or when the answer to objection is so lengthy as is likely to hinder the uniform impact of the sales talk, the answer can be postponed after taking the customer into confidence.
(viii) Forecast the probable objection while planning sales talk. Nearly 90 per cent of the objections can easily be anticipated by the seasoned and experienced salesman.

Answers to these objections are incorporated in the sales story itself. This prevents a negative and favourable attitude on the part of the customer. The customer does not get a chance to take a stand and making it a prestige point. This procedure is, therefore, considered best by many salesmen.

(viii) Some of the petty objections and excuses raised by prospects need not be answered at all. But the salesman must be careful in classifying objections. If even genuine objections are treated as pretexts, sales will invariably be lost.

## HANDLING COMMON OBJECTIONS

**1. Slack Business.** Customers often talk of slack business and make it an excuse for not buying. Such an excuse raised by the customer is a mere pretext to postpone the purchase. The salesman should convince the customer of the advantages of buying the article immediately. He should have already with him a plan to promote the customer's sales with the help of the goods he sells. He should produce it before the customer raises the "slack business" objection. For example, a salesman for typewriter or other office equipment may describe how an office equipped with his typewriter can promote more sales.

**2. Consulting his Associates.** The customer often desires to discuss the product with his business partner or other associates before he takes the final decision. Usually, the customer puts forth such a plea only when he himself is convinced about the usefulness of the product but does not feel confident to make a purchase. In such cases, the salesman may try to feather the vanity of the customer and tactfully persuade him to act on his own decision. If he still insists on consulting his associates, the salesman should make it a point to meet both of them once again to present his goods. It is because the customer cannot have the necessary zeal in convincing his associate. The salesman must himself convince other associates so as to obtain their consent.

**3. Postponing Purchase.** The customer often asks for time to think. It may be a valid objection or may be mere excuse. In any case, the salesman should not agree to a future sale. He should convince the customer of the immense benefit of buying the product immediately. He should present a story of someone who lost good business in postponing purchases.

**4. Not Interested.** If the customer tells the salesman that he is not interested in the product, the salesman may ask him a straight question "why?" The customer may give reasons which the salesman should answer intelligently and properly. He can present his sales story in a new way if the earlier versions of the talk had failed to arouse sufficient interest.

**5. Price objection.** As the customer may complain of the high price of the goods, it is essential to bring the price factor into discussion immediately after the value of the product is described. It is easy to impress upon the customer the unique qualities and outstanding features of the product to justify its high price. If the customer says, "I can't pay", the salesman can suggest several solutions. He may say: "Sir, who wants you to pay just now? To good customers like you I always give credit. Money may be paid in due course. If you don't like to pay all at one time, pay as and when you please and order on the basis of your six monthly requirements for this you need not pay all at once. Out of the ordered quantity I will supply you whatever you want. During all these six months, the same price will be charged even if market price goes up substantially."

**6. Poor quality.** Where such an objection is raised, the quality must be proved by comparing it with that of the competitors, producing laboratory reports, opinions of the experts, etc. and demonstrating once again to the satisfaction of the customer.

After the objections are met, the salesman waits for the reaction or response of the customer to the proposition placed before him. If the buying decision is unfavourable, a tactful salesman does not get disappointed. He takes next step and tries his cards again. But then the techniques he employs at this reaction point are different.

## CLOSING SALES TALK

### Importance

Closing is the last step in a sales talk. It is necessary when the customers give no indication of yielding. Closing is the action of concluding the sales transaction on the part of the salesman. It is the climax of the sales talk. He who wins the last battle wins the war. The end justifies the means. Closing is the acid test of every salesman. Even first-rate salesmen sometimes fail to close a sale in spite of their success at every other stages, *i.e.* winning attention arousing interest, convincing and arousing desire, etc. After struggling hard throughout the interview if the salesman finds that he is not able to close a sale, he takes it as a personal defeat and is afraid of facing it again. Therefore, closing the sale is the most delicate point in the whole selling process. To achieve success, the salesman needs a psychological awareness and ability to make judgements at a correct moment.

**Obstacles in Closing a Sale**

There are two main obstacles in closing a sale successfully.

**1. The Buyer's pleas.** A buyer, however much he may be convinced about the quality and desirability of purchasing the goods is never confident. When he purchases the goods, he fears that the product may not be his money's worth for the purchase. He fears all the time that the product may not prove up to the quality described by the salesman. He is afraid of what others will say about the purchase. All these fears should either be tackled before they crop up in the mind of the customer or should be eradicated after they are expressed by the customer by repeating the sales story more effectively particularly emphasising the sales points.

**2. The Salesman's Attitude**. Sometimes the salesman becomes tense and over anxious at the final stage. As feelings are contagious, customers also are likely to become nervous and either postpone or cancel purchases. There is thought in the mind of the salesman, that if he fails it will be definite loss in his income. Therefore, in the closing stage, the salesman must remain composed and reassured. He must not lose heart and keep up his composure.

**Reaction Point (Trial Close)**

The salesman should be watchful to find out indications from the prospect of his readiness to purchase. Closing signals of the prospects are indicated by their facial expressions and by physical actions or by oral expressions. He leans forward in his claim to finally re-examine the article. When such signals are detected, a salesman should not lose the opportunity to use trial closes. A trial close is a leading question which calls for a decision on a minor point, e.g. "Which colour or model would you prefer?" Even if the trial close fails, the salesman does not close the door for further talk. He usually keeps certain telling points in reserve. He allows the customer a few more advantages and uses the trial close again. The salesman never presumes the sales to be lost when the buyer negatives a trial close. He continues with his presentation again.

A trial close serves three purposes :

1. It is the sample way to ask the prospect to buy;
2. It enables the salesman to gauge the thinking of the buyer and lastly;
3. It guides the salesman while protecting him against failure.

The psychological time is when the customer is psychologically ready to buy. This is also called the Reaction point — a point at which the customer reacts favourably to buying proposal from the salesman. If the salesman misses this point he fails in spite of his effective coverage of the earlier steps of the presentation. Opportunity rarely taps at your door more than once and once you lose it, you lose it for ever.

One of the most useful ways of closing a sale is to suggest a finish :

"Now how much material will you require?"

"We can deliver by tomorrow morning."

"Will you be sending the order or can you place it now?"

"I think black is the most suitable, do you agree?"

The entire selling process should work to the objective of closing the sale and progress naturally towards it.

**Summing up Techniques**

**1. To take for Granted.** The salesman should proceed in his talk taking it for granted all the time that the customer is going to buy the article. At the end of his talk he straight away places his order form before him and quotes the price and tries to pack up. This is the smallest aid at times to an effective close.

**2. Inducements.** At the end of his sales talk, the salesman offers certain extra inducements, concession or special consideration to the buyer who is happy in the expectation of extra gains.

**3. Business Stories.** The salesman should narrate stories of persons who had benefited earlier by the purchase of such goods. These stories must be real and not imaginary. They be interesting and convincing and relevant to the subject matter.

**4. Fear of Loss.** The salesman uses the "fear" motive in effecting a successful close. He may describe a probable loss if the goods are not purchased.

**5. Affirmative Close.** The salesman gets the prospect to agree to a number of questions. Answers in the affirmative to a few initial questions, leaves the prospect no other alternative except giving "yes" answers to the subsequent questions which lead to a successful close with techniques tactfully utilised the salesman has excellent chances for an effective close. However, there are equal chances of failure and the salesman should be prepared even for a flat refusal though his attitude on the whole should be confident success. Obstacles and hurdles are there to teach him the grim realities of life. Failures are highway road to success in life.

## SALES RESPONSIBILITIES

The primary responsibility of a salesman is to conclude sales successfully. This task involves the identification of customer's needs, presentation and demonstration, handling objections and closing the sale. The secondary responsibilities are :

(a) Prospecting *i.e.* searching for and calling upon customers who have not purchased the product.

(b) To maintain customer records and information feedback.

(c) Self management and plan *e.g.* deciding call frequency or dividing the territory for visit purposes.

Besides the salesman has to implement sales and marketing strategies.

## QUESTIONS FOR EXERCISE

1. What is the importance of sales talks? What are the essentials of effective sales talks?
2. What is the meaning of the term "awakening interest"? What are the factors in the process of awakening interest?
3. What are objections? How should they be handled?
4. What is meant by closing? What is the importance of closing and its chief methods?

# 25

# SALES RECORDS

Sales records are written statements of a salesman's activities during a specific period of time in a particular area. These are used by sales management as a means of controlling the activity and expenses of the sales force. They are also used as a means of collecting information about the market, present activity and anticipated activity. Sales records fall into two categories :

(a) Control of the sales force and

(b) An aid to market research and planning.

## ELEMENTS OF EFFECTIVE SALESMANSHIP

A man who has natural abilities, some experience and the correct degree of training should prove a good salesman but by these virtues alone he will not become an effective salesman. There is a lot of difference between a salesman and an effective salesman. Effective selling is made possible by a sensible routine, an understanding of the territory, a predetermined presentation and most important, clear objectives and a personal goal. A salesman who leaves home in the morning, wets his finger to which way the wind blows and follows it, will not be effective.

Following elements determine effectiveness :

1. Efficient coverage of the territory.
2. Sensible use of selling time.
3. Effective journey planning.
4. Ability to combine regular calls on established customers with creation of new customers.
5. Ability to determine customers' needs.
6. Correct use of territory customer records.
7. Ability to vary selling techniques according to the situation and circumstances.

The salesman alone is not responsible to use all the elements making for efficiency. By continuous supervision and training, sales management must see that he understands his goals, his products and is acquainted with the methods known to be best in reaching them. Management of the sales force cannot be effective without the element of control. Discipline will be used mainly for two purposes :

(i) to determine where faults lie which prevent salesmen reaching their goals and

(ii) to show how activities may be used more efficiently.

**Sensible Controls**

Sales management is ultimately responsible for any weakness in the sales force. The sales force cannot display periodic or sudden bouts of efficiency. It must be trained, equipped and motivated to run continuously at maximum efficiency. The sales manager is responsible for assessing the individual salesman's performance. Individual salesman's performance can be judged by :

**1. Determining Suitable Goals.** A salesman's ability to achieve his sales figures against goals is a tool for sales managers to use in determining the overall efficiency of the sales force as well as of the individual salesman. While it is effective as a means of discovering the less efficient salesman (the idler will not have lasted long enough to need control system to discover him) its more important purpose is to motivate the sales force through a spirit of competition and challenge, with a bonus to those who attain the largest increase in their sales over their goals.

**2. Ensuring Sensible Control Systems.** Control begins with the allocation of sales territories to salesmen. Territories provide a sales area which allows for adjustment, if necessary, without the loss or otherwise negating of existing sales records or customer records. The organisation of the sales force is usually on a basis of allocating specific territories to each representative. This enables a salesman to specialise in one territory with its customers and conditions and leads to a development of customer/salesman relationship. The territory is also the usual basis for planning and budgeting of the sales force and allocating quotas. Sales and statistical records derived from them will enable the sales manager to exercise control over the sales force by making use of the figures immediately available. These figures will also be kept in terms of the areas or groups into which the sales force is organised and will be a check on the efficiency of the managers responsible. A continuity of records becomes necessary to distinguish between the results of the salesman on his territory and the territory itself as a facet of the organisation structure. This need necessitates separate information being compiled which is capable of independent analysis. The distinctiveness is important as discontinuity may arise from :

(1) Changes in territorial organisation,

(2) Increasing the number of salesmen and

(3) Changes in salesman due to dismissal, promotion, retrenchment or illness.

Each of these factors causes decisions to be taken on the continuity of sales records.

### Controlling Salesman

If the salesmen are within reach, it is easy to control them but if they are working at different places, a personal, direct contact is out of question. The methods adopted for this purpose are as follows :

**1. Setting Performance Standards.** Improving selling effectiveness through installation and operation of control procedures require the setting of quantitative performance standards. These standards define both the nature and desired levels of performance expected of a salesman. This helps in measuring the performance and also in stimulating good performance.

**2. Sales Quota.** It is the estimated volume of sales that a company expects to secure within a definite period of time. It is a "good of sales accomplishment, a task objective or a standard that a sales organisation strives to attain." The quota may be set in terms of value or in terms of unit of sales. The quotas may be fixed for a geographical area to be attained within a definite period of time. A smaller area and a short period would generally provide greater direction and control. An attainable quota must be fixed taking into consideration the following elements :

(i) *Set scientifically* : It must be set scientifically. Past records, changed environments, etc. should be considered. Marketing research throws light on these problems.

(ii) *Flexibility Plans* : The quota fixed must also be flexible.

(iii) *Incentive Plans* : The incentive plans for remuneration are to be attached with quotas.

(iv) *Must be Attainable* : The quota should be attainable by an average salesman.

## DECIDING SALES FORCE SIZE

For deciding the sales size, the rate of sales turnover is to be seen. If a concern has 50 salesmen and if it needs 50 for the coming year to get 10% annual turnover, then 10 more persons be appointed. The sales force turnover rate is defined as a number of salesman separated, resigned and so happens in 50 salesmen. Every sales force must have some turnover. When there is no turnover, the sales force is idle. Inefficient salesmen must be removed. Management must act so as to get the turnover.

Management's decision on the size of sales force is needed for getting the consumers sales objectives.

The sales manager should make estimates for each of the personal selling objectives, the purpose in each case being that of determining the total number of men needed to achieve the objective. Difficulties in making these objectives change both the objective and nature of salesmen's activities. It is difficult to estimate the number of men required to reach a quantitative objective like total sales than to get qualitative objective of securing customers' cooperation and build goodwill among customers.

## PERSONAL SELLING APPROPRIATION

Determining the personal selling appropriation depends on the selling objectives set by the top management for the period just ahead. These may be put to effect by the management who must estimate the costs for its conversion. As an increase in the sales volume may need more salesmen, new appointments are made. Further they are trained. So management must :

(i) Estimate the volume of performance for each required activity and

(ii) Convert these performance volumes into cost estimates.

The kind and size of sales force are the main determinants of the total size of the personal selling appropriation. The management must make further decisions as to how to spend. Should they spend the amount on the same salesmen or should they train other new hands, depends on forethought. If these are resolved rationally, there would bee an equating of the marginal productivities of alternative ways of spending the personal selling appropriations. But practically such allocations are made intuitively. Management experiments constantly. It is always striving for an improved allocation pattern. As there is no known way for measuring or predicting the relative effectiveness of expenditures on the different activities, such allocations continue to be made on the basis of management's best judgement.

The formula for calculating the rate of sales force turnover is :

$$\text{Rate of sales force turnover} = \frac{\text{Number of Separations}}{\text{Average Size of Sales Force}} \times 100$$

The formula for determining the number of salesmen needed is expressed as :

$$N = \frac{S}{P} + T\,(S/P).$$

$$\text{Which reduces to } N = \frac{S}{P} + (1 + T)$$

When X is the number of salesmen.

S is the forecasted sales volume.

P is the sales productivity of an individual.

T is the allowance for rate of sales force turnover.

And S/P is the average size of sales force desired over the year.

## REPORT WRITING

The sales manager, area managers, group leaders and the salesmen all have to do a certain amount of report writing. The amount will tend to increase further up the organisation structure. It will be necessary if each element is to work effectively. While this should form relatively a small part of the total work, particularly at the lower level, it is important. It is essential to stress that the main responsibility of the salesman is to sell and he should not be overburdened with an excessive amount of report writing.

The sales organisation depends a great deal upon sources of information both about the customers and the products. Salesmen have a useful task in providing information to aid sales management in planning and controlling. The use of information is illustrated in Figure 25.1. A schematic management information circuit shows how the plan is desired, implemented, measured, compared with predicted effect and subject to revision Figure 25.2. The reports from the sales force along with achieved work are a source of information for revision of the plan.

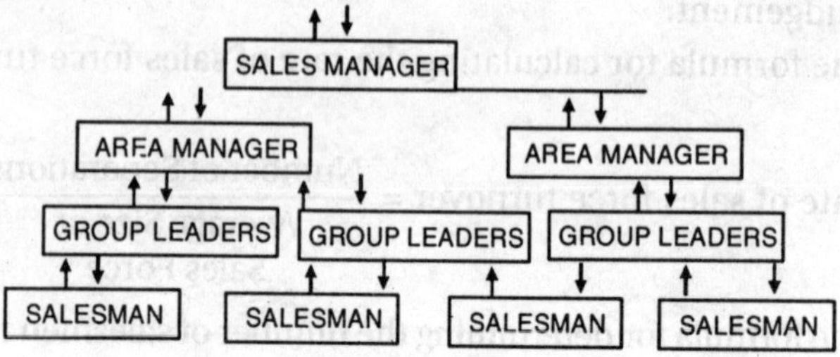


Fig. 25.1 Flow of Information

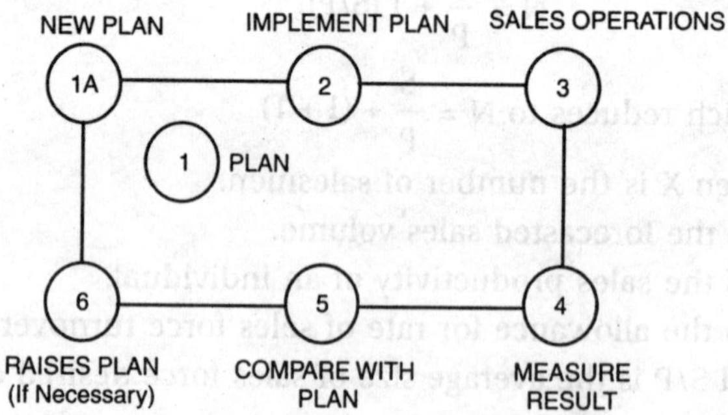


Fig. 25.2 Management Information Circuit

These reports should be clear, concise and conclusive. Where facts can be used, they must be but where opinion has to suffice it should be made clear that it is only opinion. Reports need not be long and should not take the writer more than a quarter of an hour at the most. Ideally they should be written as soon after the interview as possible, but where this cannot be done, at least the essential details should be noted in rough form. Many firms issue report pads or memorandum pads, and the salesman should be prepared to make use of them.

The information is needed by all the elements in the sales organisation. It comes in two flows :

(i) upwards from sales force to management and
(ii) downwards from management to sales force.

Figure 25.3 shows the main flows in an organisation structure and the nature of information.

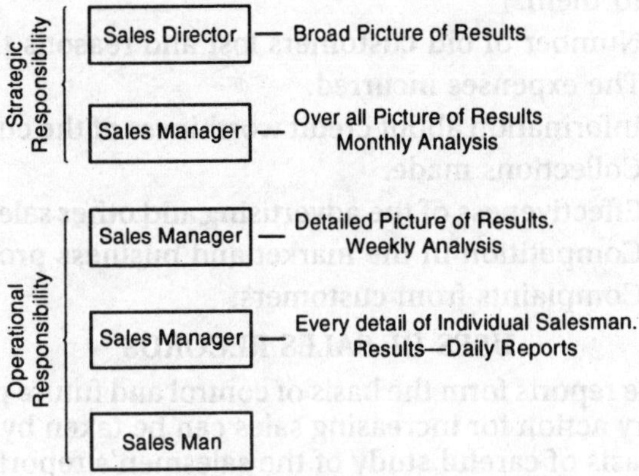


Fig. 25.3 Differing Record Needs

The different levels of management have particular needs for records. At the level it is broad analysis of results as an aid to strategic planning. Lower management want much specific information as a means of operational control. It is possible to summarize the details of the needs as shown in Fig. 25.3.

## RECORD OF PERFORMANCE

**Content of Record.** Record of each salesman's performance is prepared on the basis of the reports received from him. These records give a clear picture of every salesman's work with particular reference to the following :

1. Selling expenses for each order secured.
2. Average size of order.
3. Sales of different lines of products.
4. Number of new customers obtained.
5. Number of old customers lost.
6. Number of repeat orders booked.

**Content of Report**

Reports are sent periodically by salesmen working in different territories or areas. These reports are analysed in the sales office. These reports give information about the following :

1. Number of calls made with relevant total details about each call.

2. Total volume and value of sales made.
3. Number of new customers contacted and sales made to them.
4. Number of old customers lost and reasons thereof.
5. The expenses incurred.
6. Information about credit worthiness of the customers.
7. Collections made.
8. Effectiveness of the advertising and other sales efforts.
9. Competition in the market and business prospects.
10. Complaints from customers.

## USES OF SALES RECORDS

These reports form the basis of control and future planning. Necessary action for increasing sales can be taken by the firm on the basis of careful study of the salesmen's reports. It also helps the salesman to develop the useful habit of self-analysis. The different levels of management have particular needs for records. At the top level it is a broad analysis of results as an aid to strategic planning. Lower management want much more specific information as a means of operational control.

## CONTENTS OF VARIOUS REPORTS

**1. Report by Sales/Marketing Director**. It is summary of analysed results of performance against planned performance. This involves :

(i) Sales figure,
(ii) Selling and related costs,
(iii) market trends,
(iv) activity of competitors,
(v) anticipated business for next period and
(vi) variation from plan.

**2. Report by Sales Manager**. It has details of overall sales organisation's performance, including areas, product, customer categories, new accounts, lost accounts and selling costs.

**3. Report by Area Managers.** Detailed analysis of area results on a weekly basis :

(i) by territory,
(ii) number of calls per day,
(iii) how many new contacts and
(iv) breakdown of sales by product range.

**4. Report by Group Leaders :** It is comprehensive information on performance of the salesmen under their direct control on a daily basis. It includes :

(i) Number of calls per day; (ii) percentage of new contacts; (iii) number of interviews; (iv) number of presentations; (v) number of sales; (vi) size of orders; (vii) future anticipated business; (viii) name and status of contact; (ix) if salesman is working to plan and (x) if salesman is making effective use of training in presentation, technique and samples.

The salesman is the source of the information needed by the management to determine whether its sales policies are being applied successfully. In completing his records it is necessary for the salesmen to give explanations for any variation in their work from the prescribed plan.

## REPORTING BY EXCEPTION

If management has to be free from unnecessary clutter so that it can concentrate on the really essential details, it must increasingly delegate the routine matters. Reporting by exception is an adaptation of this concept to the sales force. It leaves the day-to-day operations to the man on the spot so long as it can be sure that it will be informed of any problem that is either beyond the salesman's authority or jurisdiction.

The salesman has to complete a number of forms or records in the period of a month. There are daily reports, weekly reports, monthly reports and expenses from. As far as possible the salesman should not be too much encumbered with long reports.

Report by exception can be summed up in the phrase : "If every thing is allright, don't tell me."

## JOURNEY CYCLES

A journey cycle is the period it takes a salesman to make a complete round of his journey of his territory in a particular route assumed to be best. A recorded system of journey cycle will do the following :

1. Ensure the logical and complete working of the territory;
2. Enable prior planning of the journey;
3. Provide customers with a known frequency of calls on particular days and
4. Aid a new man to take over with the minimum of disruption.

All the aspects listed above aid the salesman in efficient working of his territory. In consumer selling, the regular calling frequency is most important if the customer is going to develop a loyalty to products or bands. He must know when the salesman will call. For the industrial salesman, a planned schedule of call ensures that the salesman has a clear understanding of who he is going to see, enable firm appointments to be made, and ensure he has the right samples and any other additional information he will need.

Planning the journey cycle depends essentially upon the ordering frequency of the customer. If the customer buys every week, month or season then that will be the period of the cycle. The buying period by determining the frequency of the call, also affects the size of territories. If the salesman selling groceries has to call upon shops every week, he must have a territory that can be covered in a week.

The industrial salesman may also have a regular calling frequency dictated by customer buying habits. Electric lamps are a product sold to industrial users on a regular recorder basis. But there are industrial products where the need arouses from a problem and the cycle can be longer.

## QUESTIONS FOR EXERCISE

1. What is the purpose of sales records? What are the essential requirements that make the difference between a salesman and an effective salesman?
2. What are the factors influencing the determination of the personal selling appropriation? How is the size of the sales force decided?
3. Report writing is essential to all engaged in sales. List the essential points of good report writing.
4. What are the flows of information in the sales ogranisation?
5. Write notes on (i) Reporting by exception. (ii) Journey cycles.